STUDY GUIDE TO ACCOMPANY MICROECONOMICS

FOURTH EDITION

Also available from McGraw-Hill Ryerson:

MICROECONOMICS, Fourth Edition
by Blomqvist/Wonnacott/Wonnacott
ISBN: 0-07-551538-5

MACROECONOMICS, Fourth Edition
by Blomqvist/Wonnacott/Wonnacott/Fried
ISBN: 0-07-551540-7

STUDY GUIDE to accompany MACROECONOMICS, Fourth Edition
by Blomqvist/Wonnacott/Wonnacott/Hobson
ISBN: 0-07-551541-5

STUDY GUIDE TO ACCOMPANY

MICROECONOMICS

FOURTH EDITION

ÅKE BLOMQVIST
University of Western Ontario

PAUL WONNACOTT
University of Maryland

RONALD WONNACOTT
University of Western Ontario

McGraw-Hill Ryerson Limited
Toronto Montreal New York Auckland Bogotá Caracas Lisbon
London Madrid Mexico Milan New Delhi Paris San Juan
Singapore Sydney Tokyo

STUDY GUIDE to accompany MICROECONOMICS
Fourth Edition

ISBN: 0-07-551539-3

3 4 5 6 7 8 9 10 W 3 2 1 0 9 8 7 6 5

Printed and bound in Canada.

Sponsoring Editor: Jennifer Mix
Supervising Editor: Margaret Henderson
Copy Editor: Maura Brown
Cover Design: Dianna Little
Printing & Binding: Webcom Limited

TABLE OF CONTENTS

PREFACE

This study guide is intended to help any student who is taking an introductory economics course using the fourth Canadian edition of *Microeconomics* by Blomqvist, Wonnacott and Wonnacott. Our task in preparing this study guide was to revise the version that was prepared to accompany the third edition of the textbook. In so doing, we have reorganized and updated and rewritten material to correspond with changes (often quite substantial) made in the fourth edition of the textbook. Most of the multiple-choice questions, true-false questions and exercises are, however, carried forward from the earlier edition. In doing this, we owe a debt of gratitude to Peter Howitt, Paul Wonnacott and Ron Wonnacott, all of whom contributed extensively to what was good about the earlier versions of this study guide. In this edition, we have provided suggested answers for all the end-of-chapter problems in the textbook (which have been extensively revised in the corresponding edition of the textbook). Those problems now contain a mix of many of the "standard" assignment and examination questions, common to introductory courses in most Canadian universities, as well as extensions and applications of the issues and analysis developed within each chapter. In short, what we hope we have accomplished is a full integration between the textbook and the study guide as complementary elements of a total learning package. The remaining elements are, of course, the student and the instructor.

TO THE STUDENT:

Each chapter of the study guide is designed for you to read and work through after reading the corresponding chapter in the textbook. Each study guide chapter contains nine sections:

1. **Learning Objectives**. This section consists of a list of tasks you should be able to accomplish after you have studied (read and worked through) the chapter in the textbook and in the study guide. The purpose of this section is twofold. First, it should help to give you purpose and direction while studying the chapter. Second, it should serve as a useful checklist to test your comprehension after reading the chapter and working through related problems.

2. **Chapter Summary**. This section contains a summary and discussion of the important points of the chapter. Its main purpose is to reinforce the textbook by going over these key points from a somewhat different perspective and, sometimes, adding illustrative examples. To a student learning a subject for the first time, everything in the textbook is likely to

appear equally important. This section should help sort out the more important from the less by focusing more narrowly than the textbook and by drawing attention to the particularly important material.

3. **Important Terms**. This section lists most of the key terms and phrases which occur in the chapter. Your task is to write out your own brief definition of each term or phrase.

4. **True-False**. This section sets out a series of statements concerning issues arising from the chapter. Your immediate task is to determine whether the statement is true or false. However, you should go beyond this and write down a brief explanation as to why the statement is true or false, including, where relevant, a diagram.

5. **Multiple Choice**. This section provides a sampling of multiple choice questions relevant to the subject matter of the chapter. These questions provide a useful self-test of your comprehension of the chapter. You should initially answer these questions as a block without reference to the textbook. For each question, write down a brief rationale for your selection of "best" answer. In many cases, you may confirm your choice of answer by an appropriate diagram. Having completed the "self-test," you should then confirm your answers against those given in the study guide. Where you selected an incorrect answer, you should be able to write down why your answer was incorrect and a rationale for the correct selection, perhaps with reference to the textbook.

6. **Exercises**. This section provides a number of pertinent exercises, working through structured problems that require you to fill in blanks (based on side calculations that you have made) or selecting answers from a list of alternatives. This section is designed to help you learn by doing, within a framework that provides significant guidance. Besides providing reinforcement through repetition, many of the exercises are designed to guide you toward discovering ideas that are not explicitly discussed in the chapter or will not be introduced until a later chapter.

7. **Essay Questions**. This section is designed to help you apply important concepts that have been developed in the chapter, as well as to stimulate your imagination as to the broad applications of economic theory to the business of daily life. Often the questions will encourage you to pull

together the principal ideas from the chapter. Sometimes, the questions will encourage you to extend those ideas.

8. **Answers**. This section provides answers to the true-false questions, the multiple choice questions and the exercises. It is crucial that you ensure you understand why a given answer is correct. It's not as important, at this stage, to get the right answer as it is to understand how to go about arriving at the right answer. Economics is like a jigsaw puzzle — you start by turning all the pieces face up, then you begin to fit together the corners and the edges, and gradually you fill in the middle until you see exactly how the rest of the puzzle comes together. Typically, you should not expect the answer to a question to jump out of the page at you, nor should you seek divine inspiration. Rather, you have to impose some structure on the problem and work towards the solution. This is the difference between regurgitation and processing/analysis.

9. **Answers to Problems from the Text**. In this section we have provided complete answers to virtually every problem from the end of each chapter in the textbook. These problems, unlike the exercises in the study guide, are unstructured — that is, no guidance is provided in developing an answer. In part, then, by providing complete answers, we hope to give you a safety net as you venture out in often uncharted waters. As it turns out, the textbook problems contain many of the "standard" assignment and examination questions, common to introductory courses in most Canadian universities. With practice, you will become adept at solving these problems in their many versions. As well, many of these problems provide extensions and applications of the issues and analysis developed within each chapter. Working through them, therefore, will provide a true test of your comprehension of the subject matter. Finally, some of the questions provide an excellent basis for class discussion, and you should urge your instructor to occasionally permit such interactive sessions.

TO THE INSTRUCTOR:

As class sizes become increasingly large in Canadian universities, it is becoming increasingly difficult to interact with students through the conventional package of assignments and a mid-term examination. This package traditionally provided both instructors and students with an indication of "progress to date" in the complex process of communicating ideas. Yet, increasingly, students are demanding that there be some form of continuous assessment as well as frequent assignments that provide "model" questions and answers. Economics is particularly challenging in its early stages because students must not only assimilate new ideas but also develop analytical skills. There is no substitute for practice in this latter task.

It is our hope that this revised study guide will begin to fill what we perceive to be a growing void in the learning package. It is designed to provide students with a form of self-tutorial, focusing attention on key concepts and gradually building understanding through repetition, structured problem solving, and essay writing. Students often express their frustration that, having attended lectures and read the relevant material, believing that they understood the subject matter, they nonetheless perform poorly on assignments and exams. Working through the study guide as well as the end-of-chapter problems in the textbook will go a long way towards relieving this frustration. Students only come to understand economics by working at problems, making their mistakes, gradually recognizing the common themes in the analytical approach, and, piece by piece, fitting the jigsaw puzzle together. In the modern university, the study guide must substitute for direct interaction with the instructor in this important process.

Ideally, then, the study guide will be part of the "required reading" for the course. In this, it is important that instructors make frequent reference to the relevant parts of the study guide as well as the textbook during lectures. It is also possible to provide a direct incentive for students to work though the study guide by adapting questions for purposes of class tests. It is our view that the study guide, properly integrated into the course, obviates the need for formal assignments. Reference to the end-of-chapter problems in the textbook (and their answers in the study guide) as well as the true-false questions, multiple choice questions and exercises in the study guide should make it clear that simply adapting these for purposes of exams will indeed ensure that students are provided with the opportunity for the sort of sequential development of skills and continuous assessment which are the cornerstones of modern education.

ACKNOWLEDGEMENTS

We would like to acknowledge the interest, patience, encouragement and occasional discipline of the sponsoring editor, Jennifer Mix, who, having bought into the idea of the study guide as part of a total learning package, was then committed to the difficult task of ensuring its timely completion. We also wish to acknowledge the contribution of Margaret Henderson who was responsible for editing this study guide in the face of an erratic production schedule and tight deadlines.

Finally, we wish to express our appreciation to Paul Wonnacott and Ronald Wonnacott. Their intense interest in all aspects of economic policy and their strong commitment to clear and simple exposition of sometimes difficult material has resulted in an introductory economics textbook that is, in many ways, unique. Because of this, we have been able to develop exercises in the study guide that at once hone students' analytical skills while showing how the basic economic tool kit can be applied to fundamental policy issues. The major changes occurring in the economic policy field at the present time make it all the more important that we breed a generation of students who are able to critically assess what is being done. Their ability to do so will be crucial in shaping the society in which they will live and work. Accordingly, we dedicate this study guide to all those who learn from it — our students.

Åke Blomqvist
London, Ontario

and

Paul A. R. Hobson
Wolfville, Nova Scotia

STUDY GUIDE TO ACCOMPANY
MICROECONOMICS
FOURTH EDITION

PART ONE

BASIC ECONOMIC CONCEPTS

CHAPTER 1

Economic Problems and Economic Goals

LEARNING OBJECTIVES

After you have studied this chapter in the textbook and study guide, you should be able to

- List five major economic goals
- Define terms such as unemployment rate, depression, recession, inflation, hyperinflation, economic efficiency, equitable distribution of income
- Describe, in broad terms, what has happened to Canadian unemployment, inflation, growth, and the distribution of income in recent decades
- Explain why it is harder to identify the problems created by inflation than those created by unemployment
- Distinguish the views of Adam Smith and J.M. Keynes with respect to the role of the government in the economy
- Distinguish between allocative efficiency and technological efficiency
- Describe briefly how changes in relative prices may contribute to allocative efficiency
- Explain the distinction between equity and equality
- Explain how some goals may be complementary, while others are in conflict

If you have studied the appendix to Chapter 1 in the textbook, you should also be able to

- Describe some of the ways in which people may be misled by graphs
- Explain what is meant by the slope of a line and how to measure it
- Determine the slope of a curve at each point along its surface
- Determine the point of intersection between two curves

- Determine the point of intersection between two curves
- Explain the advantage of using a ratio (or logarithmic) scale
- Explain the difference between a nominal and a real measure

CHAPTER SUMMARY

The objective of economic theory is to discover and explain the basic principles and laws that govern economic life. We use economic theory to help us analyze problems such as unemployment and inflation and issues such as the determination of price and output in the marketplace for goods and services, wage rates in labour markets, or interest rates and exchange rates in money markets. We use it to evaluate the functioning of the economy: the mix of goods and services produced; the distribution of income across individuals; the problem of environmental pollution. We use it to analyze the economic role of government and the economic effects of government spending programs, taxes, tariffs and quotas, as well as government regulation of industry.

Economic theory and **economic policy** go hand-in-hand. Just as a physician needs to know how the human body works in order to heal patients, so the economic policy maker needs to understand economic theory in order to prescribe economic policies that will be successful. Scientific studies of how things work are often inspired by a policy motive – to do something about problems. Thus, scientists strive to unlock the mysteries of the human cell in order to find out why cancer occurs and, ultimately, to be able to cure cancer. Similarly, studies of how the economy works are often motivated by the desire to solve economic problems such as large-scale unemployment, spiralling inflation, wide-spread poverty, environmental deterioration.

Perhaps the most hotly contested issue in all of economics is the question of how much the government should intervene in the economy. Many of those in government are motivated by the desire to promote the public welfare. But well-meaning policy makers do not always adopt policies that work in practice. Furthermore, the government may be used to benefit individuals or groups at the expense of the public as a whole.

In the late 1700s, Adam Smith attacked many governmental interventions in the economy as being contrary to the public interest and wasteful of resources. Smith conceived of the private economy as a self-regulating mechanism. By pursuing their own interests, individuals would unwittingly contribute to the common good. There was no need for extensive government interference to ensure that things would come out all right.

A century and a half later, J.M. Keynes was sceptical of Smith's message of laissez-faire. Things were not coming out all right. The economy was in a deep depression, with many people out of work. It was the responsibility of the government, said Keynes, to do something about this tragic situation. He recommended government spending on roads and other public works as a way to provide jobs.

Full employment is one of the major economic objectives. Four others are also described in this chapter: a stable average level of prices, efficiency, an equitable distribution of income, and economic growth. Other goals might be added to this list, such as environmental protection, economic freedom, and economic security.

The first two goals – full employment and stable prices – come under the heading of maintaining a stable equilibrium in the economy. There has been, in fact, considerable instability in the Canadian economy. The most notable disturbance occurred during the Great Depression of the 1930s, when output and employment dropped sharply and remained at very low levels for a full decade. During World War II, there was an effort to produce as many munitions as possible. Unemployment ceased to be a significant problem, but prices began to rise substantially. Since the end of World War II in 1945, we have avoided severe disturbances comparable to those from 1929 to 1945. However, there have been periodic recessions, with rising unemployment, notably the recent recession from which the economy is still recovering. Inflation was severe during the late 1940s and the 1970s. During the decade of the 1970s, the average level of prices doubled. A major aspect of monetary policy in Canada in recent years has been the fight to eliminate inflation.

Of the major economic problems, unemployment is perhaps the most obvious. When employment declines, we have less output to enjoy. We not only forgo the output that might have been produced, but we also must face the demoralization that comes with unemployment.

The problems with inflation are less obvious. When people buy goods, they obviously dislike higher and higher prices. But there are two sides to every transaction – the buyer's side and the seller's. With widespread inflation, not only do the prices of what we buy increase, but wage rates also go up as do the prices of what we sell. It is not clear whether individuals are net gainers or net losers.

However, there are certain segments of the population that do lose. Those who have pensions set in money terms lose: As prices rise, their pensions buy less. (However, some pensions, including the Old Age Security and Canada Pension Plan benefits paid by the government, are increased to compensate for inflation.) Those who own government bonds or other interest-bearing securities lose. Through the years, they receive payments whose value (purchasing power) becomes smaller and smaller as prices rise. On the other hand, people who have borrowed can benefit: They repay their loans in money whose value has declined.

Inflation generates a feeling that the economic system is unfair. There are arbitrary redistributions of income and wealth, such as the gains to debtors and losses to bond owners. Inflation can also make it more difficult to make wise and well-informed decisions. Prices provide an important source of information to the business executive and consumer. During periods of rapid inflation, when all prices are rising at a brisk pace, the message carried by prices may be obscured. It becomes more difficult to make good decisions.

If inflation accelerates to very high rates – such as 1,000% per year – it becomes known as hyperinflation. Money is losing its value so rapidly that people may refuse to accept it. Because money is practically useless, sellers may feel compelled to barter their products for other goods. Such barter transactions are very cumbersome and time-consuming.

Most inflations do not accelerate into hyperinflation. Hyperinflation is relatively rare, except during wartime or early postwar periods in countries that have been defeated in wars. There are, however, a few cases where countries have had very rapid rates of inflation even though they have not been defeated in a war – for example, during some periods in Brazil.

There are two important types of efficiency. **Technological efficiency** means getting the most output from a given set of inputs (labour, machinery, raw materials). **Allocative efficiency** occurs when the economy is producing the best combination of outputs, using the lowest-cost combination of inputs. Allocative efficiency means producing the goods and services that the Canadian consuming public wants most, or that can be sold in foreign countries in exchange for goods and services that are difficult to produce here. It is possible for an economic system to produce "white elephants" in a technologically efficient manner. But this system would not be producing what people want; it would not be allocatively efficient. Similarly, if everyone were a lawyer and no one a doctor, there would be allocative inefficiency – even if everyone were a superb lawyer.

Equity means fairness, and that raises the question of what fairness means. There can be obvious disagreements. Those with low incomes are likely to argue that a more equal distribution of income would be fairer. Those with higher incomes often argue that their high incomes are the result of hard work; it is fair for them to be paid more because they have worked harder.

Most people agree that the government should take steps to help those who are poverty-stricken, for example, by taxing the rich to provide services for the needy. The question arises, however, as to how far this process should be taken. Clearly, if the government confiscated all incomes above the average and gave the revenues to low-income people, then it would severely interfere with the incentive to work hard. (This would also greatly increase the incentive to cheat on taxes!) Even less drastic steps to redistribute income can decrease incentives, and thus decrease the size of the national "pie." The size of the pie depends in part on how it is cut up.

Economic growth is often advocated for its own sake. In a growing economy, we enjoy more goods and services. Furthermore, growth may make it easier to meet other goals, such as reducing poverty. However, we should not simply assume that the more growth, the better. Growth comes at a cost. Most obviously, if we produce more machinery and equipment to help us grow, then we will give up the current consumer goods that might have been produced instead of the machinery and equipment. And, in recent years, we have become increasingly aware of the potentially devastating consequences of the pollution that industrial growth may cause, unless it is properly controlled.

Some goals – such as a high level of employment and an elimination of poverty – are complementary. Progress on the one contributes to progress on the other. If jobs are provided for people, they are less likely to be poor.

Other goals are in conflict. If people buy more goods and services, they will help to increase the number of jobs. But they will also make it easier for sellers to raise their prices. Thus, if the government takes steps to encourage spending, it may help ease one problem (unemployment) while making another worse (inflation). In such circumstances, good policies may be particularly difficult to develop.

IMPORTANT TERMS

1. Laissez-faire
2. Great Depression
3. Labour force
4. Inflation
5. Relative prices
6. Economic efficiency
7. Technological efficiency
8. Allocative efficiency
9. Distribution of income
10. Equity

TRUE-FALSE

T F 1. Adam Smith argued that the government should build public works whenever needed to reduce the rate of inflation.

T F 2. By definition, a depression occurs whenever the output of the nation falls.

T F 3. During the Great Depression of the 1930s, the unemployment rate rose above 15% of the labour force.

T F 4. Between 1965 and 1986, output per person in the 30 poorest countries in the world grew at an average annual rate of less than 1.25%, much slower than in most advanced countries.

T F 5. Since 1970, recessions have been much less severe than those of the 1950s and 1960s.

T F 6. A recession is a decline in total output, employment, and income, and is marked by a widespread contraction in many industries.

T F 7. Changes in the average level of inflation make an important contribution, since they are the key to improvements in allocative efficiency.

T F 8. Throughout the 1980s, the percentage of the population living in poverty declined slowly but consistently.

T F 9. Over the past three decades, there has been a consistent trend in Canada: the rich have gotten richer, and the poor have gotten poorer.

T F 10. Inflation is caused by a decline in purchases by consumers.

MULTIPLE CHOICE

1. Since 1900, output per capita in Canada
   a. has approximately doubled, while the length of the work week has declined
   b. has grown more than fivefold, while the length of the work week has declined
   c. has approximately doubled, while the length of the work week has remained stable
   d. has grown more than fivefold, while the length of the work week has remained stable
   e. has remained stable, while the length of the work week has declined sharply; all the gains have come in the form of more leisure

2. Between 1980 and 1990, which of the following countries grew most rapidly?
   a. France
   b. Canada
   c. Japan
   d. United States
   e. West Germany

3. By the phrase "invisible hand," Adam Smith was expressing the idea that
   a. there are no economic conflicts among nations
   b. there would be no economic conflicts among nations if countries would eliminate tariffs
   c. there are no conflicts between what is good for an individual and what is good for society as a whole
   d. by pursuing their own individual interests, people frequently promote the interests of society
   e. business executives have a natural interest in keeping prices down and preventing inflation

4. Suppose that the American government is considering increasing the tariffs on steel imported from Canada. Which organizations in the United States are most likely to oppose such an increase?
   a. steelworkers' union and auto workers' union
   b. General Motors and Caterpillar
   c. steelworkers' union and the U.S. Treasury
   d. U.S. Steel and the U.S. Treasury
   e. U.S. Steel and General Motors

5. In his *General Theory*, Keynes' principal concern was with the goal of
   a. stable prices
   b. low unemployment
   c. allocative efficiency
   d. technological efficiency
   e. an equitable distribution of income

6. Unemployment is likely to be highest during
   a. war
   b. peacetime prosperity
   c. rapid growth
   d. recession
   e. depression

7. Between 1929 and 1933 (the early part of the Great Depression), total output in Canada
   a. declined about 30%
   b. declined about 20%
   c. declined about 10%
   d. declined about 5%
   e. remained approximately stable; the Depression represented an interruption of growth, not an actual decline in output

8. Which of the following is counted as being unemployed?
   a. someone who has just retired at age 65
   b. a full-time student not looking for a job
   c. someone who has recently graduated from college and is looking for his or her first full-time job
   d. convicts in prisons
   e. all of the above

9. A moderate rate of inflation (of, say, 4% per annum)
   a. creates no problems in the economy
   b. hurts people living on fixed money incomes
   c. hurts people who have borrowed money
   d. occurs whenever money wages rise more rapidly than prices
   e. is likely to be caused by war

10. The key role in promoting allocative efficiency is played by changes in
   a. the average level of prices
   b. the rate of inflation
   c. the rate of growth
   d. relative prices
   e. the distribution of income

11. Economists distinguish changes in the average level of prices and changes in relative prices. Changes in the average level of prices are generally considered
   a. undesirable, while changes in relative prices can perform a useful function in promoting efficiency
   b. undesirable, but changes in relative prices are even more undesirable, since they hurt some people while helping others
   c. undesirable, but changes in relative prices are neither good nor bad; they just happen
   d. desirable, but the government should attempt to prevent changes in relative prices
   e. desirable, but changes in relative prices are even more desirable, and the government should take steps to increase changes in relative prices

12. Suppose that every factory worker were in the job best suited for him or her, working as productively as possible, but producing cars that nobody wanted to buy. This would be an example of
    a. technical inefficiency and allocative inefficiency
    b. technical efficiency and allocative inefficiency
    c. technical inefficiency and allocative efficiency
    d. technical efficiency and allocative efficiency
    e. technical efficiency and allocative efficiency, but slow growth

13. During the past two decades, the prices of computers have fallen, while the price of oil has risen. As a result, manufacturers and other businesses have used more computers, and have conserved on energy. This switch toward more computers and less energy consumption is an illustration of
    a. allocative efficiency
    b. technological efficiency
    c. the effects of inflation
    d. a less equal distribution of income
    e. a more equal distribution of income

14. Which is the best example of technological inefficiency?
    a. producing too many cars, and not enough housing
    b. slow growth
    c. inflation
    d. inequality of incomes
    e. sloppy management

15. Equity in the distribution of income means
    a. equality
    b. fairness
    c. more for everyone as a result of growth
    d. more for those who can't work
    e. more for those who work hard

16. Suppose that the incomes of all families are perfectly equal. Then what share of total income will the poorest 10% of the families get?
    a. 5%
    b. 10%
    c. approximately 15%
    d. 20%
    e. 25%

17. Which of the following pairs is the clearest example of conflicting goals?
    a. less unemployment and less inflation
    b. less unemployment and less poverty
    c. less unemployment and more growth
    d. less unemployment and more efficiency
    e. more efficiency and less poverty

18. If, during the coming six months, there is a boom in the purchases of machinery by businesses, then we would be most likely to observe
    a. an increase in the rate of inflation and a decline in the rate of unemployment
    b. a decrease in the rate of inflation and a decline in the rate of unemployment
    c. an increase in the rate of inflation and an increase in the rate of unemployment
    d. a decrease in the rate of inflation and an increase in the rate of unemployment
    e. a decrease in inflation, growth, and unemployment

19. Economists study
    a. inflation
    b. unemployment
    c. efficiency
    d. poverty
    e. all of the above

(Appendix)

20. A reason for using a logarithmic or ratio scale on the vertical axis of a chart is that this
    a. makes it easier to start measuring from zero
    b. allows readers to quickly see when the rate of increase was most rapid
    c. avoids the necessity of choosing an arbitrary beginning year
    d. shows when profits were at a maximum
    e. shows when profits were at a minimum

EXERCISE

In the following passage, choose the correct word or phrase from those given in the brackets.

Economic history is a story of both progress and problems. Some evidence of progress shows up in Figure 1-1 in the textbook. Here we see that output per person has increased by a little more than (150%, 200%, 300%) since 1926, and about (25%, 100%, 200%) since 1960. If we were to look at total output of the economy – rather than at output per person – we would find that total output has increased by (an even greater percentage than output per person, a somewhat smaller percentage).

The right-hand panel of Figure 1-1 shows another source of gain. Not only have we produced more, but we have done so with a shorter work week. The decline in the work week was approximately (20%, 40%, 60%) between 1926 and the mid-1980s. Notice also the very sharp drop between 1926 and 1935. This decrease was the result of (a much more rapidly improving economy which allowed more leisure, the Depression which reduced the demand for output, a loss of the work ethic).

Successes and problems also show up in Figure 1-3 in the textbook. The (upward trend in output, downward trend in unemployment, both) since 1950 show(s) how things have improved. However, from time to time there have been problems such as in 1981/82 when (the unemployment rate increased, output declined, both). This was only one of several instances since 1950 when the Canadian economy suffered from the problem of (recession, depression, inflation, poverty).

Figure 1-4 shows the average level of prices. A rise in this curve is an indication of inflation. The more rapid is inflation, the steeper is the curve. We see that inflation was particularly rapid between (1950 and 1960, 1960 and 1970, 1970 and 1980).

Finally, Figure 1-5 shows the percentage of the population living in poverty; a decline in the percentage is a sign of success. Observe that, at the beginning of the period shown, the incidence of poverty declined, from about (15%, 22%, 35%) in the mid-1960s to about (8%, 11%, 14%) in the mid-1980s.

ESSAY QUESTION

A major policy dilemma of the 1990s is coping with high budget deficits and high levels of government debt. Outline the conflicts in economic goals which have arisen from governments' attempts to cope with this problem in recent years.

ANSWERS

True-False: **1**F, **2**F, **3**T, **4**T, **5**F, **6**T, **7**F, **8**F, **9**F, **10**F

Multiple Choice: **1**b, **2**c, **3**d, **4**b, **5**b, **6**e, **7**a, **8**c, **9**b, **10**d, **11**a, **12**b, **13**a, **14**e, **15**b, **16**b, **17**a, **18**a, **19**e, **20**b

Exercise: 300%, 100%, an even greater percentage than output per person, 40%, the Depression which reduced the demand for output, upward trend in output, both, recession, 1970 and 1980, 35%, 11%.

ANSWERS TO PROBLEMS FROM THE TEXT

1-1. In the first instance, the butcher gets money in exchange for the meat. In turn, this money can be used to buy the things the butcher wants – clothing, housing, etc. The butcher and the baker find that, by specializing in the preparation of food, they can obtain more clothing and housing than they could make themselves in an equivalent time.

1-2. Unemployment is the major problem of a depression. After a collapse, as many as 10% or 25% of the labour force may be unable to find jobs. Furthermore, joblessness tends to be of much longer duration during a depression than in more normal times. Unemployment is particularly severe for young people. During hard times, those who have jobs try to keep them. It is the new entrants into the labour force who are hit particularly hard when job openings dry up.

1-3. There is no "right" answer. This would be a good question to pose to your instructor as the basis for a class discussion.

1-4. This question asks you to think about a potential conflict between the goal of technological efficiency and that of low unemployment. The rapid rate of technological change in the workplace in recent years resulting from the widespread introduction of computer technology has displaced not only many clerical workers but also a wide range of unskilled labour.

1-5. (a) Presumably, the main reason that the length of the work week has declined is that as real incomes have increased, people have felt that they could afford more leisure. In Sweden, tax rates are very high. This means that the "price of leisure" (that is, the after-tax income you forgo by not working) is relatively low, which may explain why Swedes choose more leisure. The difference between Canada and the United States also may be explained by higher taxes here.

(b) No; if people value leisure, they may be happy to give up some growth in income in order to have more leisure.

APPENDIX

This appendix provides additional information and practice for those who have already studied the appendix to Chapter 1 in the textbook.

Graphs

During rainy spells, sales of lawn furniture decline. A simple version of the relationship between weather and the sales of lawn furniture is illustrated in Figure 1.1 below.

The two measures used in this graph – sales of furniture and rainfall – are examples of variables. A *variable* is something that can change, or vary, from time to time or from place to place. For example, the amount of rain in April is generally different from the amount in July.

The statement that the sales of lawn furniture decline during rainy weather means that there is a relationship between the two variables in Figure 1.1. In particular, it means that when rainfall increases, sales decline. This idea can be illustrated in the figure.

The two axes, marked with numbers, meet at the origin 0. The vertical axis shows the quantity of lawn furniture sold. The horizontal axis shows the amount of rainfall. The relationship between the two variables is depicted by the line marked with the letters *A* through *F*. For example, point *A* shows that when the rainfall is 1 cm per month (measured along the horizontal axis), there are $6,000 worth of sales of lawn furniture (measured up the vertical axis). Likewise, at point *B*, 2 cm of rainfall result in sales of $5,000. In this way, each time you read a point on the line you get one bit of information. These "bits" are shown in Table 1.1.

Table 1.1

Point	A	B	C	D	E	F
Rainfall	1	2	3	4	5	6
Sales	6	5	4	3	2	1

Thus, the rule for reading the graph is as follows: If you want to find out how much furniture will be sold when there is some particular amount of rain (say, 3 cm), go along the horizontal axis to 3 units, then go directly up to the line. This shows sales of $4,000 worth of furniture when the rainfall is 3 cm. Question 1 at the end of this appendix provides an exercise in reading graphs.

Slope

Figure 1.1 shows not only that rainfall and sales are related. It shows the direction of that relationship.

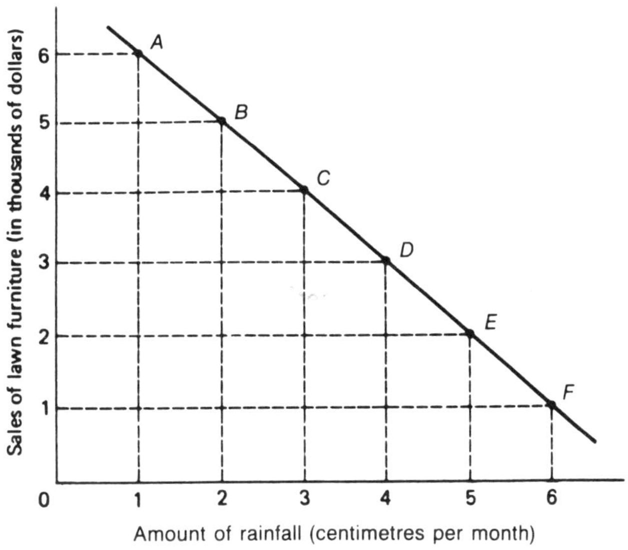

Figure 1.1

Specifically, when rainfall increases, sales decrease. In other words, sales are *negatively* or *inversely* related to rainfall. This negative relationship means that the line in Figure 1.1 slopes downward to the right. As you move to the right (as rainfall increases), the height of the line decreases (sales decrease). For example, by comparing points *A* and *B*, we see that when rainfall increases from 1 to 2 cm, sales decrease from $6,000 to $5,000.

A **positive** or **direct relationship** is illustrated in Figure 1.2; both variables change in the same direction. When snowfall increases, sales of skis increase, too. This means that as we move to the right (more snow), the line slopes upward (more sales of skis).

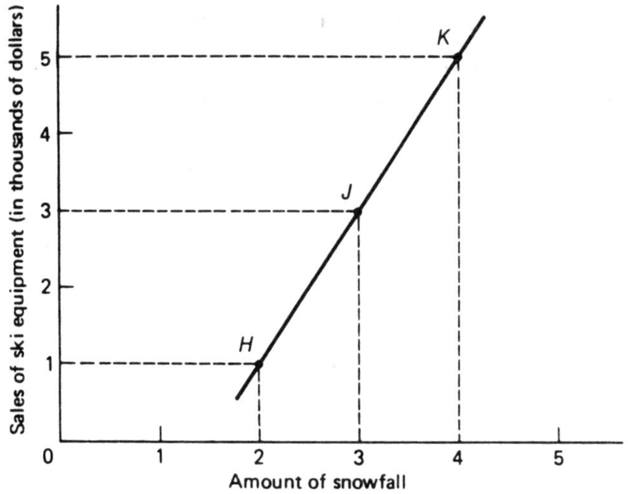

Figure 1.2

A graph such as Figure 1.2 shows not only the direction of the relationship between the two variables, it also shows the strength. For example, it shows that when snow increases by 1 cm (from 2 to 3 cm), 2000 more skis are sold. The strength of the relationship is shown by the slope of the line. The slope of the line is defined as the amount by which the height of the line changes when you go one more unit to the right on the horizontal axis. In Figure 1.2, the slope is 2; a 1-unit increase in snow causes a 2-unit increase in the sales of skis. Alternatively, the slope of a line between two points (such as *H* and *K* in Figure 1.2) is defined as the rise (that is, the vertical change of 4 units) divided by the run (the horizontal change of 2 units). Again, we see that the slope of the line is 2 (that is, 4 divided by 2).

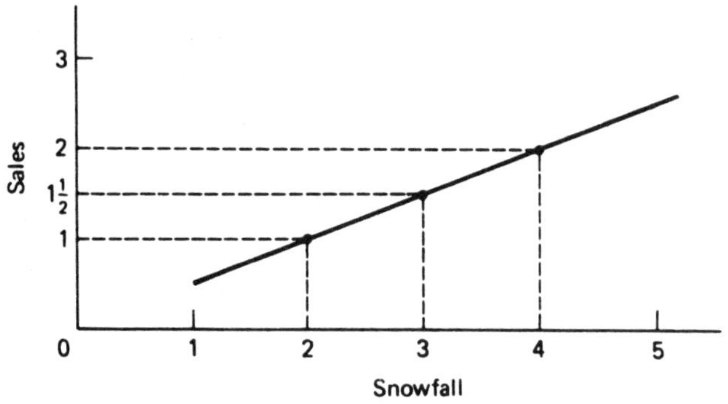

Figure 1.3

Observe that ski sales respond much more strongly to snow in Figure 1.2 than in Figure 1.3. In Figure 1.3, the much weaker response is illustrated by the relatively flat curve; when snowfall increases by 1 unit, ski sales increase only a half unit; the slope is only 1/2.

Back in Figure 1.1, an increase in one variable (rain) caused a decrease in the other variable (sales of lawn furniture). The line slopes downward; that is, the slope is negative. (For example, between points *A* and *C*, the rise is 2 while the run is 2; thus the slope is 1.) A negative slope means, therefore, that the two variables are **negatively** or **inversely** related.

In summary, the slope of the line shows two ideas – the direction and strength of the relationship between two variables. The direction of the relationship depends on whether the line slopes up or down – that is, whether the slope is positive or negative. The strength of the relationship depends on the steepness of the line. Questions 3 and 4 at the end of this appendix deal with the concept of slope.

Linear Equations

Sometimes the relationship between two variables is shown not by a graph, but by an equation. For example, suppose that you are told that my expenditures on consumer goods (C) each month depend on my income (Y) according to the equation:

$$C = \$400 + 0.50Y$$

(Economists almost always use the letter Y for income. I is used to denote investment.)

In simple English, this equation says that I spend $400 plus half of my income that month. As my income varies from month to month, the equation tells you how my expenditures will vary. Whatever my income (Y) is, you can figure out how much I am likely to spend for consumer goods (C).

For example, choose some convenient value for my income, such as $1,000. Then substitute this into the equation to get $C = 400 + 0.5 \times 1{,}000 = 400 + 500 = 900$. This tells us that when my income is $1,000, my expenditure on consumer goods is $900. Now choose any other convenient value, such as $1,100. Substituting this value into the equation shows us that when my income is $1,100, my expenditure on consumer goods is $400 + 0.5 \times 1{,}100$ or $950. Each time you choose a value for Y and make this substitution, you get one bit of information. These two bits are shown in Table 1.2. As an exercise, fill in the rest of the table.

Table 1.2

Y	100	200	300	400	500	600	700	800	900	1000	1100
C										900	950

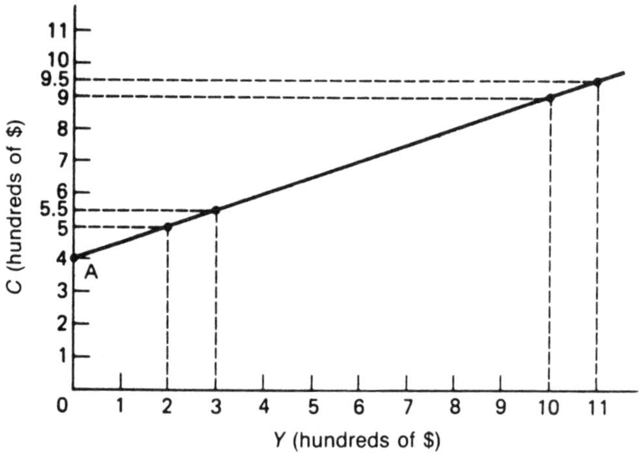

Figure 1.4

Figure 1.4 shows this relationship in a graph. The slope of the line is 0.5. This is because every time my income increases by $100 (shown as a move of one unit along the horizontal axis), I spend another $50 (shown as a rise of 0.5 of a unit). In contrast, the equation $C = 400 + 0.75Y$ represents the behaviour of individuals who spend $400 plus three-quarters of their income. In this case, the slope of the line would be 0.75, because every increase of $100 in income would cause an increase of $75 in consumption.

In general, any equation of the sort $C = a + bY$ represents a line with a slope equal to b. Such an equation is a linear equation. For example, the **linear equation** illustrated in Figure 1.4 has $a = 400$ and $b = 0.5$.

The number b (in this example, 0.5) is known as the **coefficient** of the variable Y. It indicates the slope of the line. The number a (400) shows how high the line is where it meets the vertical axis (point A). Thus, a is often called the **vertical intercept** of this equation. For example, the vertical intercept in Figure 1.4 is 400; this corresponds to the equation where $a = 400$.

At this time, you should do questions 5 and 6, which deal with linear equations.

Curves

So far we have drawn only straight lines. A straight line is easy to use because it has a **constant slope**. For example, in Figure 1.1, the slope of the line is the same between *A* and *B* as it is between any other two points on the line.

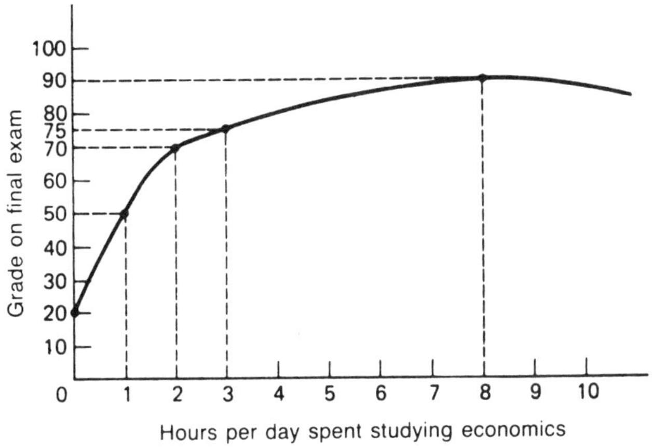

Figure 1.5

However, sometimes a relationship is described better by a curve, like the one in Figure 1.5, which illustrates how a student's final grade depends on how many hours he or she spends studying during the average week. A curve does not have a constant slope; as you move to the right on this curve, it gets flatter. For example, the first hour of studying causes an increase in the grade by 30 points – from 20 to 50. However, the second hour makes it rise by only 20 more (to 70), and the third hour causes an increase of only 5 more points. Each move to the right of 1 hour per week causes a smaller increase in the grade. In this example, it would obviously be impossible for the relationship to continue in a straight line in the way it began. The first hour caused an increase of 30 points. Four hours obviously couldn't cause an increase of 120 points, for the simple reason that the exam has a maximum grade of 100 points.

In this curve, as before, the slope is still identified as the amount by which the height of the curve changes as you go one more unit to the right along the horizontal axis. But, in this case, the slope changes as you go to the right. For the first hour, it is 30; for the second, 20; then 5; and so on.

The decreasing slope in Figure 1.5 indicates that as the student spends more and more time studying, each additional hour may raise the grade, *but not by as much as the previous hour*. The first hour raises the grade by 30 points, the next by only 20. This is an example of diminishing returns; the payoff (in terms of a higher grade) diminishes as a person studies more and more.

Notice that, according to Figure 1.5, the curve reaches its maximum. No matter how much time the student spends studying, he or she can't get more than 90. Indeed, after 8 hours, the student gets tired and stale. Any more time with the books will be counterproductive. The slope of the curve becomes negative; each additional hour results in a lower grade.

Other Graphs

Sometimes, in presenting a general argument, we don't bother to put numbers on the axes. For example, the linear relationship in Figure 1.6 shows no numbers (except for the 0 at the origin). Without numbers, we can't tell exactly how strong the relationship is between the variables *X* and *Y*. But the graph still provides important information – that the relationship is linear, with a constant direction and slope. In this diagram, we can put in letters as points of reference. Point *E* represents 0*A* units of *X*, and its height is measured as 0*C* units of *Y*.

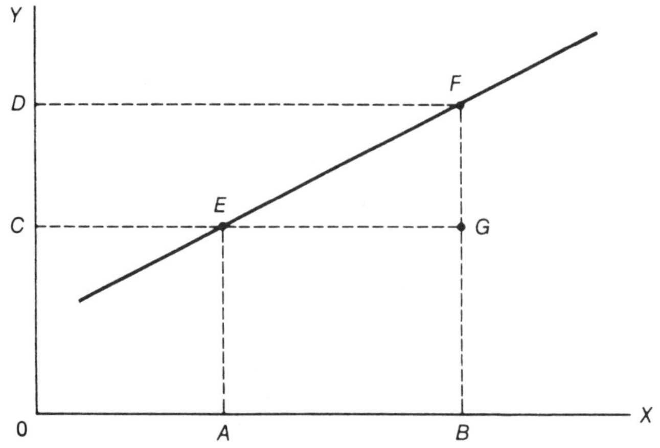

Figure 1.6

When describing the movement from *E* to *F* along the line, it helps to look at triangle *EFG*. The change in *X* is the difference between distance 0*B* and 0*A*, that is, distance *AB*. Likewise, the change in *Y* can be read from the vertical axis as *CD*, or from the triangle as distance *GF*.

The Ratio Scale

In the standard diagram (such as Figure 1.2) each vertical increase of one notch represents the same increase – in this example, an increase of 1000 skis. Equal distances along an axis represent equal changes in the variable.

But there is an important exception to this rule. Look at Figure 1.7. In this graph, going up one notch on the vertical axis doesn't always mean the same change in the price level. The first notch takes you from 25 to 50 – a change of 25. But, when you move up to the second notch, the price level goes from 50 to 100 – a change this time of 50. The vertical axis measures the price level, not on the usual scale, but on the **ratio scale**, or **logarithmic scale.**

As you move up a ratio scale, equal distances represent equal *percentage* changes. Going up from 25 to the first notch, the price level goes up by 100% to 50. Going to the second notch, it again goes up by 100% – this time to 100. In this case, every notch higher represents a price level that is 100% higher.

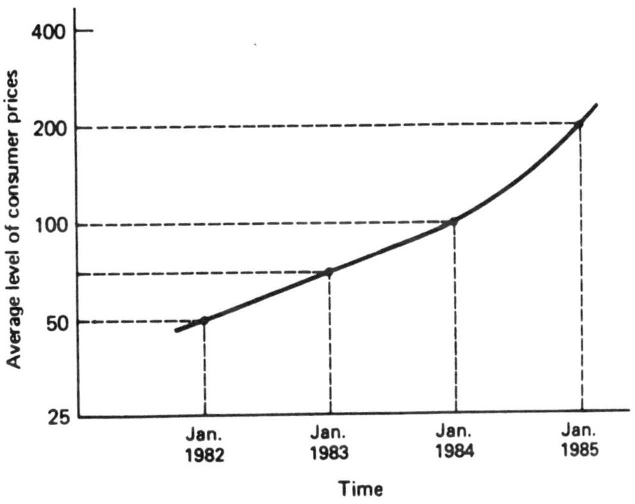

Figure 1.7

In economics, a ratio scale is used most frequently along the vertical axis, with time shown on the horizontal axis (as in Figure 1.7). Such a diagram is used when we're interested in the percentage rate of growth of something – for example, the percentage rate of growth of population or the percentage increase in prices. When such a curve becomes steeper, the percentage rate of increase in population or prices is becoming greater. We can identify the period when the rate of growth was the most rapid. It is the period when the curve is the steepest.

QUESTIONS

1. Point *A* in Figure 1.8 has a height of ____ and lies distance ____ to the right of the origin. Thus, it indicates that when there is a light rainfall of ____ centimetres during rush hour, ____ thousand workers will arrive at work on time. If rain is heavier, at 6 cm, only ____ thousand workers will be on time. With a very heavy rain of 10 cm, ____ thousand workers will be on time.

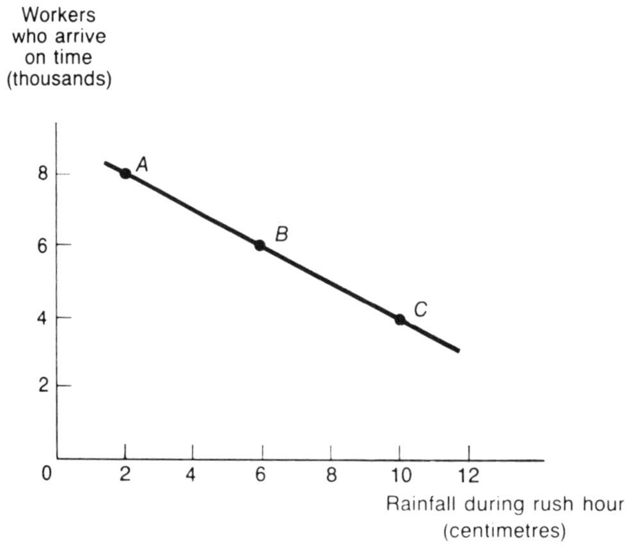

Figure 1.8

2. From Figure 1.2, fill in Table 1.3.

Table 1.3

Amount of snow	2	3	4
Sales of skis			

3. There are six different lines in Figure 1.9. In Table 1.4, fill in the slope of each line.

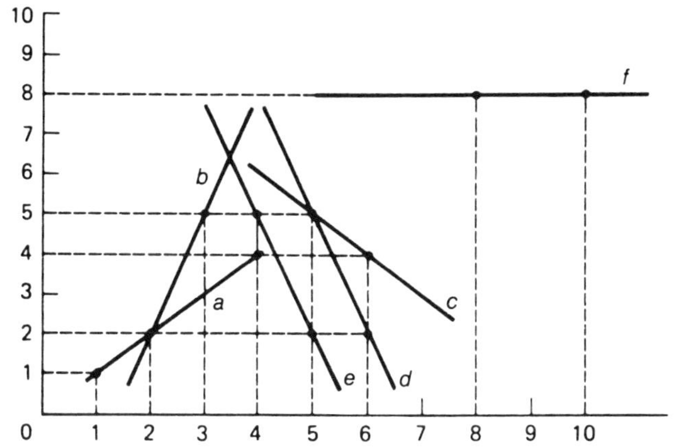

Figure 1.9

Table 1.4

Line	a	b	c	d	e	f
Slope						

4. Which of the lines in Figure 1.10 shows a positive relationship between variables *X* and *Y*? ____. When *X* increases by 1 unit, which of these lines shows the greatest increase in *Y*? ____. When *X* increases by 1 unit, which of these lines shows the greatest decrease in *Y*? ____.

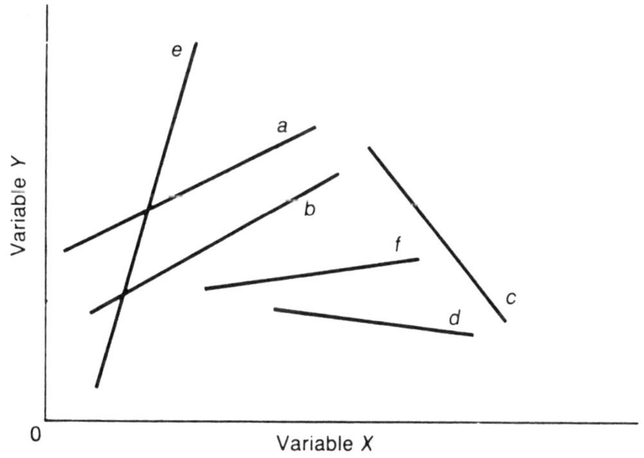

Figure 1.10

5. Consider two variables, X and Y, that are related according to the linear equation $Y = 8 - 2X$. From this equation, fill in Table 1.5.

Table 1.5

X	0	1	2	3	4
Y					

Draw the line representing this equation in Figure 1.11. The slope of this line is ____. The vertical intercept is ____.

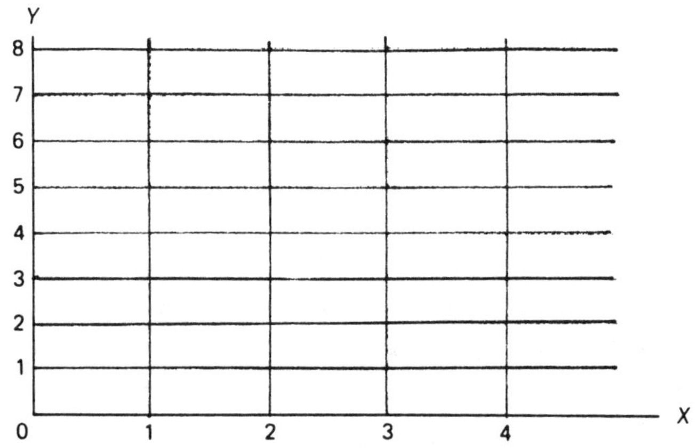

Figure 1.11

6. The following linear equations show how one variable, Y, depends on another variable, X.
(a) $Y = 90 + 10X$
(b) $Y = 50 + 15X$
(c) $Y = 80 - 5X$
(d) $Y = 3X$
(e) $Y = -10 + 5X$
(f) $Y = 50$

Line ____ has the largest vertical intercept and line ____ has the largest slope. When X increases by 1 unit, which line shows the largest increase in Y? ____. When $X = 0$, the highest line is ____.
Which equations show a positive relationship between X and Y? ____. Which

a negative relationship? ____. What is the slope of (f)? ____. Which line has a vertical intercept of zero? ____. Which line passes through the origin? ____.

ANSWERS

Table 1.2 completed:

Y	100	200	300	400	500	600	700	800	900	1000	1100
C	450	500	550	600	650	700	750	800	850	900	950

1. 8, 2, 2, 8, 6, 4

2. **Table 1.3 completed:**

Amount of snow	2	3	4
Sales of skis	1	3	5

3. **Table 1.4 completed:**

Line	*a*	*b*	*c*	*d*	*e*	*f*
Slope	1	3	-1	-3	-3	0

4. (*a, b, e, f*), *e, c*

5. **Table 1.5 completed:**

X	0	1	2	3	4
Y	8	6	4	2	0

   -2, 8

6. *a, b, b, a,* (*a, b, d, e*), *c,* 0, *d, d*

CHAPTER 2

Scarcity and Choice: The Economic Problem

LEARNING OBJECTIVES

After you have studied this chapter in the textbook and study guide, you should be able to

- Understand why the combination of limited resources and unlimited wants requires us to make choices
- Define the three major factors of production
- Explain the difference between real capital and financial capital
- Explain the functions of the entrepreneur
- Explain the concept of opportunity cost
- Explain why the production possibilities curve (PPC) slopes downward to the right
- Explain why the PPC usually bows outward from the origin
- Explain why production occurs within the PPC if there is large-scale unemployment
- Explain the effects on the PPC of an increase in the capital stock in Canada through a capital inflow from foreign countries
- Distinguish between the effects on the PPC of a general increase in society's endowment of resources (labour and capital) and an improvement in the technology of clothing production.
- Distinguish between positive and normative economics

CHAPTER SUMMARY

The major purpose of this chapter is to introduce the concept of **scarcity**. Because of limited resources, we cannot have all the goods and services that we want. Therefore, we must *make choices*, picking some items and forgoing others. This idea – that we face scarcity and therefore have to make choices – is at the centre of economics. A standard definition of economics is "the study of the allocation of scarce resources to satisfy alternative, competing human wants."

The ideas of scarcity and choice are illustrated by the production possibilities curve (PPC). This illustrates the idea of scarcity because we are limited to a point on (or within) the curve; we cannot go outside the curve with our present resources and technological capabilities. The curve also illustrates the need to make choices. When we pick one point on the production possibilities curve, we pass over all the other points and forgo the goods that we might have had if we had picked some other point.

When we make choices, we pick some goods and services and forgo others. If we pick a college education, for example, we may have to put off buying a car for several years. The opportunity cost of our education is the car and other goods and services that we forgo to pay tuition and room and board. Similarly, for the society as a whole, opportunity cost is an important concept. For example, when we decide to produce more weapons, we forgo the consumer goods and services we might have produced instead. Individuals, corporations, and governments are constantly making choices among the options open to them. The slope of the PPC shows how much of one good we must forgo when we choose more of another. In other words, the slope shows the **opportunity cost** of choosing more of a specific good.

The PPC has two important properties. First, it slopes downward to the right. This means that if we decide to produce more of one good, we give up some of the other. The idea that there is an opportunity cost when we produce more of one good is illustrated by the downward slope of the PPC curve.

The second feature of the typical PPC curve is that it is bowed out – that is, it is **concave** to the origin. This is so because resources are **specialized**. If we decide to produce more and more wheat, we will use land that is less and less suited to the production of wheat, even though it was very good for producing wool. For each additional unit of wheat, we will have to give up more wool. Thus, the outward bend in the PPC illustrates the idea of *increasing opportunity cost*.

It is worth emphasizing that a downward slope and an outward bow are two *different* features. A PPC can slope downward without bowing outward. A downward slope means that the opportunity cost is **positive**. An outward bow means that the opportunity cost increases as more of a good is produced.

One of the important choices facing the society is the choice between consumer goods and capital goods. If we produce only a little capital, we will be able to enjoy a large quantity of consumer goods now. But, with little investment, we will have slow growth. In other words, there is a *trade-off between a high current level of consumption and high growth*. This trade-off or choice is illustrated when we draw a PPC curve with consumer goods on one axis and capital goods on the other. For example, Figure 2.6 in the textbook illustrates the difference between a high-growth and a low-growth strategy. A high-growth strategy requires that a sizeable fraction of our resources be committed to investment in plant and equipment (capital goods). But this makes possible a rapid growth – that is, a rapid outward movement of the PPC.

When a nation is receiving a capital inflow from foreign countries, its stock of capital goods may expand rapidly even if the nation's citizens use most of their resources for present consumption. But there is an offsetting disadvantage: Part of the increased future production that is made possible by the nation's larger capital stock will have to be paid to the foreign investors or lenders who initially supplied the capital inflow, as a return on their investment.

This chapter also provides a brief introduction to economic theory. When we develop economic theories, we must simplify. The world is much too complex to describe in all its detail. The objective of theory is to strip away the non-essential complications in order to see the important relationships within the economy. Theory should not be dismissed because it fails to account for everything, just as a road map should not be discarded as useless just because it doesn't show everything. But, because of simplifications, theory must be used carefully. Just as last week's weather map is useless for planning a trip in a car, so the theory that helps to explain one aspect of the economy may be inappropriate or useless for explaining others.

Finally, this chapter explains the distinction between **positive** and **normative economics**. Positive or *descriptive economics* is aimed at explaining what has been happening and why. Normative economics deals with policies; it deals with the way things ought to be.

IMPORTANT TERMS

1. Economic resources
2. Natural resources
3. Labour
3. Physical capital
4. Scarcity
5. Choice
6. Opportunity cost
7. Production possibilities curve (PPC)
8. Technical change
9. Positive economics
10. Normative economics

TRUE-FALSE

T F 1. Resources are said to be scarce because they are incapable of producing all the goods and services that people want; therefore, choices must be made.

T F 2. Wants were "unlimited" during the early days of the study of economics in the eighteenth and nineteenth centuries. But they are no longer unlimited in the affluent countries of North America and Western Europe.

T F 3. Suppose that a production possibilities curve meets the axes at 5 units of clothing and at 20 units of food. This illustrates that the society can have a total of 5 units of clothing plus 20 units of food, but no more.

T F 4. The production possibilities curve bends outward because resources are not uniform in quality; some are better at producing one good than the other.

T F 5. Just as it is possible to select a combination of goods inside the PPC, so it is possible to choose a combination of goods that lie outside the PPC.

T F 6. An increase in the quantity of labour causes the production possibilities curve to shift outwards from the origin.

T F 7. Suppose that two countries, A and B, were identical in 1979. Suppose that, between 1979 and 1989, the economy of A grew at 4% per annum, while B grew at 3% per annum. Then, from that fact, we may conclude that economy A was allocatively more efficient than B during the 1979-1989 period.

T F 8. Positive economics is the study of how policy makers can achieve desirable (that is, "positive") social goals.

T F 9. Less developed countries have a special problem: If they want to grow through creating more capital, they have to forgo some consumer goods or import capital. In the affluent countries in North America and Western Europe, no such choice is necessary.

T F 10. An inflow of American capital into Canada would help shift Canada's PPC outward from the origin.

T F 11. In most less developed countries, an increase in the population and in the quantity of labour will make it more difficult to raise income per person. In such a country, such a population increase will generally cause an inward movement of its PPC.

MULTIPLE CHOICE

1. Economists often speak of wants being "unlimited" because
   a. the cost of living has increased; it costs more to meet our basic needs now than it did twenty years ago
   b. more people live in the cities now than in an earlier age, and it is more expensive to live in cities than on the farm
   c. even though our incomes have risen, we still want "more"; we do not believe all our wants are satisfied
   d. resources such as oil have become scarcer because we have been using them up
   e. as people's incomes have risen, they have decided to take more leisure, and work fewer hours

2. By real capital, economists mean
   a. real estate, particularly land
   b. plant and equipment
   c. the real value of bonds, adjusted for inflation
   d. the real value of common stock, adjusted for inflation
   e. both c. and d.

3. The production possibilities curve has one major purpose: to illustrate the need to
   a. stop inflation
   b. cut taxes
   c. cut government spending
   d. make choices
   e. stop pollution

4. The textbook has a picture of a production possibilities curve (PPC), joining six points.
   a. all six points are equally desirable, since they all represent full employment
   b. all six points are equally desirable, since they all are consistent with zero inflation
   c. all six points are equally desirable, since they all provide for some growth
   d. all six points are possible, but the PPC curve doesn't give enough information to tell which point is best
   e. only one of the six points is presently achievable; the others can be achieved only if the economy grows

5. An outward bow in the production possibilities curve illustrates what concept?
   a. scarcity
   b. unlimited wants
   c. increasing opportunity cost
   d. unemployment
   e. inflation

6. The opportunity cost of a good is measured by
   a. the slope of the PPC
   b. how far the PPC is from the origin
   c. the slope of a line from the origin out to the PPC
   d. how far the economy is operating within the PPC
   e. how fast the PPC is shifting outward

7. Suppose the production possibilities curve for goods *X* and *Y* is a straight line. Then we know that
   a. *X* and *Y* are really the same good
   b. the problem of scarcity has been solved
   c. we can have all the *X* and *Y* we want without incurring an opportunity cost, even though the general problem of scarcity has not been solved
   d. the opportunity cost of *X* is zero, in terms of *Y* forgone
   e. the opportunity cost of *X* is constant, in terms of *Y* forgone

8. We speak of a production possibilities curve as a "frontier" because
   a. we can produce within it or on it, but not beyond it, with presently available resources and technology
   b. it reflects the concept of scarcity, and goods were particularly scarce for settlers on the western frontier in the nineteenth century
   c. it is no longer relevant, now that the frontier has been tamed and we have an affluent society
   d. unemployment problems provide the frontier for economic research
   e. differences among resources provide the frontier for economic research

9. Suppose that the society has only one objective, to maximize growth. Then, the best choice among the five points shown on Figure 2.1 is
   a. *A*
   b. *B*
   c. *C*
   d. *D*
   e. *E*

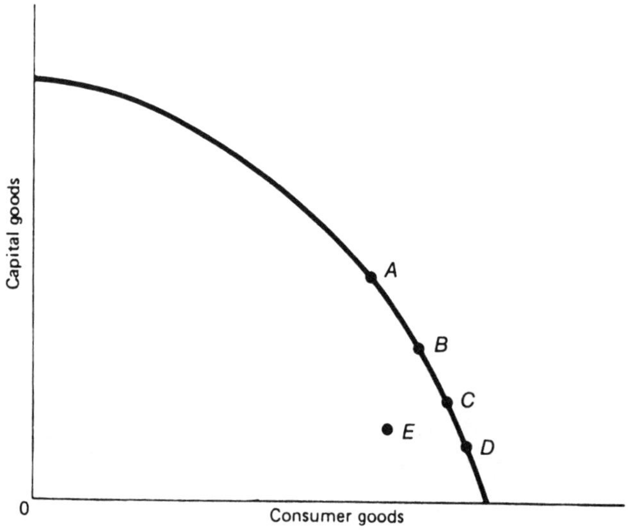

Figure 2.1

10. In Figure 2.1, a growth of the economy can be illustrated by
   a. a move from point *A* to *B*
   b. a move from point *B* to *A*
   c. a move from point *A* to *E*
   d. a move from point *D* to *E*
   e. an outward shift of the production possibilities curve

11. In Figure 2.1, suppose that the economy is originally at point *E*. Then there will be
   a. rapid growth
   b. no capital formation
   c. more capital formation than at points *A*, *B*, or *C*
   d. a high rate of unemployment
   e. rapid inflation

12. The production possibilities curve generally bends outward because
    a. sensible people want to divide their purchases; they want to choose some food and some clothing
    b. there are economies of large-scale production
    c. most people have a comparative advantage in the production of at least one good
    d. there is much less unemployment now than during the Great Depression of the 1930s
    e. resources are not uniform in quality; some are better for producing one good than the other

Table 2.1 Production Possibilities

	Options					
Products	*A*	*B*	*C*	*D*	*E*	*F*
Capital goods	0	1	2	3	4	5
Consumer goods	25	24	21	16	9	0

13. In Table 2.1, the opportunity cost of the second unit of capital goods is how many units of consumer goods?
    a. 1
    b. 3
    c. 5
    d. 7
    e. 9

14. Given the options in Table 2.1, a total output of 5 units of capital goods and 25 units of consumer goods
    a. is unattainable at present
    b. represents a situation of large-scale unemployment
    c. can be achieved only if the economy achieves technological efficiency
    d. can be achieved only if the economy achieves allocative efficiency
    e. can be achieved only if the economy achieves both allocative and technological efficiency

15. Given the options in Table 2.1, a total output of 2 units of capital goods and 10 units of consumer goods
    a. is unattainable at present
    b. represents a situation of large-scale unemployment
    c. can be achieved only if the economy achieves technological efficiency
    d. can be achieved only if the economy achieves allocative efficiency
    e. can be achieved only if the economy achieves both allocative and technological efficiency

16. The choice of option C rather than B
    a. represents a mistake, since only 23 total units are produced (that is, 2 + 21) rather than 25 (that is, 1 + 24)
    b. represents a mistake, since consumers have fewer goods
    c. means that there will be more unemployment
    d. represents a choice of more growth
    e. represents a choice of less growth

17. The production possibilities curve shifts outward, away from the origin
    a. if the number of workers increases
    b. if the skill of workers increases
    c. if there is more capital
    d. if technology improves
    e. if any of the above happens

18. Oil now being pumped in a pipeline is an example of
    a. the land resource, because oil comes out of the ground
    b. real capital, because it has been produced in the past and will be used in the production of other goods
    c. financial capital, because it is valuable and is worth money
    d. financial capital, because it can be used as collateral for bank loans
    e. financial capital, because it was costly to pump out of the ground

19. Which of the following is an example of a capital inflow into Canada?
    a. a Canadian student spends $10,000 to study business administration at a U.S. university
    b. a Japanese construction firm buys $100,000 worth of timber from British Columbia
    c. a Finnish firm builds a plant in Quebec to produce cross-country skis
    d. an American couple spends $100 for a room and meals in Niagara Falls, Ontario
    e. a Canadian tourist brings back $100 worth of Mexican currency after a vacation in Acapulco

EXERCISES

1. Consider the following production possibilities table:

Table 2.2

	Options							
	A	*B*	*C*	*D*	*E*	*F*	*G*	*H*
Consumer goods	0	1	2	3	4	5	6	7
Capital goods	23	22	20	17	13	9	5	0
Opportunity cost of consumer goods	1	2						

a. Complete the third line, showing the opportunity cost of each additional unit of consumer goods.
b. Draw the PPC on Figure 2.2.

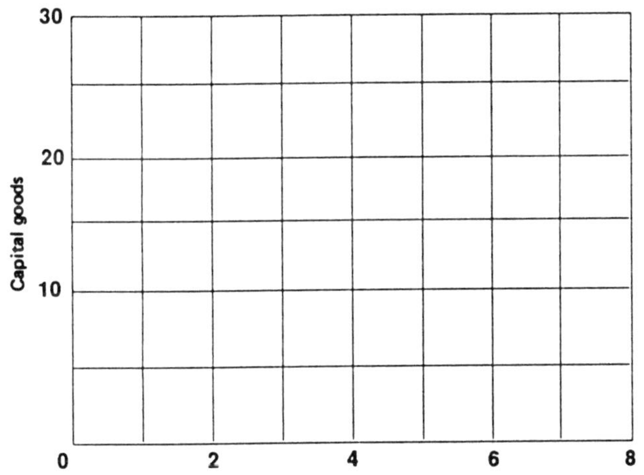

Figure 2.2

c. What is unusual about this curve?
d. In the range between points *A* and *D*, the PPC (bows outward, bows inward, is a straight line). This shows that opportunity cost is (increasing, decreasing, constant) in this range. However, between points *D* and *G*, the curve (bows outward, bows inward, is a straight line). This shows that opportunity cost is (increasing, decreasing, constant) in this range.

2. Consider a hypothetical economy with a labour force of 10 000 workers, each of whom can be put to work building either houses or roads. Each worker is available for 2000 hours per year. Thus, there are 20 million labour hours available during the year to produce houses and roads. Table 2.3 shows how many labour hours it takes to build various quantities of houses. For example, in order to build 18 000 houses, 15 million labour hours are needed. Likewise, Table 2.4 indicates how many labour hours are needed to build various amounts of roadway. In Figure 2.3, only one point, *A*, on the PPC has been plotted. It shows that if no houses are built, the 20 million labour hours can be used to produce 1000 kilometres of road. Using the data in Tables 2.3 and 2.4, plot four other points and draw a PPC to connect them.

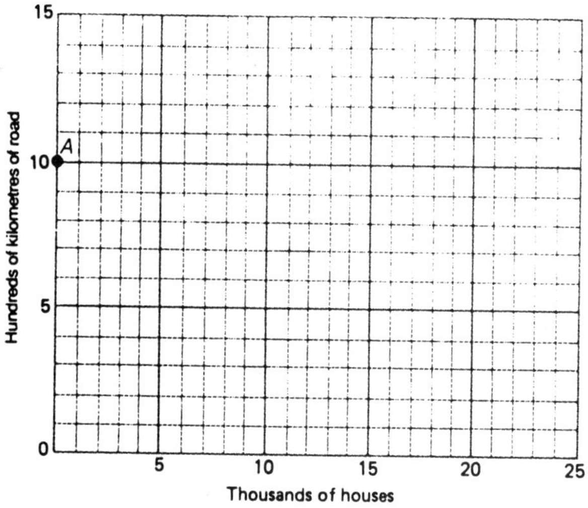

Figure 2.3

Table 2.3

Millions of labour hours	Thousands of houses
20	20
15	18
10	14
5	8
0	0

Table 2.4

Millions of labour hours	Hundreds of kilometres of road
20	10
15	9
10	7
5	4
0	0

ESSAY QUESTION

The opportunity cost principle is widely applicable in people's daily lives. Briefly discuss the opportunity cost of some of the key decisions you have made during the past year. Also, consider the opportunity cost of some of the key decisions made by (a) the federal government and (b) your provincial government during the past year. Can you think of any examples for which due consideration of opportunity cost may have altered the final decision?

ANSWERS

True-False: **1**T, **2**F, **3**F, **4**T, **5**F, **6**T, **7**F, **8**F, **9**F, **10**T, **11**F

Multiple Choice: **1**c, **2**b, **3**d, **4**d, **5**c, **6**a, **7**e, **8**a, **9**a, **10**e, **11**d, **12**e, **13**b, **14**a, **15**b, **16**d, **17**e, **18**b, **19**c

Exercises: **1a**. 3, 4, 4, 4, 5. **1c**. over part of its range, it is a straight line (between *D* and *G*). **1d**. bows outward, increasing, is a straight line, constant. **2**. Four other points are:

	B	*C*	*D*	*E*
Hundreds of kilometres	9	7	4	0
Thousands of houses	8	14	18	20

ANSWERS TO PROBLEMS FROM THE TEXT

2-1. The first definition covers the problem of unemployment, but the second does not. (If there is large-scale unemployment, production is not limited by the scarcity of productive factors.) The importance of the unemployment problem is one of the reasons Chapter 1 uses the broader definition of economics.

2-2. It may be true that Pocklington's material wants have been completely satisfied, but the vast majority of people consume less than they would if they had an unlimited budget. For society as a whole, scarce resources constrain behaviour even though some individuals may have great personal wealth. Although the wealth of very rich families is great, it is not capable of solving the economic problems of society as a whole.

2-3. No clearly correct answer; the best rate of growth is an interesting policy issue. In addressing this question, it is important to recognize that growth comes at a cost. When we direct more of our resources toward capital formation, we have less for current consumption (Figure 2-6 in text). Unless there are unemployed resources that can be directed toward capital formation, higher growth represents a choice between consumption today and consumption in the future.

2-4. Question 2-3 falls within the category of normative economics. It addresses the question of the best rate of growth of the economy.

CHAPTER 3

Specialization, Exchange, and Money

LEARNING OBJECTIVES

After you have studied this chapter in the textbook and study guide, you should be able to

- Explain why specialization and exchange go hand in hand
- Explain why barter is inferior to exchange with money
- Give an example of Gresham's Law
- Explain the two major reasons that there can be gains from specialization and exchange
- Explain the difference between absolute advantage and comparative advantage
- Explain why a country may have an absolute advantage in a product without having a comparative advantage in that product
- Explain why a country cannot have a comparative advantage in producing every product
- Explain why economies of scale may lead to substantial gains from freer international trade, especially for small countries

CHAPTER SUMMARY

In this chapter, we study specialization, exchange, and money. People specialize and engage in exchange because there are gains from doing so; people can achieve higher standards of living. There are two major sources of gain from specialization: (1) **comparative advantage**, and (2) **economies of scale**. These two phenomena are the forces that motivate specialization and exchange; that is, they are the twin engines that drive commerce.

Money, on the other hand, is the *oil* that makes the machinery of commerce run smoothly, with a minimum of friction. Without money, people would engage in cumbersome barter. **Barter** requires a *coincidence of wants* – people engaging in exchange must each be able to provide a good or service that the other wants. Furthermore, for barter to work, there must be some rough equivalence in the value of the two goods or services to be exchanged. To buy toothpaste, a farmer would scarcely offer a cow in exchange. However, with money, such problems of indivisibility do not arise. The farmer may sell the cow for $1,000 and spend just a bit of the money to buy toothpaste, using the rest for a wide variety of other purchases. Money provides people with general purchasing power; money can be used to buy any of the wide variety of goods and services on the market. Those wishing to make exchanges no longer have to search for unlikely coincidences (such as the ill-clad farmer looking for someone who not only has clothes to exchange, but who also wants to get beef in return). But, if some money helps to make the system work smoothly, we should not conclude that more money would make it work even better. Just as too much oil can gum up an engine, so too much money can cause difficulty. Specifically, it causes inflation. The Bank of Canada acts as the chief mechanic. Its task is to create the right amount of "oil" (money) – neither too much, nor too little. The operations of the Bank of Canada will be considered in detail in Chapter 12.

One reason for economic progress has been an increase in **specialization**. Individuals, cities, and countries are now more specialized than they were a hundred years ago. When production is specialized, people engage in exchange, selling the products they produce to buy the wide variety of goods and services that they want to consume. We live in a highly interdependent economy, in which each of us depends on the specialized production of others.

Because it is so useful for those who wish to engage in exchange, money is used even in rudimentary societies with little or no government. The prisoner-of-war camp provides an example of such a simple society. However, governments have gotten deeply involved in the monetary system. Every country uses paper money printed by a central bank.

One reason for the government to be involved in the monetary system is that the government can provide a *uniform currency*. In Canada, for example, every $5 Bank of Canada note (five-dollar bill) is always worth exactly the same as every other five-dollar bill, or as five "loonies" (one-dollar coins). This uniformity of the money stock is very convenient. When selling something for $5, we have to find out only if the buyer has a $5 bill or the equivalent in other standard coins and bills. Except for the rare cases where counterfeiting is suspected, we do not need to ask the much more complicated question of whether the buyer's bills or coins are inferior to someone else's bills or coins.

(Canada has not always had a uniform currency. In the nineteenth century, privately owned banks issued currency. The value of this currency depended on the soundness of the bank that issued it. Thus, sellers did have to worry about the value of the notes or dollar bills they accepted. Similar problems have arisen throughout history. For example, when gold coins were in use, their value could depend on the amount of gold they contained. Before the development of modern methods of producing coins with hard edges, such coins were sometimes clipped. That is, people chipped off bits before spending them. As a result, not every coin was worth the same as every other coin of the same denomination. People had to examine the physical condition of the coins they were accepting.)

In addition to providing a uniform currency, the Bank of Canada has the responsibility of providing an appropriate *quantity* of money. If too many bills or coins are issued, there will be "too much money chasing too few goods." Inflation will result; the currency will decline in value. On the other hand, if the quantity of money is allowed to decline sharply, spending will decline. Sellers will have a very difficult time finding buyers. Sales will fall, unemployment will rise, and prices will be under downward pressure. The authorities do not always perform their monetary duties well. In some countries – for example, Brazil – prices are galloping ahead by more than 100% per year. This reduces the convenience of money. If prices are rising rapidly, sellers feel under pressure to spend their money as soon as possible, before its value declines significantly.

With the proper quantity of money, the monetary system can work very smoothly, making transactions very convenient. But this is all that money does – it makes exchange convenient. It is not the reason that exchange is desirable in the first place.

There are two reasons that specialization and exchange can yield benefits. The first is comparative advantage. The notion of **comparative advantage** is illustrated in the textbook by the example of the gardener and the lawyer. The lawyer has an **absolute advantage** in both the law and gardening; she can do both quicker than the gardener. It follows that the gardener has an absolute disadvantage in both the law and gardening – he is slower at both. However, the gardener has a comparative advantage in gardening, while the lawyer has a comparative advantage in the law. Comparative advantage provides the basis for mutually beneficial trade. Both the gardener and the lawyer can gain from specialization and exchange. (Details are provided in Box 3-2 in the text.)

Two points should be emphasized. (1) Absolute advantage is not necessary for gain; the gardener can gain by specializing in gardening, even though he is not the best gardener. (2) A person (or a nation) cannot have a comparative disadvantage in everything. In the simple case of two people and two activities (law and gardening), if one person has a comparative advantage in one activity, the other person must have the comparative advantage in the other activity.

Economies of scale provide the second major reason that there are gains from specialization and exchange. Economies of scale exist if an increase of $x\%$ in all inputs (labour, machinery, land, steel, etc.) leads to an increase of more than $x\%$ in output. Economies of scale are the major reason that big firms have an advantage in many industries, such as automobiles and mainframe computers. Economies of scale are the major reason that costs per unit of output often decline as more is produced. For example, a car company can produce 100 000 cars at a much lower cost per car than if it produces 1000 cars. Clearly, if a person tried to put together a car in the backyard or in a small shop, it would be very expensive. There are gains when car production is left to the specialists.

Comparative advantage and economies of scale also help explain international trade and specialization among countries in producing different goods. For example, land in Florida is not used to produce trees for wood-pulp even though Florida land can produce more wood-pulp per hectare per year than land in Northern Alberta. Instead, Florida produces oranges while wood-pulp is produced in Northern Alberta, even though Alberta (like the gardener in Box 3-2) has an absolute disadvantage in both wood-pulp and oranges.

Similarly, the desire to gain economies of scale was part of the explanation for Canada entering into an agreement with the United States to allow free trade in cars and car parts (the Auto Pact) in the 1960s. With this agreement, Canadian auto plants could gain scale economies by specializing and producing a narrow range of models for the whole North American market, rather than producing a wide range of models, each on a small scale, for the Canadian market alone. And the hope for greater efficiency through increased scale economies was an important reason for Canada's decision to enter into the wide-ranging Free Trade Agreement with the United States that came into effect in 1989, and most recently the North American Free Trade Agreement (NAFTA) involving Canada, the United States, and Mexico.

IMPORTANT TERMS

1. Specialization
2. Exchange
3. Barter economy
4. Circular flow of expenditures and income
5. Medium of exchange
6. Purchasing power
7. Gresham's Law
8. Comparative advantage
9. Absolute advantage
10. Economies of scale

TRUE-FALSE

T F 1. One reason that barter is inconvenient is that many commodities cannot easily be divided into smaller parts.

T F 2. Monetary systems develop only when there is a strong national government, since strong national governments are required to provide money with value.

T F 3. Suppose that, in the prisoner-of-war camp with its "cigarette money," the value of cigarettes rises compared to the value of other items (such as beef, etc.). Such an increase is known as inflation.

T F 4. Comparative advantage is the reason wheat is grown in rural Manitoba and not in downtown Vancouver.

T F 5. If everyone had exactly the same talents and training, and exactly the same quantity of capital, then economies of scale would not exist.

T F 6. In the absence of a government, money is valuable only if it is useful. Therefore, cigarette money would be used exclusively in transactions between smokers in the prisoner-of-war camp.

T F 7. Economies of scale are the primary reason wood-pulp is produced in Northern Quebec rather than on the Niagara peninsula.

T F 8. Even if everyone has the same abilities, specialization may be beneficial if there are economies of scale.

T F 9. International trade is morc important for a country such as the United States than for Canada because large-scale U.S. factories have a more urgent need for access to world markets.

T F 10. If scale economies are important in many industries, then free international trade is likely to mean both cheaper products and a wider choice for consumers.

MULTIPLE CHOICE

1. One of the problems with barter is that it requires a "coincidence of wants." This means that
   a. everybody must want money
   b. everybody must want the same good
   c. at least two people must want the same good
   d. everybody must want my good before I am able to exchange it
   e. for there to be an exchange between individuals A and B, individual A must want what B has, while B must want what A has

2. When a monetary system first replaces barter, it becomes possible for the first time to distinguish between
   a. a good and a service
   b. the buyer and the seller
   c. private entrepreneurs and the government
   d. owners of capital and workers
   e. all of the above

3. Money is said to represent "general purchasing power" because
   a. it can be used to buy any of the goods and services offered for sale
   b. the government guarantees its value
   c. the government is committed to accept money in payment of taxes
   d. Gresham's Law no longer is valid
   e. Gresham's Law applies to other goods, but not money

4. When we draw a diagram showing the circular flow of payments between households and businesses, the two major markets we show are
   a. goods and services
   b. capital and labour
   c. capital and land
   d. consumer goods and economic resources
   e. products made by private entrepreneurs, and those provided by the government

5. In the present-day Canadian economy, what would an economist consider to be the "medium of exchange"?
   a. supermarkets
   b. corner drug stores
   c. the Sear's catalogue
   d. real estate brokers
   e. 5-dollar bills

6. When the best-tasting cigarettes started to disappear from circulation in the prisoner-of-war camp, this was an example of
   a. economies of scale
   b. absolute advantage
   c. comparative advantage
   d. inflation
   e. Gresham's Law

7. In the prisoner-of-war camp, in which cigarettes acted as money, suppose that the quantity of cigarettes coming into the camp remained constant, while the quantity of all other goods decreased. Then the most probable result would be
   a. a rise in the value of cigarettes, measured in terms of other items
   b. a fall in the prices of other goods, measured in terms of cigarettes
   c. inflation
   d. deflation
   e. bad money driving out good money

8. Suppose that a building supervisor can lay bricks more rapidly and better than a bricklayer. Then, considering only these two individuals, we may conclude that
   a. the bricklayer has an absolute advantage in bricklaying
   b. the supervisor has an absolute advantage in bricklaying
   c. the bricklayer has a comparative advantage in bricklaying
   d. the supervisor has a comparative advantage in bricklaying
   e. we can't tell which of the above is true without knowing how much bricks cost, compared to the wage for bricklayers

9. The theory of comparative advantage was put forward by
   a. Adam Smith
   b. John Maynard Keynes
   c. David Ricardo
   d. David Hume
   e. Karl Marx

10. Suppose that there are only two countries, A and B, and only two goods, food and clothing. If country A has a comparative advantage in the production of food, B is most likely to have a comparative advantage in
    a. food also
    b. clothing
    c. both food and clothing
    d. neither food nor clothing
    e. we don't have enough information to decide

11. Suppose 10 workers with 1 machine can produce 100 TV sets in a month, while 20 workers with 2 machines can produce 250 TV sets in a month. This is an example of
    a. technological efficiency
    b. allocative efficiency
    c. economies of scale
    d. comparative advantage
    e. absolute advantage

12. Suppose that (1) there are economies of scale in the production of each good, and (2) land and labour have specialized capabilities – for example, land and the climate give Brazil a comparative advantage in coffee. Then the gains from specialization will be
    a. larger than if either (1) or (2) had existed alone
    b. smaller, since (1) and (2) tend to offset each other
    c. negative, since the combination of (1) and (2) creates confusion
    d. about the same as with (1) alone, since (2) doesn't make much difference
    e. about the same as with (2) alone, since (1) doesn't make much difference

13. When tariffs among countries are reduced, this generally leads to gains from
    a. economies of scale
    b. wider use of money rather than barter
    c. comparative advantage
    d. a. and b.
    e. a. and c.

14. For there to be mutual benefits from specialization and trade, an essential element is the presence of
    a. absolute advantage
    b. comparative advantage
    c. both absolute and comparative advantage
    d. the invisible hand
    e. none of the above

15. Gresham's Law states that
    a. individuals will be promoted and specialize to their level of incompetence
    b. if anything can go wrong in an economy, it will
    c. supply creates its own demand
    d. bad money drives out good
    e. none of the above

EXERCISES

1. This exercise illustrates the idea of comparative advantage. Assume the following: A doctor working on home repairs can fix a leaky faucet in 10 minutes. A plumber takes 15 minutes. Then the (doctor, plumber) has an absolute advantage in plumbing. The doctor's time is worth $80 per hour in the practice of medicine. The plumber is paid $20 per hour.

   Suppose the doctor's house has six leaky faucets. If he fixes them himself, it will take _____ minutes. Thus, to fix the faucets, the doctor will use $ _____ worth of his time. If the plumber is hired to fix the faucets, he will take _____ minutes, which is (longer, shorter) than the doctor would take. The cost in this case is $ _____, which is (more, less) by $ _____ than if the doctor fixed the faucets himself. The (doctor, plumber) has a comparative advantage in plumbing.

2. Table 3.1 shows how many cars can be produced in a country with various amounts of inputs. Each unit of input represents a specific quantity of labour and capital. Table 3.2 provides similar information for TV sets. Table 3.1, by itself, illustrates the idea of (comparative advantage, absolute advantage, economies of scale, none of these). Table 3.2, by itself, illustrates the idea of (comparative advantage, absolute advantage, economies of scale, none of these).

   Suppose that the economy has 5 units of inputs to be devoted to cars and TV sets. Plot the PPC for these 5 units of input in Figure 3.1. How is the shape of the PPC different from the PPCs in Chapter 2? _____. The opportunity cost of producing cars (increases, decreases, remains constant) as more are produced.

Table 3.1 Production of Cars

Number of cars (millions)	Units of input
1	1
3	2
6	3
12	4
20	5

Table 3.2 Production of TV Sets

Number of TV sets (millions)	Units of input
20	1
40	2
60	3
80	4
100	5

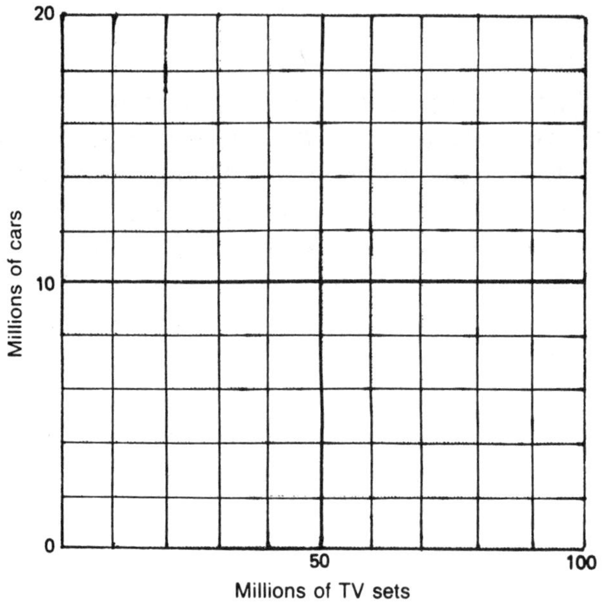

Figure 3.1

ESSAY QUESTIONS

1. The textbook explains why comparative advantage can mean that there are benefits from specialization and exchange. But it does not explain why specific people or nations might have a comparative advantage. How would you explain Saskatchewan's comparative advantage over New Brunswick in producing wheat? Why does Quebec have a comparative advantage over most American states in the production of wood-pulp and newsprint? Why does Taiwan have a comparative advantage in the production of transistor radios and TV sets?

2. There are disadvantages associated with specialization as well as advantages. What are they?

ANSWERS

True-False: **1**T, **2**F, **3**F, **4**T, **5**F, **6**F, **7**F, **8**T, **9**F, **10**T

Multiple Choice: **1**e, **2**b, **3**a, **4**d, **5**e, **6**e, **7**c, **8**b, **9**c, **10**b, **11**c, **12**a, **13**e, **14**b, **15**d.

Exercises: **1**. doctor, 60, $80, 90, longer, $30, less, $50, plumber. **2**. economies of scale, none of these, it bows inward, decreases

ANSWERS TO PROBLEMS FROM THE TEXT

3-1. The simple answer to (a) and (b) is that we export those goods in whose production we have a comparative advantage, and import those goods for which our trading partners have a comparative advantage (that is, for which we have a comparative disadvantage).

In the case of an industry like cars (item (c)), economies of scale provide a reason for exporting some models and importing others, as discussed in the text.

3-2. The important point here is to recognize that this question illustrates absolute advantage in all activities. The decision on specialization would require a comparison on the basis of comparative advantage with other individuals.

3-3. One reason for greater specialization is the development of more specialized machinery. The advantage is more output. One possible disadvantage is the boredom that can come from producing only one narrow product.

3-4. Measuring "number of wills per week" on the vertical axis and "flowers planted per week" on the horizontal axis, the lawyer's PPC will be a straight line from 40 wills on the vertical axis to 800 flowers on the horizontal axis. It is different because it is a straight line.

*3-5. The PPC for each of the two identical cities is bowed toward the origin (the intercepts are 2500 bicycles or 2500 lawnmowers), illustrating increasing opportunity cost as more bicycles are produced (place bicycles on the vertical axis).

CHAPTER 4

Demand and Supply: The Market Mechanism

LEARNING OBJECTIVES

After you have studied this chapter in the textbook and study guide, you should be able to

- Distinguish between capitalist (or free market) economies and Marxist economies
- Explain what is meant by the market mechanism
- Distinguish between perfectly competitive and imperfectly competitive markets
- Define the term "demand curve" and explain why it slopes downward
- Define the term "supply curve" and explain why it slopes upward
- Explain the concept of market equilibrium
- Describe the forces that will cause a price that begins away from equilibrium to adjust to its equilibrium level
- List and explain three things that can shift the demand curve and four that can shift the supply curve
- Distinguish between normal and inferior goods
- Give one example each of two goods that are (1) substitutes in use, (2) complements in use, (3) substitutes in production, and (4) complements in production. In each case, you should be able to explain why they fit into the category.
- Distinguish between the term "change in quantity demanded" and the term "change in demand"
- Distinguish between the term "change in quantity supplied" and the term "change in supply"

- Explain the distinction between product markets and markets for factors of production

- Explain how the factor markets can help answer the question, *For whom?*

- Explain how changes in factor markets can affect what happens in a product market, and vice versa

- List the main strengths and main shortcomings of the market mechanism as a way of answering the questions, *What?, How?*, and *For whom?*

CHAPTER SUMMARY

This chapter is one of the most important in the book. It introduces the concepts of *demand* and *supply*, which help us to understand the market mechanism. In every economy, some mechanism is needed to decide three major questions: What will be produced? How will it be produced? And for whom will it be produced? There are two major ways of answering these questions: (1) through the market – that is, through voluntary exchanges between buyers and sellers, and (2) through governmental decision making. (Other ways are sometimes used – for example, in a family or in a monastery. But we are not primarily interested in these alternatives.)

All nations have some reliance on markets and some reliance on governmental decision making. However, there are substantial differences among nations. In Canada and the United States, the market is the most important mechanism, although the government does play a significant role in modifying the outcome of the market. In the former Soviet Union, government used to play a much more **central** role; there is now, however, an attempt to move to a **market system**.

The central feature of a market is **price**. Different prices for different goods provide *incentives* for producers to make some goods rather than others, and incentives for consumers to purchase cheap goods rather than expensive ones. Prices also provide signals and information to buyers and sellers. For example, the willingness of buyers to pay a high price acts as a signal to producers, showing that people are eager to obtain the product.

To study how buyers respond to different prices, we use a **demand curve** or **demand schedule**. This curve or schedule shows the quantity of a specific good that buyers would be willing and able to purchase at various different prices. The demand curve slopes downward to the right, illustrating that people are more eager to buy at lower prices. A major reason is that, at a lower price, people have an incentive to switch away from other products and buy the product whose price is lower instead.

On the other side of the market, the supply curve shows how much sellers would be willing to offer at various prices. It slopes upward to the right, because sellers will be increasingly eager to sell as the price rises. Again, the willingness to switch is an important reason for the slope. If the price of a good is higher, firms have an incentive to drop other products, and make more of this good instead.

What happens in the market depends on both demand and supply. To find the **equilibrium price** and **quantity**, we put the demand and supply curves together, to find where they *intersect*. At this price, the quantity offered by sellers is equal to the quantity that buyers want to purchase. There is no unfulfilled demand to pull prices up, nor any excess offers to pull prices down.

When the price is not at its equilibrium, there are pressures for it to change. If the price is below its equilibrium, for example, there are eager buyers who are unable to find the good for sale. In other words, there is a **shortage** (excess demand). Producers notice this and conclude that they can sell at a higher price. The price rises to its equilibrium level. On the other hand, if the price is initially above its equilibrium, there is a **surplus** (excess supply). Eager sellers are unable to find buyers. They are willing to sell at a lower price. The result is that price falls to its equilibrium.

When we draw a demand or supply curve, we are looking at the way in which buyers and sellers respond to price, and to price alone. In practice, of course, buyers and sellers are influenced by many other things than the price of the good – for example, buyers generally purchase more when their incomes rise, and sellers are less willing to sell when the costs of their inputs rise. But these other things are held constant when a single demand or supply curve is drawn. This is the important assumption of *ceteris paribus*, that other things do not change. If they do change, the demand or supply curve shifts. For example, an increase in income generally causes a rightward shift in the whole demand curve (so-called **normal goods**). However, in the case of **inferior goods**, the demand curve shifts left; when people can afford better alternatives, they choose them instead.

If the demand curve shifts to the right while the supply curve remains stable, then both price and quantity will increase. On the other hand, if the supply curve shifts to the right while the demand curve remains stable, then quantity will increase but price will fall. In brief, a change in demand makes price and quantity change in the same direction, whereas a change in supply makes price and quantity move in opposite directions. In practice, of course, many things can happen at once; often the demand and supply curves both shift. In this case, it becomes more difficult to predict what will happen.

Supply and demand theory is often used to study the market for a single good. However, there are strong connections among markets. When a price changes in one market, it can change conditions in other markets. For example, an increase in the price of gasoline in the 1970s caused a decline in the demand for large cars. This is an example of **complementary goods** – large cars and gasoline are used together. When the price of gasoline increases, the demand for large cars shifts left.

Whereas gasoline and cars are complements, some other products – such as bus tickets and train tickets – are **substitutes.** A person wanting to travel to the next city can go either by train or by bus. The higher is the train fare, the more people will use buses instead. Thus, a higher price of train tickets causes the demand for bus tickets to shift to the right.

Goods may also be substitutes or complements in production. Substitutes in production are goods which use the same inputs; the inputs can be used to produce either the one good or the other. For example, land can be used to produce either wheat or corn. If there is a crop failure abroad and an increase in North American exports of wheat, the price of wheat will be bid up. Farmers will be encouraged to switch out of the production of corn and produce additional wheat instead. The supply curve for corn will shift to the left.

On the other hand, complements are produced together. For example, wheat and straw are produced together. If the price of wheat is bid up, more wheat will be produced. In the process, more straw will be produced as a by-product. The supply curve of straw will shift to the right.

The question of what will be produced is decided primarily in the product market. To throw light on the other two questions – *How?* and *For whom?* – we look first at the markets for inputs. For example, the market for labour helps to answer these two questions. If the demand for labour is high compared to its supply, then wage rates will be high. Thus, wage rates are much higher in Canada than in India because there are fewer workers for each unit of land and capital in Canada. As a result of the high wage, producers in Canada have an incentive to use only a little labour, and substitute capital instead. In an Indian factory, in contrast, many more things are done by hand because of the low wage rate. The wage rate not only helps to determine how things are produced, but it also helps to determine who gets the product. Because wage rates are high in Canada, a typical worker here can buy and consume many more products than the Indian worker.

Observe that high wage rates affect what the worker can buy; with high wages, workers are more likely to buy TV sets and homes. This means that wages – determined in the factor markets in the lower box in Figure 4-8 in the textbook – have an impact on the demand for TV sets, homes, and other products in the upper box. Thus, there are important connections among markets.

Finally, this chapter summarizes the strengths and weaknesses of the market as a mechanism for answering the three central questions – *What?, How?*, and *For whom?* The strong points of the market are that (1) it encourages producers to make what consumers want; (2) it provides people with an incentive to acquire useful skills; (3) it encourages consumers to conserve scarce goods; (4) it encourages producers to conserve scarce resources; (5) it provides a high degree of economic freedom; and

(6) it provides buyers and sellers with information on market conditions, including local conditions.

The market mechanism is also subject to major criticisms: (1) some people may be left in desperate poverty; (2) markets don't work in the case of public goods such as defence and the police; (3) monopolies and oligopolies may have the power to keep production down and keep prices up; (4) the market does not provide a strong incentive for producers to limit pollution and other negative side effects; (5) a market economy may be unstable (although government policies will not necessarily increase stability); and (6) producers may simply be satisfying a want that they have created in the first place through advertising.

To evaluate the market, it is important to compare it with the alternatives that exist in fact, not with some ideal, unattainable system. The textbook outlines a few of the problems that can arise when the government sets prices – in particular, the problem of **black markets** and shortages. A number of countries that have interfered very heavily in economic activity – such as the former Soviet Union – have run into severe problems, including shortages.

IMPORTANT TERMS

1. Capitalism
2. Marxism
3. Market system
4. Centrally planned system
5. Perfect competition
6. Imperfect competition
7. Market equilibrium
8. Surplus (excess supply)
9. Shortage (excess demand)
10. Inferior good
11. Normal good
12. Substitute good
13. Complementary good
14. Price control
15. Black market

TRUE-FALSE

T F 1. Perfect competition exists only when the government fixes the price, so that no single buyer or seller is able to influence the price of the good.

T F 2. Perfect competition will not exist in a market if there is only one seller, or if there is only one buyer.

T F 3. In a perfectly competitive industry, every buyer and seller takes the quantity as given, and is left with only a pricing decision.

T F 4. Even if there are many buyers, imperfect competition can exist in a market.

T F 5. Even if there are many sellers, imperfect competition can exist in a market.

T F 6. In a capitalist economy, most of the capital equipment is owned by the government.

T F 7. A surplus drives the price down; a shortage drives the price up.

T F 8. If the price of wheat increases, the supply curve of straw will probably shift to the right.

T F 9. The demand curve for Pepsi-Cola will probably shift to the right if the price of Coke rises.

T F 10. If the price of paper increases, the supply curve of books will probably shift to the right.

T F 11. If demand increases while supply decreases, the price will increase.

T F 12. If the demand curve shifts to the right, the result will be an increase in the quantity sold and an increase in the market price.

T F 13. If both the demand and supply curves for a product shift to the right, we can expect the quantity sold to increase, but we cannot be sure whether the price will rise or fall.

T F 14. One essential characteristic of a free enterprise economy is that the government make it easier to enter businesses freely by subsidizing new businesses.

T F 15. Factor markets are different from the markets for most goods, in that goods markets are generally perfectly competitive, while the markets for factors are usually monopolized.

MULTIPLE CHOICE

1. Economists sometimes speak of a "free" market. By "free," they mean
   a. prices are low
   b. people do not have to pay admission to the marketplace
   c. transactions take place with little or no government interference
   d. the government is not a buyer or seller in the market
   e. there is perfect competition in that market

2. The Canadian government uses four major ways to influence what will be produced, how, and for whom. It uses every one of the following except one. Which one does not belong on this list?
   a. spending
   b. taxes
   c. regulation
   d. comprehensive central planning
   e. public enterprises

3. What is the most important characteristic of perfect competition?
   a. each seller has at least one powerful competitor to worry about
   b. there is at least one powerful, efficient producer who acts to keep prices down
   c. every buyer can go to at least three or four sellers to see who has the lowest price
   d. every buyer and seller is a price taker; none has any power to set price
   e. there must be many buyers, and at least three or four sellers

4. A market with one seller and a few buyers is an example of
   a. monopoly
   b. oligopoly
   c. perfect competition
   d. technological inefficiency
   e. a black market

5. It is most accurate to speak of Abitibi Paper Ltd. as
   a. a plant
   b. a firm
   c. an industry
   d. a monopoly
   e. a perfect competitor

6. A surplus of turnips exists when
   a. turnip production is lower than last year
   b. turnip production is higher than last year
   c. turnip production exceeds the production of all other vegetables combined
   d. the quantity of turnips demanded exceeds the quantity supplied
   e. the quantity of turnips supplied exceeds the quantity demanded

7. Suppose that a surplus exists in a market. Then we may conclude that
   a. the price is below the equilibrium
   b. the price is above the equilibrium
   c. the government has imposed a price ceiling
   d. the quantity demanded has decreased
   e. the quantity supplied has increased

8. When we draw the demand curve for a product, we assume that
   a. there are many sellers
   b. there are only a few sellers
   c. all "supply shifters" are held constant
   d. all "demand shifters" are held constant
   e. both c. and d.

9. When incomes increase, the demand curve for an individual good
   a. usually shifts down
   b. always shifts down
   c. usually shifts to the right
   d. always shifts to the right
   e. doesn't move, since only price affects demand

10. Suppose that we know that an increase in the price of good A will cause a rightward shift in the demand curve for good B. Then we may conclude that
    a. producers of A and B use the same set of inputs
    b. consumers of A and B have the same levels of income
    c. consumers of A and B have different incomes
    d. A and B are complementary goods
    e. A and B are substitutes

11. Tennis rackets and tennis balls are
    a. substitutes
    b. complementary goods
    c. inferior goods
    d. independent goods
    e. monopolistic goods

12. Apples and textbooks are
    a. substitutes
    b. complementary goods
    c. inferior goods
    d. independent goods
    e. monopolistic goods

13. Which illustrate best the idea of substitutes in production?
    a. copper and aluminum
    b. wheat and barley
    c. wheat and bananas
    d. beef and leather
    e. cream and sugars

14. Peanuts and tobacco can be grown on similar land. Therefore, they are
    a. substitutes in production
    b. joint products
    c. inferior goods
    d. normal goods
    e. an oligopoly

15. Suppose that the demand for beef increases. This is most likely to cause
    a. a rightward shift in the supply curve for beef
    b. a leftward shift in the supply curve for beef
    c. a fall in the price of beef
    d. a fall in the price of leather
    e. an upward shift in the demand for leather

16. In a typical market
    a. an increase in demand, with no change in supply, will result in a fall in price
    b. an increase in demand, with no change in supply, will result in a decrease in quantity
    c. an increase in demand, with no change in supply, will result in an increase in both price and quantity
    d. an increase in supply, with no change in demand, will result in a decrease in quantity
    e. an increase in supply, with no change in demand, will result in an increase in price

17. Suppose that, between year 1 and year 2, the demand curve and the supply curve for wheat both shift to the right. From this information, we may conclude that, in year 2,
    a. the quantity of wheat sold will be larger, while the price will be higher
    b. the quantity of wheat sold will be larger, while the price will be lower
    c. the quantity of wheat sold will be larger, while we do not have enough information to tell if the price will be higher or lower
    d. the quantity of wheat sold will be smaller, while we do not have enough information to tell if the price will be higher or lower
    e. we do not have enough information to tell what will happen to either the price or the quantity

18. Incomes are determined primarily in the markets for
    a. goods
    b. services
    c. factors of production
    d. machinery
    e. parts

19. The advantages of the market mechanism (as contrasted to government controls) as a way of deciding *What?*, *How?*, and *For whom?* include
    a. prices provide incentives for producers to make what the public wants
    b. prices provide incentives for producers to conserve scarce resources
    c. prices provide incentives for consumers to conserve scarce goods
    d. high wages in skilled occupations act as an incentive for workers to undertake training
    e. all of the above

20. A black market is most likely to exist when
    a. the government controls the price of a good
    b. the supply of a good is controlled by a monopolist
    c. the supply of a good is controlled by two or three producers
    d. the government imposes an excise tax on a good
    e. the government urges producers to produce more to promote the general welfare of the public

EXERCISES

1. Using the demand schedule in the first two columns of the table below, plot the demand and supply curves in Figure 4.1. Label the axes and mark in appropriate numbers on each axis. Then fill in the last column of the table.
    a. The equilibrium quantity is _____.
    b. The equilibrium price is _____.
    c. At the equilibrium price, what is the surplus or shortage shown in the last column? _____. Does this confirm that this price is an equilibrium?
    d. Now suppose that the government sets a price of 60 cents. At this price, there will be a (surplus, shortage) of _____.

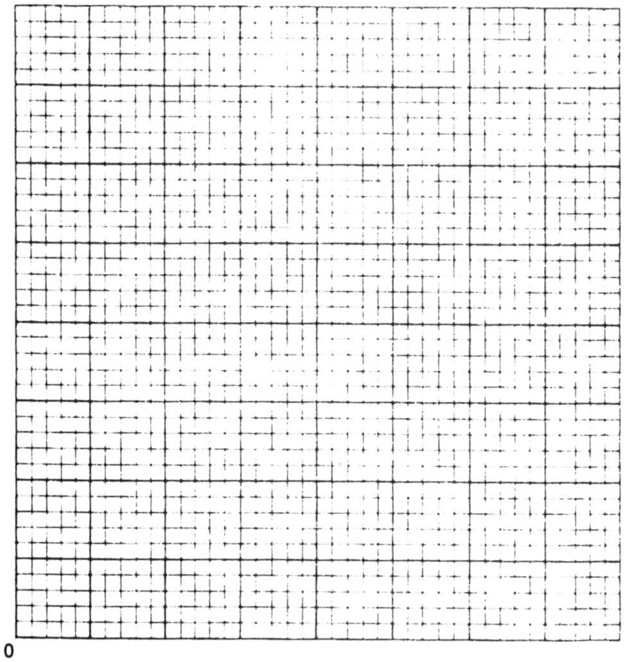

Figure 4.1

Price of Hamburgers	Quantity Demanded (thousands per week)	Quantity supplied (thousands per week)	Surplus (+) or Shortage (-)
$1.40	200	700	
$1.20	240	600	
$1.00	300	500	
$0.80	400	400	
$0.60	600	300	
$0.50	800	250	

2. Figure 4.2 illustrates some of the issues that arise when the government undertakes price supports (for example, in agriculture). *D* shows the demand curve, and S_1 the supply curve. Initially, the equilibrium quantity is _____ million bushels, and the price is _____. Now suppose that the government passes a rule that says that wheat cannot be sold at a price less than P_3. The result of this law will be a (surplus, shortage) amounting to _____ million bushels.

   If all the government does is set a high price, not all wheat farmers will be better off. Those who are better off will be those who (cut back production, sell their wheat at the high price). On the other hand, some will be worse off, specifically those who (are unable to sell their wheat at the high price, sell their wheat at a low price). To ensure that wheat farmers are better off, the government can (buy the surplus wheat, reduce the price to P_1).

   Now, suppose that the government undertakes irrigation projects to help agriculture in dry areas. This will cause an increase in supply from S_1 to S_2, and the (surplus, shortage) of wheat will (increase, decrease) to ____ million bushels. The government will find the costs of its price support program (increasing, decreasing). If it now eliminates the price support, the free market price will settle at _____.

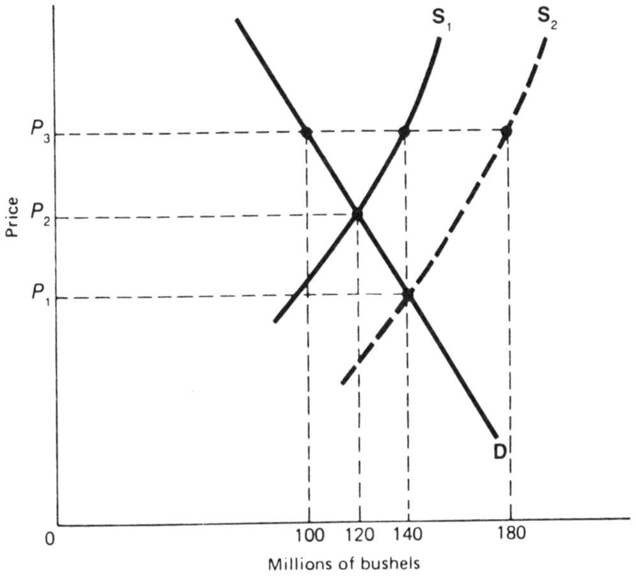

Figure 4.2

3. Suppose that supply is given by the equation:

$$Q = -30 + 4P$$

This supply is plotted in Figure 4.3 in the following way. First, choose some convenient value for P, such as 10. Put this value into the equation to get $Q = -30 + 40 = 10$. This means that when $P = 10$, $Q = 10$, so that point A is on the supply "curve." Then, choose another value of P, say, 15. Substituting this into the equation, we find that the corresponding $Q =$ _____. This is plotted as point B. The supply relationship is a straight line; there are no squared terms or other reasons for supply to bend. Thus, with the two points A and B, we can draw the straight-line supply S_1.

a. Suppose that demand is also a straight line:

$$Q = 20 - P$$

Then, if $P = 15$, $Q =$ _____, and if $P = 5$, $Q =$ _____. Plot demand in Figure 4.3 and label it D_1. On this figure, we see that the equilibrium price is _____ and the equilibrium quantity _____. Confirm these figures by solving the two equations algebraically, to find P and Q.

b. Suppose now that income increases and demand consequently increases, with 15 more units being demanded at each price. Thus, the new demand is

$$Q = 35 - P$$

To plot this new demand, we find two points. For example, if $P = 15$, $Q =$ _____, and if $P = 5$, $Q =$ _____. Plot the new equilibrium demand, labelling it D_2. At the new equilibrium, $P =$ _____ and $Q =$ _____. Again, confirm these numbers by solving the demand and supply equations. The price has (increased, decreased), and the quantity has (increased, decreased) as a result of this increase in demand.

c. Now, suppose we are back with the original demand, D_1, but that supply is now:

$$Q = -10 + 2P$$

If $P = 10$, $Q =$ _____, and if $P = 15$, $Q =$ _____. Plot this new supply and label it S_2. With supply S_2 and demand D_1, the equilibrium price is _____, while quantity is _____. Again, confirm these numbers by solving the demand and supply equations.

d. Finally, suppose that demand shifts from D_1 to D_2, while supply remains at S_2. At the new equilibrium $P =$ _____ and $Q =$ _____. When the demand curve shifted this time, why is it that the price rose more, and the quantity rose less, than in part b?
Answer: _____.

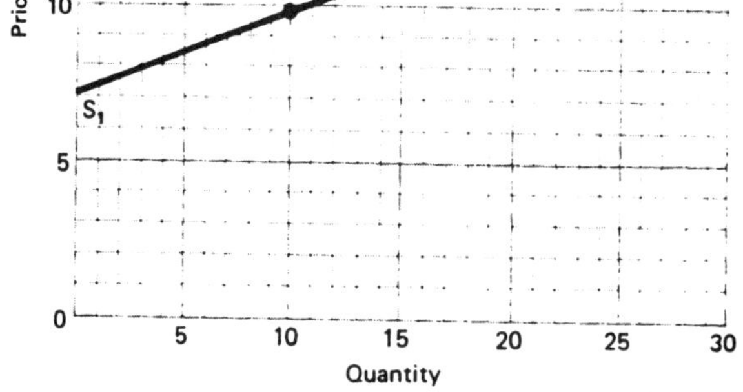

Figure 4.3

ESSAY QUESTIONS

1. A demand or supply curve applies to a specific time and a specific location. For example, the market for maple syrup in London, Ontario, is not the same thing as the market for maple syrup in Winnipeg, Manitoba. Would you expect the price of maple syrup in these two cities to be similar? Precisely the same? Explain.

2. Suppose that, as a result of an increase in the number of pancake eaters in Winnipeg, there were an increase in the demand for maple syrup in that city. If you were an all-powerful social planner, you would probably want to persuade people in London to give up some of their maple syrup in order to provide for the higher demand in Winnipeg. What sort of rationing scheme might you devise to accomplish this goal? How would you know how much to allocate to each family? How large a staff do you think you would need?

   Suppose, alternatively, that you allowed market forces to work freely. What would happen to the price of maple syrup in London, Ontario? What would happen to the quantity? How would the changing conditions in London affect the supply curve for maple syrup in Winnipeg? What would happen to the price of maple syrup in Winnipeg? To the quantity? Draw demand and supply curves for London and Winnipeg to illustrate what is happening. Would your intentions as a social planner be carried out by the market instead? Which policy – rationing or the market – works more efficiently? Are there any disadvantages to the more efficient system?

3. The prices printed on a restaurant menu apply whether the restaurant is crowded or half empty on any particular evening. If you ran a restaurant,

   a. would you charge higher prices on Friday and Saturday evenings, when the restaurant is crowded, than on other evenings?
   b. would you charge higher prices during the evening than for an identical meal at lunch? Why or why not? (Or, under what circumstances might you?)
   c. Does McDonald's behave in the way you have suggested? How do you explain that?

ANSWERS

True-False: 1F, 2T, 3F, 4T, 5T, 6F, 7T, 8T, 9T, 10F, 11T, 12T, 13T, 14F, 15F

Multiple Choice: 1c, 2d, 3d, 4a, 5b, 6e, 7b, 8d, 9c, 10e, 11b, 12d, 13b, 14a, 15d, 16c, 17c, 18c, 19e, 20a

Exercises: **1a.** 400, **b.** \$0.80, **c.** zero, yes, **d.** shortage, 300

2. 120, P_2, surplus, 40, sell their wheat at the high price, are unable to sell their wheat at the high price, buy the surplus wheat, surplus, increase, 80, increasing, P_1

3. 30, **a.** 5, 15, 10, 10, **b.** 20, 30, 13, 22, increased, increased, **c.** 10, 20, 10, 10, **d.** 15, 20, because S_2 is steeper than S_1.

ANSWERS TO PROBLEMS FROM THE TEXT

4-1. When there is a freeze on the coffee plantations, the supply of coffee shifts to the left, causing the price to rise. Because tea and coffee are substitutes, the rise in the price of coffee causes a rightward shift in the demand for tea. This causes an increase in the price of tea. The effects are the same as those shown in Figure 4-7.

4-2. Some other relevant questions in deciding careers are these: Is a job interesting? Does it provide satisfaction? Are the surroundings pleasant? Does the job offer prestige? Do you get to meet interesting people? Are you likely to get along with your colleagues? Is the job safe?

4-3. (a) The supply will shift to the left. The demand will also shift to the left, to the extent that social pressures mean less drinking.
(b) The demand for and supply of funds will likewise shift left. Profitability may go up or down, depending on whether the demand or supply shifts more.

4-4. The supply will shift left or upward. Suppliers will not be willing to offer the item unless they are compensated for the risk of prison. The demand is likely to shift to the left, too, although we cannot be certain. (The thrill of doing something mildly illegal may appeal to some users.) The quantity will therefore probably fall, and the price will probably rise. The money incomes of sellers will probably increase (although their risk-adjusted returns will probably fall, unless there is a perverse outward shift of the demand curve).

*4-5. The problem is that the statement departs from the *ceteris paribus* assumption. The demand for both oil and insulation is high in Winnipeg because of the cold winters. The following would be a correct statement: In Winnipeg, the winters are cold, and, therefore, homes are well insulated but still use a lot of oil. If the price of oil goes up, people will have an incentive to substitute insulation for oil; the demand for insulation will increase while the quantity demanded of oil decreases. Therefore, oil and insulation are substitutes. Of course, people who live in Miami use relatively little oil and insulation because their winters are relatively mild. (Actually, insulation can be used to keep houses cool in summer – in Miami, electricity used for air conditioning and insulation are substitutes!)

CHAPTER 5

The Economic Role of the Government

LEARNING OBJECTIVES

After you have studied this chapter in the textbook and study guide, you should be able to

- Describe the four ways in which the government affects the economy
- Describe the major programs of the three levels of government
- Explain the difference between government spending for goods and services, and transfer payments
- Explain the difference between a progressive and a regressive tax, and give an example of each
- Describe the five major reasons for government intervention in the economy
- Explain the role and significance of Crown corporations in the Canadian economy
- Explain the objectives that should be kept in mind when designing a tax system
- Explain the difference between the benefit principle and the ability to pay principle in tax design
- Explain why the Canadian tax system is less progressive than we might guess by looking at the income tax schedule
- Describe the major elements of Canada's federal tax reform initiated in 1989.

CHAPTER SUMMARY

The economic role of government is to compensate for the limitations of the market system which were outlined at the end of Chapter 4. Government affects the economy in four major ways: (1) spending, (2) taxation, (3) regulation, and (4) public enterprises.

Spending

In dollar terms, government spending has risen very rapidly in Canada, from about $4 billion during the 1950 fiscal year to over $300 billion during the 1991 fiscal year. However, if we look at the size of the government relative to the economy, we get a much less spectacular picture. For example, government purchases of goods and services have increased relatively slowly as a percentage of GDP since the mid-1940s, and the percentage remains well below what it was during World War II. Nevertheless, if **transfer payments** to individuals are included, government spending has risen substantially as a percentage of GDP in recent decades; in the mid-1980s this percentage surpassed its wartime peak. Thus, most of the increase in the relative size of government reflects the increase in transfer payments such as Old Age Security and Unemployment Insurance benefits, family allowances, and so on.

A large part of government spending at the federal level consists of revenue transfers to provincial governments, both as general equalization payments (to provinces with deficient revenue-generating capacity), and as specific purpose transfers for provincial health care and post-secondary education and welfare. Provincial governments, in turn, transfer substantial amounts to local governments.

Taxes

The primary purpose of taxes is to raise the revenue to finance government spending (including interest payments on government debt). The personal income tax is the largest revenue raiser, by a large margin, for the federal and provincial governments. Other important sources are the corporate income tax, sales taxes (including the federal GST as well as provincial retail sales taxes) and local government property taxes. At the federal level, unemployment insurance contributions and mandatory contributions to the Canada/Quebec Pension Plans represent another important revenue source.

Other than raising revenues, there are a number of other objectives that should be considered in designing a tax code.

1. One objective is equity, or fairness. As we suggested in Chapter 1, there is some controversy over just what is fair. Nevertheless, discussions of fairness usually begin with one of two approaches to taxation:

   a. Ability to pay. According to this idea, taxes should be imposed according to income or wealth; people with high incomes should pay more because they are better able to do so. The **progressive income tax** is one application of this principle.

b. Benefit principle. According to this idea, taxes should depend on who benefits most from government programs. Those who benefit most should pay the most.

2. Simplicity is an important objective in the tax system. Discussions of tax reform in recent years have often centred around the criticism that the income tax has become hopelessly complicated.

3. Neutrality. As a starting point, most economists believe that the tax system should be designed to disturb market forces as little as possible. It should not capriciously introduce incentives for people to change their behaviour in order to avoid taxes.

4. Meeting social objectives. Nevertheless, in some cases it may be desirable to encourage people to change their behaviour. For example, in order to encourage people to give to charities, the government allows people to deduct their contributions to charities from their taxable income. Taxes may also be used to discourage businesses from polluting the air or water.

In the 1980s, efforts were made to improve the federal tax system in Canada through a number of reforms. While some of the specific measures were controversial, there was widespread support for the basic underlying principles of the reform program: that the tax base should be broadened by reducing the number of **loopholes**; that income tax rates should be reduced; and that there should be more emphasis on tax credits (specific dollar reductions in the amount of tax payable) than on deductions from taxable income, as a way of reducing the tax burden on various categories of individuals. These elements were all present in the reforms implemented between 1989 and 1991, which included not only income tax reform but also the replacement of the former narrowly based federal manufacturers' sales tax (MST) with the broad-based goods and services tax (GST).

Regulation

More direct means are available for encouraging some behaviour, and discouraging other activities. For example, there are regulations limiting the amount of pollutants that factories are allowed to discharge into the air and water. In the early days of regulation, about a hundred years ago, the government took steps to discourage monopolistic behaviour by the industrial cartels – "combines" – that were being organized at the time. Other regulations are aimed at protecting the safety of workers and discouraging discrimination.

Government regulations are generally aimed at reducing major problems. Nevertheless, regulation has been a source of controversy. There are two major problems with regulation: (1) regulatory agencies may require major reporting efforts from business, and sometimes generate expensive red tape of little value; and (2) regulatory agencies sometimes come under the control of the industry they are supposedly regulating. The government may become the means for an industry gaining oligopolistic or monopolistic power.

Public Enterprise

Another important way in which the government influences the economy is through **Crown corporations**, government-owned firms that derive much of their revenue from selling goods or services to the public. In the 1980s, it was estimated that Crown corporations were responsible for as much as 15% of all capital investment in Canada.

Federal and provincial governments establish Crown corporations for a variety of reasons: as an alternative to regulation in the case of a natural monopoly; as a way of ensuring the provision of certain services (such as transportation and communications) to communities that would be inadequately served by private firms; to stimulate investment in risky ventures involving new technology. Sometimes Crown corporations are created when the government takes over a financially ailing firm as a way of protecting employment opportunities in particular communities.

A possible problem with Crown corporations has to do with lack of **accountability**. If the political control over the corporation's managers is weak, there may be inadequate control over costs, and some corporations may end up running deficits far higher than can be justified by the special objectives they are supposed to serve. One possible way of overcoming this problem is **privatization** – that is, selling Crown corporations to private shareholders. In the 1980s, a number of instances of privatization occurred at both the provincial and federal levels.

Reasons For Government Activity

The government becomes involved in the economy for many reasons. Here are the five most important:

1. Governments often provide goods and services that the private sector would otherwise fail to provide or would provide only with difficulty and at a high cost. Roads are one example. If the roads within a city were run by private entrepreneurs, motorists would have to stop frequently to pay tolls. National

defence is unlikely to be organized and paid for privately. There is a problem of free riders – people who let others pay because they will reap the benefits even if they don't contribute. If people benefit whether they pay or not, we have an example of a **public good**.

2. The government may intervene when side effects prevent people from making socially desirable decisions. For example, vaccinations protect not only the individuals who are vaccinated; they also protect the public from communicable diseases. Smallpox has been eradicated by the combined action of governments and international organizations. Benefits that go to people other than those who are vaccinated (or their doctors) are known as **external benefits**. There also can be external costs, such as the cost to people downwind from a polluting factory. Just as the government encourages activities with external benefits – such as vaccinations – so it may discourage those with external costs.

3. The government may provide **merit goods** or services, such as education, that it considers very desirable from a social viewpoint.

4. The government has programs to help the poor; for example, subsidized housing and welfare programs. Generally, a significant part of what governments actually do involves the redistribution of income within society.

5. The government may increase or decrease its expenditures in order to promote economic stability. For example, during a period of high unemployment, it may undertake public projects in order to provide jobs.

IMPORTANT TERMS

1. Transfer payments (to individuals)
2. Progressive tax
3. Proportional tax
4. Regressive tax
5. Average tax rate
6. Marginal tax rate
7. Intergovernmental transfers
8. Crown corporation
9. Accountability
10. Privatization
11. Public goods
12. Externality

13. Merit good
14. Tax loopholes
15. Tax incidence

TRUE-FALSE

T F 1. Payments to the unemployed are a form of transfer payment.

T F 2. If we include all levels of government (federal, provincial, and local), then government spending on goods and services is more, as a fraction of GDP, than it was even at the height of World War II in 1943/44.

T F 3. Since 1960, transfer payments through the federal government have risen, both as a fraction of total federal government expenditures and as a fraction of GDP.

T F 4. Public enterprise in Canada is about the same size (in relation to the economy as a whole) as public enterprise in the United States.

T F 5. A tax is progressive if high-income people pay a larger percentage of their income than low-income people.

T F 6. Suppose that a province imposes a tax of 5% on all income. Because it "hits the poor as hard as the rich," such a tax is regressive.

T F 7. Suppose that the government imposes a federal sales tax of 7%. Because high-income people buy more than low-income people, they will pay more sales tax. Therefore, such a tax is progressive.

T F 8. According to the benefit principle of taxation, government expenditures should be undertaken whenever they benefit the public.

T F 9. According to the ability-to-pay principle of taxation, only those who have enough income that they are able to save should be required to pay taxes.

T F 10. The term "merit good" is used in describing a feature of the British economy. Specifically, a "merit good" is one that the upper class consumes more heavily than the lower classes.

T F 11. Since poor people are more likely than rich people to live in rented housing, the non-taxation of the implicit return on homeowners' equity makes the Canadian tax system less progressive.

MULTIPLE CHOICE

1. Which of the following is the best example of government expenditure for goods or services?
   a. salaries of judges
   b. Old Age Security benefits paid to the elderly
   c. social assistance payments to poor people
   d. unemployment compensation
   e. the progressive income tax

2. Of the following categories of expenditure for the federal government, which two are the largest: "Debt charges" (interest on the public debt); "Protection of Persons and Property" (national defence, etc.); "Education"; "Social Services" (including transfers to individuals, etc.)?
   a. debt charges and protection of persons and property
   b. protection of persons and property and social services
   c. debt charges and education
   d. debt charges and social services
   e. education and social services

3. The two largest categories of expenditures for provincial and local governments combined are
   a. health care and interest
   b. health care and education
   c. education and social services
   d. health care and social services
   e. interest and social services

4. Over the past three decades, transfer payments by the federal government have been rising as a percentage of GDP. From this we may conclude that
   a. transfer payments have become too large
   b. transfer payments may or may not be too large now, but they were too small in 1960
   c. transfer payments are still too small, since they continue to rise
   d. transfer payments will sooner or later bankrupt the government
   e. we don't have enough information to come to any of the above conclusions

5. In 1988, each person over the age of 65 was allowed to subtract about $550 when computing the amount they had to pay in federal income tax. This illustrates
   a. that the federal income tax is progressive
   b. the benefit principle of taxation
   c. a tax deduction
   d. a transfer payment
   e. a tax credit

6. Of the following, which provides the largest source of revenue for the federal government?
   a. sales taxes
   b. corporate income taxes
   c. personal income taxes
   d. customs duties
   e. excise taxes on cigarettes and alcohol

Table 1 Income Tax Rates (hypothetical)

Income	Tax
$10,000	$1,000
$20,000	$3,000
$30,000	$5,000

7. For a person with an income of $20,000, the average tax rate in Table 1 is
   a. 10%
   b. 15%
   c. 20%
   d. 30%
   e. we don't have enough information to tell what the average tax rate is

8. For a person with an income of $20,000, the marginal tax rate in Table 1 is
   a. 10%
   b. 15%
   c. 20%
   d. 30%
   e. 50%

9. If a tax takes $1,000 from someone with an income of $10,000, and $2,000 from someone with an income of $50,000, that tax is
   a. neutral
   b. progressive
   c. regressive
   d. proportional
   e. marginal

10. If unemployment insurance contributions are considered as a tax, then it would be characterized as
    a. neutral
    b. marginal
    c. mildly progressive
    d. highly progressive
    e. regressive

11. Last year, the government's debt increased by the amount of last year's
    a. tax revenues - expenditures
    b. interest payments
    c. transfer payments
    d. surplus
    e. deficit

12. During the past decade, the federal government has
    a. run a surplus every year
    b. run a surplus most years, but not every one
    c. had about the same number of surpluses as deficits
    d. run a deficit most years, but not every one
    e. run a deficit every year

13. Prior to 1977, the federal government reimbursed half the total spending of each provincial government for health care and post-secondary education. This was an example of
   a. government provision of public goods
   b. equalization payments
   c. unconditional federal-provincial transfers
   d. the federal government's laissez-faire approach to economic policy
   e. conditional federal-provincial transfers

14. According to the "neutrality" principle of taxation
   a. income taxes should be progressive
   b. taxes should be imposed only on goods about which people are neutral (that is, neither very enthusiastic nor very negative)
   c. taxes should be imposed on tobacco and alcoholic beverages
   d. taxes should be designed to disturb market forces as little as possible
   e. the government should rely on the corporate profits tax, not the personal income tax

15. A public good
   a. creates no positive externalities
   b. creates no negative externalities
   c. cannot be produced by a private corporation
   d. can be enjoyed by all, even those who do not pay for it
   e. must be provided by the federal government if it is to be provided at all

16. Which of the following is the best example of a negative economic externality?
   a. an increase in the international price of oil
   b. an increase in the international price of grain
   c. air pollution created by a steel mill
   d. the rise in the price of steel when the government requires steel mills to reduce pollution
   e. vaccinations

17. Which of the following is designed specifically to be non-neutral?
   a. a proportional income tax
   b. a general sales tax of 5%
   c. a tax on polluting activities
   d. all of the above
   e. none of the above

18. The presence of externalities means that
    a. a tax system that seems to be progressive will, in fact, be regressive
    b. a tax system that seems to be regressive will, in fact, be progressive
    c. the market system will generally not work as well as it would in the absence of externalities
    d. the rich will generally get richer, and the poor poorer
    e. the federal government will find it much more difficult to balance its budget

EXERCISES

1. The table below shows two different taxes – Tax A and Tax B. For each of these taxes, fill in the column showing the average tax rate at various incomes, and the marginal tax rate. Also note on the last line whether the tax is proportional, regressive, or progressive.

	TAX A			TAX B		
Income		Average Rate	Marginal Rate		Average Rate	Marginal Rate
$10,000	$1,500	_____%	_____%	$1,500	_____%	_____%
$20,000	3,000	_____%	_____%	3,500	_____%	_____%
$30,000	4,500	_____%	_____%	6,000	_____%	_____%
$40,000	6,000	_____%	_____%	9,000	_____%	_____%

Type of tax: ______________________; ___________________________

2. Suppose that a family has an income of $35,000, which includes $5,000 in benefits from a pension plan. Suppose the family is allowed to deduct that $5,000 when calculating its taxable income. As a result, taxable income falls from $35,000 to $30,000. This would mean a reduction of $ _____ in tax payable under Tax A, and a reduction of $ _____ under Tax B. Thus, the higher is the marginal tax rate, the (greater, less) is the tax saving from a deduction.

ESSAY QUESTIONS

1. What would it be like to live in Canada if there were no federal or provincial government regulatory agencies? Describe what would happen if specific agencies, such as the CRTC, were absent. What do you think the effects were when the government revamped, and sharply reduced the role of, the Foreign Investment Review Agency (FIRA) in 1986?

2. In most communities, the following services are provided by the local government:
   a. police
   b. elementary education
   c. street cleaning
   d. garbage collection

   Could these be provided by private enterprise? Is there any advantage in having them provided by the government? Would there be any advantage in having them provided by the private sector?

3. What externalities are created by individuals who:
   a. drive on a highway
   b. mow the lawn
   c. smoke in a theatre

   In each case, do you think that the government should do anything to encourage or discourage the activity? If so, what? and why? If not, why not?

ANSWERS

True-False: **1**T, **2**F, **3**T, **4**F, **5**T, **6**F, **7**F, **8**F, **9**F, **10**F, **11**T

Multiple Choice: **1**a, **2**d, **3**b, **4**e, **5**e, **6**c, **7**b, **8**c, **9**c, **10**e, **11**e, **12**e, **13**e, **14**d, **15**d, **16**c, **17**c, **18**c

Exercises: **1.** Tax A. Average rates: 15%, 15%, 15%, 15%. Marginal rates: 15%, 15%, 15%. The tax is proportional. Tax B. Average rates: 15%, 17.5%, 20%, 22.5%. Marginal rates: 20%, 25%, 30%. The tax is progressive. **2.** $750, $1,500, greater.

ANSWERS TO PROBLEMS FROM THE TEXT

5-1. There is no "right" answer to this question. The issues should be assessed on the basis of standard economics criteria – efficiency and equity. For class discussion, you may wish to consider the grounds for public-sector involvement in delivery of health care and education. On efficiency grounds, might it not be the case that the private sector should be relied on to deliver such services? What is the equity case for public-sector involvement here?

5-2. Again, there is no "right" answer to this question; it is well suited to a lively class discussion. In some federal systems of government, education is a federal responsibility, in others it is a state responsibility. In Canada, some provinces have centralized primary and secondary education, others maintain a high degree of responsibility at the school board level. What are the pros and cons here on grounds of efficiency and equity? (You may also wish to discuss delivery of social programs generally – what are the advantages and disadvantages associated with decentralization in, say, health care and income security?)

5-3. In the case of defence research, a major reason is the need for secrecy. In the case of agricultural research, it may be necessary for government to do it since individual farmers produce on too small a scale to justify the high cost of doing research just to increase production on their own farms. Moreover, agricultural research often involves technology that cannot be patented or sold under licensing agreements. Thus, a private firm could not cover the cost of its research by selling the rights to its inventions (the way inventors in other sectors some times are able to do).

5-4. So-called "tax expenditures" (policy goals achieved through tax reductions/ exemptions rather than cash expenditures) are both pervasive and significant within the Canadian system. They are, however, not reported on a regular basis. The main point of this question is to recognize that equity/efficiency goals must be assessed on the basis of the net impact of the tax and expenditure sides of the budget; there is little to be achieved by examining either side in isolation from the other. Many equity goals, for example, are delivered through the expenditure side of government budgets, e.g., public provision of health care and education is primarily justified on redistributive grounds.

5-5. If the tax is progressive/proportional/regressive then T/Y rises/remains constant/falls as Y rises. Now, dividing through by Y, $T/Y = \bar{T}/Y + t$. For $\bar{T} > 0$, the tax is regressive. For $\bar{T} = 0$, the tax is proportional. For $\bar{T} < 0$, the tax is progressive. (Plot the tax function on a sheet of graph paper assuming $t = .4$ and for $\bar{T} = 100/0/\text{-}100$.

PART TWO

FOUNDATIONS OF MICROECONOMICS: THE COMPETITIVE MODEL

CHAPTER 6

Applications of Demand and Supply: The Concept of Elasticity

LEARNING OBJECTIVES

After you have studied this chapter in the textbook and the study guide, you should be able to

- Define and calculate elasticity of demand and elasticity of supply
- Describe how a move to a lower point on a demand curve may increase or decrease the total revenue from the sale of a product, depending on the elasticity of demand
- Compare the elasticity of two demand curves that pass through the same point, showing why the flatter one is more elastic, and explain why flatness and elasticity are not the same when curves do not pass through the same point
- List four factors that increase the elasticity of demand for a good
- List three factors that increase the elasticity of supply for a good
- Show how a straight-line supply that is elastic will, when extended, intersect the vertical axis, while a supply that is inelastic will intersect the horizontal axis
- Explain how an excise tax will affect buyers and sellers of a good, and why the group that is most sensitive to price (most elastic in its response to a price change) will be able to push the burden of the tax onto the other group
- Understand how the government's ability to raise revenue with an excise tax depends on the elasticities of demand and supply for the good being taxed
- Show the effects of rent control
- Explain how an inelastic demand for their products makes it difficult for some of the world's heavily indebted nations to increase their export earnings and repay their debts

- Define and calculate the income elasticity of demand and the cross elasticity of demand

If you have studied the appendix to Chapter 6, you should be able to

- Describe some of the special problems of agriculture and how they can be related to the concepts of price and income elasticity of demand

CHAPTER SUMMARY

In this chapter, we begin the detailed study of microeconomics by picking up the supply and demand curves developed in Chapter 4. In that earlier analysis, we saw how a demand curve describes how buyers increase their purchases of a product if its price falls. For some products, this response by buyers will be very strong; for others it may be weak. To illustrate, visualize two demand curves with different slopes that pass through the same point. The flatter one describes buyers who are sensitive to price; they buy much more when price falls. On the other hand, the steeper demand curve describes buyers who are less responsive to price; the amount they buy changes relatively little as price falls. In this chapter we develop a measure – called the **elasticity of demand** – to describe this responsiveness of buyers to price.

A similar concept – **supply elasticity** – is developed to measure the responsiveness of sellers to price. An important question is then addressed: Why are demand and supply elastic in some cases, but inelastic in others? Finally, this chapter includes illustrations of how important elasticity may be in answering policy questions such as: Who bears the burden of a sales tax on a product – the buyers or sellers? How much revenue will the government raise from this tax? and, What are the short-run and long-run effects of rent control?

Elasticity of Demand

This is defined as

$$\text{elasticity of demand} = \frac{\text{\% change in quantity demanded}}{\text{\% change in price}} \qquad (1)$$

To illustrate this formula, suppose that, as a result of a shift in the supply of a good to the right, equilibrium moves downward to the right along the demand curve. With the decrease in the per unit price (the denominator above), there is an increase in the amount demanded (the numerator). If these two are equal – that is, if the price and the quantity demanded change at the same rate – then the elasticity of demand in equation (1) above is equal to 1. Moreover, the total payment buyers make to sellers does not change. To see why this is so, suppose that when the price P paid by buyers falls by 20%, the quantity Q that they purchase rises at the same rate. Then the decrease in P is offset by the increase in Q, and there is no change in P times Q, the total payment made by buyers. This is the first conclusion: When the elasticity of demand is 1, there is no change in the total payment by buyers – that is, in the total revenue received by sellers.

Now suppose buyers are more responsive to a price change – as in panel (*a*) of Figure 6.1 below where the quantity they demand increases by 200% (from 400 to 1200 units) when the price falls by 25% (from $8 to $6). In this case, demand elasticity exceeds 1 in equation (1) above, and there is an increase in PQ, the total revenue received by sellers from buyers. In this case, demand is described as "elastic."

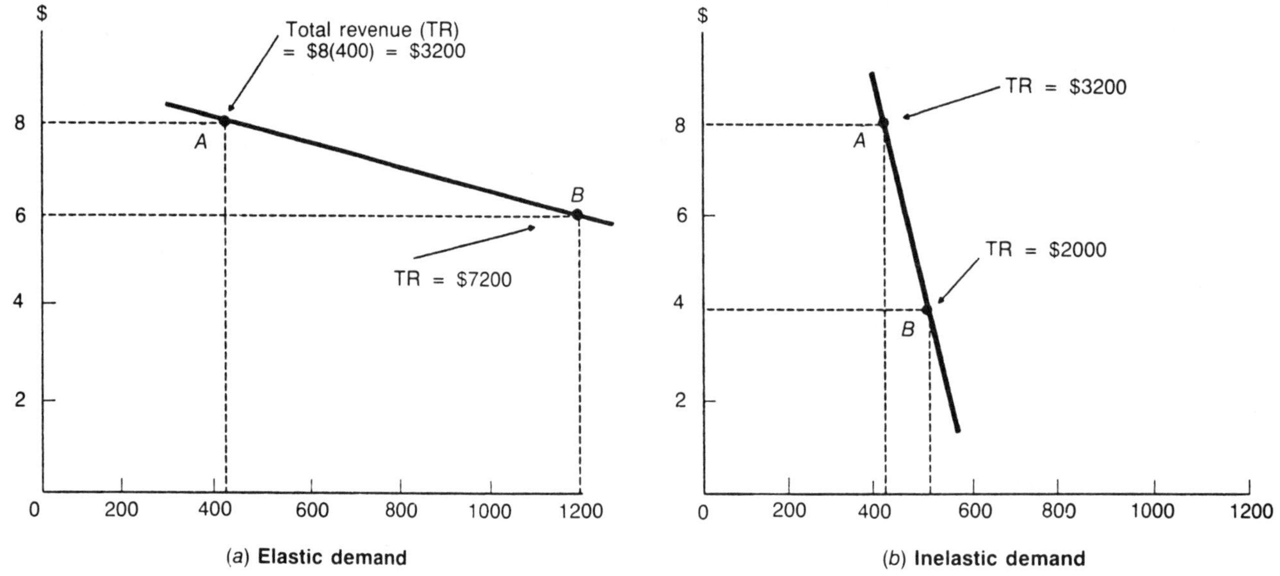

Figure 6.1

In panel (*b*) of Figure 6.1, buyers are less responsive to a price change: The quantity demanded increases by only 25% when the price falls by 50%. This is the unresponsive, inelastic case; the elasticity ratio in equation (1) above is less than 1, and there is a decrease in the total revenue received by sellers. Before you leave Figure 6.1, it is essential that you are comfortable with the way elasticity and total revenue are related.

In that diagram, slope and elasticity seem to be closely related: The flatter curve in panel (*a*) is the more elastic. Is this generally true? The answer is yes – but only if the two curves being compared pass through the same point. (In Figure 6.1, the common point is *A*.)

Once you have mastered these simple and essential ideas of elasticity, return to the text and ensure you understand why, in actual calculations, the midpoint formula should be used.

Elasticity of Supply

This can also be calculated, using a ratio like the one in the equation above. The only difference is the obvious one – quantity demanded is replaced with quantity supplied.

$$\text{elasticity of supply} = \frac{\text{\% change in quantity supplied}}{\text{\% change in price}} \qquad (2)$$

Whereas elasticity of demand has an important "total revenue" interpretation, elasticity of supply does not. The reason is that a move upward and to the right on any supply curve – regardless of its elasticity – will increase total revenue. The one intuitive interpretation of **elasticity of supply** is this: If a straight-line supply curve passes through the origin, it has an elasticity of supply of 1. If it intersects the vertical axis, it is elastic, and if it intersects the horizontal axis, it is inelastic.

What Determines Demand and Supply Elasticity?

Demand elasticity tends to be greater if (1) the product is a luxury rather than a necessity; (2) it is a large item in purchasers' budgets rather than a small one; (3) it is easy for buyers to replace it with substitutes in consumption; (4) we are considering the long-run rather than the short-run demand. The elasticity of supply tends to be greater if (1) the commodity can be inexpensively stored – that is, if it is not perishable and has low storage costs; (2) it is easy for it to be replaced with substitutes in production; (3) we are considering the long-run rather than the short-run supply.

One of the most important of these influences on both supply and demand is time – the short run versus the long run. The reason is simple: If people – whether they are consumers or producers – are given a longer time to adjust to a change in price, they will be able to do more adjusting than if they are given only a short time.

Using Elasticity to Analyze the Burden of a Tax

The first important application of the concept of elasticity is in analyzing whether buyers or sellers bear the burden of a commodity tax. The conclusion from this analysis is important because it applies to any marketplace where two groups face each other, with buyers on the one hand and sellers on the other. The "inelastic" group that can't back away from the market but must complete the transaction almost without regard to price will bear more of the burden of a new tax or any other similar disturbance than will the more "elastic" group that is prepared to resist a price change by backing away from the market.

Using Elasticity to Analyze the Amount of Revenue that Will Be Raised by a Sales Tax

A sales tax will raise the price of the good to buyers, and lower the price received by sellers. Thus, typically, both are hurt by the price change. If demand and supply are elastic, both buyers and sellers will be sensitive to this price change and will be willing to reduce their purchases and sales. Therefore, the quantity that will be sold will be substantially reduced. The government's revenue (which is this quantity times the tax) will be disappointing.

If demand and supply are inelastic, then buyers and sellers won't cut back their purchases and sales substantially. The quantity sold will not be reduced very much, and government revenues will not be disappointing.

Rent Control

The key issue here is that the supply of apartments is inelastic in the short run, but more elastic in the long run. When the government keeps rents – the price paid for the use of apartments – below the market equilibrium, the inelastic short-run supply means that there will only be a small reduction in the supply of apartments. But in the long run, the more elastic supply means that there will be an even greater reduction in the supply of rental apartments and thus an even more severe shortage. (New apartments won't be built, and some existing ones may be turned into condominiums – that is, sold to new owners who then occupy them and thus take them out of the rental market.)

When rent controls are removed, there is an initial large increase in rents because short-run supply is inelastic; there is not yet enough time for new apartments to be built. Once new apartments are built – that is, once the supply becomes more elastic in the long run – the new units coming into the market will moderate the price increase and eliminate the shortage. Thus, tenants benefit in the long run. The problem is: How can a government survive the short run when rents take a big jump? One answer is for the government to gradually phase out controls.

Income Elasticity of Demand and Cross Elasticity of Demand

Just as price elasticity of demand measures how much the quantity demanded will respond to a change in price, the **income elasticity of demand** measures how much the quantity demanded will respond to a change in income, and the **cross elasticity of demand** measures how much the quantity demanded of X will respond to a change in the price of Y.

All three of these measures can be described in the following way:

$$\frac{\text{\% change in quantity demanded of X}}{\text{\% change in whatever is influencing it}} \tag{3}$$

If the influence on demand in the denominator is the price of X, this ratio becomes the price elasticity of demand. If the influence in the denominator is income, this ratio becomes the income elasticity of demand. If the influence in the denominator is the price of good Y, this ratio becomes the cross elasticity of demand. Note that in each case, the numerator measures how much the demand for X responds to that influence.

IMPORTANT TERMS

1. Total revenue
2. Elasticity of demand
3. Elasticity of supply
4. Income elasticity of demand
5. Cross elasticity of demand
6. Unit elasticity of demand
7. Elastic demand
8. Inelastic demand
9. Midpoint formula
10. Joint products
11. Incidence of a tax
12. Inferior goods
13. Normal goods
14. Substitutes
15. Complements

TRUE-FALSE

T F 1. A move to a new lower price equilibrium on an elastic demand curve means that total revenue falls.

T F 2. A straight-line demand curve has the same elasticity at each point on the curve.

T F 3. If the elasticity of demand is one, then a 1% change in price will lead to a greater than 1% change in the quantity demanded.

T F 4. Elasticity of demand is measured as

(% change in price / % change in quantity demanded)

T F 5. Elasticity of demand describes how responsive buyers are to a change in price, while elasticity of supply describes how responsive sellers are to a change in price.

T F 6. The elasticity of supply is greater in the short run than in the long run.

T F 7. The elasticity of demand tends to be higher for luxuries than for necessities.

T F 8. The supply of hides tends to be inelastic because hides and beef are joint products.

T F 9. The better the substitutes in production, the more elastic the supply; and the better the substitutes in consumption, the more elastic the demand.

T F 10. Over time, demand becomes less elastic, while supply becomes more elastic.

T F 11. The past downward trend in farm prices (relative to other prices) has occurred because improvements in farm technology have shifted the supply curve to the right more rapidly than the demand curve has been shifting.

T F 12. Because agricultural prices tend to be very stable in the short run, the only price problem in agriculture has been a long-term downward trend.

MULTIPLE CHOICE

1. When there is a rightward shift in the supply curve, total revenue
   a. must rise
   b. must fall
   c. will rise only if the demand curve is elastic
   d. will rise only if the demand curve is inelastic
   e. will rise only if the supply curve is inelastic

2. If people reduce their consumption of coffee by very little, even when its price skyrockets, we can conclude that
   a. supply is elastic
   b. supply is inelastic
   c. supply has zero elasticity
   d. supply has unit elasticity
   e. demand is inelastic

3. If the elasticity of demand is greater than 1, then a 10% reduction in price will result in
   a. no change in quantity demanded
   b. an increase of less than 10% in the quantity demanded
   c. a decrease of less than 10% in the quantity demanded
   d. a decrease of 10% in the quantity demanded
   e. an increase of more than 10% in the quantity demanded

4. If the elasticity of supply is 3, then a 1% increase in price will
   a. reduce the quantity supplied by 3%
   b. increase the quantity supplied by 3%
   c. increase the quantity supplied by 1%
   d. triple the quantity supplied
   e. increase the quantity supplied by one-third

5. A move to a new, higher-price equilibrium on a supply curve means that total revenue
   a. will not change
   b. may rise or remain unchanged
   c. may fall or remain unchanged
   d. must fall
   e. must rise

6. If the price of X goes from $1.50 per dozen to $2.50 per dozen, and suppliers are willing to increase from 9000 to 11 000 the amount they offer for sale, then the midpoint elasticity of supply is
   a. 0.10
   b. 0.4
   c. 0.8
   d. 2.5
   e. 4.0

7. If the supply curve for apples shifts to the left
   a. the rise in price will be greater in the short run than in the long run
   b. the rise in price will be less in the short run than in the long run
   c. the rise in price will be the same in the long and short run
   d. the fall in price will be the same in the long and short run
   e. the price will fall in the short run, and rise in the long run

8. In the long run, the elasticity of demand for foreign travel is high because
   a. it is a necessity
   b. it is a luxury
   c. airliners can easily switch from transporting goods to transporting people
   d. travel has no substitutes in consumption
   e. travel has no substitutes in production

9. A technological change that shifts the supply curve to the right will cause total revenue to
   a. rise if demand is elastic
   b. fall if demand is elastic
   c. rise if demand is inelastic
   d. rise if the elasticity of demand is 1
   e. fall if the elasticity of demand is 1

10. If the government places a sales tax on a perfectly competitive good, then the seller will bear the heavier part of the burden (incidence) if
    a. demand is elastic and supply is inelastic
    b. demand is inelastic and supply is elastic
    c. both demand and supply are inelastic
    d. both demand and supply are elastic
    e. the elasticity of supply is infinite

11. The burden (incidence) of a commodity tax is borne entirely by buyers
    a. in any case
    b. if supply has unit elasticity
    c. if demand has unit elasticity
    d. if demand has infinite elasticity
    e. if demand has zero elasticity

12. A bumper crop will lower farm income
    a. regardless of demand and supply elasticity
    b. if demand is elastic
    c. if demand is inelastic
    d. if demand and supply have equal elasticity
    e. if demand elasticity is infinite

13. If demand for good X is less elastic than the government estimates, then the revenue it will raise from a sales tax on X will be
    a. impossible to collect
    b. changed, but it is impossible to know in which direction
    c. lower than predicted
    d. higher than predicted
    e. unaffected

14. Annual government revenue from a sales tax on a specific product will be
    a. higher in the long run than in the short run
    b. lower in the long run than in the short run
    c. higher in provinces with a small population
    d. higher in provinces with large cities at the border
    e. none of the above

15. For most renters, government imposition of rent control
   a. provides gains in the short run and the long run
   b. imposes losses in the short run and the long run
   c. provides gains in the short run but losses in the long run
   d. provides losses in the short run but gains in the long run
   e. has no effect

16. Relative to other prices, farm prices have been
   a. stable in the short run, with a long-term upward trend
   b. stable in the short run, with a downward long-term trend
   c. unstable in the short run, with neither an upward nor a downward long-term trend
   d. unstable in the short run, with a long-term downward trend
   e. unstable in the short run, with a long-term upward trend

17. The income elasticity of demand
   a. is positive for an inferior good
   b. is negative for a normal good
   c. is zero for an inferior good
   d. is negative for an inferior good
   e. a. and b.

18. If, other things equal, the demand for X falls by 20% while the price of Y increases by 10%, then the cross elasticity of demand is
   a. 0.5
   b. -0.5
   c. unknown
   d. 2
   e. -2

19. The income elasticity of demand is the percentage change in
   a. quantity demanded divided by the percentage change in price
   b. income divided by the percentage change in quantity demanded
   c. price divided by the percentage change in quantity demanded
   d. quantity demanded divided by the amount of income
   e. quantity demanded divided by the percentage change in income

20. The cross elasticity of demand is the percentage change in the quantity demanded of X divided by the percentage change in
   a. quantity demanded of Y
   b. quantity supplied of Y
   c. income
   d. the price of X
   e. the price of Y

EXERCISES

1a. If equilibrium is at *A* in Figure 6.2, total revenue is area _____, which is $_____. Total revenue at point *B* is area _____, that is, $_____. D_1 is (elastic, inelastic, unit elastic) because, as price falls, total revenue (increases, decreases). To be more precise, we can calculate the elasticity of D_1 from the formula:

(% change in _____ / % change in _____) = _____ / _____ = _____

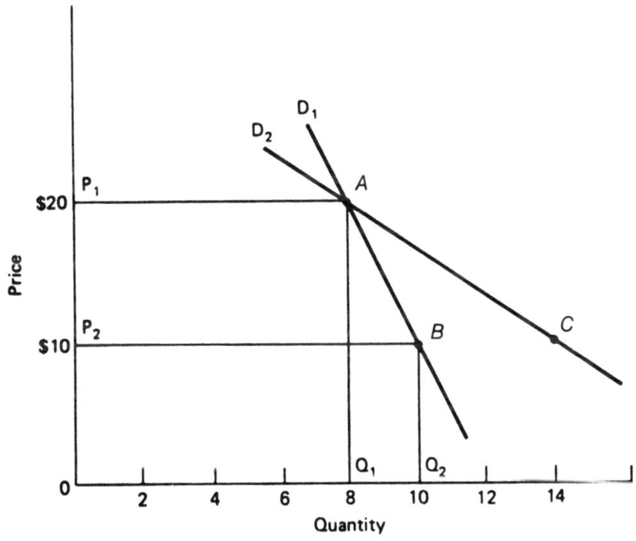

Figure 6.2

1b. D_2 is (more, less) elastic than D_1 because the elasticity of D_2 is:

(% change in _____ / % change in _____) = _____ / _____ = _____

2. In Figure 6.2, draw in a supply curve through point A and mark it S_1. Draw in another supply curve through point B and mark it S_2. Mark the point where S_2 cuts D_2 as F. If supply is initially at S_1, and it shifts to S_2, then the change in price is greater if demand is (D_1, D_2); that is, the change in price resulting from a shift in supply is greater if demand is (more, less) elastic.

3a. In Figure 6.3, supply curve S_1 is (elastic, inelastic, unit elastic) because it _____. If price rises from P_1 to P_2, then the equilibrium on S_1 moves from point _____ to point _____. On the other hand, for supply curve S_2, this change in price would move equilibrium from point _____ to _____. The quantity response to this change in price is (greater, less) for S_2 than for S_1. S_2 is therefore (more, less) elastic than S_1. It is (true, not true) that if two supply curves pass through the same point – such as A – the flatter one is the more elastic. This conclusion is (the same as, quite different from) the one we arrived at in comparing slopes of demand curves. In general, if any straight-line supply curve such as S_2 cuts the quantity axis, it is (elastic, inelastic).

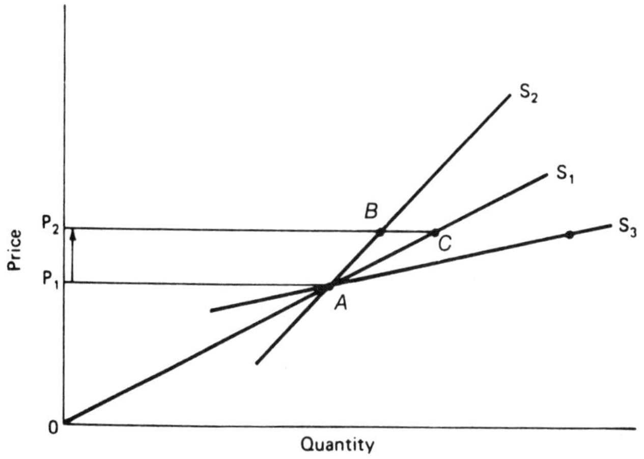

Figure 6.3

3b. Now consider S_3. As price rises from P_1 to P_2, the quantity response is (greater, less) than for S_1. S_3 is therefore (more, less) elastic than S_1. It is (true, not true) that if two supply curves pass through the same point – such as A – the flatter one is the more elastic. In general, if any straight-line supply curve like S_3 cuts the price axis, it is (elastic, inelastic).

4. In Figure 6.3, draw in a demand curve through point A and mark it D_1. Draw in another parallel demand curve through point B and mark it D_2. Mark the point where D_2 cuts S_1 as F. If demand is initially at D_1, and it shifts to D_2, then the

change in price is greater if supply is (S_1, S_2), that is, the change in price resulting from a shift in demand is greater if supply is (more, less) elastic.

5a. The data in Table 6.1 describe hypothetical demand and supply curves for apples. Plot these curves in Figure 6.4 and mark them *S* and *D*. Mark the equilibrium as point *A*, where the price of apples is $____ per bushel, and the equilibrium quantity is _____ million bushels. Suppose the government sets a price floor at $19, making it illegal to sell apples at a price below this. Mark the new equilibrium in Figure 6.4 as *B* and draw in an arrow showing the excess (demand, supply). Mark this arrow *BC*.

Table 6.1

Price per bushel	Millions of bushels demanded	Millions of bushels supplied
$ 5	25	5
10	20	10
15	15	15
20	10	20
25	5	25

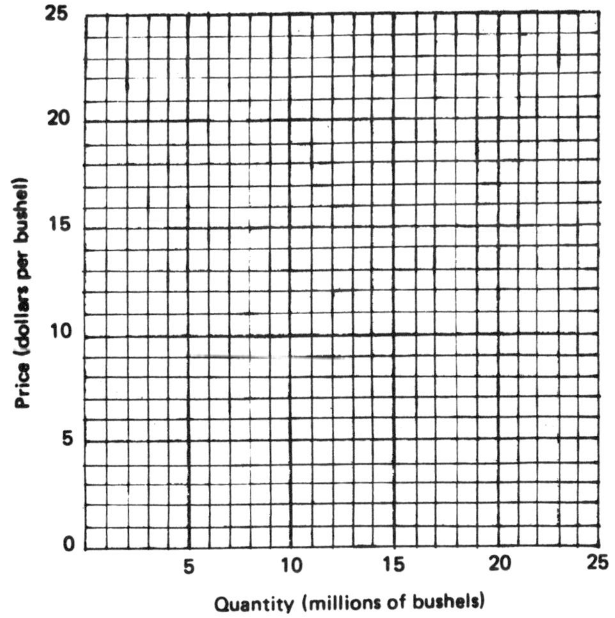

Figure 6.4

5b. In moving from *A* to *B*, the percentage change in price is _____ ; the percentage change in quantity demanded is _____ ; and the elasticity of demand is _____. The percentage change in quantity that sellers would like to supply is approximately _____; therefore, the elasticity of supply is _____.

6a. Suppose now that the government cancels its price floor, and instead requires the sellers of apples to pay a sales tax of $10 per bushel. When the buyers now pay $15 per bushel, the sellers get to keep only $_____ per bushel after they pay the $10 per bushel tax. Thus, according to Table 6.1, they will supply _____ million bushels. Fill in the rest of Table 6.2.

Table 6.2

(1) Price per bushel paid by demanders (including tax)	(2) Amount per bushel received by sellers	(3) Millions of bushels supplied
$10	$ 0	0
15	________	________
20	________	________
25	________	________

6b. Plot the new supply curve in Figure 6.4 and mark it S_2. The new equilibrium price (paid by demanders) is $_____, and the new equilibrium quantity is _____. Of the $10 per bushel paid in sales tax, sellers are paying $_____, and buyers are paying $_____.

7. Draw a straight-line demand curve D_2 passing through point *A* which is more elastic than *D*. If this new demand curve were to replace the old demand curve, the equilibrium price before the imposition of the tax would be (higher, lower, no different); and the equilibrium quantity before the tax would be (higher, lower, no different). The equilibrium price after the tax would be (higher, lower, no different) than with the old demand curve, and the equilibrium quantity would be (less, more, no different). With the new demand curve, the amount of tax paid by buyers would be (more, less) and the amount paid by suppliers would be (more, less) than with the old demand curve.

ESSAY QUESTIONS

1. Suppose you are a monopolist (a single seller) and you can set your price. If you discover that the demand for your product is inelastic, would you want to raise your price or lower it? Why? How far would you want to change it?

2. It has been argued that stores issue trading stamps to discriminate against people who cannot be bothered collecting, licking, and redeeming the stamps. These people end up paying a higher price for their purchases than those who use the stamps, because only the users receive a "discount" in the form of the items they get with the stamps. Suppose you were the owner of a large chain of stores and you wanted to engage in this kind of price discrimination. (That is, raise the price to nonusers of stamps, and lower it to users.) What would happen to your total revenue if the demand by users of stamps was elastic and the demand by nonusers was inelastic? What would happen to your total revenue if the demand by users was inelastic and the demand by nonusers was elastic?

ANSWERS

True-False: **1F, 2F, 3F, 4F, 5T, 6F, 7T, 8T, 9T, 10F, 11T, 12F**

Multiple-Choice: **1c, 2e, 3e, 4b, 5e, 6b, 7a, 8b, 9a, 10a, 11e, 12c, 13d, 14b, 15c, 16d, 17d, 18e, 19e, 20e**

Exercises:

1a. P_1AQ_10, \$20 × 8 = \$160, P_2BQ_20, \$10 × 10 = \$100, inelastic, decreases, quantity, price, 25, 50, 0.5 (or using the more appropriate midpoint formula, E_d = 0.333)

1b. more, quantity, price, 75, 50, 1.5

2. D_1, less

3a. unit elastic, passes through the origin 0, *A*, *C*, *A*, *B*, less, less, true, the same as, inelastic

3b. greater, more, true, elastic

4. S_2, less

5a. \$15, 15, supply

Figure 6.4 completed

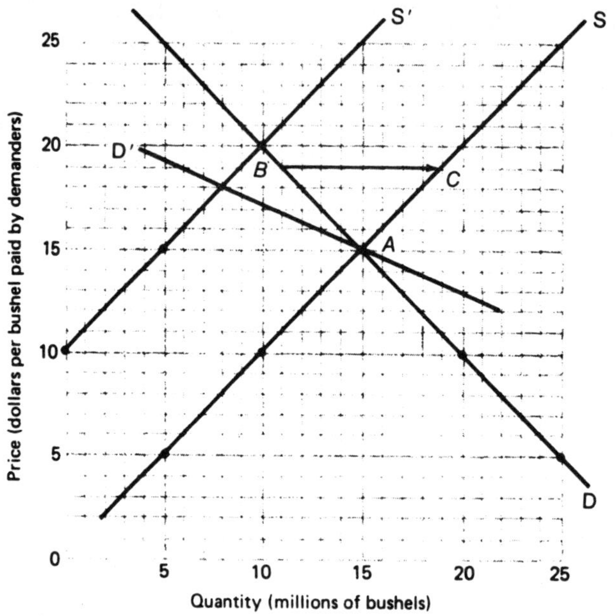

5b. 27%, 27% (slightly different using the midpoint formula), 1, 27%, 1
6a. \$5, 5

Table 6.2 completed

(1) Price per bushel paid by demanders (including tax)	(2) Amount per bushel received by sellers	(3) Millions of bushels supplied
\$10	\$ 0	0
15	5	5
20	10	10
25	15	15

6b. \$20, 10, \$5, \$5
7. no different, no different, lower, less, less, more

ANSWERS TO PROBLEMS FROM THE TEXT

6-1. It provides information on the elasticity of demand. To evaluate this, use equation 6-1 in the text.

$$\frac{\text{\% change in quantity demanded}}{\text{\% change in price}} = \frac{10\%}{50\%} = \frac{0.1}{0.5}$$

Therefore, demand is inelastic – (.1/.5) = .2

If the more precise midpoint formula for elasticity is used, the numbers change a bit, but not the conclusion that demand is inelastic.

6-2. *c, b, a, d, a*

6-3. We need a measure that is independent of the scale in which *P* and *Q* are measured. Elasticity is, but flatness is not. Thus, the quote in part (b) is correct and is the answer to the question in part (a).

6-4. Elasticity falls as it moves down along the demand curve. The statement is false – a reduction in price by 1 is much more significant in percentage terms starting from *C* rather than *D*; the corresponding increases in quantity are, respectively, much less significant in percentage terms.

6-5. (a) Yes, because with higher prices of imported goods, Brazil would use less foreign currency to pay for imports; thus more money would be available for debt repayment.

(b) If a low U.S.-dollar price of exports lowers total dollar earnings, it follows that a higher U.S.-dollar price would lead to larger dollar earnings, even though the quantity of exports would decrease. Thus, Brazil could try to increase its dollar earnings by reducing the quantity of its exports.

6-6. Yes. If the price rises, all that residents can do in the short run is turn down their thermostats. In the long run, however, they may convert to other forms of fuel and/or improve insulation of homes. Thus, oil purchases will fall more significantly in the long run.

6-7. The demand for restaurant meals should be more income elastic than the demand for food (home meals). Since food is a necessity, people must purchase roughly the same amount, whether or not incomes rise or fall. On the other hand, as income rises, people may eat out more often. (They can now afford it.)

CHAPTER 7

Demand and Utility

LEARNING OBJECTIVES

After you have studied this chapter in the textbook and the study guide, you should be able to

- Show how the market demand curve is constructed by adding up the individual demand curves
- Define marginal utility and show how it is related to total utility
- Define marginal benefit and explain how it differs from marginal utility
- Describe the principles of diminishing marginal benefit and diminishing marginal utility
- Explain consumer equilibrium which occurs when purchases have been made up to the point where marginal benefit is just equal to price
- Use the demand curve to illustrate consumer surplus and to measure how consumers lose when price rises
- Use Adam Smith's diamonds/water paradox to explain the importance of total benefit as well as marginal benefit
- Explain the concepts of indifference curves and of the marginal rate of substitution between goods, and how the "normal" shape of an indifference curve implies a diminishing marginal rate of substitution
- Relate the concept of marginal rate of substitution to the ratio of marginal utilities
- Relate the concept of marginal rate of substitution to that of the consumer's willingness to pay for the last unit of a good – her marginal benefit
- Explain the concept of the consumer's budget line

- Explain why the consumer's utility is maximized by moving along the budget line to the highest attainable indifference curve (Figure 7-10 in the text)

- Explain how a consumer's utility maximizing choice can, equivalently, be represented as a point where the marginal utility of a dollar spent on any one good is equal to the marginal utility of a dollar spent on any other good

- Explain how the consumer's demand curve can be derived from an indifference map

- Decompose the effects of a price change on quantity demanded into a substitution effect and an income effect (Figure 7-14 in the text)

- Explain the phenomenon of a Giffen good

- Show why purchasers must take into account not only price, but also transactions costs, including search (information) costs

- Explain why search costs include not only out-of-pocket costs, but also time costs, and why time costs are also important in using a product

CHAPTER SUMMARY

In the last chapter, we measured elasticity of demand and elasticity of supply and saw how important they are in analyzing policy problems. In this chapter, we describe the fundamentals of demand – we examine the foundations of the individual consumer's demand curve.

Specifically, the four most important objectives in this chapter are (1) to analyze how the consumer, facing a given price, arrives at equilibrium, (2) to examine and measure how much the consumer benefits when the price of a product falls, (3) to describe how a consumer makes a choice among several goods, and (4) to decompose the effects of a price change into an income effect and a substitution effect.

The first fundamental characteristic of the demand curve that must be recognized is an obvious one: A market demand curve is simply the sum of all the individual demand curves. This is illustrated in Figure 7-1 in the textbook. In turning to the other characteristics of demand, we begin by examining the demand curve of one individual consumer.

The First View of the Consumer: What Does the Demand Curve Tell Us?

Underlying each individual demand curve are the two basic concepts introduced in Chapter 2 – scarcity and choice. Thus, the consumer can be viewed as choosing between scarce movies and all other scarce products – that is, between movies and money, since money is the means of acquiring all other goods. The key to describing this choice is to look at the value to the individual of an additional unit of a commodity such as movies. We can conceptualize this value by looking at what happens to the individual's utility (an index of "satisfaction") as he or she enjoys one more movie. This concept of marginal utility – that is, the addition to total utility as one more unit is consumed – has traditionally been used to study consumer behaviour. However, a problem with this concept is that there is no obvious way of actually measuring marginal utility. To get around this problem, we may ask instead how much an additional unit is worth to the individual in terms of money. That is, we may ask how much the individual would be willing to pay for an additional unit.

Willingness to pay is typically a good indicator of how highly the consumer values each additional unit of a commodity such as movies – that is, willingness to pay measures the marginal benefit of movies. The more a consumer buys, the less marginal benefit is derived from another movie. In other words, the further to the right the consumer goes in making more and more purchases in Figure 7-3, the shorter the lines (arrows) of marginal benefit (willingness to pay) become. In the simplest terms, the more movies you watch, the less interested you become in watching any more. Formally stated, this is the law of **diminishing marginal benefit** (or its close cousin, the law of **diminishing marginal utility**), which states that as more and more of any product is acquired, eventually the additional benefit (or utility) provided by one more unit must fall.

Consumer Equilibrium: A First Look

As the text explains, the curve that describes how an individual's marginal benefit for a good falls as more units are consumed is precisely what we need to describe the equilibrium of the consumer – namely, his or her demand curve for the good. Because the benefit of, say, the third movie – as shown by the associated vertical line through $Q = 3$ in Figure 7-3 of the textbook – is higher than the market price of $4, the consumer buys that movie. For the same reason, the consumer buys a fourth and fifth movie. Purchases cease at six movies because the marginal benefit has fallen to the level of price. (Beyond that, where marginal benefit has fallen below price – that is, below the marginal cost to the buyer – further purchases are obviously not justified.) This, then, provides an important conclusion: In equilibrium, the consumer purchases up to the point where the marginal benefit of a product equals its price. Thus, we can read the quantity a consumer will demand at any price right off the consumer's marginal benefit curve. This confirms that the demand curve is nothing other than the consumer's marginal benefit curve.

Notice that here we are taking a different approach to the demand curve than we did in previous chapters. Earlier, we viewed the demand curve as telling us, at each given price, how many units (the quantity) the buyer would purchase. As an example, consider Figure 4-1 in the text. At a given price of $4 we horizontally measured the quantity (400) that a buyer would purchase. Now, we are viewing the demand curve as telling us, at each given quantity, how much money the consumer is willing to pay for another movie – as shown by the set of vertical lines in Figure 7-3 of the text.

Consumer's Surplus

Figure 7-4 in the text shows the concept of **consumer's surplus.** In purchasing the third movie, the consumer enjoys a $3 surplus; the individual is willing to pay $7 for that movie, but it only costs $4. Similarly, there is a $2 surplus on the next movie, and so on. The consumer purchasing six movies acquires a surplus equal to all these arrows above the $4 price line, that is, a surplus equal to the area of the shaded triangle. Thus, consumer surplus is the area of the triangle to the northwest of the point of equilibrium on the demand curve.

Figure 7-5 of the text shows how much the consumer benefits from a price reduction. At the original price of $10 and with equilibrium at E_1, the consumer surplus is area 1. When the price falls to $6 and equilibrium moves to E_2, the consumer surplus is area 1 + 2 + 3, for an increase of 2 + 3 – that is, the area enclosed to the left of the demand curve between the old and new price. This area measures the benefit to the consumer if the price falls from $10 to $6 (or, of course, the consumer loss if the price rises from $6 to $10) – that is, the change in consumer's surplus resulting from the price change.

The Paradox of Value

Why is the price of water, which is essential to human survival, so low relative to the price of diamonds, which are mere trinkets? As is illustrated in Figure 7-6 in the text, even though the marginal benefits associated with the first few units of water are extremely high, because it is in plentiful supply, the marginal benefit associated with the last units consumed (washing the car or having a water fight) will be quite low. The story is the exact opposite for diamonds, resulting in a **high marginal benefit** (and, therefore, price) but a comparatively small total benefit.

Consumer Equilibrium: A Second Look

In using the demand curve so far, we have only been studying how a consumer chooses between one product (movies) and money, that is, all other products. In the text, we also show how a rational consumer will choose among movies, apples, shoes, and all other items. So we are no longer concentrating on the purchase just of movies; instead we are examining the purchase of each of the available products. Faced with this variety, what does the consumer do?

One approach here is that of **indifference curve analysis**. An indifference curve shows the various combinations of available goods among which the consumer will be indifferent – combinations that yield the same satisfaction or utility. The consumer's indifference map shows the whole set of indifference curves representing different levels of utility. Higher indifference curves (viewed from the origin in Figure 7-8 in the text) represent higher levels of utility (or satisfaction). Indifference curves are drawn as bowed towards the origin, reflecting the concept of diminishing marginal rate of substitution. This latter concept is related to that of diminishing marginal benefit introduced previously. Specifically, the consumer's willingness to pay for the last unit of food in Figure 7-8 in the text is measured by the marginal benefit from its consumption. This is measured as the consumer's marginal rate of substitution of food for money – the slope of the indifference curve. More precisely, the marginal rate of substitution (MRS) measures the amount of money the individual is willing to give up (and, therefore, units of all other goods) in order to obtain an additional unit of food.

Faced with a **budget line** (Figure 7-9 in the text) which shows the various combinations of goods which can be purchased by an individual with a given money income and facing a given set of prices, the consumer's best choice (utility maximizing choice) is to find the point along the budget line which permits the attainment of the highest possible indifference curve. This point is found where the budget line is just tangent to an indifference curve (Figure 7-10 in the text).

One way of characterizing this equilibrium is as a situation in which the marginal utility of the last dollar spent on food is equal to the marginal utility of the last dollar spent on all other goods. You can derive this fundamental principle – which appears formally on page 135 of the text – by applying the same sort of reasoning that mathematicians frequently use: Assume that this principle does not hold, and then show how the consumer will then change purchases until it does. For example, if the consumer is getting more utility from the last dollar spent on movies than on shoes, total utility can be increased by switching purchases from shoes to movies until the utility from the last dollar spent on each is equal. (Take a close look at Box 7-2 in the text.)

Deriving a Demand Curve From an Indifference Map

The consumer's demand curve can be easily derived, based on this model of consumer equilibrium. As shown in Figure 7-13 in the text, as the price of food changes, the budget line pivots about its vertical intercept. Accordingly, the consumer selects a different equilibrium consumption combination of food (and all other goods) for each different price of food. Each price-quantity combination represents a point along the consumer's demand curve for food; connecting the set of all such points describes the consumer's demand curve for food.

The Results of Price Changes: Substitution and Income Effects

The effects on a consumer's equilibrium due to a price change can be decomposed into a **substitution effect** and an **income effect**. The substitution effect isolates the effect of the change in the relative price of food on food consumption, holding real income constant. The income effect isolates the effect of the change in the consumer's real income – the purchasing power of income – resulting from the price change.

In Figure 7-14 in the text, the substitution effect is isolated by holding real income constant (before and after the price change). By this we mean that income is adjusted after the price change such that the consumer is just able to attain the original utility level. Thus, the substitution effect is the change in the quantity purchased that occurs purely as a result of the change in relative prices (real income is held constant). The shape of the indifference curve guarantees that the substitution effect will lead the individual to buy more food (and less of other goods) when the relative price of food falls.

The income effect is the change in the quantity purchased that would occur as a result of a change only in real income. For normal goods, the increase in real income associated with a reduction in the relative price of food will lead the individual to buy more food. For inferior goods, however, the income effect will be in the opposite direction – that is, the increase in real income associated with a reduction in relative price will result in the individual buying less of the good. Thus, for normal goods, the substitution and income effects reinforce each other, moving in the same direction. For normal goods, demand curves slope downwards unambiguously. For inferior goods, on the other hand, the substitution and income effects work against each other; the possibility exists (the **Giffen good** case) that demand curves may not slope downwards for inferior goods.

Costs to the Consumer in Addition to Price

The price of a good is not the only cost to a buyer. In addition, the buyer may also face **transaction costs.** These may include dealer or brokerage fees in making the actual purchase, plus costs of any search **(information costs)** that must be undertaken. **Search costs** are the costs incurred in making a purchasing decision. For example, if you are buying a car, search costs will include any out-of-pocket costs of buying magazines that compare cars, plus the "time costs" involved in studying these magazines. There are also time costs in using products once they are purchased. If your new car turns out to be a lemon, you will incur a lot of time costs in taking it back and forth for repair. Thus, if your time is worth a great deal, you are more likely to buy a reliable car that minimizes this time cost. In general, it is important in any purchasing decision to consider not only price, but all of these other costs as well.

IMPORTANT TERMS

1. Total benefit (total utility)
2. Marginal benefit (marginal utility)
3. Law of diminishing marginal benefit (diminishing marginal utility)
4. Consumer's equilibrium
5. Consumer's surplus
6. Indifference curves
7. Diminishing marginal rate of substitution
8. Budget line
9. Utility maximizing consumption point
10. Substitution effect
11. Income effect
12. Giffen good
13. Transactions costs
14. Search cost (information cost)

TRUE-FALSE

T F 1. If marginal benefit has fallen below the price of a good, the consumer has bought too much.

T F 2. If a consumer's purchase of a good is less than the equilibrium amount, marginal benefit will still be greater than the price of the good.

T F 3. The reason a demand curve slopes downward to the right is that ultimately each consumer's marginal benefit falls as the individual consumes more.

T F 4. Because diamonds sell for a higher price than water, they must provide more total benefit to society.

T F 5. When the price of a good falls, the consumer's surplus that an individual receives from that good will rise.

T F 6. If the price of a good falls, then both marginal and total benefit will increase as the consumer reaches the new equilibrium.

T F 7. It is possible to draw an indifference curve bowed away from the origin that is consistent with the principle of diminishing marginal rate of substitution

T F 8. Indifference curves can cross, but only once

T F 9. All points to the right of the consumer's budget line are necessarily preferred to points along or to the left of the budget line

T F 10. A consumer who gets twice as much marginal utility from a pound of beef as a loaf of bread will be in equilibrium if the price of a loaf of bread is twice as high as the price of a pound of beef.

T F 11. For inferior goods, the substitution effect associated with a price reduction will be such that consumption falls

T F 12. Demand curves necessarily slope downwards

T F 13. Time costs are incurred in using, but not in purchasing, products.

T F 14. If a consumer is purchasing only 2 goods, and continues to do so until the ratio of the marginal utilities of these 2 goods is equal to their price ratio, then that consumer is in equilibrium.

T F 15. Time-saving devices are more prevalent in low-wage countries than in high-wage countries.

MULTIPLE CHOICE

1. The market demand for a good is the
   a. vertical sum of the individual demands
   b. average of the individual demands
   c. horizontal sum of the individual demands
   d. vertical product of the individual demands
   e. horizontal product of the individual demands

2. The market demand curve has
   a. less slope than the individual demand curves
   b. more slope than the individual demand curves
   c. more slope or less; you can't tell in general
   d. the same slope as the individual demand curves
   e. more slope, if the individual demand curves are elastic

3. The height of a demand curve is
   a. the price consumers would be willing to pay plus consumer surplus
   b. the price consumers would be willing to pay minus consumer surplus
   c. the price consumers would be willing to pay minus the price they actually paid
   d. the price consumers would be willing to pay plus the price they actually paid
   e. the price consumers would be willing to pay

4. Marginal benefit can be viewed as
   a. the height of the demand curve plus the price consumers actually pay
   b. the height of the demand curve minus the price consumers actually pay
   c. the price consumers would be willing to pay plus the price they actually pay
   d. the price consumers would be willing to pay minus the height of the demand curve
   e. the height of the demand curve

5. A consumer will continue to purchase a good until its
   a. marginal benefit falls to zero
   b. marginal benefit falls to the level of its price
   c. total benefit falls to the level of its price
   d. total benefit falls to zero
   e. total benefit rises to the level of its price

6. The amount of a good that a consumer purchases should depend on its
   a. marginal benefit only
   b. search cost only
   c. price only
   d. price and search cost only
   e. marginal benefit, search cost, and price

7. A consumer with diminishing marginal benefit for a good will be willing to pay
   a. more and more for each additional unit
   b. less and less for each additional unit
   c. the same amount for each additional unit
   d. nothing for this good
   e. less than nothing for this good; the individual will have to be subsidized to take it

8. According to the law of diminishing marginal utility
   a. the utility from another unit can never rise
   b. marginal utility must always be negative
   c. marginal utility must always be positive
   d. marginal utility must rise at first, but eventually it may fall
   e. marginal utility may rise at first, but eventually it must fall

9. If water and champagne, both measured in litres, had the same upward-sloping supply curve
   a. they would certainly sell for the same price
   b. the would be likely to sell for the same price
   c. champagne would be more expensive
   d. water would be more expensive
   e. no prediction could be made about their prices

10. If we know only the selling price of a perfectly competitive good, then we know
    a. the total benefit it provides
    b. the total cost of producing it
    c. its total cost and total benefit
    d. the marginal benefit it provides
    e. none of the above

11. If price increases, there is
    a. a gain to the consumer equal to the area to the left of the demand curve between the old and new price
    b. a loss to the consumer equal to the area to the left of the demand curve between the old and new price
    c. a loss to the consumer equal to the area to the left of the supply curve between the old and new price
    d. a gain to the consumer equal to the area to the left of the supply curve between the old and new price
    e. no effect on the consumer

12. Consumer surplus is a "triangle," with two sides being
    a. the vertical axis and the horizontal axis
    b. the horizontal axis and the price line
    c. the horizontal axis and the demand curve
    d. the vertical axis and the price line
    e. none of the above

13. In which case do consumers enjoy the least consumer surplus? (Assume in each case that they face the same price and purchase the same quantity.)
    a. demand elasticity is 1
    b. demand is highly inelastic
    c. demand is highly elastic
    d. supply elasticity is 1
    e. supply is highly elastic

14. If the price of good A increases, then, as the consumer reaches his or her new equilibrium
    a. marginal benefit will decrease, and total benefit will increase
    b. marginal benefit will increase and total benefit will decrease
    c. marginal benefit will decrease, but by less than total benefit decreases
    d. marginal benefit will decrease by more than total benefit decreases
    e. marginal and total benefit will both increase

15. For a normal good, the demand curve will slope downwards
    a. only if the income effect dominates the substitution effect
    b. only if the substitution effect dominates the income effect
    c. only if price falls
    d. only if income rises
    e. none of the above

16. If all prices double and income doubles, then
    a. the consumer's budget line pivots about the vertical axis
    b. the consumer's budget line shifts out parallel
    c. the consumer's budget line shifts in parallel
    d. both the slope and the position of the budget line will be altered
    e. none of the above, the budget line is unchanged

17. The more willing the public is to bear search costs
    a. the more variation there will be in prices quoted by sellers
    b. the less variation there will be in prices quoted by sellers
    c. the higher will be the price quoted by sellers
    d. the greater the overcharging by wholesalers and retailers
    e. the greater the overcharging by retailers, but not wholesalers

18. Time costs are
    a. greater in a high-income (than a low-income) country, and this is one reason that less reliable cars are purchased there
    b. greater in a high-income country, and this is one reason that more expensive and reliable cars are purchased there
    c. less in a high-income country, and this is one reason that more expensive and reliable cars are purchased there
    d. less in a high-income country, and this is one reason that less expensive and reliable cars are purchased there
    e. less in a high-income country, but this doesn't affect the cars that are purchased there

19. A consumer buying two goods will be in equilibrium if
    a. the ratio of the marginal utilities of these goods is greater than their price ratio
    b. the ratio of the marginal utilities of these goods is less than their price ratio
    c. the ratio of the marginal utilities of these goods is equal to 1
    d. the ratio of the marginal utilities of these goods is equal to their price ratio
    e. some other condition is met; any condition involving marginal utilities is irrelevant

20. If the price of apples rises, the consumer will buy
    a. fewer apples, thus increasing his marginal utility from apples
    b. fewer apples, thus reducing his marginal utility from apples
    c. more cherries, thus reducing his marginal utility from cherries
    d. more cherries, thus increasing his marginal utility from cherries
    e. a. and c.

21. If the marginal utility of a pound of beef is twice as great as the marginal utility of a loaf of bread, then the consumer will be in equilibrium if
    a. the price of a pound of beef is twice the price of a loaf of bread
    b. the price of a pound of beef is four times the price of a loaf of bread
    c. the price of a pound of beef is half the price of a loaf of bread
    d. their prices are the same
    e. their prices are related in some other way

22. According to the substitution effect, a fall in the price of apples results in
    a. an increase in the purchases of apples because other goods have become cheap relative to apples
    b. an increase in the purchases of apples because apples have become less expensive relative to other goods
    c. a decrease in the purchases of apples because apples have become less expensive relative to other goods
    d. a decrease in the purchases of apples because the buyer's real income has risen
    e. an increase in the purchases of apples because the buyer's real income has risen

EXERCISES

1a. If the price for the product shown in Figure 7.1 below is $7, then _____ units will be purchased, because this is the quantity where marginal benefit, as given by the height of the _____ curve, is equal to _____. There are two interpretations of any point such as *R* on an individual's demand curve. The first is that *R* indicates the quantity that will be purchased at a certain price of, say, $7. This interpretation is shown by arrow _____. The second is that *R* indicates, at a given quantity, the maximum price that the buyer is willing to pay for the marginal unit – in this case, the 100th unit. This second interpretation is shown by arrow _____. Since this arrow indicates how much the consumer will be willing to pay to acquire that 100th unit, it measures the value the consumer puts on that unit – that is, the (total value of all 100 units, marginal benefit of that 100th unit).

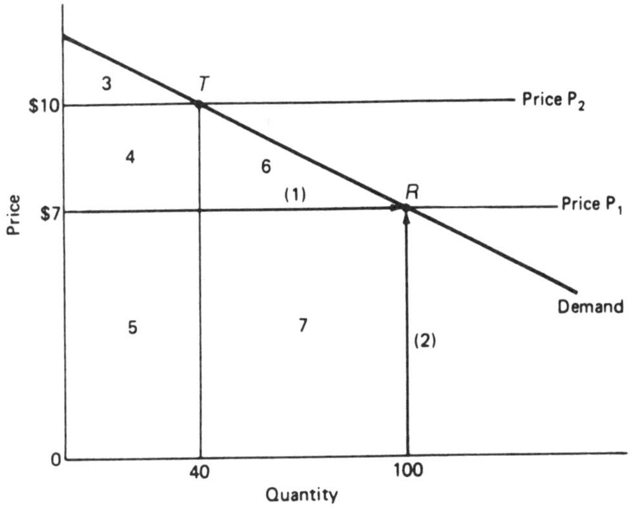

Figure 7.1

1b. The total benefit the consumer gets from all 100 units purchased is area _____, which is the sum of all the (horizontal, vertical) marginal benefit arrows like _____ enclosed beneath the _____ curve throughout the range of quantities between _____ and _____. However, this purchase costs the consumer area _____, which is the quantity of _____ units multiplied by the $_____ price. Therefore, the net benefit to the consumer of this purchase is area _____, which is sometimes called _____.

2. If price increases to $10, the new equilibrium is at _____, where the quantity purchased is _____ units. The demand curve between *R* and *T* is (elastic, inelastic) because the % change in quantity is (less, more) than the % change in price. The total benefit from this smaller purchase is area _____. However, the cost is area _____, which is the quantity of _____ units times the $_____ price. Therefore, the net benefit to the purchaser when price is $10 is area _____.

3a. Since the net benefit to the purchaser when the price was $7 was area _____, and that benefit was reduced to area _____ when the price rose to $10, the burden of this price increase on the consumer is area _____, which is the area enclosed to the (left, right) of the _____ curve between the old price and the new price.

3b. Let's look at this from another point of view. Because price has risen, the consumer is buying _____ units less. The total benefit the consumer used to get on these units – and has now lost – is area _____. However, the consumer is no longer incurring the cost, shown by area _____, of purchasing these units, since they are no longer being bought. Therefore, the net loss to the consumer on these units that are no longer purchased is area _____. In addition, the consumer is hurt because of the greater price that has to be paid on the first 40 units (that continue to be purchased). The higher cost to the consumer on these units is area _____, which is the $_____ increase in price times those 40 units.

Thus, in summary, we confirm that the loss to the consumer because of the price increase is area _____. This is made up of a loss of area _____ because purchases are reduced, plus a loss of area _____ because of the higher price that must be paid on purchases that continue to be made.

4a. In the same vein as Figure 7-12 in the text, use an indifference curve-budget line diagram to illustrate the effect of a sales tax on food (the good on the horizontal axis).

4b. Contrast the effects of a sales tax on food alone with those of an equal-rate sales tax on all goods, including food.

4c. Contrast the effects of a sales tax on all goods with those of a general income tax.

ESSAY QUESTIONS

1. People derive more benefit from the water they use than they do from all the champagne they drink. Yet champagne costs far more than water. Would champagne be more expensive than water if the two had the same supply curve and were thus equally scarce? Explain your answer.

2. To judge by the amount of time spent, most people seem to derive more utility from watching television than from going to movies. Yet they will pay $4 or $5 to go to a movie, when they could stay home and watch television for nothing. Can you explain this?

3. When Henry Ford invented the mass production of automobiles, what effect do you suppose this had on the typical marginal benefit schedule for horse-drawn carriages? What do you suppose it did to the price and sales of horse-drawn carriages?

4. Heroin addicts find that the more they consume, the more they want. Does this contradict or illustrate diminishing marginal utility? Can you use this heroin example to illustrate the law of diminishing marginal utility?

5. "Higher indifference curves (viewed from the origin) are associated with higher levels of utility." Does this therefore require that utility be measurable (like height or weight) in order for indifference-curve analysis to be relevant to the real world?

ANSWERS

True-False: **1**T, **2**T, **3**T, **4**F, **5**T, **6**F, **7**F, **8**F, **9**F, **10**F, **11**F, **12**F, **13**F, **14**T, **15**F

Multiple Choice: **1**c, **2**a, **3**e, **4**e, **5**b, **6**e, **7**b, **8**e, **9**d, **10**d, **11**b, **12**d, **13**c, **14**b, **15**e, **16**e, **17**b, **18**b, **19**d, **20**e, **21**a, **22**b

Exercises: **1a**. 100, demand, price, (1), (2), marginal benefit of that 100th unit

1b. 3 + 4 + 5 + 6 + 7, vertical, (2), demand, zero, 100, 5 + 7, 100, $7, 3 + 4 + 6, consumer surplus

2. *T*, 40, elastic, more, 3 + 4 + 5, 4 + 5, 40, $10, 3

3a. 3 + 4 + 6, 3, 4 + 6, left, demand

3b. 60, 6 + 7, 7, 6, 4, $3, 6 + 4, 6, 4

4a. The sales tax pivots the budget line inwards about the vertical axis

4b. An equal-rate sales tax on all goods would shift the budget line in parallel

4c. An income tax is equivalent in its effects on the budget line to an equal-rate sales tax on all goods.

ANSWERS TO PROBLEMS FROM THE TEXT

7-1. Unit elasticity. Market demand is constructed as in Figure 7-1 in the text. It is flatter than the individual demand, but not more elastic. (Flatness indicates elasticity only if we are comparing demand curves that pass through the same point – and these do not.)

7-2. A good question for class discussion. A popular example is consumption of bottles of beer.

7-3.

	Hamburgers (price = $2)		Novels (price = $2)	
Unit	**MU**	**MU per $**	**MU**	**MU per $**
1	12	6	16	8
2	10	5	12	6
3	8	4	8	4
4	6	3	4	2
5	4	2	2	1

(i) With income of $10, buy 3 hamburgers and 2 novels, or vice versa.
(ii) Increases from 1 to 2 (or 3).
(iii) Three of each

7-4. The slope of the budget line is equal to the negative of the ratio of the price of the good on the horizontal axis to that of the good on the vertical axis. If the price of the good on the horizontal axis falls when more is purchased, then the slope of the budget line is no longer a constant; rather it falls as the quantity of the good on the horizontal axis rises. Thus, the "budget line" will, in fact, be a curve bowed towards the origin.

7-5. See exercise 4 above for a similar question in the context of taxes. (*a*) For equal cost to the government, the lump-sum payment will yield the greatest increase in utility. A utility-maximizing individual will therefore prefer Policy B. (In order to see this, first show the effect of a 50% subsidy on dental services on the consumer's budget line – it pivots outwards – and depict the new tangency with an indifference curve (point *A*). A lump-sum payment in the same amount as the subsidy would shift the original budget line out parallel, passing through the point *A*. It is then possible to draw an indifference curve tangent to this new budget line (point *B*) that represents a higher level of utility than at point *A*). (*b*) Note, however, that point *A* represents a higher level of consumption of dental services. A government which wishes to maximize individuals' consumption of dental services would therefore choose Policy A.

7-6. At a price of 25, the individual consumes no meals; at a price of 5, the individual consumes 200 meals; at a price of zero the individual consumes 250 meals. Plot the demand curve. The maximum amount the individual would be prepared to pay by way of a club membership fee would be the amount of consumer's surplus at P = 5. This area works out to be equal to (1/2)(200)(25 - 5) = 2,000 – that is, the maximum membership fee the individual would be willing to pay is $2,000 per year.

7-7. How people rank alternative commodity bundles will depend on the indifference map. It is entirely possible for a bundle that can be afforded (i.e., one along or to the left of the budget line) to be preferred to one that cannot be afforded (i.e., one to the right of the budget line) – it must simply lie along a higher indifference curve.

7-8. This is simply the reverse case of that in Figure 7-14 in the text. Here, the price of the good on the horizontal axis (gasoline) rises. So, you should be able to turn the analysis of Figure 7-14 on its head. This is a good class exercise.

CHAPTER 8

Business Organization and Finance

LEARNING OBJECTIVES

After you have studied this chapter in the textbook and study guide, you should be able to

- Describe the three major types of business organization, and explain the major advantages and disadvantages of each
- Explain the purpose of the dividend tax credit
- Describe the ways in which a corporation can raise funds for expansion
- Explain the advantages and disadvantages to the corporation of issuing common stock (shares) rather than bonds
- Explain the advantages and disadvantages of buying common stock (shares) rather than bonds
- Explain what the concept of leverage means
- Explain how greater leverage can create risks for both corporations and bondholders
- Describe the major motives of the people who buy securities, and the major motives of those who issue securities
- Contrast the two basic types of business accounts – the balance sheet and the income statement
- Contrast the principle of opportunity cost with that of accounting cost
- Define and contrast normal profit and economic profit

CHAPTER SUMMARY

The major purposes of this chapter are to (1) explain the three forms of business organization, (2) describe how businesses finance expansion, (3) describe some of the problems that arise in the financial markets, (4) introduce the concepts of balance sheets and income statements, and (5) explain the distinction between accounting cost and economic cost.

There are three major types of business organization:

1. The single **proprietorship**, owned and operated by an individual. Many small businesses are single proprietorships.

2. The partnership, which is quite similar to the single proprietorship, except that there are several owners and operators. With a few exceptions, partnerships are quite small businesses.

3. The corporation, which is the standard organization for large businesses. The corporation provides **limited liability** to the shareholder-owners. This is a great advantage, because the shareholder-owners don't have to worry about being stuck with the obligations undertaken by the corporation. (In contrast, a partner is liable for the obligations undertaken by the partnership.) Because of limited liability, a large, well-known corporation may be able to sell shares of **common stock** (that is, shares of ownership) to a wide variety of people. Thus, the corporate form of organization has the advantage of making it easier to finance growth. A third advantage of the corporation is that it has automatic continuity. When one of the stockholder-owners dies, the stock goes to the heirs. The corporation continues uninterrupted. Because of the protection offered by limited liability, an heir need not be concerned about accepting the stock.

Many small corporations are not well-known, and the desire to raise funds is not the reason for incorporation. For many small businesses, tax considerations are important in the decision whether to incorporate or not. The income of a proprietorship or partnership is taxed as personal income of the owner or owners. Corporate profits are taxed differently; they are subject to the corporation income tax. For small corporations, the corporate tax rate is relatively low, and may be substantially less than the rate at which the owner's personal income is taxed. Thus, there may be an advantage in incorporating, especially if most of the corporation's profits will be reinvested rather than paid out to the owner as dividends. (Profits paid out as dividends are taxed as part of the owner's personal income, just like the profits from a proprietorship or a partnership. However, under Canadian tax law, shareholders who receive dividends from Canadian corporations are given credit for the corporate income tax that has already been levied on the profits from which the dividends are paid.)

Ways in which the corporation can raise funds include (1) issuing additional shares of common stock, each representing a fraction of the ownership of the corporation; (2) selling **bonds**, which is a way of borrowing money for a long period of time from the person who buys the bond; (3) issuing shorter-term debt, such as notes or **commercial paper**; and (4) borrowing from a bank or other financial institution.

Each of the first three items can normally be bought and sold in markets. For example, a person who owns stock or bonds of a corporation may sell them to anyone who is willing to buy. Transactions in such securities are usually facilitated by **brokers** or investment dealers. (Brokers bring buyers and sellers together. A dealer may be the actual buyer or seller of a bond.) Similarly, government bonds and shorter-term securities may be sold by the present holder to someone else. Thus, if the government or corporation issues long-term bonds, it has a guaranteed use of the funds for a long period of time. But the buyer is not necessarily tying up funds for a similar long period: the bond may be sold at any time. Thus, the financial markets provide liquidity to bondholders.

The prices of securities in the financial markets are determined by supply and demand; the prices of common shares, bonds, and other financial **assets** can fluctuate as conditions change. The major determinant of the price of common stock is the expected profitability of the corporation. The person who buys the share will participate in the good fortune (if any) of the corporation. Even though bonds provide a fixed contract – for, say $12,000 in interest payments each year over 20 years – they may nevertheless fluctuate in value. In the marketplace, people have the choice of buying new bonds or old bonds. If a new bond will pay more interest – say $14,000 – then the amount people will be willing to pay for the old bond (with $12,000 interest per year) will go down.

Although interest payments on bonds are set by the bond contract, the payment of interest is not guaranteed. If the issuing corporation runs into trouble, it may not have the funds to pay interest. In this case, the bondholder has the legal right to sue, and may push the corporation into the bankruptcy courts. Even then, there is no assurance that the bondholder will be paid, because the corporation may simply not have enough assets to cover its **liabilities**. If a corporation is in difficulty, there may be an agreement among bondholders and other creditors to give it more time to pay, and perhaps take smaller interest payments.

Because bondholders are not guaranteed payment, they must be concerned with the prospects that the issuer will, in fact, be able to make interest payments on schedule, and repay the principal when the bond reaches maturity. If a corporation is shaky, people will avoid its bonds unless they offer an extra amount of interest to compensate for the risk – the so-called **risk premium**. Because of differences in risk, some bonds offer substantially higher interest rates than others.

In deciding which securities to buy, potential bond buyers weigh a number of factors – risk, return, and liquidity. Issuers of securities also have a number of factors to consider. One of their most important decisions is whether they will issue additional common stock or additional bonds. If they issue stock, they will be taking on additional part-owners. Thus, they will have to share their future profits among more people. If they issue additional bonds, they will be increasing the **leverage** of the corporation. If the business does well, the owners will only have to pay the interest; they will not have to share their profits with the bondholders. But they will be legally committed to pay the interest, whether the firm does well or not. Thus, leverage can add to the risks that the company may fail in the future.

The major function of financial markets is to allocate the saving of society to the various investment projects that can be undertaken. On the whole, the financial markets do a fairly good job in allocating funds among various projects. People who buy bonds or stocks have an incentive to put their funds into the corporation with the best prospects. Nevertheless, major mistakes are made. Some mistakes are inevitable in a risky and uncertain world – the best buggy whip manufacturer in North America became obsolete with the invention of the motor car. But some mistakes can be avoided if people have more information. This is where government regulation of financial markets plays an important role. It requires corporations to disclose their financial condition. By enforcing a reasonable rule – that information be disclosed – the government can help the private capital markets work better.

The basic sources of information about a firm's past performance and future prospects are its accounts and financial reports, as periodically issued. There are two basic types of business accounts. The firm's **balance sheet** shows (1) assets, (2) liabilities and (3) **net worth** at a point of time. The **income statement**, on the other hand, records the flow of payments into and out of the firm over a period of time.

The concept of cost (and of profits) used by economists is not quite the same as that of accountants. By cost, economists mean "**opportunity cost**" – that is, the value or return that a particular resource could get in its best alternative use. Thus, economists include not only the explicit accounting costs, but also implicit costs such as the **normal profit** on capital invested in the firm. The economist's concept of profit is, therefore, that of **above-normal** profit – that is, revenues in excess of all opportunity costs. It is **economic profit** (or loss) which provides the key signal for resources to move into or out of a particular activity.

IMPORTANT TERMS

1. Proprietorship
2. Limited liability
3. Double taxation
4. Common stock
5. Bond
6. Commercial paper

7. Leverage
8. Risk premium
9. Broker
10. Balance sheet
11. Asset
12. Liability
13. Net worth
14. Book value
15. Income statement
16. Depreciation
17. Opportunity cost
18. Normal profit
19. Above-normal (economic) profit

TRUE-FALSE

T F 1. Partnerships have "unlimited liability." This means that there is no limit to the amount of bonds and other liabilities they can issue.

T F 2. A partnership with two partners (A and B) has its income taxed twice – once as the income of A, and once as the income of B.

T F 3. Under Canadian income tax rules, income received as dividends from a Canadian corporation is taxed at a lower rate of personal income tax than other types of income.

T F 4. A government bond is generally more liquid than a house.

T F 5. Issuing additional common stock increases the leverage of a corporation.

T F 6. Issuing more bonds increases the leverage of a corporation.

T F 7. Businesses that increase their leverage usually do so to reduce the risk of bankruptcy.

T F 8. A corporation's balance sheet shows its sales and costs over a period of time.

T F 9. A situation of zero economic profit suggests that resources could be better employed in some alternative use

MULTIPLE CHOICE

1. In a standard partnership, each partner
   a. must pay personal income tax on all the income of the partnership
   b. has unlimited liability, but only for the debts which he or she undertook personally
   c. has unlimited liability, but only for his or her share of the debts of the corporation
   d. has unlimited liability for all the debts of the partnership, including those undertaken by the other partners
   e. can lose the amount of his or her initial investment, but no more

2. The partnership form of business organization
   a. provides each partner with a liability limited to his or her share of the business
   b. normally issues common stock to raise the funds for expansion
   c. can have a maximum of five partners (since any larger number means that incorporation is required)
   d. does not provide the automatic continuity that a corporation does in the event of the death of one of the owners
   e. is generally used by banks

3. Corporations provide "limited liability." This means that
   a. the stockholder-owners are not personally liable for debts of the corporation
   b. the corporation is not legally liable for debts of more than one-half its net worth in any one year
   c. officers of the corporation cannot be held legally liable for any fraudulent activities of the corporation
   d. the corporation is legally required to make contributions to the pension fund of its employees only in the years when it is profitable
   e. all of the above

4. The profits earned by a partnership
   a. are taxed twice
   b. are often retained by the firm, in which case, they escape taxation
   c. are treated as personal income of the partners, and are therefore subject to personal income tax
   d. are treated as capital gains for tax purposes
   e. are never taxed

5. Under Canadian tax law, shareholders who receive dividends from a Canadian corporation
   a. receive a tax credit representing their share of the income tax already paid by the corporation
   b. do not have to include the dividend income in their taxable income
   c. are taxed at double the rate on income from a partnership
   d. must report their dividend income to a provincial securities commission
   e. receive a tax credit that reduces the corporation's income tax the following year

6. Profits earned by a small Canadian corporation
   a. are subject to both corporation income tax and personal income tax if they are paid out as dividends to shareholders
   b. are taxed at a lower rate than profits from large corporations
   c. are not treated as taxable income of the shareholders if they are reinvested in the business
   d. do not add to retained earnings if they are paid out as dividends
   e. all of the above

7. Each share of common stock represents
   a. a debt of the issuing corporation
   b. an asset of the issuing corporation
   c. a fraction of the ownership of the corporation
   d. a claim on the stocks of inventories held by the corporation
   e. a right to receive dividends, even if interest cannot be paid on bonds

8. Normally, the riskiest type of security to buy is a
   a. federal government bond
   b. short-term debt of the federal government
   c. provincial government bond
   d. corporate bond
   e. common share

9. A major purpose of provincial government commissions that regulate financial markets is to require corporations to
   a. issue stock periodically so as to decrease leverage
   b. issue stock periodically so as to increase leverage
   c. issue bonds periodically so as to decrease leverage
   d. issue bonds periodically so as to provide bondholders a stable source of income
   e. make information available to the public

10. Financial leverage is measured by
    a. the trend in net worth, measured in dollars
    b. the trend in debt, measured in dollars
    c. the trend in debt, after adjustment for inflation
    d. the ratio of debt to net worth
    e. the price-earnings ratio

11. Leverage generally adds to the risks faced by
    a. the stockholders of the leveraged company
    b. the bondholders of the leveraged company
    c. suppliers to whom the leveraged company owes money
    d. the banks which have made loans to the leveraged company
    e. all of the above

12. The net worth of a company is equal to
    a. assets minus liabilities
    b. liabilities minus assets
    c. profits minus costs
    d. costs minus profits
    e. profits minus taxes

13. A commitment by a bank to lend up to a predetermined limit to a specific customer is known as a
    a. form of leverage over the bank
    b. stock option
    c. commercial paper
    d. line of credit
    e. illegal overdraft

14. Whenever a corporation issues bonds, rather than raising funds by issuing new common stock, it
    a. increases its leverage
    b. decreases its leverage
    c. decreases the risks faced by stockholders
    d. decreases the risks faced by bondholders
    e. increases the tax it has to pay

15. The book value of a share of common stock is equal to
    a. the value of the share when it was initially issued by the corporation
    b. today's price of a share on the books of investment dealers
    c. the market price of a share when the books were closed at the end of the most recent fiscal year
    d. retained earnings of the company divided by the number of shares outstanding
    e. net worth of the company divided by the number of shares outstanding

16. In the 1930s, the yield on many high-grade corporate bonds was as low as 5%, while the yield on lower grade corporate bonds was as much as 10% or more. The difference was
    a. a tax premium
    b. a risk premium
    c. an inflation premium
    d. an incentive for risky businesses to borrow
    e. a sign of the breakdown of capital markets

17. Interest rates on bonds of private corporations are normally several percentage points higher than the rates on Government of Canada bonds of comparable term to maturity. The difference represents
    a. a tax premium
    b. a risk premium
    c. an inflation premium
    d. an incentive for risky businesses to borrow
    e. a sign of the breakdown of capital markets

18. Interest rates on government bonds are most likely to rise during
    a. recessions
    b. depressions
    c. deflationary periods
    d. periods of rising inflation
    e. the period just prior to income tax time in April of each year

19. In the balance sheet of a corporation
    a. net worth = assets + liabilities
    b. assets = net worth - liabilities
    c. assets = liabilities - net worth
    d. assets = liabilities + net worth
    e. profits = sales - depreciation

20. What appears on the income statement of a corporation?
    a. depreciation
    b. income before taxes
    c. income after taxes
    d. all of the above
    e. none of the above

EXERCISE

1a. The following numbers apply to the XYZ Corporation. Prepare a balance sheet for the XYZ Corporation in Table 8.1 below. There are no assets and liabilities other than those listed below. However, not all items should be included in the balance sheet: USE ONLY THE ONES THAT BELONG.

Accounts payable	$800,000
Sales during year	$1,900,000
Accounts receivable	$900,000
Wages paid during year	$850,000
Long-term bonds of XYZ Corp. outstanding	$1,000,000
Plant and equipment (current value, after depreciation)	$2,000,000
Inventory on hand	$300,000
Revenue from service contracts	$250,000
Bank deposits and other cash items	$200,000
Depreciation during year	$300,000
Net interest paid	$150,000
Other costs	$250,000
Accrued liabilities	$150,000
Number of shares of common stock outstanding	100,000
Holdings of notes issued by ABC Corp.	$50,000

Table 8.1 (thousands of dollars)

Assets	**Liabilities**
	Net Worth
Total Assets =	Total Liabilities and Net Worth =

1b. Some of the numbers not used in part a. belong in the income statement. Use them to complete the income statement in Table 8.2. Assume that this corporation pays 30% of its income in taxes.

Table 8.2 Income Statement (thousands of dollars)

1. Revenues:

   Total:

2. Costs:

   Total:

3. Profit before taxes:
4. Tax:
5. Net profit:
6. Addendum: profit per share:

1c. The book value of each share of stock of the XYZ Corp. is ($15, $19.50, $20.00, $34.50).

2. Fill in a table similar to Table 8-4 in the textbook, showing how an accountant and an economist would describe the costs and profit of Peter Davidson, who owns and operates a farm. His total revenue in this particular year is $180,000. His expenses include $27,000 to hire farm labour, $12,000 for fertilizer and seed, $10,000 rent for an adjacent farm, and $20,000 for gas and other costs. Although his accountant tells him that, relative to his neighbours, he's extremely successful, he sometimes considers giving up farming to take a job managing a farm supply business nearby where he has been offered a $65,000 salary. If he did so, he would sell his farm and invest the proceeds in government bonds that would yield a $62,000 per year interest income.

   What is his accounting profit and his economic profit? Assuming that he finds farming and managing the farm supply business equally attractive, what would you recommend that he do? Why?

ESSAY QUESTIONS

1. To find net worth, what do we subtract from assets? Is it possible for the net worth of a corporation to be negative? If so, what could we say about the book value of each share of common stock of a corporation with a negative net worth? Would it ever pay to buy shares in a firm with a negative net worth? If it is not possible, explain why not. Specifically, explain what will happen as the net worth of the corporation shrinks toward zero.

2. Suppose that you are in charge of finance for a large corporation. How would you go about raising funds to (a) finance the construction of a large plant, with an expected useful life of 25 years, (b) acquire larger inventories of raw materials, and (c) meet a temporary shortage of cash resulting from a decision by your customers to wait an extra month before paying their bills? Under what circumstances might you issue new common stock rather than borrow? Might it ever be a good idea to cut the dividend by, say, 50% to pay for any of the above? Explain why or why not. Might it ever be a good idea to cut the dividend for other reasons? Explain.

ANSWERS

True-False: **1F, 2F, 3T, 4T, 5F, 6T, 7F, 8F, 9F**

Multiple Choice: **1d, 2d, 3a, 4c, 5a, 6e, 7c, 8e, 9e, 10d, 11e, 12a, 13d, 14a, 15e, 16b, 17b, 18d, 19d, 20d**

Exercises:

1a.

Table 8.1 completed (thousands of dollars)

Assets		Liabilities	
Cash	$200	Accounts payable	$800
ABC note	50	Accrued liabilities	150
Accounts receivable	900	XYZ bonds	1,000
Inventory	300	(Total liabilities 1,950)	
Plant & equip.	2,000	Net Worth	1,500
		Total Liabilities	
Total Assets =	3,450	and Net Worth =	3,450

1b.

Table 8.2 Income Statement completed (thousands of dollars)

1. Revenues:	
Sales	$1,900
Service contracts	250
Total:	$2,150
2. Costs:	
Wages	$850
Depreciation	300
Net interest	150
Other	250
Total:	$1,550
3. Profit before taxes:	$600
4. Tax:	$180
5. Net profit:	$420
6. Addendum: profit per share:	$4.20

1c. $15.

2. The table you derive should look like this:

Costs and profits, evaluated by:

1. An accountant			**2. An economist**		
Total revenue		$180,000	Total revenue		$180,000
			Costs:		
Costs:			Explicit:		
Labour	27,000		Labour	27,000	
Fertilizer, seed	12,000		Fertilizer, seed	12,000	
Rent	10,000		Rent	10,000	
Gas, etc.	20,000		Gas, etc.	20,000	
Total costs		69,000	Implicit:		
			Owner's salary	65,000	
			Normal profit	62,000	
			Total costs		196,000
Accounting profit		111,000	Economic (above-normal) profit		-16,000

His accounting profit is \$111,000, but his economic profit is -\$16,000.

His best course of action is to sell the farm, buy bonds with the proceeds, and take the other job, since he is now earning \$16,000 less in farming than he could if he followed this alternative course of action. That is, his economic loss in farming is \$16,000; his \$111,000 of accounting profit is \$16,000 less than his opportunity cost of \$65,000 + \$62,000 = \$127,000.

ANSWERS TO PROBLEMS FROM THE TEXT

8-1. Consider why the builder may wish to establish limited liability. Also, consider the tax implications for a "small" corporation.

8-2. Consider the issue of risk as viewed by individuals at different stages in the life cycle. There is no clearly right answer. Standard advice for the 50-year-old involves a combination of stocks and longer-term bonds. Because of the large increases in interest rates and corresponding fall in the prices of bonds, longer-term bonds turn out to have been a bad investment in the past. The combination depends in part on the tax bracket of the individual. Those in high tax brackets should avoid corporation bonds, and choose instead stocks whose gain is likely to come in the form of appreciation rather than high current dividends. For the future homebuyer, liquidity is important. Money market funds give a combination of high liquidity, a reasonably good return, and safety.

8-3. (a) The owner of a share gains additional leverage. This means the potential of higher earnings if the company does well; the stockholder will own all the returns from the borrowed funds in excess of the interest payments. But if the company does not prosper, leverage can hurt the stockholder: The payment of interest may leave little or no profit for the stockholder.

(b) Additional bond sales are generally against the interest of the present bondholders, since they can increase the risk of bankruptcy. However, if additional bonds help the corporation to expand in a healthy way, they can improve the security of present bondholders by strengthening the company. (Also, the bonds of a large corporation are generally more liquid than those of a smaller company.)

8-4. (a) Probably by issuing 20-year bonds (unless the corporation already has such a large debt load that it would have to pay a very high interest rate). If you are right and the total value of the company rises as investors discover how profitable the mine is, the increase in the value per share is larger the fewer the number of shareholders. (Bondholders, of course, do not share in the increased value of the company.)

(b) If other people expected the mine to be very profitable, they would be willing to pay a relatively high price for the company's shares. As an existing shareholder, you would benefit from this. By the same token, if you are right and the mine is not very profitable, the total value of the company will fall as investors discover this. The reduction in the value per share will be smaller if there are many shareholders.

8-5. This is a good question for class discussion. To some extent, the dividend tax credit does ensure "fairness" with regard to the tax treatment of interest income and dividend income. However, this is not entirely so; dividend income is, in fact, taxed at a higher rate. The corporate income tax acts, imperfectly, as a withholding tax on undistributed profits; once they are distributed, they become taxable as income in the hands of the owners of the corporation. In both cases, the usual case for a more favourable treatment of dividend income and corporation profits is based on providing incentives for risk-taking and job creation.

8-6. $350 – the opportunity cost of labour.

8-7. He won't provide any statement on the opportunity cost of his own time and effort (the wage or salary he could earn in another occupation) or the opportunity cost of the capital he has invested (the return it could earn in its best alternative use). Thus, his accounting costs may seriously understate the true cost of the resources he is using.

CHAPTER 9

The Costs of Production

LEARNING OBJECTIVES

After you have studied this chapter in the textbook and the study guide, you should be able to

- Explain why, in the short run, some costs are fixed and some are variable while, in the long run, all costs are variable
- Define total, variable, fixed, and marginal costs; also average total cost, average variable cost, and average fixed cost
- Define the short-run production function and explain the concepts and determination of marginal and average productivity
- Explain the law of (eventually) diminishing returns, and why this law means that marginal costs must eventually rise
- Explain, using a diagram, why a firm's average cost curve is cut, at its minimum point, by its marginal cost curve (Figure 9.1(*b*))
- Explain why an increase in the quantity of fixed factor will shift the short-run production function upwards (Figure 9.3)
- Explain the concept of an isoquant
- Explain the concept of an iso-cost line
- Explain why the least-cost combination of inputs that can be used to produce a given level of output is found where an iso-cost line is just tangent to the corresponding isoquant (Figure 9-5)
- Show in a diagram how long-run and short-run average cost curves are related to each other by an envelope relationship
- Define economies of scale and diminishing returns, clearly distinguishing between the two. You should also be able to explain why a firm may face both.

CHAPTER SUMMARY

Businesses make profits by selling at a price that exceeds costs (measured according to the opportunity cost principle). Price depends on the type of market in which they sell – the market structure. In this chapter, we examine costs with special reference to how they differ in the short run and the long run. First, we focus on the **short run** – the period in which the firm cannot change the amount of plant and equipment it is using. Then, we turn to the **long run**, when the firm is able to vary the amount of capital and equipment it uses – in the long run, all factors are variable.

The Long Run vs. the Short Run

In the short run, one or more inputs are fixed. The capital the auto producer has is fixed. The land a farmer has is set. The decision is a narrow one: How much should the firm use of the variable inputs? In this simplified treatment, we consider only one variable input – namely, labour.

In the long run, all inputs are variable. The firm now has to decide not only how much labour it should use, but also how much land and capital it should use. (In this simplified analysis, we assume that there is only one of these inputs – capital.)

The short run when capital is fixed isn't specified in number of years. For a college entrepreneur typing term papers, it may take only a matter of days to acquire more capital – that is, a small computer. But, for the company generating electrical power, the short run may be 10 years or more – the time necessary to build a new power-generating plant.

Costs in the Short Run

To understand short-run costs, there is no substitute for working your way across Table 9-1 in the text – at least the first three rows for outputs 0, 1, and 2. Thus, in the first row, at an output of zero (in column 1) there is no variable cost (in column 3); since the firm is producing nothing, it hires no labour and therefore has no **variable costs**. But it does have that $35 of **fixed cost** (in column 2) that it cannot escape – for example, its capital equipment will depreciate and will have to be insured against fire even if it's producing nothing. Since such charges are incurred regardless of the firm's output, this $35 always remains the same as you go down column 2. However, in column 3, variable costs do rise to $24, then $40, and so on, as the firm increases its output and hires more labour.

With this in hand, you can now finish working your way across the first three (or more) rows, showing how each of the figures you calculate appears in Figure 9-1. As you proceed, you cover all the definitions of various concepts of cost in the text.

The Relationship Between Average and Marginal Costs

MC intersects ATC at the lowest point on ATC. The reason is that initially the marginal value (MC) is below the average value (ATC), so it's dragging the average value down. But when MC rises above ATC (as it does after output 5 in this example) MC begins to pull ATC up. If you follow baseball at all, Box 9-1 will make this idea transparent.

The Short-Run Production Function: Marginal Product and Marginal Cost

The **law of eventually diminishing returns** guarantees that the short-run marginal cost curve, MC, will ultimately rise – as indeed it does in Figure 9-1(*b*). To understand this law, consider the short-run situation of a firm producing bicycles with a given stock of capital and only one variable factor, labour. As the firm initially hires more labour, each additional worker increases the firm's output by a substantial amount. But, ultimately, as its labour force grows and its capital equipment is operated closer and closer to capacity, an additional worker will add only a small amount to the firm's output. All the new employee can do is work on odd jobs or stand around waiting for one of the machines to be free. In other words, the **marginal product** of labour – that is, the number of additional units of output (bicycles) which result from using one more worker – must eventually decrease. This illustrates the law of (eventually) diminishing returns: If more of one factor (labour) is employed while all other factors (capital, etc.) are held constant, eventually the marginal product of that one factor (labour) must fall.

In Part 4 of the text, it will become clear that the law of diminishing returns is a key to explaining wages and other income payments. For now, it is important because it explains why **marginal costs** must ultimately rise. In our example, the law of diminishing returns means that eventually an extra worker in the bicycle factory is able to do only odd jobs and produce very little. Most of her time is wasted. True, the firm can still produce another unit of output; but when it's done by a worker like this who is wasting most of her time, this unit of output comes at a very high marginal cost. Thus, the law of diminishing returns ensures that marginal costs must eventually rise.

Costs in the Long Run

In the short run, labour is variable but capital is fixed. However, in the long run, both labour and capital are variable. The firm now has to decide how much capital it should install. As illustrated in Figure 9-3 in the textbook, an increase in the amount of capital increases the output that can be produced by a given number of workers.

Thus, by increasing capital, the firm can produce the same level of output but with a smaller number of workers – the firm has substituted capital in place of labour.

An alternative way to illustrate that different combinations of inputs can be used to produce a given amount of output at different levels of cost involves the use of isoquants and iso-cost lines. A point on an isoquant (such as point B on Figure 9-4 in the textbook) represents a possible combination of inputs (6 units of capital and 30 workers) that the firm can choose to produce a given quantity of output (140 units). Isoquants (like indifference curves) are normally drawn as bowed towards the origin and "higher" isoquants correspond to higher levels of output. An iso-cost line shows different combinations of inputs that can be bought for a given total cost (examine the line CD in Figure 9-5 of the textbook). The least-cost input combination that can be used to produce a given level of output (140 units in Figure 9-5) is found where the lowest possible iso-cost line just touches the isoquant (point J in Figure 9-5).

Notice that the corresponding ATC can be found in the usual way by dividing TC (the value associated with the iso-cost line at point J). Necessarily, this point represents a point for which SAC and LAC will be equal. Holding the amount of capital fixed, however, will result in TC associated with each output level that is higher than it would be if all inputs were variable. This is the reason why the LAC curve turns out to be the envelope cost curve that encloses all the SAC curves from below (see figures 9-7 and 9-9 in the textbook).

Figure 9-9 in the text shows how a firm's long-run average cost curve (LAC) can be related to its short-run average cost curves (SAC). (Each of its SAC curves applies to a specific amount of capital.) Note in that diagram how the firm's LAC curve is the envelope curve enclosing all the SAC curves from below. LAC shows how a firm wishing to produce any specified level of output – say, $q = 100$ – can select the appropriate amount of capital. Specifically, the firm minimizes its average cost of producing $q = 100$ at point *B* in Figure 9-7 in the textbook by selecting capital stock K_0. (SAC_1, of course, is the short-run average cost curve that applies if the firm has capital stock K_0.) Alternatively, if the firm wished to produce output $q = 150$, it would do so at minimum average cost by producing at *C* using capital stock K_1. Thus, the LAC "planning curve" tells the firm what its minimum average cost will be for each level of output when, in the long run, it is free to select any capital stock.

Economies of Scale and the Law of (Eventually) Diminishing Returns

Economies of scale exist when a 10% increase in output requires less than a 10% increase in all inputs – in other words, when input costs increase less rapidly than output. In this situation, the average cost of producing output falls as output increases – LAC slopes downward and to the right. An important conclusion follows: When there are **economies of scale**, the LAC slopes downward.

Figure 9-11 shows how a firm facing economies of scale – with a downward-sloping LAC shown by arrow *e* – can also be facing diminishing returns (arrow *f*). The reason is that diminishing returns occur when the short-run marginal cost curve SMC_1 rises. Although economies of scale refer to falling costs (specifically, a downward-sloping LAC) and diminishing returns refer to rising costs (an upward-sloping marginal cost curve), the two are not in contradiction. Diminishing returns apply to the short run, when the firm cannot change its capital stock. On the other hand, economies of scale apply to the long run, when the firm is not constrained in this way and can do better – that is, achieve lower costs – by changing its capital stock. To see this in more detail in Figure 9-11, note that in the short run the firm cannot change its fixed capital stock. Increasing only its labour results in rising marginal cost (SMC_1) – that is, diminishing returns. However, in the long run, when the firm can vary both labour and capital, it can operate on LAC. Because this is falling, the firm enjoys economies of scale.

IMPORTANT TERMS

1. Short run
2. Long run
3. Short-run production function
4. Marginal product
5. Average product
6. Law of (eventually) diminishing returns
7. Fixed costs
8. Variable costs
9. Total cost
10. Average total cost
11. Marginal cost
12. Isoquant
13. Iso-cost line
14. Least-cost (cost minimizing) input combination
15. Economies of scale

TRUE-FALSE

T F 1. If output is zero, variable costs must be zero.

T F 2. The law of diminishing returns states that the marginal product of any factor must eventually fall if other factors are held constant.

T F 3. In a firm's short-run production function, the firm's labour and plant are held constant, while its machinery is allowed to vary.

T F 4. The law of diminishing returns is unrealistic because it implies that we could feed the world from our back garden.

T F 5. An isoquant shows the minimum cost input combinations which may be employed to produce a given level of output.

T F 6. The least-cost input combination for producing a given level of output can always be achieved in the short run.

T F 7. Diseconomies of scale exist if a 15% increase in output requires a 16% increase in all inputs.

T F 8. It is not possible for a firm to be facing diminishing returns if its long-run average cost curve is falling.

T F 9. In the long run, there are no variable costs.

T F 10. The law of eventually diminishing returns describes a short-run situation in which labour varies but fixed factors do not.

T F 11. Whereas each indifference curve of a consumer represents a specific number of units of satisfaction, each isoquant in a production function represents only a "higher" or "lower" level of output.

MULTIPLE CHOICE

1. An example of a variable cost is:
   a. wage payments
   b. rental payments on a long-term lease
   c. interest payments on a mortgage
   d. depreciation costs
   e. all of the above

2. As output increases in the short run:
   a. fixed costs increase, but variable costs do not
   b. fixed costs decrease, but variable costs do not
   c. both fixed costs and variable costs change
   d. neither fixed costs nor variable costs change
   e. variable costs increase, but fixed costs do not

3. As output increases in the short run:
   a. fixed cost falls
   b. fixed cost rises
   c. fixed cost has less and less influence on average total cost
   d. fixed cost has more and more influence on average total cost
   e. average fixed cost rises

4. A firm's costs are related in the following way:
   a. average cost ATC cuts marginal cost MC at the minimum point of MC
   b. average cost ATC cuts average variable cost AVC at the minimum point of AVC
   c. MC cuts ATC at the minimum point of ATC
   d. MC cuts total cost at the minimum point of total cost
   e. AVC cuts ATC at the minimum point of ATC

5. If total costs are rising, then marginal cost must be:
   a. rising
   b. falling
   c. positive
   d. negative
   e. zero

6. The law of diminishing returns means that, as output increases in the short run,
   a. fixed cost will eventually fall
   b. fixed cost will eventually rise
   c. marginal costs will eventually rise
   d. marginal costs will eventually fall
   e. marginal costs will eventually become constant

7. In the long-run decisions of a firm:
   a. employment of labour is held constant, while its use of capital is allowed to increase
   b. employment of labour is held constant, while its use of capital is allowed to decrease
   c. use of capital is held constant, while its employment of labour is allowed to vary
   d. both are allowed to vary
   e. neither is allowed to vary

8. To calculate all the short-run costs of a firm with two inputs – labour and capital – all we need to know is:
   a. the firm's short-run production function
   b. the firm's short-run production function and its fixed costs
   c. the firm's short-run production function and its wage rate
   d. the firm's short-run production function, its wage rate, and its fixed costs
   e. none of the above is enough

9. If a firm's fixed cost is $100, and its total cost is $200 to produce one unit and $310 to produce two, then the marginal cost of the second unit is:
   a. $100
   b. $110
   c. $200
   d. $210
   e. $310

10. If a firm's fixed cost is $100, and its total cost is $200 to produce one unit and $310 to produce two, then its average variable cost for each of the two units is:
   a. $50
   b. $100
   c. $105
   d. $110
   e. $155

11. If a firm's fixed cost is $100, and its total cost is $200 to produce one unit, and $310 to produce two, the firm is:
   a. already facing diminishing returns
   b. not yet facing diminishing returns
   c. not yet facing constant returns
   d. already facing increasing returns
   e. facing constant returns

12. If there are economies of scale:
    a. short-run average cost rises
    b. short-run average cost is constant
    c. short-run average cost falls
    d. long-run average cost falls
    e. long-run average cost rises

13. If there are diminishing returns:
    a. short-run marginal cost falls
    b. short-run marginal cost rises
    c. short-run marginal cost is constant
    d. long-run marginal cost falls
    e. long-run marginal cost is constant

14. Fixed costs are:
    a. fixed only in the short run
    b. fixed only in the long run
    c. fixed in both the long and short run
    d. fixed in neither the long nor the short run
    e. variable in the short run

15. In the long run, a firm has to decide on:
    a. how much plant and equipment it uses, but not how much labour
    b. how much plant it uses, but not how much equipment and labour
    c. how much equipment and labour it uses, but not how much plant
    d. how much labour it uses, but not how much plant and equipment
    e. how much of all three it uses

16. A firm's long-run average cost curve is the envelope of its short-run:
    a. marginal cost curves
    b. fixed cost curves
    c. average variable cost curves
    d. average cost curves
    e. total cost curves

17. The long-run average cost curve is constructed by:
    a. joining the minimum points on all the short-run marginal cost curves
    b. joining the minimum points on all the short-run average cost curves
    c. joining the minimum points on all the short-run average variable cost curves
    d. joining the minimum points on all of the firm's planning curves
    e. none of the above

18. If a firm is simultaneously facing diminishing returns and economies of scale, then:
    a. its long-run average cost curve is falling, while its short-run marginal cost curve is rising
    b. its long-run average cost curve is rising, while its short-run marginal cost curve is rising
    c. its long-run average cost curve is rising, while its short-run marginal cost curve is falling
    d. its long-run average cost curve is falling, while its short-run marginal cost curve is falling
    e. its long-run average cost curve is neither rising nor falling, while its short-run marginal cost curve is rising

19. In reading a long-run production function table, any evidence of:
    a. economies of scale would be found along a row, with diminishing returns along a diagonal
    b. economies of scale would be found along a diagonal, with diminishing returns along a row
    c. both economies of scale and diminishing returns would be found along a row
    d. both economies of scale and diminishing returns would be found along a diagonal
    e. economies of scale would be found along a column

20. At the long-run equilibrium for the firm:
    a. an isoquant of the long-run production function is tangent to an equal-cost line
    b. an isoquant of the short-run production function is tangent to an equal-cost line
    c. an isoquant of the long-run production function intersects an equal-cost line
    d. an isoquant of the short-run production function intersects an equal-cost line
    e. an indifference curve is tangent to an equal-cost line

EXERCISES

1a. Table 9.1 below shows 2 short-run production functions for a firm that uses only 2 factors: labour and capital. Each production function describes the amounts of labour the firm would require to produce various amounts of output. The left panel shows the short-run production function if the firm has 20 units of capital; the right panel shows its short-run production function if it has 40 units of capital.

Table 9.1 Two Short-run Production Functions

20 units of capital			40 units of capital		
Output	Capital	Labour required	Output	Capital	Labour required
0	20	0	0	40	0
1	20	8	1	40	7
2	20	14	2	40	12
3	20	28	3	40	20
4	20	45	4	40	30
5	20	65	5	40	46
6	20	90	6	40	66

The cost of labour to the firm is $500 per unit and the cost of capital is $250 per unit. Thus, producing, say, 3 units of output with 20 units of capital cost would total $19,000; that is, $5,000 in fixed costs (20 units of capital at $250 per unit) plus $14,000 in variable costs (28 units of labour at a $500 per unit wage rate). This $19,000 is entered in Table 9.2 below. Fill in the rest of this table.

Table 9.2 Costs Calculated from the Two Short-run Production Functions in Table 9.1 Given a Wage of $500

Output	Total cost	Fixed cost	Variable cost	Average cost	Average variable cost	Marginal cost	Total cost	Fixed cost	Variable cost	Average cost	Average variable cost	Marginal cost
0				____	____	0				____	____	0
1												
2												
3	19,000	5,000	14,000	6,333	4,667							
4												
5												
6												

1b. If the firm is making a long-run decision and wishes to produce 2 units of output, how much capital should it acquire – 20 units or 40? Why?

1c. Answer question 1b. if the firm wishes to produce 5 units of output.

2. Table 9.3 below presents average cost figures for 4 of the large number of plant sizes that a firm can select in the long run. (Note that plants B and C have costs similar – but not identical – to those you calculated for the 2 plants in Table 9.2.) In Figure 9.1, graph the 4 average cost curves. Label them A, B, C, and D and mark the minimum point of each M_A, M_B, M_C and M_D. Sketch in a rough long-run average cost curve (LAC) for this firm. Does it pass through all the minimum points? In particular, does it pass through M_A and M_D? Through M_C? Why?

Table 9.3

	Average cost, if fixed cost is:			
	$2,000	$5,000	$10,000	$15,000
Output	Plant A	Plant B	Plant C	Plant D
1	$ 7,100	$9,000	$13,500	$13,900
2	6,700	7,000	8,000	8,500
3	6,800	6,300	6,700	6,900
4	8,000	6,900	6,200	6,600
5	9,600	7,600	6,600	6,500
6	12,000	8,700	7,200	6,600

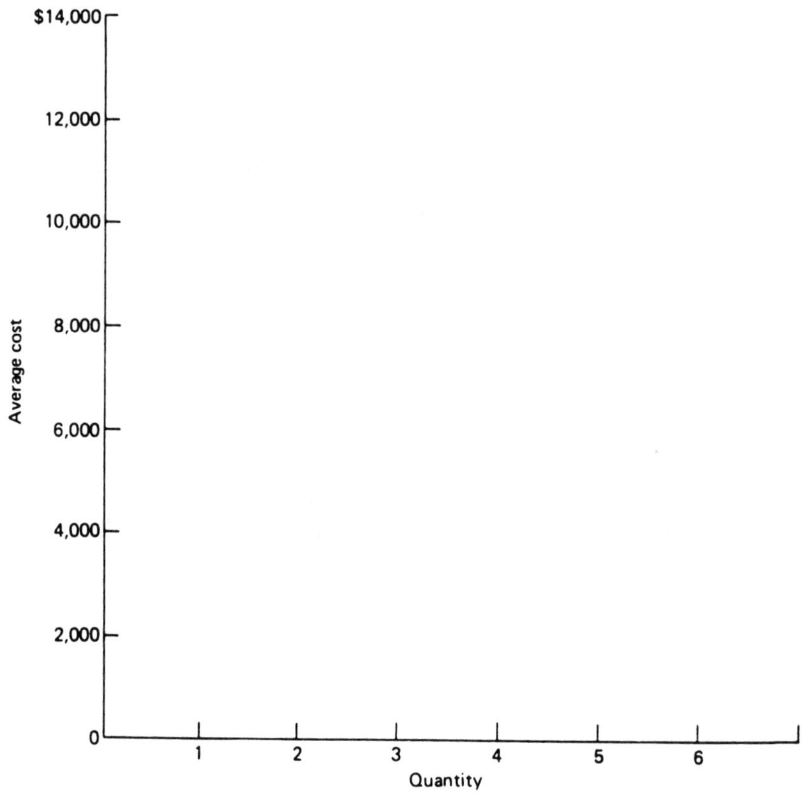

Figure 9.1

ESSAY QUESTIONS

1. Draw a U-shaped average cost curve. Then, draw in the corresponding MC curve and, finally, the AVC curve. In red, show the new curves after a cost-cutting technological innovation. What effect do you think this would have on the firm's supply curve?

2. Would you expect the short run to be longer for a gardening service or a steel company? Explain.

3. In Figure 9-2(*b*) in the text, the marginal product curve cuts the average product curve at the highest point on the average product curve. Explain why this must be so, using an argument similar to the one used to establish that the MC curve intersects the AC at the lowest point on the AC curve.

4. "The law of diminishing returns ensures a dismal economic future, because it tells us that as the labour force grows, it will eventually produce a lower and lower marginal product." Do you agree? Why or why not?

5. Do you agree with the following statement? Explain why or why not. "If a firm producing 1000 units of output is on its long-run average cost curve, then the combination of capital and labour that it is using costs less than any alternative combination which could be used to produce 1000 units of output." Illustrate your answer with a diagram, showing two or three of the other combinations.

ANSWERS

True-False: **1**T, **2**T, **3**F, **4**F, **5**F, **6**F, **7**T, **8**F, **9**F, **10**T, **11**F

Multiple Choice: **1**a, **2**e, **3**c, **4**c, **5**c, **6**c, **7**d, **8**d, **9**b, **10**c, **11**a, **12**d, **13**b, **14**a, **15**e, **16**d, **17**e, **18**a, **19**b, **20**a, **21**c

Exercises:

1a. Table 9.2 completed

Output	Total cost	Fixed cost	Variable cost	Average cost	Average variable cost	Marginal cost	Total cost	Fixed cost	Variable cost	Average cost	Average variable cost	Marginal cost
0	5,000	5,000	0			0	10,000	10,000	0			0
1	9,000	5,000	4,000	9,000	4,000	4,000	13,500	10,000	3,500	13,500	3,500	3,500
2	12,000	5,000	7,000	6,000	3,500	3,000	16,000	10,000	6,000	8,000	3,000	2,500
3	19,000	5,000	14,000	6,333	4,667	7,000	20,000	10,000	10,000	6,667	3,333	4,000
4	27,500	5,000	22,500	6,875	5,625	8,500	25,000	10,000	15,000	6,250	3,750	5,000
5	37,500	5,000	32,500	7,500	6,500	10,000	33,000	10,000	23,000	6,600	4,600	8,000
6	50,000	5,000	45,000	8,333	7,500	12,500	43,000	10,000	33,000	7,167	5,500	10,000

1b. 20 units; its average cost will be \$6,000, rather than \$8,000 **1c.** 40 units; its average cost will be \$6,600, rather than \$7,500

2. no, no, yes, because M_C is the lowest of all the minimum values

Figure 9.1 completed

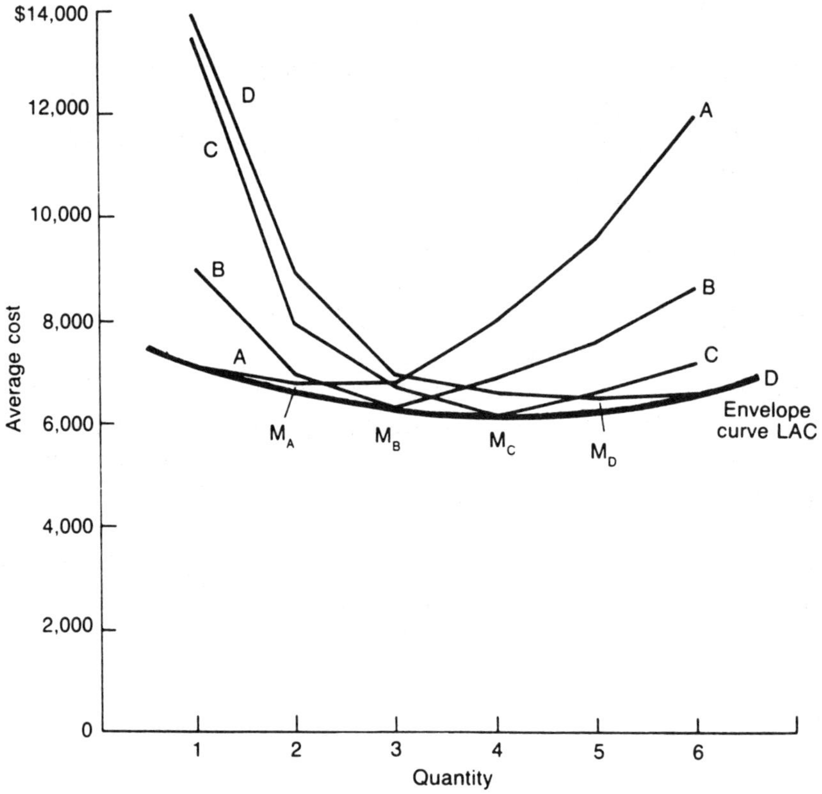

ANSWERS TO PROBLEMS FROM THE TEXT

9-1. The calculations follow the same pattern as in Table 9-1. Note that $500 replaces $35 throughout column 2.

(a) No. Because variable cost remains the same, so does marginal cost. (Marginal cost is the increase in either total cost or variable cost.)

(b) While nothing happens to MC, AC shifts up dramatically. Its minimum point – the point where it passes through MC – will be at a greater quantity of output (as long as MC slopes up to the right).

9-2. (a) False. MC could be rising, but still be below ATC, and therefore pulling ATC down.

(b) This statement is false for AVC, just as it was for ATC in part (a). MC could be rising, but still be below AVC, and therefore pulling AVC down.

(c) True. Since MC is higher than ATC, it is pulling ATC up.

(d) True. Since MC is higher than AVC, it is pulling AVC up.

(e) False. AFC always falls. MC is not related to fixed costs.

(f) False. No reason it should. For example, see falling MC on the left of Figure 9-1(b), even though ATC is above it.

9-3. (a) Cost rises from $120 to $165 – an increase of $45.

(b) Cost falls from $130 to $120 – a saving of $10.

9-4. (a, b) Diseconomies of scale or constant returns to scale – TC bends upwards (it is increasing at an increasing rate) from a positive vertical intercept (reflecting fixed costs); correspondingly, SAC is U-shaped. (In the short run, doubling output will more than double TC.)

(c) Economies of scale – the effect on TC (in the short run) of doubling output is uncertain – it could more than double, double, or less than double. Hence the shape of SAC is uncertain also.

9-5. (a) The isoquants are straight lines.

(b) The isoquants are "L-shaped."

(c) "L-shaped" isoquants imply that inputs must be used in fixed proportions – there is no substitutability. Thus, this case is most favourable to rising wages since there will be no substitution into capital resulting from relatively higher wages.

9-6. (a) Increasing returns to scale – doubling both inputs more than doubles output.

(b) No. Additional units of one input, holding the quantity of the other input fixed, result in constant increases in output.

(c) (i) Costs will be minimized by hiring 6 units of labour and 4 units of capital. (ii) Costs will be minimized by hiring 4 units of labour and 6 units of capital.

CHAPTER 10

Supply in a Perfectly Competitive Market

LEARNING OBJECTIVES

After you have studied this chapter in the textbook and the study guide, you should be able to

- Define perfect competition, explaining each of the five important requirements
- Distinguish between the demand curve of an individual buyer and the demand curve facing an individual seller
- Define the concept of marginal revenue
- Show why the condition for profit maximization by any firm is to produce until "marginal cost = marginal revenue"
- Show, as one specific case of this general principle, that the condition for profit maximization by a perfectly competitive firm is to produce until "marginal cost = price"
- Demonstrate why the short-run supply curve of a perfectly competitive firm is its marginal cost curve (above its average variable cost curve)
- Distinguish between the individual firm's short-run supply curve and the short-run market supply curve
- Analyze the long-run effect of the entry of new firms on an industry's supply
- Describe how an industry adjusts to an increase in demand, clearly distinguishing between the short-run increase in price, and the long-term drift of that price back down toward its original level as new firms enter the industry
- Explain why the long-run supply curve may be horizontal, upward sloping, or downward sloping
- Explain what it means for a firm to produce at its efficient scale

- Show how the gain to producers from a price increase can be read off a supply curve, just as a change in consumer surplus can be read off a demand curve

- Distinguish between the primary and excess burdens of an excise tax

CHAPTER SUMMARY

In Chapter 7 we saw how a demand curve reflects the desire of buyers to acquire a good. In this chapter, our attention turns to supply. It will be shown that, in a **perfectly competitive** market, a supply curve reflects the marginal cost of producing a good. Specifically, just as you can visualize a whole set of marginal benefit arrows rising up to a demand curve, you can also visualize a whole set of marginal cost arrows rising up to a supply curve. To establish this important conclusion, we analyze a profit-maximizing, perfectly competitive firm's response to various market prices.

Supply in the Short Run

The stage is now set for addressing the question: Given the firm's marginal cost (MC) and other cost schedules described in Chapter 9, how much will the firm supply at any given price? The rule for any profit-maximizing firm is to produce until its MC equals its **marginal revenue** (MR), where MR is its additional revenue earned from producing one more unit of output.

This general rule – that a firm will produce until MC = MR – can be stated in an alternative way for a perfectly competitive firm: Such a firm will produce until its MC = price. The reason is that such a firm takes the price of its output as given. Therefore, its MR is just the price that it faces. For example, if it sells apples for a price *P* = $2 a basket, then each additional basket provides $2 of extra revenue MR. This conclusion that a competitive firm continues to produce until MC = *P* is important. It means that when it is faced with any given market price *P*, it will supply a quantity of output that can be read off its MC curve; in other words, the firm's supply curve depends on its MC curve. Be sure that you fully understand Figure 10-2 and Table 10-1 in the textbook. These most clearly demonstrate why the firm will produce until MC = *P* and why, therefore, the firm's supply curve is the same as its marginal cost curve.

In making this statement about the firm's supply, however, we must recognize one important reservation. Price must be above a certain minimum level or the firm won't supply anything at all. This minimum level is the price that will generate enough revenue to cover the firm's variable costs. More specifically, price must be at least as high as the firm's "**shutdown point**" on its average variable cost (AVC) curve – that is, at least as high as point *K* in Figure 10-4 in the textbook. As long as price is at least this high, then in the short run the firm will supply this product. This is true, even if the price is still below the "**breakeven point**" (*H* in the same diagram) where the firm is just barely able to cover its total costs, including both its variable costs and its fixed costs. Even though a firm operating between these two points is incurring a loss, it is still able to cover part of its variable costs and have at least something left over to cover its fixed costs. Therefore, it is better to continue to operate than to close down altogether. (If it were to close down, it would be worse off because it would be unable to cover any of its fixed costs.)

This, then, leads to the conclusion that, as price falls, the firm's short-run supply curve will follow its MC curve down until it reaches the shutdown point where MC intersects AVC.

The short-run industry supply curve is the horizontal summation of the short-run supply curves of all of the individual firms, as shown in Figure 10-6.

Supply in the Long Run

In the long run (unlike the short run) there are no fixed costs – all costs are variable. Therefore, the firm is able to operate on its flatter long-run ATC (envelope) curve. There is another important difference between the short run and the long run: In the long run, firms can enter or leave the industry, in response to profit incentives.

In deriving **long-run supply**, two cases should be distinguished.

Case 1: Long-run supply is completely elastic (Figure 10-8 in the text). Suppose new firms can produce at the same cost as old firms. (For this to happen, inputs acquired by new firms would have to be as productive as those used by existing firms; and the industry would have to be small enough so that new firms can purchase inputs without bidding up their price.) In such circumstances, an increase in demand for this industry's output can, in the long run, be met entirely by new firms entering the industry and selling at the same price as old firms. Since supply can increase without any increase in price, the long-run supply is completely elastic; an example is S_L in Figure 10-8.

It is true that when demand initially increases, price does rise in the short run before new firms can enter. It is this increase in price and, hence, profit to existing firms that becomes the incentive for new firms to enter the industry. As new firms enter, supply shifts to the right. As a result, profit is reduced. This process continues until price falls back all the way to its original level, **above-normal (economic) profit** is eliminated, and there is therefore no incentive left for new firms to enter.

Case 2: A rising long-run supply curve (Figure 10-10 in the text.) In this case, price does not fall all the way back to its original level following a long-run adjustment to an increase in demand. The reason is that, as the number of firms in the industry increases, costs rise. This may happen because new firms cannot purchase inputs without bidding up their price, or because these firms cannot acquire inputs of the same quality as those used by existing firms. (For example, new entrants into farming may find that the only available land is less productive.) Because new firms are incurring higher costs, their profits will disappear before price falls all the way back to its original level. At this point, there will be no incentive left for more firms to enter; thus, the new equilibrium price will be higher than its original level. In this case, therefore, the long-run supply curve slopes up; an example is S_L in Figure 10-10.

The Benefit to Producers from a Higher Price

When, in response to a higher price, producers move from E_1 to E_2 in Figure 10-11 in the textbook, they acquire two benefits:

1.They get a higher price on their original 30 units of sales; thus, their profit increases by area 1.

2. On the additional 20 units they now sell, their costs are given by the height of the supply curve. But they receive the higher $700 price. Thus, profit increases by the difference between the two – area 2. Therefore, when price rises, producers benefit by the area to the left of the supply curve between the old and new price.

Reprise: The Burden of an Excise Tax

A $1 tax in Figure 10-12 shifts the S curve up from S_1 to S_2, with consumer equilibrium moving from E_1 to E_2.

Consumers lose areas 1 + 2, the area to the left of the demand curve between the old and new prices.

Producers must take a price reduction (after tax) from $2 to $1.60. Thus, they lose areas 3 + 4 to the left of the supply curve.

The government gains 1 + 3 of tax revenue – a $1 tax on each of the 3000 units sold.

Thus, there is a transfer of 1 + 3 from consumers and producers to the government (i.e., to taxpayers). This is the primary burden of the tax. The rest of the loss (area 3 + 4) is referred to as the excess burden of the tax. This area represents the loss in economic efficiency that results when people change their behaviour in response to the tax.

IMPORTANT TERMS

1. Perfect competition
2. Marginal revenue
3. Profit-maximizing output
4. Short-run supply
5. Break-even point
6. Shutdown point
7. Long-run supply
8. Efficient scale
9. Producers' gain
10. Above-normal (economic) profit

TRUE-FALSE

T F 1. Marginal revenue is total revenue less the cost that results when one more unit is produced.

T F 2. If a competitive firm is producing slightly less than the profit-maximizing amount, then price is greater than marginal cost.

T F 3. In the short run, the firm stops producing if price falls below its minimum average total cost.

T F 4. As you move up a firm's short-run marginal cost curve to the right, you reach the shutdown point before the break-even point.

T F 5. A firm maximizes its profits where the vertical distance between its total cost and total revenue curves is minimized.

T F 6. If a firm is operating at capacity – that is, with a completely inelastic supply (MC) curve – then an increase in market price will result in no increase in its total revenue or output.

T F 7. In the short run, a firm that is operating at its shutdown point is earning no economic profit or loss.

T F 8. Unless there are economies of scale, a perfectly competitive firm's short-run supply curve cannot slope upward to the right.

T F 9. An increase in demand for a perfectly competitive good will result in a short-run increase in the output and profit of existing firms.

T F 10. If new entrants to an industry can obtain the same quality of inputs as existing firms, and inputs are available at stable prices, then the long-run industry supply will be upward-sloping.

MULTIPLE CHOICE

1. For a perfectly competitive firm, marginal revenue is
   a. less than the price of its output
   b. equal to the price of its output
   c. greater than the price of its output
   d. greater than the price of its output if the elasticity of demand for its output is greater than 1
   e. not related to the price of its output

2. The short-run supply curve slopes upward because of
   a. the law of eventually diminishing returns
   b. economies of scale
   c. the upward slope of the marginal cost curve
   d. a. and c.
   e. b. and c.

3. In a perfectly competitive industry, there are
   a. so few buyers and sellers that each one can influence price
   b. so few buyers and sellers that none can influence price
   c. so many buyers and sellers that none can influence price
   d. so many buyers and sellers that each one can influence price
   e. just the right number of buyers and sellers so that each can influence the price

4. In a perfectly competitive market, an individual consumer determines
   a. price but not the quantity to purchase
   b. quantity to purchase, but not price
   c. neither the quantity to purchase, nor price
   d. both the quantity to purchase, and price
   e. both the quantity to purchase and price, but only if the product is standardized

5. In perfect competition, the demand by individual buyers is
   a. perfectly elastic while the demand facing individual sellers is not
   b. perfectly elastic like the demand facing individual sellers
   c. not perfectly elastic while the demand facing individual sellers is perfectly elastic
   d. not perfectly elastic, nor is the demand facing individual sellers
   e. perfectly elastic while the demand facing individual sellers can be either elastic or inelastic

6. In perfect competition, the per unit profit of an individual firm is
   a. its total cost minus its total revenue
   b. its total revenue minus its total cost
   c. its average total cost minus the price at which it sells
   d. its average total cost plus the price at which it sells
   e. its selling price minus its average total cost

7. In perfect competition, total profit of an individual firm is its
   a. marginal revenue minus its average total cost
   b. total revenue minus its average total cost
   c. total revenue minus its total cost
   d. marginal revenue minus its total cost
   e. marginal revenue minus its marginal cost

8. Consider a perfectly competitive industry, where there are many identical firms initially producing with zero (excess) profit. If demand decreases, then in the short run
   a. each firm will produce more and operate at a loss
   b. each firm will produce more and operate at a profit
   c. each firm will produce more and continue to operate with zero profit
   d. each firm will produce less and operate at a profit
   e. each firm will produce less and operate at a loss

9. The shutdown point is
   a. the minimum point on the average total cost curve
   b. the minimum point on the average variable cost curve
   c. the minimum point on the marginal cost curve
   d. the minimum point on the average fixed cost curve
   e. the point where marginal cost cuts the average fixed cost curve

10. Beneath a supply curve, you can visualize a set of vertical
    a. marginal revenue arrows
    b. marginal benefit arrows
    c. marginal cost arrows
    d. average cost arrows
    e. average benefit arrows

11. In the short run, the break-even point is
    a. at the intersection of the marginal cost curve and the average fixed cost curve
    b. below the intersection of the marginal cost curve and the average fixed cost curve
    c. the same as the shutdown point
    d. above the shutdown point
    e. below the shutdown point

12. In the short run, the perfectly competitive firm's break-even point occurs at
    a. a greater quantity of output than the shutdown point
    b. a smaller quantity than the shutdown point
    c. the same quantity as the shutdown point
    d. a lower price than the shutdown point
    e. the same price as the shutdown point

13. If a firm's total cost and total revenue curves (TC and TR) are plotted, the firm can earn a profit and maximize it where
    a. its TC cuts its TR from above
    b. its TC cuts its TR from below
    c. its TC is parallel to and above its TR
    d. its TC is parallel to and below its TR
    e. its TC is horizontal

14. Removing restrictions on entry by new firms will
    a. shift the industry's supply curve to the left
    b. shift the industry's demand curve to the left
    c. shift the industry's supply curve to the right
    d. have no effect on the industry's supply curve
    e. have no effect on the industry's supply and demand curves

15. If demand decreases in a perfectly competitive industry, then price will
    a. rise in the short run and fall in the long run
    b. rise in the short run and rise further in the long run
    c. fall in the short run and fall further in the long run
    d. fall in the short run and rise back towards the original price in the long run
    e. fall in the short run and thereafter remain constant at that level

16. Suppose demand has increased in a perfectly competitive industry, and each firm has moved to a new short-run equilibrium. Then, in the further process of long-run adjustment, the individual firm will face
    a. falling price and decreasing profit
    b. falling price and increasing profit
    c. falling price and constant profit
    d. increasing price and decreasing profit
    e. increasing price and increasing profit

17. For long-run industry supply to be completely elastic (horizontal)
    a. the industry must be large enough so that it can influence the price of its inputs
    b. inputs of uniform quality must be available to old and new firms alike
    c. both of the above
    d. neither of the above
    e. It is not possible for an industry supply curve to be completely elastic

18. The long-run supply curve for an industry will be upward-sloping if
    a. new firms bid up the price of inputs
    b. the quality of inputs deteriorates as new firms purchase more
    c. a. or b.
    d. neither a. nor b.
    e. It's impossible for a long-run supply curve to be upward-sloping

19. If price rises and output increases, then the gain to the producing firm is
    a. the increase in the firm's revenue, plus the increase in its costs
    b. the increase in the firm's revenue, minus the increase in its costs
    c. the increase in the firm's revenue
    d. the increase in the firm's costs, minus the increase in its revenue
    e. the decrease in the firm's costs

20. If price falls, then producers
   a. benefit by the area to the left of the supply curve between the old and new price
   b. benefit by the area to the left of the demand curve between the old and new price
   c. are worse off by the area to the left of the demand curve between the old and new price
   d. are worse off by the area to the left of the supply curve between the old and new price
   e. are not affected

21. When the government imposes an excise tax on a product
   a. the consumers' and producers' loss is less than the government's tax collections
   b. the consumers' and producers' loss is the same as the government's tax collections
   c. the consumers' and producers' gain is the same as the government's loss of tax collections
   d. the consumers' and producers' gain is less than the government's loss of tax collections
   e. the consumers' and producers' loss is greater than the government's tax collections

EXERCISES

1a. If the price is P_1 in Figure 10.1 below, the quantity supplied will be _____, total revenue will be area _____, average cost will be _____, and multiplying this by the number of units sold yields a total cost of area _____. Thus economic profit will be area _____.

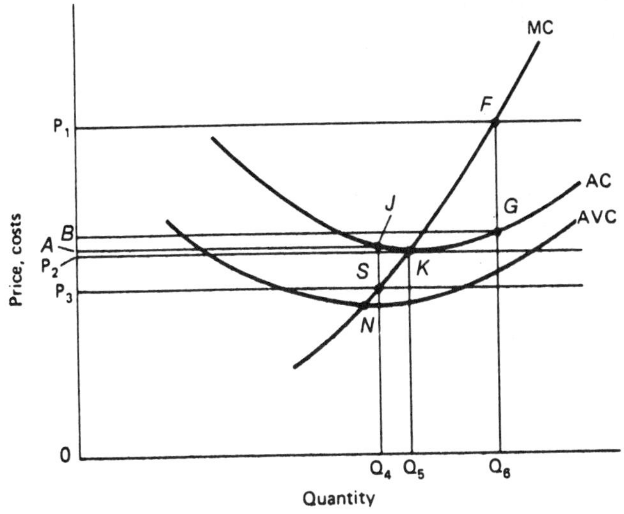

Figure 10.1

1b. Alternatively, we can arrive at this same profit by noting that the firm's average revenue is its price P_1, its average cost is _____ and, therefore, its profit per unit of output is _____. Multiplying this by its quantity of output yields its total profit of area _____.

1c. If the price is P_2, the firm will supply quantity _____, total revenue will be _____, average cost will be _____, total cost will be _____, and economic profit will be _____. Therefore, the (break-even, shutdown) point is _____.

1d. If the price is P_3, the firm will supply _____, total revenue will be _____, average cost will be _____, and total cost will be _____. Therefore, total economic (profit, loss) will be _____. If price stays at P_3, then the firm will continue to operate in the _____ run, but not in the _____ run. Despite its loss, it makes this short-run decision because price P_3 is still above the firm's (shutdown, break-even) point at _____. Another way of viewing this decision is that the firm is operating above its (MC, AC, AVC) curve. Therefore, it can more than cover its _____ costs and, thus, have some left over partly to cover its _____ costs. Shade in and mark for future reference the firm's profit when its price (in this case, P_1) is above the minimum point *K* on its AC curve; and its loss when its price (in this case, P_3) is below *K*.

2. Table 10.1 describes some of a firm's long-run costs. Fill in the rest of this table. Note, in particular, that column 3 is to show its envelope curve LAC.

When the price of this firm's output is $70, the firm's long-run profit-maximizing output is _____, and its economic profit is _____. When the price is $85, the firm's profit-maximizing output is _____, and its profit is _____.

Table 10.1 A Firm's Long-run Costs

Output	Total cost	Average cost (LAC)	Marginal cost	Total revenue if price equals $70	Economic profit if price equals $70	Total revenue if price equals $85	Economic profit if price equals $85
1	$120		$120				
2	150						
3	200						
4	270						
5	350						
6	440						

When price rises from $70 to $85, there is a (gain, loss) to this firm of _____.

3. In Figure 10.2, supply is S_1 in panel (*b*). When D_1 decreases to D_2, price falls from _____ to _____ as the short-run equilibrium of the industry shifts from _____ to _____. Each firm in panel (*a*) responds by moving along its supply curve from _____ to _____. Each firm now has a (profit, loss) of _____. As firms therefore (enter, leave) the industry, the industry supply in panel (*b*) shifts from _____ to _____, and industry equilibrium moves from _____ to _____. The initial 30% leftward shift in demand has been offset by a ____% shift in supply, and price (moves to, returns to) _____. Long-run supply is constructed by joining all points such as _____ and _____. It is (completely elastic, unit elastic, inelastic).

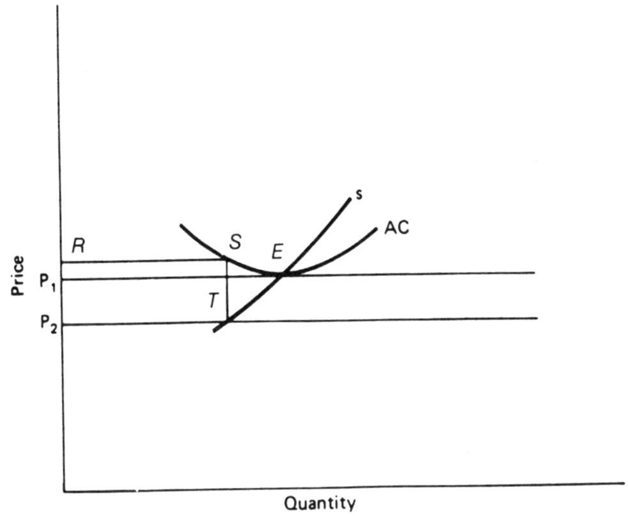

(a) An individual firm ...

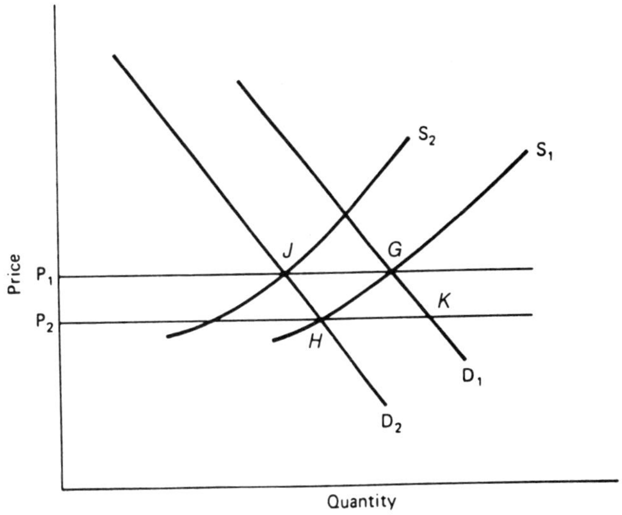

(b) ... in a perfectly competitive industry

Figure 10.2

4. If price is P_1, the total revenue of the perfectly competitive industry shown in Figure 10.3 is _____. If price falls to P_2, its total revenue is _____, for a (decrease, increase) in revenue of _____. However, this is partially offset by a decrease in _____ of _____. Therefore, the producers lose by _____.

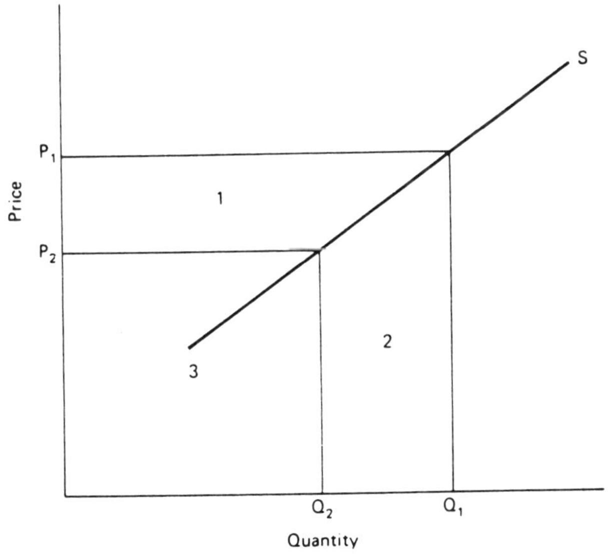

Figure 10.3

ESSAY QUESTIONS

1. "If a firm's overhead costs increase by, say, 20% because of an increase in its property taxes, its output will not be affected." Evaluate this statement, clearly distinguishing between the short and long run.

2. Draw a U-shaped average cost curve. Then, draw in the corresponding MC curve and, finally, the AVC curve. Show the new curves after a cost-cutting technological innovation. What effect does this have on the firm's supply curve?

3. "In the short run, a perfectly competitive firm will not produce at any point where its average cost is still falling." Do you agree? Why or why not?

4. "If demand for a perfectly competitive product shifts downward, price must fall." Do you agree? Explain, clearly distinguishing between the long and short run.

ANSWERS

True-False: **1F, 2T, 3F, 4T, 5F, 6F, 7F, 8F, 9T, 10F**

Multiple Choice: **1b, 2d, 3c, 4b, 5c, 6e, 7c, 8e, 9b, 10c, 11d, 12a, 13d, 14c, 15d, 16a, 17b, 18c, 19b, 20d, 21e**

Exercises: **1a.** Q_6, P_1FQ_60, *B*, BGQ_60, P_1FGB

1b. *B*, BP_1, P_1FGB

1c. Q_5, P_2KQ_50, P_2, P_2KQ_50, zero, break-even, *K*

1d. Q_4, P_3SQ_40, *A*, AJQ_40, loss, $AJSP_3$, short, long, shutdown, *N*, AVC, variable, fixed.

2. Table 10.1 completed

Output	Total cost	Average cost (LAC)	Marginal cost	Total revenue if price equals $70	Economic profit if price equals $70	Total revenue if price equals $85	Economic profit if price equals $85
1	$120	$120	$120	$ 70	$-50	$ 85	$-35
2	150	75	30	140	-10	170	20
3	200	66⅔	50	210	10	255	55
4	270	67½	70	280	10	340	70
5	350	70	80	350	0	425	75
6	400	73⅓	90	420	-20	510	70

4, \$10, 5, \$75, gain, \$65.

3. P_1, P_2, *G*, *H*, *E*, *T*, loss, *RST*P_2, leave, S_1, S_2, *H*, *J*, 30%, returns to, P_1, *G*, *J*, completely elastic.

4. 1 + 2 + 3, 3, decrease, 1 + 2, costs, 2, 1.

ANSWERS TO PROBLEMS FROM THE TEXT

10-1. Assuming P > AVC, the firm should expand production since MR (= P) > MC. The firm's profit from producing an additional unit would be \$90 - \$50 = \$40.

10-2. (a) Add 2 columns to the right of Table 10-1, just like the last two columns of Table 10-2, except that they are headed "Price = \$55 = MR." The profit-maximizing output is 7 units, where MC = MR = \$55. Profit is 7(\$55) - \$245 = \$140.

(b) 6 units. Nothing. Price must be at least as high as MC = \$55 before the 7th unit will be justified.

10-3. (a) Add \$35 to each item in column (2) and follow exactly the same calculations as before.

(b) Nothing happens to MC, but ATC shifts up. Profit falls.

(c) Because ATC shifts up you can visualize its minimum point shifting up along the MC curve to a greater level of output. (The MC curve slopes upward to the right.) Therefore, it is generally true that heavier fixed cost makes ATC fall over a wider range of output – although, in this particular case, this effect isn't quite strong enough to trigger a change; minimum ATC still occurs at 5 units of output. (To clearly see ATC falling through a wider range, increase fixed costs to \$1,000.)

(d) AVC remains unchanged. (It has nothing to do with fixed cost.)

(e) Since fixed cost is included in ATC, ATC is affected by it. But AVC is not; fixed costs are not included in AVC.

(f) In columns 5 and 7 of Table 25-2, we see that AVC = MC = \$20 at 3 units of output. This is the shutdown point whether fixed cost is \$30, \$70, or any other amount. It doesn't matter how you change fixed costs, AVC and MC are both unaffected; therefore, so is the shutdown point. (However, the break-even point is affected because that is on ATC which is influenced by fixed cost.)

10-4. (a) Yes. Its short-run supply extends down its short-run marginal cost curve SMC until SMC intersects its short-run AVC curve. The firm won't supply at a price below this because it is the shutdown point.

(b) Since its price has fallen below its break-even point at H, the firm would view its original decision to get into this industry as a mistake. In the short run it would continue to produce (as long as price is at least as high as the shutdown level). However, in the long run it won't produce at all. This makes long-run supply more elastic because it reflects firms leaving the industry, while short-run supply does not.

10-5. What this illustrates is the efficiency of the perfectly competitive market equilibrium, the topic of the next chapter. Note from your diagram that there is a transfer from producers to consumers associated with the initial number of units when price falls. The net gain to society is reflected in the triangle. Suppose, for example, that the supply curve is perfectly elastic (a horizontal line). Then, the net gain to society is captured wholly by the change in consumers' surplus.

10-6. Sketch the AC curve. Note that min AC = 10. Sketch the MR curve, below AC. Note that MR (= P) = 8. Draw in the MC curve, cutting AC from below at its minimum point. Since P (= 8) < MC (= 10, since MC cuts AC at min AC), the firm should reduce output to the profit-maximizing level. Note that if P < AVC, the firm should, in fact, cease production.

10-7. Normal profit reflects the opportunity cost of capital and/or entrepreneurship. Economists measure cost using the opportunity-cost principle; hence normal profit is included as a cost. Above-normal profits are a signal for entry into the industry.

CHAPTER 11

Perfect Competition and Economic Efficiency

LEARNING OBJECTIVES

After you have studied this chapter in the textbook and the study guide, you should be able to

- Explain why the condition "marginal cost to society = marginal benefit to society" is necessary for there to be (allocative) efficiency

- Explain why perfect competition results in allocative efficiency when there are no externalities

- Show how perfect competition tends to promote technical efficiency

- Demonstrate, in a diagram similar to Figure 11-3 in the text, that a deadweight loss (efficiency loss) to society results if either more or less than the efficient quantity of output is produced

- Illustrate the efficiency of perfect competition using indifference curves

- Explain why perfect competition tends to promote dynamic efficiency in certain ways; but why, in some other ways, other types of markets may provide greater dynamic efficiency

- Show not only the great virtues of a perfectly competitive market, but also its limitations; in particular, be able to explain why an efficient outcome is not necessarily best, and why there are many possible efficient outcomes

- Explain why speculation sometimes benefits society, and why it sometimes damages society

- Explain why government agricultural support programs may improve efficiency by stabilizing prices, but may reduce efficiency if they stabilize prices and quantities at the wrong levels

CHAPTER SUMMARY

The primary objective in this chapter is to demonstrate that, under certain conditions, a perfectly competitive market provides an efficient outcome. Thus perfect competition must be studied carefully, even though it doesn't describe a large part of the economy, precisely because of its efficiency properties. In contrast, some other market structures, such as monopoly (discussed in the next chapter) are not efficient, and we will be able to see why in later chapters only if we now develop a full understanding of the conditions under which perfect competition is efficient.

Another important topic of later chapters will be those instances in which even perfect competition fails to achieve an efficient allocation. So, efficiency is seldom completely achieved. But it must be understood to ensure that policies to cure inefficiency do indeed move the economy in that direction, rather than making matters worse. Thus, understanding what efficiency means and why it is sometimes achieved in perfectly competitive markets is our major task in this chapter.

You sometimes hear it said that we should learn to cooperate more with each other rather than compete. But the economist will say that, on the contrary, competition is often the best method of ensuring harmony. This is the message of Adam Smith's "invisible hand," as described in Chapter 1. In pursuing our own self-interest, each of us is led by market forces – as if by an invisible hand – to promote the interests of others as well. In this chapter we show how this does indeed often happen in perfectly competitive markets. (In other markets, it often does not.) We also show that, even when they are (allocatively) efficient, perfectly competitive markets do have some shortcomings.

Perfect Competition and Allocative Efficiency

The core idea of this chapter is that, under certain conditions, perfectly competitive markets produce an efficient outcome. Consider first the concept of **allocative efficiency**, defined in Chapter 1. This requires that the marginal social cost of any activity be equal to its marginal social benefit – otherwise, a net gain can be acquired by changing the level of that activity. For example, if the marginal benefit of producing wheat is less than its marginal cost – that is, if the benefit of one more bushel of wheat exceeds its cost – then there is a net benefit from producing that additional bushel. The output of wheat should be increased. Moreover, it should continue to be increased until marginal benefit and cost are equal. Only then will the incentive for increasing output disappear; this output is efficient.

Under perfect competition, output is efficient because **marginal social benefit** (MB_S) and **marginal social cost** (MC_S) are equalized. The reason is that under perfect competition, supply equals demand. Supply reflects the marginal cost of producers and demand reflects the marginal benefit to consumers. Therefore, the equality of supply and demand means that the marginal cost of producers is equal to the marginal benefit to consumers. Provided these are the only benefits and costs – as carefully assumed in Equations 11-1 and 11-2 of the text – it follows that the marginal cost to society is equal to the marginal benefit to society, and an efficient outcome results. Thus, in a perfectly competitive market, the pursuit by producers and consumers of their own private interest promotes the interest of society as a whole.

Figure 11-2 in the textbook is particularly useful in clarifying this. In panel (*a*), consumers pursue their self-interest by responding as perfectly competitive price takers to the $10 market price. In panel (*b*), perfectly competitive producers pursue their self-interest by also responding as price takers to the same $10 market price. The result in panel (*c*) is an efficient outcome for society as a whole. We emphasize that this occurs in perfect competition, because both producers and consumers are price takers, who respond to the same market price.

In succeeding chapters we will examine markets that, for one reason or another, are not efficient. One possible reason is that producers are not perfectly competitive price takers. A second reason is that consumers are not perfectly competitive price takers. In either case, the market is not perfectly competitive and, therefore, is inefficient. But sometimes a market is inefficient, even though it is perfectly competitive. There are two reasons. The first is that consumers are not the only ones to benefit from a good; there are benefits that go to others in society as well. (When you have landscaping done around your home, the benefits may go not only to you, but also to your neighbours, since they too will enjoy the improved appearance of your garden.) The second reason is that producers may not be the only ones who face a cost when a good is produced. (For example, those living downstream from a chemical factory face a cost when the factory dumps waste into a river.) Note that, in each case, inefficiency arises because of the violation of one of the key assumptions made in this chapter.

Perfect Competition and Other Kinds of Efficiency

Perfect competition also tends to promote **technical efficiency**. Technically inefficient firms that are operating above their AC curves aren't likely to survive competition with technically efficient firms that are operating on their AC curves.

The situation is different with respect to **dynamic efficiency**. Discovering innovations that generate economic growth is usually very expensive. The perfectly competitive firm may be too small to be able to afford such expenditures. Moreover, it has less incentive to undertake them; a farmer who discovers a new strain of wheat would find that most of the benefit would go to the millions of other farmers.

However, when innovations are discovered, they will be quickly adopted by perfectly competitive firms. These firms have no choice: If they don't make these changes, their competitors will drive them out of business.

Other Reservations about Perfect Competition

Efficiency isn't everything. There are problems that the perfectly competitive market doesn't solve. One is how the nation's income should be distributed. Perfect competition provides no answer here. The reason is that for every possible distribution of income there is a different perfectly competitive equilibrium. While each is efficient, the economist has no objective way of deciding which of these efficient outcomes is "best." This is an important point: Make sure you can explain it using Figures 11-1 and 11-10 in the textbook.

Another possible drawback of a perfectly competitive market is that it may be subject to severe fluctuations in price and quantity – especially when there is a time lag between the production decision and the delivery of the product to the market. In the case of the hog cycle, the text shows how the expectation that future price will be the same as today's price leads to cyclical fluctuations in price and quantity.

Speculation

The text describes how price fluctuations may be reduced by speculators. For example, if private speculators make accurate forecasts they will tend to iron out fluctuations in the market. They do this by buying when there is an oversupply (and thus keeping price from falling even more) and by selling when there is a scarcity (and thereby keeping the price from rising even higher).

A speculator who succeeds in this strategy will not only make a personal profit, but will also benefit society by helping to iron out the instability in this market. On the other hand, a speculator who gets it wrong – for example, one who buys when the good is cheap and is forced to sell when it is even cheaper – will lose money and will damage society as well. But such individuals typically go out of business.

Another type of speculation that is against the public interest is the attempt to **corner a market** in order to reduce sales and thus raise price. The resulting contrived scarcity is damaging to society. There may also be costs to society even if those who are trying to corner a market don't succeed, if their purchases trigger severe price fluctuations. An example was the apparent attempt by the Hunt brothers to corner the silver market.

Farm Programs

Ideally, a government price-support policy can be viewed as playing the same socially desirable role that speculators play – that is, stabilizing by buying when the item is in oversupply and selling when it is scarce. In practice, it is not that simple. Just as speculators damage society when they err in their predictions, so, too, can the government. (Some would say that this problem is more serious for a government, since its decisions may sometimes be made by those without experience or talent in predicting the future.) Government price-support policies are also complicated because they are often used not just to stabilize price, but also to raise it. In this case, farmers may respond to an artificially high price by increasing their output above the efficient level (and the government may have to dispose of a surplus at bargain-basement prices in the world market). Alternatively, if the government limits the amount that each producer is allowed to put on the market, the result may be an output below the efficient level.

IMPORTANT TERMS

1. Marginal social benefit (MB_S)
2. Marginal social cost (MC_S)
3. Allocative efficiency
4. Efficiency loss (deadweight loss)
5. Technical efficiency
6. Dynamic efficiency
7. Moral hazard
8. Adverse selection
9. Speculation
10. Cornering a market
11. Pareto optimum(Box 11-1)
12. Pareto improvement

TRUE-FALSE

T F 1. Perfect competition guarantees an efficient solution.

T F 2. For a good with external benefits, marginal benefit to buyers is less than marginal social benefit.

T F 3. The typical firm in perfect competition must strive to eliminate technical inefficiency because it could be driven out of business otherwise.

T F 4. For each distribution of income, there is a different efficient solution.

T F 5. The best possible distribution of income is the only distribution that can lead to an efficient outcome.

T F 6. The only efficient outcome is the one in which everyone receives the same income.

T F 7. The greater the cost of storing a good, the greater will be the gap in its price between two years.

T F 8. A speculator may try to corner a market in order to be able to create a future shortage and thus raise the price.

T F 9. For a good with external costs, marginal cost to producers is greater than marginal cost to society.

For those who have studied the appendix to Chapter 11:

T F 10. Canadian farm price supports provide a subsidy that is larger in dollar terms to the poor farmer than to the rich farmer.

T F 11. Producers maximize their income by producing at a point of tangency between their production possibilities curve and the highest income line they can reach.

MULTIPLE CHOICE

1. In a perfectly competitive market where supply equals demand, the marginal benefit of each consumer will
   a. be greater than the marginal cost of each producer
   b. be equal to the marginal cost of each producer
   c. be less than the marginal cost of each producer
   d. be less than the average variable cost of each producer
   e. be less than the average fixed cost of each producer

2. A perfectly competitive market generates an efficient outcome if all but one of the following conditions holds. Which of the conditions below does not hold?
   a. social costs are the same as private costs
   b. social benefits are the same as private benefits
   c. consumers equate marginal benefit and price
   d. producers equate marginal cost and price
   e. consumers equate marginal benefit and total cost

3. If more than the efficient output is being produced, then
   a. marginal social benefit MB_S is equal to marginal social cost MC_S
   b. MB_S is less than MC_S
   c. MB_S is more than MC_S
   d. MB_S is zero
   e. MC_S is zero

4. To be efficient, a perfectly competitive market requires that
   a. benefits from the good are widely dispersed among buyers and non-buyers
   b. all benefits of the good go to its purchasers, with none going to others
   c. costs of the good are borne by all producers and some non-producers
   d. all costs of the good are borne by non-producers
   e. costs of the good are borne by all members of society

5. If a firm is prevented from entering an industry because of failure to obtain a government licence, then
   a. more will be produced at a higher price
   b. more will be produced at a lower price
   c. less will be produced at a lower price
   d. less will be produced at a higher price
   e. less will be produced at the same price

6. In a perfectly competitive market
   a. price is a rationing device that determines which buyers will acquire a good, and which sellers will produce it
   b. price is a rationing device that determines only which buyers will acquire a good
   c. price determines only which sellers will produce a good
   d. price determines neither the buyers nor the sellers of a good; price determines only how wealthy sellers will be
   e. none of the above

7. Perfect competition is superior to monopoly in terms of
   a. dynamic efficiency, but not necessarily allocative efficiency
   b. allocative efficiency, but not necessarily dynamic efficiency
   c. allocative efficiency, but not technical efficiency
   d. dynamic and technical efficiency
   e. dynamic and allocative efficiency

8. It is sometimes argued that perfect competition is inferior to other market forms in creating innovation because the typical small firm
   a. has an incentive, but not the funds to finance large R&D expenditures
   b. has lots of funds, but doesn't have an incentive to spend them on R&D, since it would gain only a small share of the benefits
   c. has neither the funds nor the incentive to spend them on R&D
   d. has both the funds and the incentive to spend them on R&D, but it is just mismanaged
   e. knows that once it has created an innovation, the government will not allow it to be widely applied

9. If we are initially in an efficient, perfectly competitive equilibrium, and we take income from Smith and give it to Jones, then
   a. the quantities of goods that each will acquire will remain unchanged
   b. there will be a move to a new, efficient equilibrium where Smith acquires fewer goods and Jones more
   c. there will be a move to a new, efficient equilibrium where Jones acquires fewer goods and Smith more
   d. there will be a move to a new, inefficient equilibrium where Smith acquires fewer goods and Jones more
   e. there will be a move to a new, inefficient equilibrium where Jones acquires fewer goods and Smith more

10. If the price in a hog cycle is
   a. low this year, then there will be decreased production, and price will be even lower next year
   b. low this year, then there will be increased production, and price will be even lower next year
   c. high this year, then there will be reduced production, and price will be even higher next year
   d. high this year, then there will be increased production, and price will be even higher next year
   e. high this year, then there will be increased production, and price will be lower next year

11. In a market with only a few sellers (when some have influence over price) which of the following efficiency conditions for perfect competition is violated?
    a. there are costs of a product to others than producers
    b. there are benefits of a product to others than buyers
    c. sellers equate their marginal cost and price
    d. buyers equate their marginal benefit and price
    e. none of the above

12. Speculation will be most effective in moderating a hog cycle if
    a. speculators buy pork when it is cheap and sell it when it is dear
    b. speculators sell pork when it is cheap and buy it when it is dear
    c. speculators buy pork when it is cheap and buy it again when it is dear
    d. speculators sell pork when it is cheap and sell it again when it is dear
    e. speculators lose money on the transaction

13. Suppose speculators buy in the first year and sell in the second. Then
    a. if price is higher in the second year, this speculation results in an efficiency loss for society, but a profit for speculators
    b. if price is higher in the second year, this speculation results in an efficiency gain for society, but a loss for speculators
    c. if price is lower in the second year, this speculation results in an efficiency loss for society, and a loss for speculators
    d. if price is lower in the second year, this speculation results in an efficiency loss for society, but a profit for speculators
    e. if price is lower in the second year, this speculation results in an efficiency gain for society, but a loss for speculators

14. Speculation that stabilizes price and quantity
    a. is beneficial to society because goods are moved from a year of glut to a year of scarcity when they are valued more highly
    b. is beneficial to society because goods are moved from a year of scarcity to a year of glut when they are valued more highly
    c. is damaging to society because goods are moved from a year of glut to a year of scarcity when they are valued more highly
    d. is damaging to society for other reasons; supplies are not moved from one year to another
    e. has no effect on society

15. A perfectly competitive market is likely to rank
    a. high in developing new technology but low in adopting it
    b. low in developing new technology but high in adopting it
    c. low in both
    d. high in both
    e. high in neither

16. British deregulation of the London financial markets in 1986
    a. raised the cost of financial services
    b. left the cost of financial services unchanged
    c. made entry of new firms easier
    d. made entry of new firms more difficult
    e. had no effect on the entry of new firms

17. For a good with an external cost, the
    a. marginal benefit to society is more than the marginal benefit to buyers
    b. marginal benefit to society is less than the marginal benefit to buyers
    c. marginal cost to society is the same as the marginal cost to sellers
    d. marginal cost to society is greater than the marginal cost to sellers
    e. marginal cost to society has an unknown relationship to the marginal cost to sellers

18. At a Pareto optimum
    a. it is possible to make someone better off without hurting someone else
    b. it is impossible to make someone better off without hurting someone else
    c. many Pareto improvements can still be made
    d. a few Pareto improvements can still be made
    e. none of the above

19. According to economists, moral hazard occurs when
    a. people stop celebrating religious holidays
    b. those who are insured become more careful in protecting themselves against risk
    c. those who are insured become less careful in protecting themselves against risk
    d. those who are insured don't change their attitude toward risk
    e. a. and b.

20. Cornering a market is
   a. selling a whole block of city property
   b. selling a large block of the common stock of a company
   c. selling enough of a good to be able to raise its price in the future
   d. none of the above
   e. all of the above

21. Marketing board quota systems
   a. are used primarily in deficiency payment programs
   b. are used primarily in price-support programs to ensure that there is enough production to meet export demand
   c. are used primarily in price-support programs to avoid costly surplus disposal
   d. require minimum production levels from each participating farmer
   e. are used to ensure that each province gets an equal share of total farm exports

EXERCISES

1a. Figure 11.1 shows the supply and demand for wheat. (This question also draws on Chapter 10.)

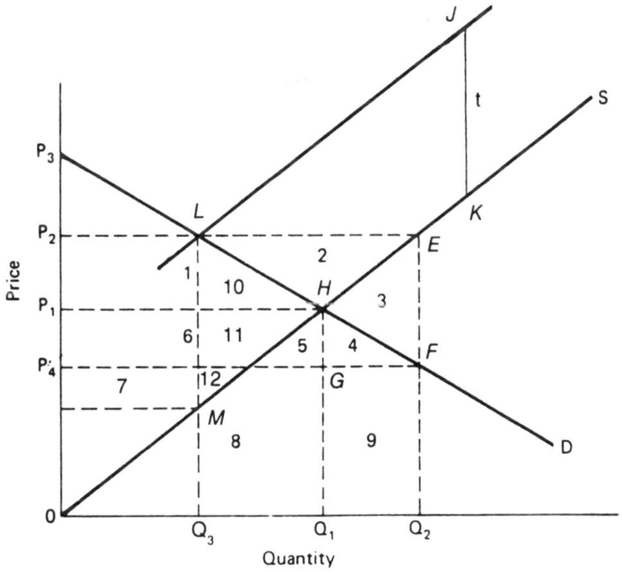

Figure 11.1

If the market supply curve is S, the equilibrium price is _____, and the equilibrium quantity is _____. Now suppose that the government imposes a sales tax t = *JK* = *LM*. The new equilibrium price is _____ and quantity is _____. The efficiency (gain/loss) is 10+ _____ because output has been (increased above/reduced below) its efficient level. Consumers (gain, lose) area _____, while producers (gain/lose) area _____. The government (gains/loses) area _____. The difference between all the losses and all the gains is a (gain/loss) of area _____, which is recognized to be the _____.

1b. Now suppose that, instead of this tax, the government sets a floor price on wheat. It stands ready to buy whatever amount of wheat may be necessary to keep its price from falling below P_2. The new equilibrium price and quantity sold are _____ and _____. The public purchases quantity _____ while the government (buys/sells) quantity _____. The efficiency (gain/loss) is _____ because output has been (increased above/reduced below) its efficient level _____. The cost to the government of (increasing/decreasing) its stockpile of wheat is the rectangle with base _____ and height _____.

1c. Repeat question 1b., assuming the government imposes a price floor at P_4.

2a. The purpose of this next exercise is to demonstrate the social benefit that can be produced by the existence of markets. Figures 11.2 and 11.3 represent the markets for a manufactured good in New Brunswick and Quebec.

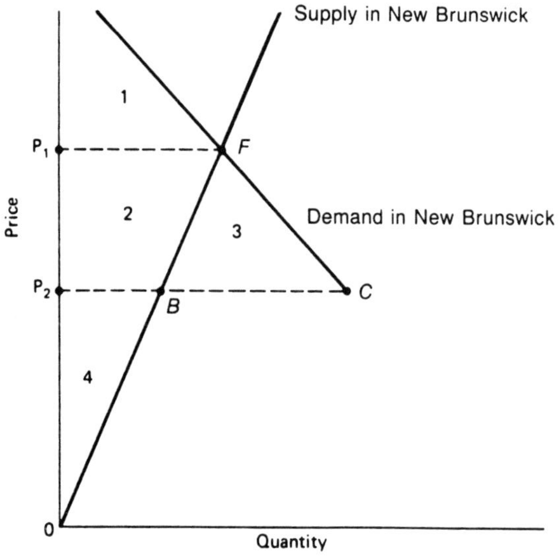

Figure 11.2

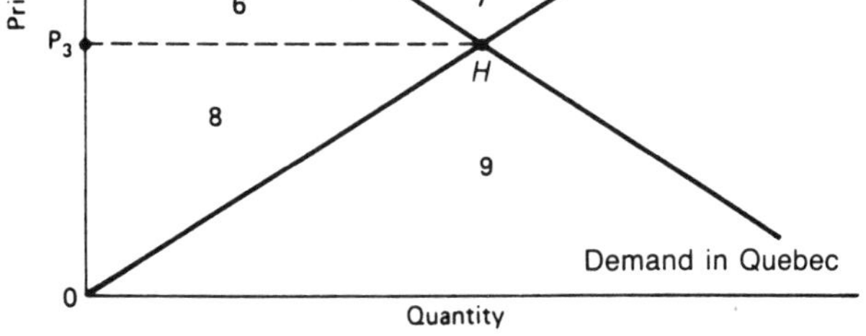

Figure 11.3

Suppose that initially there was no trade between the two provinces; that is, no market in which people from one province could trade with people from the other. Then the equilibrium price in New Brunswick would be ____ and the equilibrium price in Quebec would be ____.

2b. Next, suppose that a group of traders organized a market in which Quebeckers could trade with New Brunswickers. Suppose that there were no transportation costs or any other kind of cost to separate the market of the two provinces. Then, there would be only one market that included both provinces. A single equilibrium price would be established such that the total amount supplied in the two provinces together was just equal to the amount demanded in the two provinces together (suppose no other provinces are involved). Therefore, the excess of supply over demand in one province must equal the shortfall in the other. In Figures 11.2 and 11.3 this equilibrium price is ____. At that price New Brunswick has an excess (demand, supply) of ____. This is an equilibrium price because the excess (supply, demand) of Quebec is ____, which is equal to the excess (supply, demand) of New Brunswick.

2c. As a result of trade between the two provinces, consumers in New Brunswick have realized a (gain, loss) of ____, producers in New Brunswick are (worse, better) off by ____ ; so the net (benefit, loss) to New Brunswick is ____.

2d. Consumers in Quebec have realized a (gain, loss) of ____, and producers in Quebec are (better, worse) off by ____. Therefore, the overall (gain, loss) to Quebec is ____.

These two triangles provide estimates of the gains to the two provinces from creating a market in this good.

ESSAY QUESTIONS

1. In exercise 2 immediately above, who would be the winners and who would be the losers from the opening up of trade between the two provinces? What sort of arguments do you suppose the losers might propose in favour of a government prohibition of such trade? How could these arguments be countered? Can you imagine any way in which the winners might compensate the losers? Would the total gain in each province be enough so that after such compensation everybody could end up a winner? Would this then be a Pareto improvement?

2. According to the economist's theory of how markets work, butchers provide the public with meat in an economically efficient manner, not because they hate to see people go hungry, but because they are interested in making as large a profit as possible. In this chapter we have seen that this is true in perfect competition where there are so many buyers and sellers that none can affect price. But is it true if there is a monopoly – that is, a single seller with power to raise price? Specifically, suppose there is a monopolist who raises price from P_1 to P_2 in Figure 11.1 above. Is the outcome then an efficient one? Explain your answer.

3. Argue the case that perfect competition tends to promote at least two different kinds of efficiency.

4. Apply the analysis of this chapter to show in a diagram the triangular efficiency loss from a rent-control policy.

5. Earlier we stated that the demand and supply of a product are defined in terms of a certain time and certain place. What is the "place," that is, the geographical extent of the market for the firms supplying the following items?
   a. pastries
   b. haircuts
   c. copper

6. The text gave reasons that a perfectly competitive firm would not engage in much R&D expenditure. Is the same true of advertising expenditure? Explain why. Do you think it might make sense for all perfect competitors in an industry to advertise?

ANSWERS

True-False: **1**F, **2**T, **3**T, **4**T, **5**F, **6**F, **7**T, **8**T, **9**F, **10**F, **11**T

Multiple Choice: **1**b, **2**e, **3**b, **4**b, **5**d, **6**a, **7**b, **8**c, **9**b, **10**e, **11**c, **12**a, **13**c, **14**a, **15**b, **16**c, **17**d, **18**b, **19**c, **20**d, **21**c

Exercises: **1a**. P_1, Q_1, P_2, Q_3, loss, 10 + 11 + 12, reduced below, lose, 1 + 10, lose, 6 + 7 + 11 + 12, gains, 1 + 6 + 7, loss, 10 + 11 + 12, efficiency loss

1b. P_2, Q_2, Q_3, buys, Q_3Q_2, loss, 3, increased above, Q_1, increasing, Q_3Q_2, Q_3L

1c. This floor has no effect because the market price is already above it.

2a. P_1, P_3

2b. P_2, demand, *BC*, supply, *KL*, demand

2c. gain, 2 + 3, worse, 2, benefit, 3.
2d. loss, 6, better, 6 + 7, gain, 7

ANSWERS TO PROBLEMS FROM THE TEXT

11-1. This statement is correct, except for the proviso that price must reflect MB_S and MC_S. Equations 11-1 and 11-2 make the assumption that private benefits and costs are the same as social benefits and costs. If this is not the case – because of externalities – competitive markets will fail to allocate resources efficiently, precisely because external benefits/costs are not taken into account in decision making.

11-2. Rent controls will maintain price below the equilibrium price for rental accommodation. On a diagram, illustrate the transfer between consumers and producers at the initial quantity when price is allowed to rise to its equilibrium level. Illustrate the net gain to society from allowing price to rise to its equilibrium level.

11-3. On a diagram, draw in a horizontal MC curve. Above it, draw in a horizontal MC_S curve. The vertical height between these (call it T) represents marginal congestion costs. P = MC will result in excessive road use. However, a congestion toll set at level T raises price such that P = MC + T = MC_S. Now, the efficient level of road use will result.

11-4. This question should be taken up as a class discussion question. The essential point is that the sales tax on clothing will increase the relative price of clothing, whereas the income tax leaves relative prices unchanged. Hence, the sales tax is distortionary – it causes people to choose to buy fewer units of clothing, sliding up to the left along the PPC. In principle, the deadweight loss (efficiency loss) of the tax on clothing can be measured as the amount by which income would have to be increased starting from the new consumption point in order to achieve the original level of utility (associated with the indifference curve tangent to PPC at E in Figure 11-5). (This is akin to the method used to determine the income effect in chapter 7.)

11-5. (a) Inadequate fireproofing when houses are built, and insufficient fire protection once they are occupied.

(b) Inadequate stormproofing when houses are built, and they may be constructed in areas where the risks from storm damage (due to, say, flooding) is high.

(c) Inadequate care by the insured to avoid health risks to themselves and to their families.

(d) It appears that there would be very little moral hazard here. Who is going to risk his life to get insurance that he won't be around to spend?

An example of a case where insurance reduces the chance of an unfavourable outcome may be health insurance that encourages individuals to have regular check-ups; this may lead to early detection and cure of disease that otherwise might have become serious.

11-6. More elastic demand makes the program in panel (*a*) more expensive, while at the same time making the program in panel (*b*) less expensive. With elastic demand, program (*b*) satisfies the criteria, whereas inelastic demand leads to the choice of program (*a*).

PART THREE

THE MARKET MECHANISM: SOME PROBLEMS

CHAPTER 12

Monopoly

LEARNING OBJECTIVES

After you have studied this chapter in the textbook and the study guide, you should be able to

- Provide four reasons for the existence of monopolies
- Describe the cost conditions that lead to a natural monopoly, and explain how, in these circumstances, competition will eliminate all firms but one
- Show why a monopolist's demand and marginal revenue are quite different from a perfect competitor's
- Explain why, for a monopolist, marginal revenue (MR) is less than price (P)
- Explain why a monopolist – like a perfect competitor – maximizes profit by selecting output where marginal cost equals marginal revenue (Figure 12-4(*a*))
- Demonstrate the alternative method of selecting this output by maximizing the rectangle defined between the firm's average cost and demand curves (Figure 12-4(*b*))
- Explain why the monopolist will only produce where demand is elastic
- Explain why there is no such thing as a supply curve in the case of a monopolist (in contrast with a perfect competitor)
- Show why a monopoly produces too low a level of output to achieve allocative efficiency
- Explain why the appropriate government policy toward collusive monopoly is to break it up or prevent it from being formed in the first place

- Explain why, in some sectors of agriculture, the government has helped organize monopolistic marketing boards, and also describe some of the problems that this has created

- Demonstrate why marginal cost pricing is the appropriate government policy toward natural monopoly, provided it is feasible; and why, if it is not feasible, average cost pricing may be used

- Show why, in very special circumstances, price discrimination by a monopolist may benefit all concerned – both the producer and consumers of the product

If you have studied the appendices to Chapter 12, you should be able to

- Explain what is meant by a perfectly discriminating monopolist, and why it results in an allocatively efficient level of output

- Explain why the theory of second best would suggest that monopolies such as transit authorities should set price below marginal cost in the face of severe roadway congestion

CHAPTER SUMMARY

We have now completed our analysis of one extreme of the market spectrum – perfect competition. Key assumptions in the theory of perfect competition are (1) that there is freedom of entry (at least, in the long run) and (2) that there are so many buyers and sellers that none can influence price – individuals and firms are price takers. Our focus now turns to the other extreme – monopoly. Key assumptions here are (1) that there are barriers to entry and (2) that there is a single seller who can not only influence price, but can actually determine it, subject only to demand conditions. The following questions will be addressed: Under what conditions does monopoly arise? How does the monopolist's price and quantity compare with the perfect competitor's? Is the monopolist's output level efficient? What instruments are available to governments for controlling monopoly? Are there conditions under which a monopoly should be free not just to set its price, but to go beyond this to set several prices that discriminate between buyers?

Why Does Monopoly Exist?

Monopolies exist for any or all of the following reasons: (1) the monopoly may possess something valuable that is not available to a potential competitor (for example, some talent, property, or **patent**); (2) government may have created the monopoly by making competition illegal, as in the case of certain kinds of mail carried by the post office, or in some sectors of agriculture; (3) there may be a **natural monopoly**; or (4) the existing sellers may have colluded – that is, agreed to act in cooperation rather than competition.

The case of natural monopoly is perhaps the most important. It exists whenever there are economies of scale through a wide range of outputs – that is, whenever a firm has an average cost curve that continues to fall until its output becomes about large enough to satisfy the entire industry demand. (See panel (*b*) in Figure 12-1 in the textbook.)

How Does a Monopoly Maximize Its Profit, and How Do Its Price and Output Compare with a Perfect Competitor's?

A monopoly, just like a perfectly competitive firm, maximizes profit by choosing the level of output where its marginal revenue (MR) equals its marginal cost (MC). But, whereas the perfect competitor's MR equals the market price, the monopoly's MR is less than the market price; that is, its MR curve lies below its demand curve. This is because the perfectly competitive firm is so small in relation to the entire market that it doesn't have to take into account the minute effect that any increase in its own sales will have on the market price. Thus, such a firm effectively faces a horizontal demand curve. When the firm sells one more unit, its extra revenue MR is just the existing market price. Compare this to a monopoly, which is the only seller in the market: It has to recognize that the demand curve for its good slopes downward to the right. When this firm sells one more unit, it has to recognize that the price doesn't stay the same. Thus, the monopoly's extra revenue (MR) is the price that it receives from selling the extra unit, minus the loss it incurs because selling this extra unit lowers the price it receives for all the other units it sells in the market.

Since the monopoly's MR curve lies below its demand curve, it intersects the MC curve at a smaller output, as you can see in Figure 12-4 in the textbook. Thus, the monopoly exploits its advantage by reducing its output. By making the product scarce, it is able to raise price.

Like the perfectly competitive firm, the monopoly produces where MR = MC only if it is able to cover its costs. This requires that the demand curve overlap the AC curve; that is, the demand curve must not always be below the AC curve. Moreover, since MR is positive only over the elastic portion of the demand curve, a profit-maximizing monopolist will only produce when demand is elastic.

Is Monopoly Efficient?

The efficient output is the one under perfect competition, where supply (MC) equals demand (the marginal benefit of this good). When competitors collude to form a monopoly, output is reduced because the new monopoly is equating MC, not with price, but instead with MR which is below the price (that is, below the demand curve). Because this reduces output below the efficient, perfectly competitive level, monopoly is inefficient. This is the main disadvantage of monopoly. But a complete verdict on any particular monopoly is not possible without also taking into account other factors such as the technical inefficiency that may exist because there is no competition to force the monopoly to fight rising costs. It is also necessary to take into account the transfer of income from consumers to the monopoly that results from the monopoly's higher price. Strictly speaking, we can't be sure whether this transfer is desirable or undesirable, because there is no objective way of comparing one person's gain with another's loss. However, it is often reasonable to assume that these **transfer effects** cancel; that is, each dollar transferred is valued as highly by the person losing it as the person receiving it. If this assumption is reasonable, then the **efficiency loss of monopoly** implies a **welfare loss**.

As an example, the case of agricultural **marketing boards** is discussed. To their critics, these boards should simply be interpreted as government-sanctioned collusive monopolies that keep farm prices high by restricting supply. Supporters of marketing boards claim that their principal effect is to stabilize the prices of agricultural commodities, not to raise them toward the level that an unregulated monopolist would set. Moreover, they often argue that marketing boards have favourable transfer effects, since they make it possible for smaller family-based farm operations to remain in business.

What Should Government Policy Be toward Monopoly?

To answer this question, it is first necessary to specify what sort of monopoly is being considered. If it is a collusive monopoly of firms that would otherwise be highly competitive, then the solution is to break up the monopoly – or, better still, prevent it from being formed in the first place. This is a problem of competition policy that is discussed in Chapter 14. On the other hand, if it is a natural monopoly because of extended economies of scale, then breaking it up is no longer a simple solution. The reason is that this policy would create smaller-volume firms, thereby raising costs of production; this would impose an unnecessary cost on society. The preferred approach in this case is to leave the firm as a monopoly and continue to benefit from its relatively low costs of production; at the same time, impose a government policy that forces the monopoly to act as though it were a price-taking perfect competitor. That is, take away its market power to raise its price by imposing a ceiling on that price.

The question is, at what level should that price be set? The simple answer is **marginal cost pricing**, shown in Figure 12-9 of the text; set the price at the efficient level where the marginal cost of producing this good (MC) equals the marginal benefit it provides – as reflected in the market demand curve.

Unfortunately, in many instances this policy is not feasible because forcing the price down this much would turn the monopoly into a money-loser, and drive it out of business in the long run. This is the case examined in Box 12-2, where the government would have to supplement marginal cost pricing with whatever subsidy would be necessary to keep the firm in business; or, equivalently, put the firm under government ownership and subsidize its operations in this way. A final often-used alternative is **average cost pricing**: Instead of driving the price all the way down to the level required by marginal cost pricing, drive it down only part way – specifically, to the level where demand intersects average cost rather than marginal cost. Because price equals average cost, the firm breaks even. It is not turned into a money-loser, and the problem of going out of business does not arise.

However, since price is reduced only part way, monopoly inefficiency is only reduced part way; it is not eliminated. There is also a problem which applies not only to average cost pricing, but also to marginal cost pricing – and indeed to any government policy to control natural monopoly. Firms lack adequate incentive to keep costs down: If their costs rise, they know that the government-administered price will rise, because price is tied to costs.

Price Discrimination

So far we have assumed that the monopoly charges a single price to all consumers. But the firm will usually find it more profitable if it can charge different customers different prices – that is, if it can divide its market and charge a higher price to the group of customers with less elastic demand than to those with more elastic demand. Such a pricing policy by a monopoly may be beneficial to all concerned if the firm would not otherwise exist. In that case, allowing the firm to discriminate may not only allow the firm to cover its costs, but also provide a benefit to consumers who would not otherwise be able to buy this product.

On the other hand, if a monopoly quoting a single price can exist, then price discrimination can no longer be defended in this way. In this case, it may be justified on other grounds, or it may not. A justified case is charging a higher toll on a highway in rush-hour periods of congestion. An unjustified case arises when a nationwide firm cuts its price in a region to bankrupt a small, emerging competitor in that region.

Finally, Appendix 12-A describes the special circumstances of the perfectly discriminating monopolist – one who is able to charge each buyer his or her maximum willingness to pay. In this case, all consumers' surplus is appropriated by the monopolist. However, monopoly output will be efficient since price for the last unit sold will be just equal to marginal cost. (For the perfectly discriminating monopolist, the MR curve is coincident with the demand curve.)

The Theory of Second Best

The theory of second best is introduced in Box 12-1. A first-best economy is one in which all industries are structured such that marginal benefit (MB) = P = MC. This would be the case, for example, under perfect competition. A second-best economy is one in which there are pre-existing distortions in some sectors of the economy – P is not equal to MC – such as the situation described in Appendix 12-2 where roadway congestion – an externality – goes unpriced. In this case, a public transit monopoly would be justified in setting P < MC; in so doing, car trips would be reduced, reducing roadway congestion. The first-best solution would be to price roadway congestion directly. Where this is not possible (or feasible), the **second-best pricing** policy determines prices in related sectors of the economy (e.g., public transit) so as to achieve the best allocation of resources given the pre-existing distortion (e.g., unpriced roadway congestion). The conclusion is that unless P = MC in all sectors of the economy, efficient pricing rules may, in fact, diverge from marginal cost pricing.

IMPORTANT TERMS

1. Market power
2. Patent
3. Legal monopoly
4. Merger
5. Natural monopoly
6. Monopolist's marginal revenue curve
7. Efficiency loss (welfare loss) from monopoly
8. Transfer effect
9. Regulated monopoly
10. Marketing board
11. Marginal cost pricing
12. Average cost pricing
13. Second-best pricing
14. Discriminating monopoly
15. Economies of scope

TRUE-FALSE

T F 1. An unregulated profit-maximizing monopoly will set a price where marginal cost intersects the demand curve.

T F 2. A monopolist will never produce over the elastic portion of the demand curve.

T F 3. A profit-maximizing monopolist will set a price above marginal cost.

T F 4. One cannot be certain that monopoly, with its efficiency loss, is damaging to society without taking into account the monopoly transfer of income.

T F 5. A likely disadvantage of breaking up a natural monopoly is that it will raise costs of production.

T F 6. One problem with government ownership or price regulation of a monopoly is this: Once the firm knows that the government will ensure that its costs are covered, the firm will have a reduced incentive to keep its costs down (technical inefficiency).

T F 7. If marginal cost pricing is feasible, it will eliminate the efficiency loss from a monopoly.

T F 8. Government fixing of a free market price may increase efficiency in one set of circumstances, but decrease it in another.

T F 9. Price discrimination is justified only if the monopolist is already earning at least a normal profit.

T F 10. If a monopoly is formed in a perfectly competitive industry, the resulting monopoly firm will act like a competitive firm.

MULTIPLE CHOICE

1. An example of a monopoly is
   a. the auto industry, while an example of an oligopoly is the steel industry
   b. the auto industry, while an example of an oligopoly is the local natural gas supplier
   c. the steel industry, while an example of an oligopoly is the local natural gas supplier
   d. the local natural gas supplier, while an example of an oligopoly is wheat production
   e. the local natural gas supplier, while an example of an oligopoly is the auto industry

2. A firm's minimum cost is $30, achievable at 1,000 units of output. This firm will be a natural monopoly if the quantity demanded at a $30 price is about
   a. 1 million units
   b. 100,000 units
   c. 10,000 units
   d. 2,000 units
   e. 1,000 units

3. Economists define market power as
   a. the ability of a firm to influence federal anti-pollution legislation
   b. the ability of a firm to influence tax legislation in its home province
   c. the ability of consumers to purchase imports rather than domestically produced goods
   d. the ability of a firm to influence Supreme Court decisions
   e. none of the above

4. A monopoly's marginal revenue is
   a. always positive
   b. always above average cost
   c. equal to the height of its demand curve
   d. less than the height of its demand curve
   e. greater than the height of its demand curve

5. Which of the following faces a completely elastic demand?
   a. Ontario Hydro
   b. an individual apple grower
   c. General Motors
   d. Air Canada
   e. an urban transit company that is not subject to government price regulation

6. The demand facing a monopoly is
   a. the same as the total market demand
   b. to the right of total market demand
   c. to the left of total market demand
   d. completely elastic
   e. more elastic than the total market demand

7. At the equilibrium output of an unregulated monopoly, marginal revenue is
   a. less than marginal cost
   b. more than marginal cost
   c. more than market price
   d. equal to market price
   e. less than the market price

8. An unregulated monopoly is inefficient because it equates
   a. marginal cost with demand rather than with marginal revenue
   b. marginal revenue with demand rather than with marginal cost
   c. marginal revenue with average cost rather than with marginal cost
   d. average cost with demand rather than with marginal revenue
   e. marginal cost with marginal revenue rather than with demand

9. If the monopolist is producing more than the profit-maximizing amount, then
   a. marginal revenue will exceed price
   b. marginal cost will exceed price
   c. marginal cost will exceed marginal revenue
   d. average cost will exceed price
   e. marginal revenue will exceed average cost

10. If a monopoly is maximizing profit, then the marginal cost of producing one more unit is
    a. equal to its marginal benefit to society
    b. more than its marginal benefit to society
    c. less than its marginal benefit to society
    d. less than its marginal benefit to the monopoly firm
    e. more than its marginal benefit to the monopoly firm

11. If a perfectly competitive industry is monopolized, the result is
    a. higher output and lower price
    b. higher output and the same price
    c. higher output and higher price
    d. lower output and higher price
    e. lower output and lower price

12. The profit rectangle for a monopoly is its quantity of output times
    a. the monopoly's average cost
    b. its price
    c. its price less its average cost
    d. its marginal cost
    e. its price less its marginal cost

13. Monopoly often results in
    a. allocative efficiency
    b. technical inefficiency
    c. allocative inefficiency
    d. a. and b.
    e. b. and c.

14. When a regulatory agency controls a monopoly by marginal cost pricing, the monopoly's
    a. price is reduced
    b. output is reduced
    c. profit is eliminated
    d. level of efficiency remains the same
    e. all of the above

15. Which of the following makes zero profit?
    a. an unregulated monopoly charging a single price
    b. an unregulated, price-discriminating monopoly
    c. a monopoly regulated by marginal cost pricing
    d. a monopoly regulated by average cost pricing
    e. a monopoly regulated by variable cost pricing

16. The theory of the second best tells us that monopolizing one industry in an economy where monopoly exists elsewhere will
    a. reduce efficiency
    b. increase efficiency
    c. have no effect on efficiency
    d. have an uncertain effect on efficiency
    e. lower price in that industry

17. Government marginal cost regulation of monopoly is designed to induce the firm to
    a. act like a perfect competitor by reducing output
    b. act like a perfect competitor by taking price as given
    c. produce to the point where above-normal profit finally disappears
    d. produce to the point where normal profit finally disappears
    e. reduce price while holding its output constant

18. A product is not being provided because the potential producer is a monopoly whose demand lies below its average cost curve AC. This problem may be solved by permitting the firm to discriminate and thus
    a. at least cover its costs
    b. shift its demand above its marginal cost curve
    c. shift its demand above its average variable cost curve
    d. shift its AC curve down so it overlaps demand
    e. shift its demand above its AC curve

19. A government-sanctioned marketing board that is introduced into a competitive agricultural industry will
    a. typically set quotas to ensure that producers will increase their sales
    b. typically set quotas to ensure that producers will reduce their sales
    c. typically set quotas to ensure that producers will maintain their previous sales levels
    d. not set quotas, but will encourage producers to sell more
    e. encourage the entry of new firms

20. If a discriminating monopolist charges a higher price to the group with the more elastic demand than to the group with the less elastic demand
    a. its profit will increase
    b. its profit will decrease
    c. its profit will remain unchanged
    d. its profit will be zero
    e. c. and d.

EXERCISES

1a. If the monopoly shown in Figure 12.1 is unregulated, it will maximize profits by selecting output _____ where _____ equals _____. The price it will quote is _____, the highest price at which this output can be sold. Its profit will be _____ for each of the units it sells, that is, a total profit of area _____. An alternative view of its decision is that it selects the point _____ on the _____ curve that maximizes this profit rectangle. The efficiency (gain, loss) is _____.

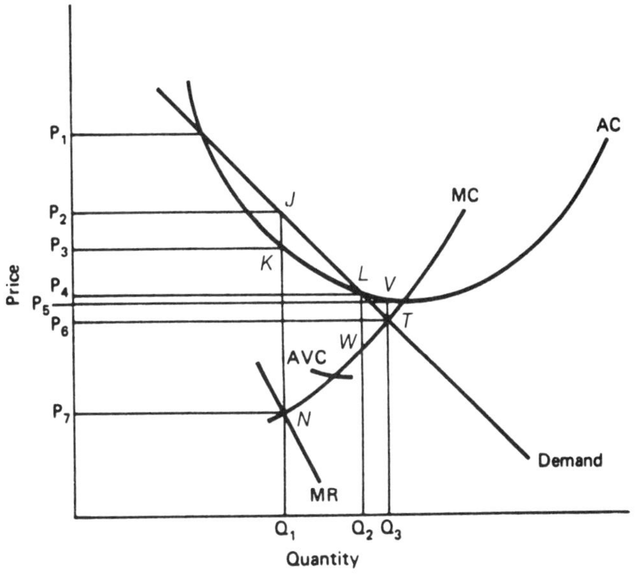

Figure 12.1

1b. A government regulatory agency that uses marginal cost pricing will set price equal to _____. The firm will respond in the short run by producing _____ output because this is where its _____ curve cuts the price line at P_6. However, in the long run, the firm would produce an output of _____ because at equilibrium *T* it is operating at a (profit, loss) of _____. To keep it in business the government would have to (provide a subsidy, impose a tax) of _____. This policy would (reduce, increase, eliminate) the previous efficiency loss of _____ ; that is, it would improve efficiency by _____.

1c. If the agency were instead to use average cost pricing, it would set price at _____. The monopolist would produce output _____ and earn a profit of _____. The subsidy now necessary to keep this firm in business would be _____. This policy would reduce the efficiency loss from the original *JTN* to _____, that is, it would improve efficiency by _____. Compared to marginal cost pricing, this average cost pricing policy improves efficiency (more, less); but it avoids the government problem of having to (subsidize, tax) this firm.

1d. With either form of regulation, the monopoly is forced to act like a (perfect competitor, oligopolist, natural monopolist) facing a fixed price.

2a. A monopoly has the demand and total cost figures shown in Table 12-1. Fill in this table, ignoring for now the last three columns.

Table 12.1

P	Quantity demanded	Total revenue	Marginal revenue	Total cost	Average cost	Marginal cost	Profit	(1) Net profit with lump-sum tax	(2) Net total revenue with excise tax	(3) Net profit with excise tax
$10	0	$0	$0	$ 2	$ -	$0	$	$	$	$
8	1	8		3						
6	2			6						
4	3			11						
2	4			18						

The monopoly's fixed cost is _____. It will choose to produce a level of output equal to _____ and charge a price equal to _____. Its maximum attainable profit is _____.

2b. Suppose that, in an attempt to capture some of this monopoly's profits for the taxpayer's benefit, the government imposes a lump-sum tax of $5. This tax may be regarded by the monopoly as a fixed cost, because it must be paid no matter how much output is produced. After the imposition of this tax, the monopoly's fixed cost is _____. Fill in (1), the third-last column, that indicates the monopoly's after-tax profit. After imposition of the tax, the monopoly will choose to produce an output equal to _____ and to charge a price equal to _____. Its maximum attainable after-tax profit will be _____.

2c. Suppose that instead of the lump-sum tax, the government decides to impose a 50% excise tax on the monopoly. In other words, the monopoly must now pay the government 50% of its total revenue. In this case, the monopoly's fixed cost is _____. Fill in the second-last column (2), showing the monopoly's after-tax total revenue, and the last column (3), showing its after-tax profit. In this case, the monopoly will choose to produce an amount of output equal to _____, and to charge a price equal to _____. Its maximum attainable after-tax profit will be _____. The amount of excise tax collected from this monopoly will be _____.

2d. From the point of view of economic efficiency the (lump-sum, excise) tax is preferable. From the point of view of maximizing the amount of tax revenue collected from the monopoly, the (lump-sum, excise) tax is preferable.

ESSAY QUESTIONS

1. Are economies of scale a barrier to entry? Explain. Is IBM a monopoly? A perfect competitor? Or in a dominant position somewhere in between? Do you think economies of scale give it an advantage over potential competitors?

2. Compare a monopoly and a perfectly competitive firm in terms of (1) their demand and marginal revenue schedules, (2) their market power, (3) their efficiency, and (4) the appropriate government policy in dealing with each.

3. "Allowing a monopolist to charge some customers more than others is not appropriate because it is unfair to those who have to pay the higher price." Evaluate this statement. Are there any circumstances in which those who pay the higher price could actually benefit?

4. Suppose the only two firms in an industry are considering a merger that would result in a reduction in costs of production through the elimination of wasteful duplication. Is it possible to argue that this action could increase efficiency? If so, how? Might it decrease efficiency? If so, how?

5. A perfectly competitive firm can sell all it wants at the existing price. Can a monopoly do that? If it tried to, what would happen? Does that mean that a monopoly is more constrained in its decision making than a perfect competitor?

ANSWERS

True-False: **1**F, **2**F, **3**T, **4**T, **5**T, **6**T, **7**T, **8**T, **9**F, **10**F

Multiple Choice: **1**e, **2**e, **3**e, **4**d, **5**b, **6**a, **7**e, **8**e, **9**c, **10**c, **11**d, **12**c, **13**e, **14**a, **15**d, **16**d, **17**b, **18**a, **19**b, **20**b

Exercises: **1a**. Q_1, MC, MR, P_2, *JK*, P_2JKP_3, *J*, demand, loss, *JNT*

1b. P_6, Q_3, MC, zero, loss, P_5VTP_6, provide a subsidy, P_5VTP_6, eliminate, *JNT*, *JNT*

1c. P_4, Q_2, zero, zero, *LWT*, *JLWN*, less, subsidize

1d. perfect competitor

Table 12.1 completed

P	Quantity demanded	Total revenue	Marginal revenue	Total cost	Average cost	Marginal cost	Profit	(1) Net profit with lump-sum tax	(2) Net total revenue with excise tax	(3) Net profit with excise tax
$10	0	$0	$ 0	$ 2	$ -	$0	$-2	$-7	$0	$-2
8	1	8	8	3	3	1	5	0	4	1
6	2	12	4	6	3	3	6	1	6	0
4	3	12	0	11	3⅔	5	1	-4	6	-5
2	4	8	-4	18	4½	7	-10	-15	4	-14

2a. $2, 2, $6, $6
2b. $7, 2, $6, $1
2c. $2, 1, $8, $1, $4
2d. lump-sum, lump-sum

ANSWERS TO PROBLEMS FROM THE TEXT

12-1. The industry will tend to become monopolized – by increasing its volume, a firm can cut its costs, lower its price, and therefore capture sales from its competitors. The advantage for society is that this good can be produced at lower cost by a monopolist operating on AC_2 than by one of the original competitors operating on AC_1. The disadvantage is that the new monopolist may be in a position to exercise market power – that is, raise the price paid by consumers. But if the government limits the exercise of this market power by regulating the monopolist, this disadvantage is removed. The result will be a good that can be produced less expensively, with the benefits of this cost reduction being passed on to the consumer.

12-2. (a) Not necessarily. If there is a labour union, it may well acquire some of this profit by negotiating for a higher wage; and the owners of a resource this firm requires may be able to increase the price they charge.

(b) Regulate price where MC intersects demand. This is best because MC = *D* (= MB), the marginal benefit to society.

12-3. You should disagree. In any market, *D* (= MB) represents the marginal benefit to society from consumption of the good or service (recall the interpretation of the demand curve as reflecting consumers' willingness to pay). Since the monopolist's MR curve lies below the demand curve, MR cannot then reflect marginal benefits. (Consider, however, the case of the perfectly discriminating monopolist discussed in Appendix 12-A.)

12-4. (a) The firm's loss L is minimized in Figure 27.2 below by setting price at P_A and selling Q_A.

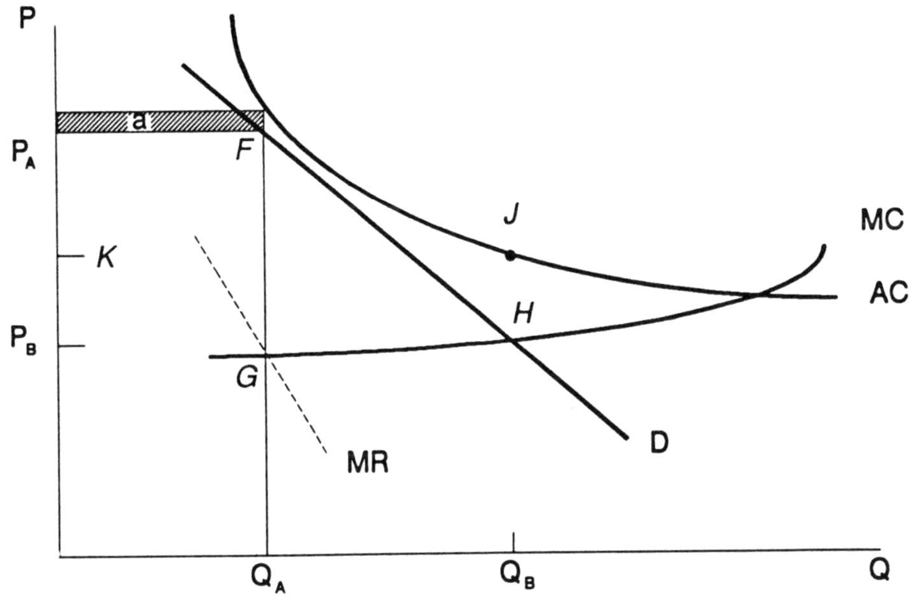

Figure 12.2

(b) No; it results in efficiency loss *FGH* because the firm is equating marginal cost MC to its own marginal benefit (MR), rather than to society's marginal benefit (*D*). The most efficient output level is Q_B, where marginal benefit to society (*D*) equals marginal cost (MC). While this eliminates the efficiency loss, it raises a problem: To reach this quantity of output, the firm would have to set price at P_B and incur an even greater loss (P_B *HJK*) than before.

(c) In Figure 12.3 below, it sets price of P_C on the first Q_C units it sells, and P_B on the rest. It sells the efficient quantity Q_B; but, because it is charging a higher price for the first Q_C units than before, it has increased its revenue by $P_C LMP_B$. This reduces its loss, or perhaps even provides it with a profit.

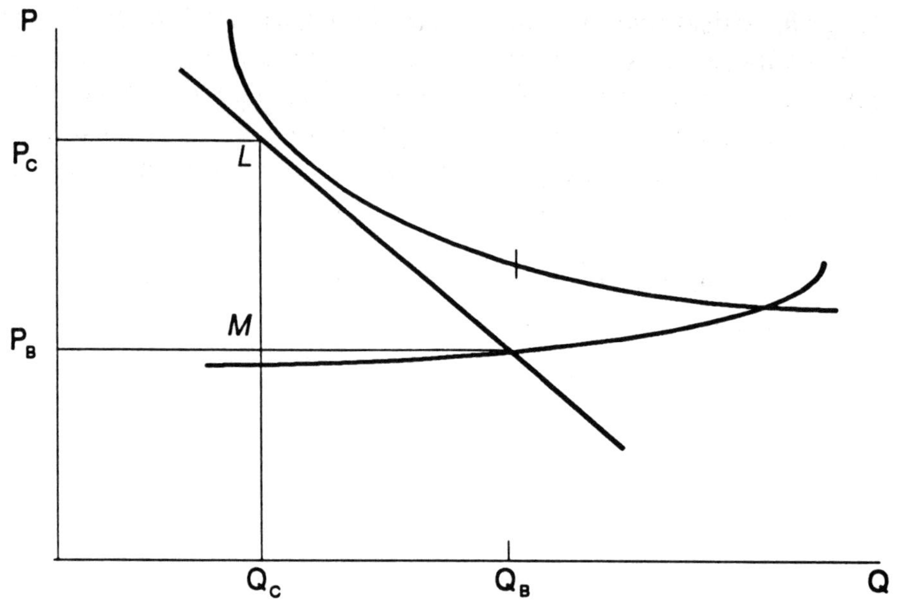

Figure 12.3

(d) Yes; it is the way to get an efficient output level, while cutting down the cost to the taxpayer of subsidizing the utility.

(e) In theory, public utilities could discriminate between buyers in, say, a wealthy area and a poor one. In practice, the electrical firm may discriminate in its dealings with each customer by charging a high rate on initial purchases, and a lower rate on purchases above a certain volume. Or, it may discriminate by charging all customers a higher price during periods of high demand.

12-5. A tax on profits will have no effect on output or price. Whatever price-quantity combination maximized profits before the tax still maximizes profits (net of tax) after the imposition of the tax.

12-6. The problem is not to know average cost at the current level of output; rather it is to know average cost where it intersects D (at E_3 in Box 12-2). Even if this problem did not exist, there would still be the problem of estimating the normal return on capital, and the amount of capital invested.

12-7. Drop a vertical line from point *B* to the horizontal axis. Profit per unit, then, is the difference between price (average revenue) and average cost (at that level of output). Total profit is found by forming the relevant rectangle. If all firms try to do the same, market price will be forced down, defeating the purpose of forming the producers' association. The important point is that there is an obvious incentive to cheat in situations like this.

12-8. The marketing board is evidently protecting the suppliers it serves, rather than the interests of consumers.

CHAPTER 13

Markets Between Monopoly and Perfect Competition

LEARNING OBJECTIVES

After you have studied this chapter in the textbook and the study guide, you should be able to

- Clearly distinguish between perfect competition, monopolistic competition, oligopoly, duopoly, and monopoly
- Explain why product differentiation is a source of market power
- Explain why the run-of-the-mill firm earns no above-normal profits in the long run in monopolistic competition, and why this market form is not necessarily inefficient, even though fewer firms could produce the same output at lower costs
- Give two reasons why oligopoly may arise
- Describe why economies of scale and advertising create barriers to entry
- Explain why oligopolists have an incentive to collude, and the effect such collusion will have on efficiency
- Explain why, as an example of a cartel, the OPEC countries were able to collude to raise the price of oil during the 1970s without imposing formal production quotas and why they at least tried to set formal production quotas in the 1980s
- Explain the underpinnings of the kinked demand curve and its implications for firms' pricing behaviour
- Describe game theory and explain why it may be useful in analyzing duopoly
- Explain why the outcome of a game may be influenced by such factors as (i) how easy it is for a player to cheat on a prior understanding and (ii) whether or not the game is repeated

- Explain the concept of price leadership, how it relates to the analysis of kinked demand, and why it is often viewed as "tacit collusion"

- Give three examples of non-price competition

- Summarize the arguments for and against advertising

- Describe a contestable market and why this concept is important

CHAPTER SUMMARY

The last two chapters have described the two extremes in the spectrum of markets: perfect competition, where there are so many sellers that none has any influence over price; and monopoly, where the single firm is free to set any price it chooses, since it has no competitors to worry about. (A monopoly is restrained only by consumer demand and the possibility of government intervention.) Most Canadian industries do not conform to either of these two extremes, but lie somewhere in between where individual firms have some influence over price. The objective in this chapter is to analyze some of the market forms that lie within this intermediate range. We begin with **monopolistic competition**, the market closest to perfect competition, and then work our way toward monopoly by considering markets with fewer and fewer firms. Thus, we describe **oligopoly**, a market with several firms, and then **duopoly**, a market with only two.

Monopolistic Competition

This is closest to perfect competition. In monopolistic competition, as in perfect competition, there is a large number of firms. There is also free entry of firms into the industry, which means that any short-run excess profit for the run-of-the-mill firm will be eliminated in the long run. The important difference between the two market forms is this: Under monopolistic competition, a firm produces a differentiated product and therefore faces a downward-sloping demand curve. Under perfect competition, the firm produces a standardized product and faces a completely horizontal demand curve. Because the downward-sloping demand curve gives a firm in monopolistic competition some influence over price, the firm quotes a higher price and therefore produces a smaller output than a perfectly competitive firm that cannot raise its price. This restricted output suggests that monopolistic competition is inefficient, but this is not necessarily the case. Lower output by each firm means more firms are satisfying total market demand. Thus, the consumer can choose from a wider range of differentiated products. This wider choice may more than make up for the disadvantage of lower output by each firm.

Oligopoly: A Market with a Few Sellers

The smaller the number of sellers, the greater the market power (the influence over price) that can be exercised by each firm. Thus, the first task is to define the degree of concentration of the industry. This has traditionally been measured by the proportion of the industry's output produced by the four largest firms. More recently, another measure, called the Herfindahl-Hirschman index, often is used instead because it takes into account all firms in the industry – not just the four largest.

An oligopoly can arise because an industry is a "**natural oligopoly**" in which the lowest-cost way of satisfying market demand is with a small number of firms. Alternatively, firms may combine or grow large, not because of cost conditions but, instead, because they seek to acquire market power.

Because there are few clear-cut principles governing the behaviour of oligopolists, the theoretical analysis is not as straightforward for oligopoly as it is for many other market forms. But the following points are important:

1. There is a tendency for oligopolists to collude – that is, to act like a monopolist and raise price so as to maximize the total profits of the industry. To maintain the high price, the product must be made scarce. Therefore, each colluding firm is required to restrict its output to a certain quota level. This reduction in output leads to the same sort of efficiency loss as in the case of monopoly. However, it is precisely this reduction in the output of each firm that creates a tendency for collusive arrangements to break down; each firm is asked to reduce its output when it has an incentive to produce more. The reason the individual firm would like to produce more is that, at its restricted level of output, the firm's marginal cost is still below its price. Therefore, it has an incentive to increase its output, if it can get away with such cheating. But if firms do cheat by producing more than their quota of output, the high price cannot be maintained, and the collusive arrangement comes apart.

In many ways, the most interesting and far-reaching example of a collusive oligopoly has been the Organization of Petroleum Exporting Countries (OPEC). This collusive arrangement succeeded in quadrupling oil prices in 1973/74, and again doubling them in 1979/80. This was even more remarkable because, during the 1970s, OPEC did not have to rely on the formal quotas on output that are typically required to keep price up and ensure that the collusive arrangement won't come apart. One of the reasons for this was the dominant role of the Saudi Arabians in producing world-traded oil. For many years they could keep the price up by restricting just their own very large output.

However, by 1985 the Saudis' production had been so far reduced in the attempt to maintain price that they were unwilling to continue to do this. They turned up their pumps and the price of oil fell sharply, to less than $10 a barrel, compared to the high of $32 a barrel three years earlier. This made other OPEC countries recognize the importance of abiding by quotas. The problem remains that they will, nonetheless, be difficult to enforce.

2. When the oligopolistic firm makes a change in, say, its price, it must take into account the possible reaction of its rivals – something that need not even be considered by a monopolist (with no rivals) or a perfectly competitive firm (whose rivals don't even notice what it's doing). This sort of complicated decision making is what makes the theory of oligopoly so interesting and difficult.

3. Oligopolistic firms sometimes face a **kinked demand curve**. If one firm raises its price, its rivals won't. Instead, they'll hope to capture some of its sales. But if the firm lowers its price, its rivals will follow suit to avoid being undersold. In such circumstances, the firm is facing the kinked demand curve shown in Figure 13-5 of the textbook; it is unlikely to change its price from the kinked level unless underlying cost conditions change a great deal. While the theory of kinked demand is controversial as an explanation of how firms behave, it is very useful in making clear the issues that firms must deal with in making their decisions. For example, the kinked demand analysis in Figure 13-5 can be modified slightly to explain price leadership.

The kinked demand curve is derived from assumptions about a firm's rivals reactions to price changes. In most oligopoly markets, a key issue is "How will competing firms react?" In duopoly, this becomes of paramount importance. **Game theory** is designed to deal with this issue, and the text provides an example of how it can be applied. In this example, the two firms are both far worse off if they both cut their price than if they both do not. It's in their collective interest not to. The problem is that it's in the individual interest of each of the firms to cut price and capture market share from the competitor. Game theory describes the possible outcomes, which depend on such questions as:

i. Is the game repeated? If it is, then the best strategy may be to "stand pat." Avoid price cutting on the first play of the game, in order to increase the chance of avoiding a mutually destructive price war. Stand pat in the hope your competitor will do the same; don't cut your price until your competitor does.

ii. How much can each firm trust the other? The more trust there is (that is, the more each firm can trust the other not to cut price) the more reasonable it is for each to refrain from price cutting.

iii. How long does it take for cheating (price cutting) to be detected and for the other firm to retaliate? The shorter the time period, the less likely it is for either firm to cheat.

4. In an industry with price leadership one firm takes on the role of being the leader in announcing a price change, on the understanding that other firms will follow. Such arrangements have often been criticized as being collusive – that is, the price leader sets the price at about the level that a monopolist would select. However, it is only "tacit collusion" because there is no communication between the

firms and it is therefore very difficult or impossible to prove that collusion has taken place. (Selling at the same price is not proof of collusion because, after all, that is what perfectly competitive firms do.)

5. Oligopolists who wish to avoid potentially destructive price competition have other options (in addition to tacit collusion in the form of price leadership). They can attempt to increase their market share by various forms of non-price competition, such as advertising or R&D expenditure to improve product quality. Advertising, in particular, is controversial. On the one hand, it may involve wasteful competition, distort people's values, and mislead consumers. On the other hand, it may make consumers better informed and help to promote product quality by making firms fearful of losing the goodwill that they achieve through advertising. Moreover, it provides financial support for the media.

6. Oligopolists often succeed in erecting **barriers to entry** against new competitors. One such barrier is advertising, which creates a favourable image of an existing firm that is difficult for new firms to overcome. But the most important barrier to entry may be economies of scale that leave room for only a few low-cost firms in the industry.

The Concept of Contestable Markets

Even if there is only one firm in an industry, it cannot act like a monopolist if the market is contestable, and new firms can freely enter and leave. Then any attempt by the firm to increase price and profit will be met by the free entry of new competitors, and any new excess profit will be competed away.

IMPORTANT TERMS

1. Product differentiation
2. Monopolistic competition
3. Excess capacity
4. Product variety (consumer choice)
5. Oligopoly
6. Concentration ratio
7. Natural oligopoly
8. Barriers to entry
9. Collusion
10. Kinked demand curve
11. Game theory
12. Duopoly
13. Prisoner's dilemma

14. Repeated games
15. Price leadership
16. Non-price competition
17. Contestable market

TRUE-FALSE

T F 1. Monopolistic competition is similar in many respects to perfect competition; but one important difference is that the product is differentiated.

T F 2. Because consumers like variety, we cannot conclude that monopolistic competition is inefficient.

T F 3. The concentration ratio is relatively low in the auto industry.

T F 4. Colluding firms in a cartel typically have an incentive to cheat by producing less than their quotas.

T F 5. All cartels, regardless of where they may exist, are illegal.

T F 6. A large firm, acting as a price leader, may decide not to retaliate against a small firm that has cut price, for fear that this may initiate a price war with other large firms.

T F 7. Price leadership may be a disguised method of collusion.

T F 8. The kinked demand curve arises mainly in monopolistic competition.

T F 9. The theory of the kinked demand curve doesn't predict the price where the kink will occur.

T F 10. All barriers to entry take the form of economies of scale.

T F 11. Duopoly firms have an individual and collective interest in cutting price if their situation is similar to the prisoner's dilemma.

T F 12. A stand-pat, collusive outcome becomes more likely if a duopoly game is repeated.

MULTIPLE CHOICE

1. Product differentiation by a firm occurs:
   a. only in perfect competition
   b. only in monopoly
   c. in monopoly and perfect competition
   d. in monopolistic competition
   e. in all market structures

2. In the long run, a firm in monopolistic competition will:
   a. face a perfectly elastic demand curve
   b. produce more than the amount that minimizes average cost
   c. produce less than the amount that minimizes average cost
   d. produce the amount that minimizes average cost
   e. earn an above-normal profit

3. In monopolistic competition:
   a. there is a standardized product, just as in perfect competition
   b. there is a standardized product, unlike the differentiated product in perfect competition
   c. entry of new firms is restricted, unlike the free entry that exists in perfect competition
   d. entry of new firms is restricted, just as in perfect competition
   e. there is a large number of sellers, just as in perfect competition

4. In monopolistic competition:
   a. there are very few sellers
   b. it is impossible for new firms to enter the market
   c. firms sell differentiated products
   d. all of the above
   e. none of the above

5. The feature of monopolistic competition that drives a firm's profits to zero in the long run is:
   a. production differentiation
   b. price leadership
   c. market power
   d. free entry
   e. collusion by sellers

6. A firm's minimum cost is $10, achievable at 20 000 units of output. The industry will be perfectly competitive if the total quantity demanded of this product at a $10 price is:
   a. 1 million units
   b. 100,000 units
   c. 40,000 units
   d. 20,000 units
   e. 10,000 units

7. If oligopolistic firms collude to raise price:
   a. each benefits, while there is an overall loss to the economy as a whole
   b. the price leader benefits, while the other firms and the economy as a whole lose
   c. each firm and the economy as a whole benefit
   d. each firm benefits, while the economy as a whole is not affected
   e. each firm and the economy as a whole lose

8. In the North American market for passenger vehicles, General Motors is a:
   a. monopolist
   b. duopolist
   c. oligopolist
   d. monopolistic competitor
   e. perfect competitor

9. A high concentration ratio in an industry typically indicates that:
   a. the dominant firms in the industry have a great deal of market power
   b. no firms in the industry have much market power
   c. no firms in the industry have any market power
   d. the industry is monopolistically competitive
   e. the industry is perfectly competitive

10. Between 1975 and 1985, Canadian industry became:
   a. less competitive, because of the decline in international trade
   b. more competitive, because of the decline in international trade
   c. less competitive, because of the growth in international trade
   d. more competitive, because of the growth of international trade
   e. more competitive, despite the decline in international trade

11. The Herfindahl-Hirschman index for an industry where one firm produces 80% of the industry output and the other two produce 10% each is:
    a. 0.84
    b. 6600
    c. 0.88
    d. 8800
    e. 1.0

12. The biggest surprise about OPEC is that it:
    a. survived for many years without a formal set of production quotas
    b. did not increase the price of oil when it had an opportunity to do so in 1973/74
    c. has made no further price increases since its spectacular success in 1973/74
    d. has been able to prevent any price reduction since 1973
    e. includes only countries from the Middle East

13. The success of the OPEC cartel in the 1970s and early 1980s was in substantial part due to:
    a. strong cultural ties among the member countries
    b. the strong sense of political unity among the member countries
    c. close social ties among the member countries
    d. all of the above
    e. the willingness of the Saudis to cut back their production

14. If a firm is at the kink in its demand curve and it raises its price, then:
    a. it will lose market share, but only to those competitors that follow its price increase
    b. it will lose market share to those competitors that don't follow its price increase
    c. its market share will not be affected
    d. its market share will increase
    e. its market share will increase, but only at the expense of those competitors that follow its price increase

15. If all firms sell at the same price:
    a. there must be price leadership
    b. there must be some other form of collusion
    c. the industry must be perfectly competitive
    d. the industry must be an oligopoly
    e. none of the above

16. The growing importance of international trade has:
    a. made Canadian firms more competitive
    b. made Canadian firms less competitive
    c. not affected the competitiveness of Canadian firms
    d. made domestic concentration ratios more meaningful
    e. b. and d.

17. Price leadership:
    a. only occurs when there is heavy advertising in an industry
    b. is a means of achieving "orderly" price changes in an oligopolistic industry
    c. indicates which senior executive within a firm will make pricing decisions
    d. frequently occurs in perfect competition
    e. frequently occurs in a monopolized industry

18. The kinked demand curve:
    a. helps to explain why oligopoly price has some degree of stability
    b. leaves unanswered the question of how price is established in the first place
    c. is based on the assumption that if a firm lowers its price, its competitors will follow
    d. is based on the assumption that if a firm raises its price, its competitors won't follow
    e. all of the above

19. Which of the following is not true about advertising?
    a. it may involve waste
    b. it may mislead consumers
    c. it provides financial support for the media
    d. it may help to promote product quality by making firms fearful of losing good will
    e. it is often undertaken by single firms in a perfectly competitive market

20. In a contestable market:
    a. there is a single firm which can act as a monopolist
    b. there is no free entry
    c. the potential entry of new firms increases the market power of the existing firm
    d. the potential entry of new firms has no effect on the market power of the existing firm
    e. if there is a single firm, it cannot act as though it is a monopolist

21. A payoff matrix shows:
   a. the difference between duopoly and oligopoly
   b. the difference between duopoly and monopolistic competition
   c. the difference between oligopoly and monopolistic competition
   d. the definition of duopoly
   e. how the outcome in duopoly depends on the policy selected by each firm

22. Once firms recognize that a game is to be repeated:
   a. the chance of a collusive, stand-pat outcome decreases
   b. the chance of a collusive, stand-pat outcome increases
   c. the chance of a collusive, stand-pat outcome is left unchanged
   d. both firms will lower their price
   e. both firms will increase their output

EXERCISES

1a. In Figure 13.1, D represents the total market demand for an industry, with MR_I being the marginal revenue curve that corresponds to D. (For any demand curve, there exists a marginal revenue curve.) MC_A and AC_A are the cost curves for firm A, one of the 5 identical firms in this industry. Draw in the marginal cost curve for the industry, and label it MC_I. Label point *R*, where MC_I and D intersect, and point *S*, where MC_I and MR_I intersect. Label as *Z* the point directly above *S* on the demand curve.

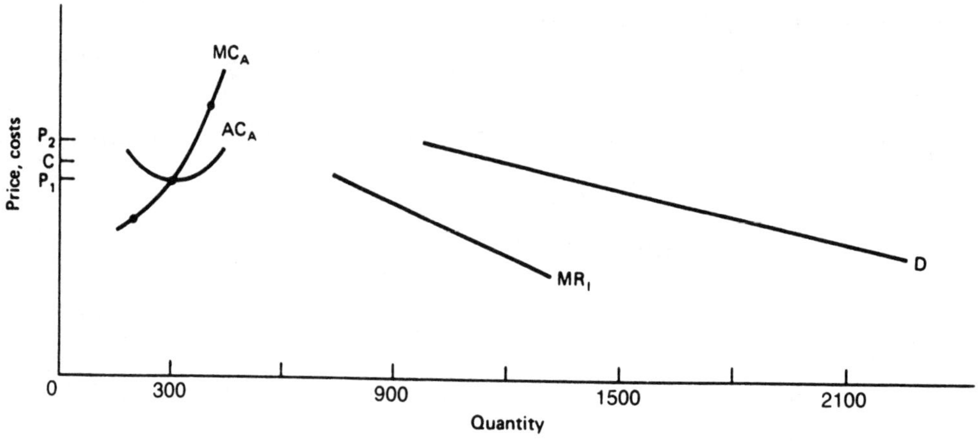

Figure 13.1

If these firms act like perfect competitors and take price as given, then MC_I becomes the industry (demand, supply) curve, and the industry equilibrium is at point _____. _____ units are sold at price _____, with each firm earning a profit of _____.

1b. Now suppose these firms collude to maximize their collective profit, which they will do by equating MC_I and _____, at an output of _____ units. They will sell this output for price _____. That is, the industry will select its profit-maximizing point _____ on the demand curve D. Since industry output has been reduced from _____ to _____ units, the output of each individual firm, such as A, must be reduced by the same proportion, from _____ units to _____. Draw in point *T*, which is the equilibrium for firm A, where this firm is now selling _____ units at price _____. Label as *V* the point on ACA directly below *T*. Shade in the new profit area _____ of firm A.

By colluding, these 5 firms have each (increased, decreased) their profit from _____ to _____. At the same time, the nation as a whole has (lost, gained) because of the efficiency (loss, gain) of area _____ that results because output has been (reduced, increased) to the (efficient, inefficient) level of _____ units from the (efficient, inefficient) level of _____ units where the marginal benefit to society shown by curve _____ equals the marginal cost to society shown by curve _____.

2a. Figure 13.2 depicts the situation of an oligopoly firm which, along with all its rivals, is currently charging price P and producing quantity Q. This firm faces the kinked demand curve that consists of the segment of D_A above the existing price P and the segment of D_B below the price P. The respective marginal revenue curves are MR_A and MR_B.

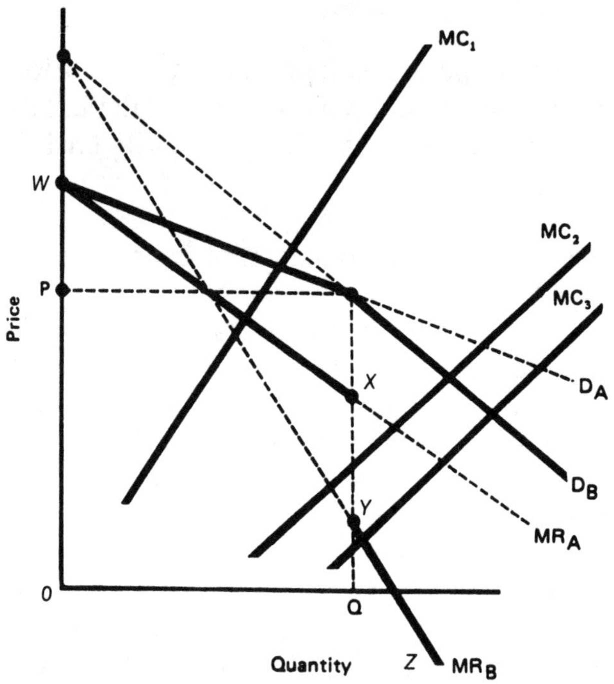

Figure 13.2

If the firm increases its output to more than Q, it faces demand curve _____, and its MR curve is therefore (MR_A, MR_B). But if it decreases its output to less than Q, if faces demand curve _____, and its MR curve is therefore (MR_A, MR_B). Therefore, its complete MR curve is (MR_A, MR_B, *WXYZ*).

2b. If its MC is MC_1, then it will charge a price that is (more than, less than, the same as) P, and it will choose a quantity that is (more than, less than, the same as) Q.

2c. If its MC is MC_2, then it will charge a price that is (more than, less than, the same as) P, and choose a quantity that is (more than, less than, the same as) Q.

2d. If its MC is MC_3, then it will charge a price that is (more than, less than, the same as) P, and choose a quantity that is (more than, less than, the same as) Q.

2e. If its MC is MC_2, we now see why the kinked demand curve results in a stable price. If MC_2 shifts up, but still intersects the vertical segment *XY*, then the firm will (raise, lower, leave unchanged) the price. Alternatively, if MC_2 shifts down, still intersecting *XY*, the firm will (raise, lower, leave unchanged) the price. In other words, marginal cost can shift up or down within the range _____ without affecting price at all.

ESSAY QUESTIONS

1. Firms in monopolistic competition have some influence over price. Why don't they use this influence to raise price above average costs and, therefore, make an above-normal profit in the long run?

2. Will firms in an industry with a high concentration ratio be more or less likely to engage in collusive activity than those in an industry with a low concentration ratio? Why?

3. Oligopoly is a market with a few sellers. But how many is a few? Does it matter if there are 4 or 14? Why? To be specific, compare the situation of an individual Canadian firm if

   (a) it has only 3 Canadian competitors, versus

   (b) a situation in which it has the same 3 Canadian competitors, plus 2 Japanese competitors, 4 U.S. competitors, and 2 other foreign competitors.

   Would the Canadian firm have the same market power in either case? Would firms be equally able to collude, tacitly or explicitly?

4. Explain why a group of oligopolists might have trouble establishing a collusive price agreement, and then have trouble keeping the agreement from coming apart.

5. It is often argued that advertising increases sales, and this permits lower prices to consumers. Explain the circumstances in which this could occur. Also explain the circumstances in which advertising would increase prices to consumers.

6. What industry characteristics distinguish oligopoly from monopoly? from perfect competition?

7. Explain some of the techniques oligopolists use to avoid price competition.

8. If it is in the collective interests of 2 duopoly firms to avoid price cutting, how can it be in the individual interest of each to engage in price cutting?

ANSWERS

True-False: **1T, 2T, 3F, 4F, 5F, 6T, 7T, 8F, 9T, 10F, 11F, 12T**

Multiple Choice: **1d, 2c, 3e, 4c, 5d, 6a, 7a, 8c, 9a, 10d, 11b, 12a, 13e, 14b, 15e, 16a, 17b, 18e, 19e, 20e, 21e, 22b**

Exercises: **1a.** supply, *R*, 1500, P_1, zero

1b. MR_I, 1000, P_2, *Z*, 1500, 1000, 300, 200, 200, P_2, P_2TVC, increased, zero, the shaded area, lost, loss, *ZSR*, reduced, inefficient, 1000, efficient, 1500, D, MC_I

Figure 13.1 completed

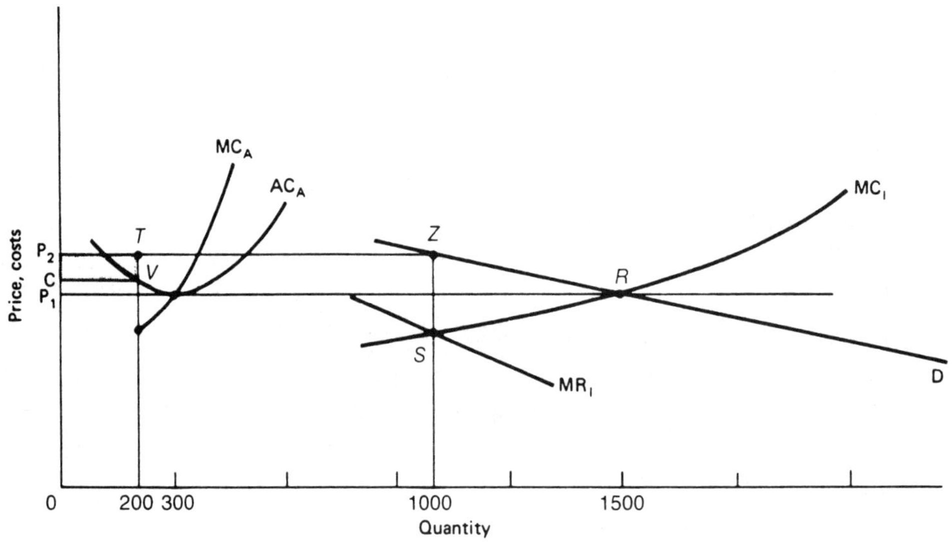

2a. D_B, MR_B, D_A, MR_A, *WXYZ*
2b. more than, less than
2c. the same as, the same as
2d. less than, more than
2e. leave unchanged, leave unchanged, *XY*

ANSWERS TO PROBLEMS FROM THE TEXT

13-1. The answer is essentially to be found in the discussion around Figure 13-4 in the textbook. Collusion would allow you to restrict your output and, accordingly monopoly price (thus achieving monopoly profits). Consumers lose (a reduction in consumers surplus due to the higher price). The major problems facing the colluding firms would be to fix quota levels, and to discipline all firms to not exceed their quota, as well as the problem of deterring potential new entrants.

13-2. (a) (i) 100/10 000, (ii) 100/3333, (iii) 100/3750

(b) HHI is better because it takes account of all firms, not just the four largest. Moreover, in part (*a*) above, it is clear that it does a better job even when there are not more than four firms in an industry. The industry in (iii) is more concentrated than the industry in (ii) because it has a dominant firm. But you wouldn't know this from the four-firm concentration ratio, which is 100 in both cases.

13-3. (a) Again, see the pros and cons of advertising in the text. To the degree that advertising just shifts customers from one firm to another (and perhaps back again), it is a waste in either industry. In such circumstances, the information provided by either tobacco or liquor companies seems to have little or no value, unless you are prepared to argue that people feel better because they are using a brand that someone in the media has told them is highly desirable.

However, advertising also leads to greater total consumption, in the case of either tobacco or alcohol. It is here that advertising is costly, since greater consumption is related to higher health care costs.

The agreement among tobacco companies to voluntarily restrict advertising may have raised total industry profits, since it eliminated the need for each company to advertise in order to offset the impact of the others' advertising.

13-4. This regulation has had much the same effect from an economic point of view as past restrictions by organized medicine (the American Medical Association, Canadian Medical Association) on the supply of doctors. It holds the price of legal services up and, consequently, less than the efficient quantity of legal service is purchased. You can judge for yourself the argument that such a floor on fees has improved the quality of legal service. ("Lawyers who don't cut prices don't have to cut down on the services they provide.") In our view, there is something in this argument, but it tends to be overstated.

Lawyers are likely to approve of such a regulation because it keeps their fees up. They may also support it because they believe it improves the quality of legal services.

13-5. They should try to get each to believe that the other has confessed. If each can be convinced of this, he will have nothing to lose by confessing and gains in the form of a shorter jail term. Thus each will confess. (Another motive: each will feel he has been double-crossed, and will confess to get even.)

As long as each thinks the other has not confessed, then he will have at least some incentive to do the same, in the hope that if they can maintain their agreement, they will be able to keep the jail sentence to both down. (He may also not want to break an agreement. There may be, indeed, honour among thieves.)

13-6. Each student will have a different matrix, but it should have the same broad characteristics as the table below, replacing the high-price option for each player with "continuing as is" and the low-price option with "market the new product." Thus, the matrix should have less profit for each in quadrant IV than in I, since their market will be damaged if both market the durable new product. Moreover, the other two quadrants will show that each could increase profit by marketing the new product – provided, of course, that the other does not.

13-7. They would jointly maximize profit if they could get an agreement to keep price up that each would stick with (quadrant I). The pressures that would make this difficult – and would almost certainly lead them to forget about the agreement and engage in price competition – are (1) the fact that such an agreement is against the law, and (2) each firm would have an economic incentive to cheat, even if the agreement were legal.

13-8. The firm selling 200 units would perceive a net gain from selling an additional 50 units (since three-quarters of the total loss on original sales would be borne by the rival). Indeed, by the same token, the firm selling 600 units would perceive a net gain from reducing its sales by 50 units. The Nash equilibrium would be restored with each firm selling 400 units.

CHAPTER 14

Government Regulation of Business

LEARNING OBJECTIVES

After you have studied this chapter in the textbook and the study guide, you should be able to

- Identify and briefly describe the legislative act that forms the cornerstone of Canada's competition policy

- Explain why it may be advantageous to have large-size firms, and why legal rules that discourage formation of large firms may involve costs as well as benefits

- Explain why competition from foreign sellers reduces the ability of large Canadian firms to exercise market power in the markets for Canadian-produced goods

- Show how economic efficiency may be promoted if the government on the one hand allows natural monopolies to exist (subject to international competition or price regulation), while on the other hand it uses competition policy to prevent the formation of collusive monopolies

- Give several reasons that "market-structure" regulation of naturally more competitive industries tends to be in the interest of the firms being regulated, rather than in the interest of consumers or the nation as a whole

- Explain the two important reasons that it is feasible for a government agency to cartelize an industry, but why it is not possible for a private group of producers to do so

- Explain how provincial trucking regulations have affected the interests of (1) established trucking firms, (2) the nation as a whole, (3) shippers on truck routes with high traffic volumes, and (4) shippers in small communities with low traffic volumes. (In explaining (3) and (4), use the concept of cross-subsidization.)

CHAPTER SUMMARY

Government regulation of business is one form of government intervention in the economy. The question is: When does such intervention enhance the functioning of the market system, and when does it get in the way? This chapter deals with two broad types of government regulation of business:

1. Competition laws that prevent collusion and other restraints to trade. While such laws are necessary, their application is critically evaluated by posing such questions as: Should mergers between large firms be discouraged even though they may create economies of scale and reduce the average cost of production?

2. Regulation of naturally competitive industries, such as trucking and the airlines, where government regulation in the past has not removed restraints on trade, but instead has created them. Certain types of government intervention of this form have often been hard to justify, and there is now a trend, in both Canada and the United States, toward deregulation of these industries. This chapter focuses on several ways in which the government regulates business.

Competition Legislation

The first category of regulation consists of legislation designed to prevent business practices that reduce competition. This legislation, which was revised in the 1980s, is contained in the Competition Act, which has its roots in laws going back as far as 1889. The main provisions in the Act relate to:

1. The prohibition of collusive agreements among firms to fix prices or limit production. (Although agreements among firms that reduce competition are generally detrimental to the public interest, there are other kinds of agreements that can be beneficial. The Competition Act lists certain kinds of agreements that are permitted or even encouraged, such as agreements to share research and development (R&D) expenditures or to limit advertising and promotional expenditures.)

2. Merger and abuse of dominant position. The purpose of these sections, which were substantially revised in the mid-1980s, is to make it illegal for a firm to create a monopoly position for itself by various forms of **cut-throat competition** to drive its rivals out of the market or, in some cases, by buying out competing firms.

With respect to mergers between large firms, the Act specifies that they must first be approved by the Competition Tribunal, which must decide whether the merger would, on balance, be against the public interest, or whether factors such as improved scale economies and better international competitiveness are sufficiently important so that the merger should be allowed to go ahead, even though it may substantially increase a firm's share of the Canadian market.

3. The prohibition of price discrimination; that is, making it illegal for a seller to charge different prices to buyers who buy goods of like quality and in the same quantity.

4. Prohibiting resale price maintenance; that is, making it illegal for a manufacturer to force retailers to charge a minimum price for the manufacturer's product.

5. Outlawing misleading advertising and prohibiting certain forms of tied selling.

The primary objective of provisions (1) and (2) is to reduce restraint on trade and the abuse of market power by monopoly and oligopoly firms. The main tactic is to prevent a single firm or group of firms from attaining a dominant position in the market. However, a policy of preventing any one firm from becoming large enough to dominate the market may carry a cost, because size has advantages:

1. Large firms can better afford the (R&D) expenditures that generate growth and technological improvements. Large firms also have more incentive to undertake R&D expenditures, because their large market share allows them to capture a large share of the benefits from any new technique or product they may develop. For example, if Northern Telecom develops a superior office telephone system, it will acquire millions of dollars of benefits from this in its huge sales of telephone equipment, so it can justify this sort of R&D. However, a Manitoba farmer can't justify a similar R&D expenditure to develop a better strain of wheat; the benefits to him would be limited to a few thousand dollars, while the millions of dollars of additional benefit would be spread among thousands of wheat farmers.

2. Because of economies of scale, large firms may enjoy lower costs per unit than smaller firms; this point was demonstrated in the case of natural monopoly in Chapter 12.

In a country with relatively small domestic markets, these advantages of large firm size effectively compel the government to allow firms to have a relatively large share of many markets. However, there are some ways in which the government may lessen the ability of such firms to exploit their potential market power.

First, for goods that can be transported long distances relatively easily, the government may make sure that domestic firms are subject to competition from foreign firms by not restricting imports of foreign goods into Canada. For goods and services that cannot be transported as easily, the small size of the market may mean that the industry comes close to being a natural monopoly. In such industries, the government's best policy may be to let a single firm monopolize the market. The problem with this second solution, of course, is that despite its cost advantage, a natural monopoly, left unregulated, will produce the efficiency loss that we studied in Chapter 12. Consequently, the policy needs to be supplemented by price regulation (or by government ownership) of natural monopolies. As we have seen, this sort of regulation is imperfect, and government ownership may have problems of its own. Thus, in practice, it might even make sense sometimes to prevent the formation of a natural monopoly, despite its economies of scale, as a way of eliminating all these problems of regulation.

The enforcement of competition legislation is a very difficult task – in part, because it is not easy to distinguish anti-competitive efforts from the normal efforts of business firms to compete in the marketplace. Consider, for example, cut-throat competition – when firms set a price below cost in order to drive competitors out of business. A problem in trying to deal with cut-throat competition is that it is never clear whether a firm is setting its price below costs because it is trying to cut the throats of its competitors, or because it is just trying desperately to make sales in a weak market – perhaps in the face of stiff foreign competition.

A second example is the objective of preventing firms from colluding to "cartelize" an otherwise competitive industry. Collusion, like cut-throat competition, is difficult to establish in the courts. For example, the fact that all firms in an industry are charging the same price doesn't prove that there has been a conspiracy to fix prices, because uniformity of price occurs in a perfectly competitive market in which there is no collusion whatsoever.

The Canadian courts' interpretation of the restrictive wording in the "collusive agreements" and "monopoly and merger" sections in the Combines Investigations Act (the predecessor of the 1986 Competition Act), coupled with the fact that under earlier legislation, the burden of proof was mostly on the prosecution, made it hard for the government to get convictions in the past. However, under the terms of the Competition Act, enforcement is easier because most competition legislation has been put under the rules of civil law rather than criminal law.

Market Structure Regulation

The textbook discusses market structure regulation mostly in terms of the example of Canada's trucking industry, which has been regulated since the 1930s, even though it certainly is not an industry with a natural monopoly. (Why not?)

The regulation of trucking had its origin in the increasing competition that trucking firms were offering the (already regulated) railroads, as more efficient trucks and better roads were being built in the 1920s and 1930s. The government authorities who were regulating rail transport had required the railroad companies to maintain rail service to small, remote communities even though it was unprofitable for the railroads. In return, the authorities had allowed the railroads to charge high freight rates and earn high profits on short-haul, high-volume freight. (This illustrates the use of cross-subsidization as a regulatory technique; the authorities were forcing the railroads to use the high profits from the high-volume routes to subsidize the low-volume service they were forced to maintain in small communities. But the high rail freight rates on the high-volume routes made it easier for trucking firms to take business away from the railroads on those routes by offering lower rates.) For this reason, the railroad companies were campaigning vigorously for regulation of trucking. The trucking firms themselves also wanted regulation of their own industry, since they were now competing not just with the railroads but also with other trucking firms.

In the mid-1980s, all provinces except Alberta had extensive legislation regulating things like entry of new trucking firms, the routes that each firm might serve, the allowable frequency of service to various communities, and types of freight that firms were allowed to carry; some provinces also regulated the rates that trucking firms were allowed to charge. Studies undertaken for the Economic Council of Canada have shown that this type of complicated network of regulation was very costly. In addition to the costs of administering the system (which are borne by the provincial taxpayers), the licensing system sometimes forced the firms to operate in inefficient ways, with high freight rates to consumers and lower profits for the firms as a result.

Price and entry regulation in industries that by themselves would be relatively competitive is not confined to trucking. Other examples include the radio and television industry and the taxi industry. Another area where regulation has become very extensive is that of government licensing and certification requirements for specific occupations; government regulation of pricing and production in agricultural markets has also grown rapidly in recent years.

By the mid-1980s, many types of regulation were coming under increasing criticism in both Canada and the United States, and steps were taken to reduce the extent of regulation in a number of sectors. In the United States, the airline industry became deregulated as early as 1979; in the late 1980s, regulation of air travel was substantially reduced in Canada as well. Federal regulations of railroad freight rates were eased, and an agreement was struck between the federal and provincial governments providing for reduced regulation of trucking as well.

Not everyone was happy with these trends. For example, some argued that deregulation was leading to both crowded skies and crowded airport terminals, making air travel both less safe and less convenient. But the benefits to the public, in the form of lower air fares and freight rates, were also becoming evident and, in the early 1990s, there was little support for proposals to return to the restrictive regulatory regimes of earlier decades.

IMPORTANT TERMS

1. Competition policy
2. Collusive agreements
3. Foreign competition
4. Cut-throat competition
5. Horizontal merger
6. Vertical merger
7. Price and entry regulation
8. Cross-subsidization

TRUE-FALSE

T F 1. Following the introduction of the Competition Act in 1986, most of Canada's competition legislation has been made part of our criminal rather than civil law.

T F 2. Predatory or cut-throat pricing is defined as setting price above average cost, but still low enough to put competing firms under pressure.

T F 3. Preventing the merger of two firms in an industry that is a natural monopoly will help maintain lower average costs of production.

T F 4. Tied selling is the requirement that purchasers buy a whole line of items in order to get the one they really want. The Competition Act outlaws certain forms of tied selling.

T F 5. So long as the acquiring firm offers to buy the target firm's stock, the management of a target firm will support the merger.

T F 6. Free access of Canadian buyers to imported substitutes for domestically produced goods reduces the market power of large Canadian firms that have a large share of the domestic market.

T F 7. All takeover bids will be resisted by target companies.

T F 8. In merger cases, the rule followed by the Competition Tribunal is to disallow all mergers that would cause the Herfindahl-Hirschman index of the industry to rise above 1000.

T F 9. In the mid-1980s, the freight rates charged by trucking firms in Alberta (where there was no trucking regulation) were substantially higher than in other provinces.

T F 10. A merger that increases the market power of the new firm will automatically be disallowed by the Competition Tribunal.

T F 11. Under cross-subsidization, the price to one group is raised so that better service or reduced price can be provided to another group.

MULTIPLE CHOICE

1. In recent years, the market power of large Canadian corporations has
   a. decreased because of the growth of foreign competition
   b. decreased because of the decline of foreign competition
   c. increased because of the growth of foreign competition
   d. increased because of the decline of foreign competition
   e. been unaffected by changes in foreign competition

2. Cut-throat competition is
   a. pricing above cost to drive competitors out of business
   b. pricing at cost to drive competitors out of business
   c. pricing below cost to drive competitors out of business
   d. decreasing advertising in order to put pressure on competitors
   e. restricting sales in order to put pressure on competitors

3. Which of the following is not dealt with in the Competition Act?
   a. collusive agreements
   b. misleading advertising
   c. cross-subsidization
   d. resale price maintenance
   e. price discrimination

4. Under the rules of the Competition Act, a merger between two large firms
   a. can't be approved if the new firm's share of the Canadian market will be more than 15%
   b. requires approval by Parliament
   c. requires approval by Cabinet
   d. all of the above
   e. none of the above

5. Government action to prevent the formation of a natural monopoly may
   a. restrict benefits from economies of scale
   b. increase benefits from economies of scale
   c. increase benefits from the law of diminishing returns
   d. decrease benefits from the law of diminishing returns
   e. have no economies-of-scale effect

6. Under Canadian law, the prices charged by manufacturers and wholesalers when they sell their products to large retail chains
   a. are required to be higher than when they sell to small retailers, to offset the large chains' cost advantage
   b. are required to be lower than when they sell to small retailers
   c. are required to be the same as when they sell to small retailers
   d. are only allowed to be lower than when they sell to small retailers if the large chains are buying goods of lower quality
   e. none of the above

7. The increasing strength of foreign competition in Canada has meant that enforcement of the legal provisions relating to merger and "abuse of dominant position" in the Competition Act has become
   a. illegal
   b. more necessary
   c. less necessary
   d. neither more nor less necessary
   e. more necessary in some respects, but less in others

8. Under the Competition Act's rules concerning mergers, the Competition Tribunal is least likely to approve a merger between two firms
   a. when both firms are small
   b. when one of the firms is large and the other is small
   c. when the two firms face intense competition from imports
   d. when one of the two firms is threatened by bankruptcy
   e. if there are no significant scale economies in the industry

9. Even though the Competition Act prohibits firms in most industries from making agreements to limit production and fix prices, provincial egg marketing organizations are allowed to limit the amount that individual egg farmers may produce and to fix the price at which eggs are sold to retailers. This is legal because
   a. the Act does not apply to a regulated industry
   b. egg marketing boards have a natural monopoly in the egg production industry
   c. if egg production were not limited, the quality of rural life would suffer because of the overpowering smell of chicken manure
   d. Canadian courts have ruled that the egg marketing arrangements do not "unduly" limit competition
   e. the price fixing applies only to egg exports, not to eggs sold in the domestic market

10. An example of collusion is
    a. an agreement to fix price
    b. an agreement to restrict sales
    c. an agreement to rig bids
    d. all of the above
    e. none of the above

11. An example of collusion that is beneficial for society as a whole might be
    a. an agreement by producers to reduce sales
    b. an agreement by chemical firms to cooperate in developing pollution-control devices
    c. an agreement by buyers to rig bids
    d. an agreement by producers to fix price
    e. all of the above

12. The practice of price leadership
    a. makes tacit collusion difficult to detect
    b. is practised by monopolies
    c. is practised only under perfect competition
    d. is used primarily in cut-throat competition
    e. is never practised by oligopolists

13. A merger of a firm and its supplier is called
    a. a vertical merger
    b. a horizontal merger
    c. a conglomerate merger
    d. a direct merger
    e. an indirect merger

14. In a takeover bid by firm A for firm B
    a. both the management and stockholders of B are almost certain to welcome the bid
    b. both the management and stockholders of B are almost certain to oppose the bid
    c. the managers may oppose it, even though the stockholders welcome it
    d. the managers of firm A typically employ their golden parachutes
    e. firm A usually regards firm B as a black knight

15. Which of the following is an example of an industry or profession with price and entry regulation in most places in Canada?
    a. the market for legal services
    b. radio and television broadcasting
    c. the taxi business
    d. milk production
    e. all of the above

16. Regulation of radio and television broadcasting by the Canadian Radio-television and Telecommunications Commission
    a. encourages competition by restricting the entry of new firms
    b. encourages competition by allowing the entry of new firms
    c. discourages competition by allowing the entry of new firms
    d. discourages competition by restricting the entry of new firms
    e. has no effect on competition because it prevents new firms from entering cities that are already served by a radio or television station

17. A cartel organized by a regulatory agency is easier to operate than a cartel in an unregulated industry because in the regulated industry
    a. the quotas are imposed by law and the firms are immune from prosecution
    b. the firms are free to engage in non-price competition
    c. the interests of the public are being served when the industry is regulated
    d. regulated firms are not forced to cross-subsidize the consumers of unprofitable lines
    e. entry of new firms is encouraged

18. Regulation of trucking in most Canadian provinces tends to benefit
    a. the established trucking firm and the nation as a whole
    b. the nation, but not the established trucking firm
    c. the established trucking firm, but not the nation
    d. neither the established trucking firm nor the nation
    e. potential new trucking firms and the economy as a whole

19. The American experience with airline deregulation suggests that the safety of all travellers taken together may have increased because
    a. it raised airline fares and thus induced Americans to switch from planes to safer cars
    b. it raised airline fares and thus induced Americans to switch from cars to safer planes
    c. it reduced airline fares and thus induced Americans to switch from cars to safer planes
    d. it reduced airline fares and thus induced Americans to switch from planes to safer cars
    e. it had no effect on airline fares

EXERCISES

1a. Suppose that the total cost for a firm producing widgets equals the fixed cost of $2 million plus a variable cost equal to $4 for every widget produced. Thus, the marginal cost of producing widgets is always (constant, increasing, decreasing), and average cost is always (constant, increasing, decreasing). The widget industry is a _____.

1b. Suppose this firm is being regulated using marginal cost pricing. Then its price would be $ _____. Suppose the firm sells 2 million units at this price. Its cost per unit would be $ _____, and its loss per unit would be $ _____. Therefore, the taxpayer would have to pay a total subsidy of $ _____ to keep the firm in operation.

1c. If the industry were broken up into two separate firms, each with the same cost structure as before, and each firm were to produce half of this quantity, then the cost per unit would be _____, which is (more than, less than, the same as) before. The loss per unit would be $ _____, which is (higher, lower, no different) than before. Therefore, the total subsidy required to keep the industry alive would be (higher, lower, no different) than before. Specifically, the total subsidy paid to both firms would be $ _____.

1d. After this monopoly is broken up and all necessary subsidies are paid, the firms would (gain, lose, be unaffected), the consumers would (gain, lose, be unaffected), and the taxpayers would (gain, lose, be unaffected). Thus, the nation as a whole would (gain, lose, be unaffected). What important principle is illustrated by this hypothetical example?

ESSAY QUESTIONS

1. Discuss the benefits and costs of breaking up a natural monopoly.

2. "Giant foreign and domestic companies such as General Motors and Canadian Airlines still dominate the production of many goods. Thus, our competition policies cannot have been effective." To what extent do you agree with this statement? Explain your position.

3. "In restricting GM's use of its market power in the North American market, the competition from Japanese auto companies has been far more effective than our Canadian competition policy or U.S. antitrust laws." Do you agree? Explain your position.

4. Why do you suppose the unions representing truck drivers are likely to be strongly opposed to deregulation of the Canadian trucking industry?

ANSWERS

True-False: **1**F, **2**F, **3**F, **4**T, **5**F, **6**T, **7**F, **8**F, **9**F, **10**F, **11**T

Multiple Choice: **1**a, **2**c, **3**c, **4**e, **5**a, **6**e, **7**c, **8**e, **9**a, **10**d, **11**b, **12**a, **13**a, **14**c, **15**e, **16**d, **17**a, **18**c, **19**c

Exercises: **1a**. constant, decreasing, natural monopoly

1b. $4, $5, $1, $2 million

1c. $6, more than, $2, higher, higher, $4 million

1d. be unaffected, be unaffected, lose, lose. From the point of view of efficiency, natural monopolies should be regulated rather than broken up.

ANSWERS TO PROBLEMS FROM THE TEXT

14-1. (a) and (b) are undesirable, because either agreement is a means whereby producers exercise market power to raise price. The result is an inefficient allocation of resources. (c) is more desirable because it is introduced for a different reason: It lowers costs to railroads of providing transport services. (In its early history, Australia had more than one size track. This raised the cost and inconvenience of running a railroad system.)

14-2. Two things are important in answering this question. First, the supply curve for wheat in Eastern Canada is the Western Canadian supply curve up to the world price, at which point it becomes a horizontal line (indicating perfectly elastic supply at the world price). Second, transport costs act like a tax (hence the reference to Figure 10-12) on wheat producers, shifting the "western" portion of the supply curve up by the amount of transport costs ("tax"). A subsidy on transport costs reduces the amount of "tax" per unit (transport costs), raising the net-of-transport-cost price received by Western producers (by the amount of transport subsidy per unit). Accordingly, there is a producers' gain (an increase in producers' surplus). The amount of subsidy paid, however, exceeds the producers' gain. Since the world price of wheat prevails in Eastern Canada, the consumers' price is unaffected by the transport subsidy; there is, therefore, no change in consumers' surplus. Thus, the net effect is a deadweight loss given by the difference between the total subsidy paid and the resulting producers' gain. In this sense, transport subsidies appear to be "bad" policy (it would be cheaper to simply make a lump sum income transfer to Western producers).

There is an interesting twist, however. If the transport subsidy is paid for by Eastern Canadians, there will be an interregional transfer effect – the gain in producers' surplus (which accrues to Western Canadians) comes at the expense of Eastern Canadians (who pay for the transport subsidy program).

14-3. Raising price for A reduces her consumer's surplus; however, lowering price for B generates a positive consumer's surplus for him. As long as the gain to B exceeds the loss to A, aggregate consumer surplus will have risen.

14-4. Agreements to restrict advertising will reduce the firms' costs, and could therefore benefit consumers by leading to lower product prices. On the other hand, without advertising, a firm that wanted to attract customers by reducing its price or increasing the quality of its products would find it more difficult to do so. Thus the intensity of competition may be reduced, leading to higher prices and/or lower product quality.

14-5. (a) One possible explanation was that Bell and Northern Telecom were effectively able to raise their combined profits by charging high prices for "optional" equipment, since Bell's requirement had created a monopoly for Northern Telecom in the market for such optional equipment.

(b) The ruling certainly increased competitiveness in the market for optional equipment, and gave consumers access to a wider range of such equipment, both in terms of price and quality.

(c) They could have tried to extend price regulation to cover various forms of optional equipment as well. On the other hand, although this might have been effective in holding prices down, it probably would have slowed down the rate of introduction of new types of equipment, in comparison to what happened as a consequence of the ruling.

PART FOUR

FACTOR MARKETS AND INCOME DISTRIBUTION

CHAPTER 15

Wages in a Perfectly Competitive Economy

LEARNING OBJECTIVES

After you have studied this chapter in the textbook and the study guide, you should be able to

- Distinguish between the real wage rate and the nominal wage rate
- Explain why, in a perfectly competitive labour market, a profit-maximizing firm will hire labour to the point where the marginal revenue product of labour (MRP) equals the wage rate (W)
- Explain why the firm's MRP curve is the same as its value of marginal product curve (VMP) if the market for output is perfectly competitive
- Explain why the curve showing a firm's demand for labour is the same as the curve showing the marginal revenue product of labour
- State two reasons the labour demand curve might shift to the right
- Explain the sense in which the demand for labour is a derived demand
- Distinguish between the demand for labour of individual firms in an industry and the industry's demand for labour
- Illustrate how the industry's labour demand curve can be used to show the total income of labour in an industry and the total income of other factors of production
- Explain why the height of the labour supply curve for an industry reflects the opportunity cost of labour – that is, labour's wage and productivity in other industries
- Explain why, in the absence of externalities, perfect competition in the labour market typically results in an efficient wage and employment level

- Measure diagrammatically the efficiency loss that results when a labour market is not perfectly competitive

- Explain why one cannot necessarily jump from the conclusion that a perfectly competitive labour market is efficient to the much stronger conclusion that a free, unregulated labour market is "best"

- Describe the effects of a minimum wage in an otherwise perfectly competitive labour market

- Discuss the effects of discrimination in a labour market

- Describe and evaluate the concept of work of equal value (comparable worth)

CHAPTER SUMMARY

In this chapter, the objective is to use the familiar tools of supply and demand developed in earlier chapters to analyze how wages are determined in perfectly competitive labour markets. As a first approximation, a wage can be viewed just like the price of any other good or service that is traded in the market. In this case, the service is labour, the demanders are employers, and the suppliers are workers. The labour market for a specific industry will be perfectly competitive if:

(a) there are so many buyers and sellers of labour service that none can affect the wage rate;

(b) labour is standardized, with all workers being equally productive; and

(c) workers are mobile and can move in and out of this industry.

The Demand for Labour

In defining its demand for labour, a firm begins by examining labour's **marginal physical product (MPP)**. This schedule, shown in column 3 of Table 15-1 in the textbook, shows how the firm's output increases – in physical units – as it hires more labour. The firm, of course, is primarily interested in how its total revenue increases when it hires additional units of labour. This concept – **marginal revenue product (MRP)** – is shown in column 5 of Table 15-1. In a perfectly competitive economy, those values are determined by multiplying the increase in physical output (MPP) by the price at which the firm can sell that output and are termed labour's **value of marginal product (VMP)**. (Note that in a perfectly competitive economy, MRP and VMP are the same thing.)

Further, in a perfectly competitive labour market, the individual firm takes the wage rate as given – that is, the firm can hire as much labour as it desires at the prevailing wage rate (the supply of labour to the individual firm in an industry is perfectly elastic). The profit-maximizing firm will demand labour up to the point where the MRP is just equal to the wage rate (W). To see why this is so, consider the case where MRP is greater than W. Then, the firm could increase its profits by hiring more workers, since the marginal benefit (the marginal revenue product) exceeds the marginal cost (the wages paid). Alternatively, if MRP were less than W, the firm could increase its profits by hiring fewer workers. Thus, the MRP curve shows how much labour the firm will hire at each possible wage. In other words, the MRP curve is the firm's **labour demand curve**.

A firm's demand for labour schedule slopes down because of diminishing returns. As a firm hires more and more labour (with other factors fixed), it eventually finds that the marginal physical product of labour – and therefore MRP – decreases. In other words, its demand for labour slopes downward.

There are several reasons why a firm's demand curve for labour might shift: (1) If the price of the firm's output falls (rises), MRP and, therefore, the demand for labour will shift down (shift up); (2) If the marginal physical product of labour shifts up (down), MRP and the labour demand curve will also shift up (down). For example, the firm's demand curve for labour will shift upwards if the firm increases the amount of capital it employs; this would increase labour's marginal physical product – make labour physically more productive – by providing it with more machinery to work with. Another example might be a technological improvement that allows a firm to get more physical output from its workers. (Often, increased capital equipment and technological change go together, but it is possible for one to occur without the other.)

The industry's demand curve for labour is simply the horizontal sum of the demand curves for labour of all the individual firms in the industry.

How the Labour Demand Curve Shows the Distribution of Income

The income going to labour and the income going to other factors of production in an industry can be read directly from the industry's demand curve for labour. Figure 15-4 in the textbook illustrates the point that the total income earned by all factors of production will be represented by the area under the MRP curve, given a quantity of labour hired. This area represents the sum of all the individual contributions – such as arrows *a* and *b* on the left – of all *N* workers in this industry. In total, this is area 1 and 2 under the labour demand curve. Of this area representing total industry income, rectangular area 2 is labour income, since it is the quantity of employment (the base of this rectangle) times the wage (the height of this rectangle). The rest – that is, area 1 – goes to other factors of production, in the form of rent, interest, and profit.

The Supply of Labour

The height of the labour supply curve indicates how much must be paid to attract one more worker into the industry – that is, the worker's **transfer price**. This is (roughly) the wage and productivity of this worker in another industry. In other words, the height of the labour supply curve is just the opportunity cost of an additional worker.

Is a Perfectly Competitive Labour Market Efficient?

Efficiency requires that labour be hired in an industry up to the point where its marginal benefit is just equal to its marginal costs. (If there are no externalities – as assumed here – then there is no difference between social and private benefits, and no difference between social and private costs.) The marginal benefit of labour is its productivity in this industry, as given by the labour demand curve. The marginal cost of labour is its **opportunity cost** – that is, its wage and productivity elsewhere; this is given by its supply curve. Since supply and demand for labour are equated in a perfectly competitive labour market, the marginal cost of labour is equal to the marginal benefit of labour, and this market is, therefore, efficient.

When a labour market has been shifted away from a perfectly competitive equilibrium, there is an efficiency loss that can be measured by the triangle between the demand curve, the supply curve, and the vertical line at the actual quantity of employment. Examples are provided in panels (*b*) and (*c*) of Figure 15-6 in the textbook. If such triangular efficiency losses are not clear, you may wish to review the similar analysis that was used in Chapter 11 in the context of efficiency losses in product markets. It is essential that you understand these fully, because they will be used frequently.

Although a perfectly competitive labour market is efficient, it does not necessarily follow that a free unregulated labour market is "best," for the following three reasons: (1) In an unregulated market, employers may discriminate against minorities, and thus violate the mobility assumption of perfect competition; (2) in an unregulated market, employers may have market power, thus violating another assumption of perfect competition; and (3) there may be externalities. Even if none of these problems arise – and an unregulated labour market is efficient – it may not be best because of the implied distribution of income.

The Effect of a Minimum Wage

There are four effects when a **minimum wage** (above the existing equilibrium wage) is introduced into a perfectly competitive labour market. (1) Employment is reduced. (2) Reduced employment leads to an efficiency loss, similar to the triangle in panel (*c*) of Figure 15-6. (The efficiency loss is even more than this if the minimum wage is imposed across all labour markets.) (3) Although the wage received by workers who are still employed in this industry rises, the wage of those who no longer have a job here falls (or disappears altogether). Therefore, on balance, the overall effect on total labour income is uncertain. (4) The amount of income going to other factors of production will definitely decrease, because the higher wage that must be paid to labour will put a squeeze on these other incomes.

While these four effects can be predicted from our simple demand-supply framework, there is another effect that experience has taught us: The unemployment created by minimum wage legislation falls most heavily on teenagers.

The important qualifications to this minimum wage analysis include: (1) Even if the minimum wage raises total labour income, workers may not feel that they benefit overall from the change. Even though jobs pay better, they are harder to find; and employers paying a higher wage may no longer feel that they can afford the cost of on-the-job training that is so beneficial to workers. (2) The more industries covered by minimum-wage legislation, the greater the unemployment it will create. The reason is that it becomes harder for an unemployed person to find a job elsewhere, because there are fewer and fewer other jobs available.

The Effects of Discrimination in the Labour Market

Figure 15-7 in the text shows the economic effects when employers discriminate by hiring women only for jobs with a low marginal product; the offensive moral and social dimensions are also recognized, even though they cannot be dealt with in this analysis.

When women are forced into jobs where they produce less, there is an efficiency loss roughly equal to the reduction in their output. Moreover, because they work in jobs where they are less productive, women receive a lower wage. Thus the entire efficiency loss in essentially borne by women. It is true that male workers benefit from a higher wage, due to the artificial scarcity of labour created in their part of the market because women are no longer able to work there. However, other factors of production lose because their interest, rent, and profit income is squeezed by the higher wage for men. Since most other factors of production are owned by families with a male wage earner, it is not clear that such families benefit overall, or that they lose overall: They gain because of the higher wage for the male earner, but lose because of the reduced income of their other factors of production; if there is a working woman in the family, the reduction in her wage constitutes part of the loss. The one clear message is that there is an efficiency loss, and this loss will be borne primarily by single women and families without a male wage earner.

Work of Equal Value

With equal pay for men and women in the same job now a widely accepted principle, the focus has shifted to the question: What should be done when men and women are in different but equally demanding jobs, and women are paid less? Should nurses be paid less than truck drivers? Proponents of the principle of "equal pay for work of equal value" say no. If these jobs are judged comparable, in terms of the education, responsibility, skills, etc., that they require, then pay should be equalized. Moreover, certain federal and provincial labour laws now reflect this principle. However, critics are concerned because this policy requires that specific jobs be compared; and these comparisons will be based on subjective and arbitrary judgements by bureaucrats or judges who will be second-guessing labour markets. They will be imposing a detailed and complex system of wage controls that will leave many labour markets in a chronic condition of excess demand or supply.

IMPORTANT TERMS

1. Real wage
2. Marginal physical product (MPP) of labour
3. Marginal revenue product (MRP) of labour
4. Value of the marginal product (VMP) of labour
5. Demand curve for labour
6. Opportunity cost of labour
7. Transfer price of labour
8. Efficient allocation of labour
9. Minimum wage
10. Discriminatory hiring
11. Equal pay for equal work

TRUE-FALSE

T F 1. The marginal revenue product curve shows the cost to the firm of hiring additional workers.

T F 2. A profit-maximizing firm that is operating in perfectly competitive labour and product markets will hire labour to the point where the value of the marginal product equals the wage rate.

T F 3. The demand for labour schedule shifts to the right whenever the marginal revenue product of labour schedule shifts to the right.

T F 4. If the marginal revenue product of labour is less than the wage, a perfectly competitive firm can increase its profits by hiring more labour.

T F 5. One effect of an increase in the minimum wage is a decrease in the income going to factors of production other than labour.

T F 6. Even if there is an external cost of employing labour, a perfectly competitive labour market will still be efficient.

T F 7. The marginal revenue product of labour is the amount the firm's revenue increases when it hires one more worker.

T F 8. The value of the marginal product of labour is the same as the marginal revenue product of labour, if the hiring firm is a monopolist in its product market.

T F 9. The demand for labour by an industry is the horizontal sum of the demand by the individual firms in that industry.

T F 10. If the wage rate rises elsewhere in the economy, the wage and employment in a perfectly competitive industry will tend to rise.

T F 11. There is a greater efficiency loss if the minimum wage is applied to only one industry rather than to all industries.

MULTIPLE CHOICE

1. The marginal physical product of labour:
   a. is based on the assumption that the firm uses a given capital stock as the employment of labour increases
   b. is based on the assumption that the use of capital increases by the same proportion as labour employment
   c. shows the additional revenue a firm can earn because it hires one more worker
   d. is set equal to the wage rate by an employer in equilibrium
   e. is the same as the value of the marginal product

2. A firm's demand curve for labour is the curve showing its:
   a. total physical product of labour
   b. average revenue product of labour
   c. marginal physical product of labour
   d. average physical product of labour
   e. marginal revenue product of labour

3. The demand for labour by a firm producing bolts shifts up in response to:
   a. a rise in the price of bolts
   b. a fall in labour productivity in the bolt-making industry
   c. a downward shift in the demand for bolts
   d. a decrease in the stock of machinery in the industry
   e. a decrease in the stock of other investment equipment in the industry

4. A leftward shift in the labour supply schedule may be the result of:
   a. a rightward shift in the marginal revenue product of labour schedule
   b. a leftward shift in the marginal revenue product of labour schedule
   c. higher available wages in other industries
   d. a fall in labour productivity
   e. a falling opportunity cost of labour

5. Perfect competition in a labour market requires the assumption that workers are:
   a. so numerous that each individual can affect the wage rate
   b. so numerous that no individual can affect the wage rate
   c. so few that no individual can affect the wage rate
   d. so few that any individual can affect the wage rate
   e. any of the above, since no assumption is required on this

6. If there is a perfectly competitive market for farm labour, and there is a fall in the price of grain and other farm outputs, then there will be:
   a. a shift to the left in the labour supply curve
   b. a shift to the right in the labour supply curve
   c. a shift to the left in the labour demand curve
   d. a shift to the right in the labour demand curve
   e. a. and c.

7. The value of the marginal product of labour is equal to the marginal revenue product of labour:
   a. always
   b. never
   c. only if the hiring firm is a monopolist in its product market
   d. only if the hiring firm is a perfect competitor in its product market
   e. only if the hiring firm is an oligopolist in its product market

8. The opportunity cost of labour in an industry:
   a. is approximately measured by the height of the labour demand schedule
   b. is approximately measured by the height of the labour supply schedule
   c. decreases as employment in the industry increases
   d. is completely vertical because labour can switch between industries
   e. is the income that capital can earn elsewhere

9. Which of the following will cause a rightward shift in the labour demand by an industry?
   a. an increase in labour productivity in this industry
   b. a decrease in labour productivity in this industry
   c. an increase in the minimum wage
   d. an increase in the transfer price of labour
   e. a decrease in the transfer price of labour

10. Labour demand by a firm will shift to the left if there is:
    a. a decrease in the minimum wage
    b. an increase in the marginal revenue product of labour
    c. a decrease in the marginal revenue product of labour
    d. an increase in wages in other industries
    e. a decrease in wages in other industries

11. The total area under an industry's demand for labour schedule to the left of the existing quantity of employment equals:
    a. the income received by other factors in the industry
    b. the total income of labour in the industry
    c. the total income of labour and all other factors in the industry
    d. total profits in the industry
    e. the marginal revenue received by the industry

12. If the labour supply curve is vertical, then a technological improvement that increases the marginal physical product of labour will cause:
    a. an increase in the wage and no change in employment
    b. an increase in both the wage and employment
    c. an increase in employment and no change in the wage
    d. a decrease in the wage and no change in employment
    e. a decrease in the wage and an increase in employment

13. In a perfectly competitive labour market for an industry, an increase in wages elsewhere in the economy will result in:
    a. a shift to the right in the labour supply curve
    b. an increase in wages and employment in this industry
    c. a decrease in wages and employment in this industry
    d. a decrease in wages, and an increase in employment in this industry
    e. an increase in wages, and a decrease in employment in this industry

14. Which of the following does not affect an individual worker's transfer price?
    a. the wage in the industry from which the worker is moving
    b. the wage in the industry to which the worker is moving
    c. financial moving costs
    d. psychological moving costs
    e. differences in the attractiveness of working conditions in the new and old industries

15. In a perfectly competitive labour market for an industry, there will be an efficiency loss unless labour is hired up to the point where:
    a. the marginal productivity of labour in this industry exceeds its marginal productivity elsewhere
    b. the marginal productivity of labour in this industry is less than its marginal productivity elsewhere
    c. the marginal productivity of labour in this industry is equal to its marginal productivity elsewhere
    d. the marginal opportunity cost of labour exceeds its marginal productivity in this industry
    e. The marginal opportunity cost of labour is less than its marginal productivity in this industry

16. If less than the perfectly competitive number of workers is hired in an industry:
    a. the marginal productivity of labour in this industry will exceed its marginal productivity elsewhere
    b. the marginal productivity of labour in this industry will be less than its marginal productivity elsewhere
    c. the marginal productivity of labour in this industry will be equal to its marginal productivity elsewhere
    d. the marginal opportunity cost of labour will exceed its marginal productivity in this industry
    e. the marginal opportunity cost of labour will be the same as its marginal productivity in this industry

17. In a perfectly competitive labour market:
    a. employers hire labour up to the point where they maximize their profit
    b. employers hire labour up to the point where their marginal benefit is equal to their marginal cost
    c. employees supply labour services up to the point where their marginal benefit is equal to their marginal cost
    d. there is an efficient level of employment
    e. all of the above

18. In Canada, the minimum wage:
    a. is set by the federal government for the whole country
    b. is higher for teenagers than for older workers in most jurisdictions
    c. covers every industry in those provinces where minimum wage legislation exists
    d. is generally higher for women than for men in federal jobs
    e. none of the above

19. A minimum wage can increase efficiency if:
    a. there is a major problem with teenage unemployment
    b. all wages in the economy are already above the minimum wage
    c. all wages in the economy are below the minimum wage
    d. all wages in the economy are the same as the minimum wage
    e. the labour market is not perfectly competitive

20. The efficiency loss from sex discrimination in a perfectly competitive labour market:
    a. is borne to a large extent by single women, whose income is reduced
    b. occurs because women are employed in more productive activities, while men are in less productive ones
    c. occurs because income is transferred from male workers to other factors of production
    d. occurs because income is transferred from female workers to non-labour factors of production
    e. occurs because the other factors of production are owned by outsiders

For those who have studied the appendix to this chapter:

21. An economy-wide labour supply curve will "bend backwards" if:
    a. an increase in the wage rate induces labour to work more
    b. workers decide to use their increase in wages to "buy more leisure"
    c. workers decide to use all their increase in wages to buy more goods
    d. the substitution effect of a higher wage dominates the income effect
    e. there is no cost of living allowance in wage contracts

EXERCISES

1a. Fill in the missing data in Table 15.1 for a hypothetical firm with a given stock of capital which sells its output in a competitive market at a constant price.

Table 15.1

Number of workers	Total physical output	Marginal physical product of labour	Marginal revenue product (MRP) when price of output is $10 per unit	Marginal revenue product (MRP) when price of output is $15 per unit
0	0			
1	12			
2	19			
3	24			
4	28			
5	30			

Now answer the following questions. If the wage rate is $55 per worker per day, then the firm will want to hire _____ workers if the price of its output is $10, and _____ workers when this price is $15.

1b. Fill in the missing data in Table 15.2 for another hypothetical firm, assuming that the wage it faces is $40 per worker per day and the price of its output is $5.

Table 15.2

Number of workers	Total physical output	Marginal physical product	Marginal revenue product
0	0	—	—
1		10	
2		9	
3		8	
4		7	
5		6	

Now answer the following questions. The firm will be willing to hire no more than _____ workers. With this amount of employment, the firm's total revenue will be _____, its total wage payment will be $_____, and the income of other factors will be $_____.

2. Plot the labour demand schedule of this firm in Figure 15.1. Draw a horizontal line at the wage rate of $40 per worker per day. Label as 1 the area representing labour income. Label as 2 the area representing the income going to other factors.

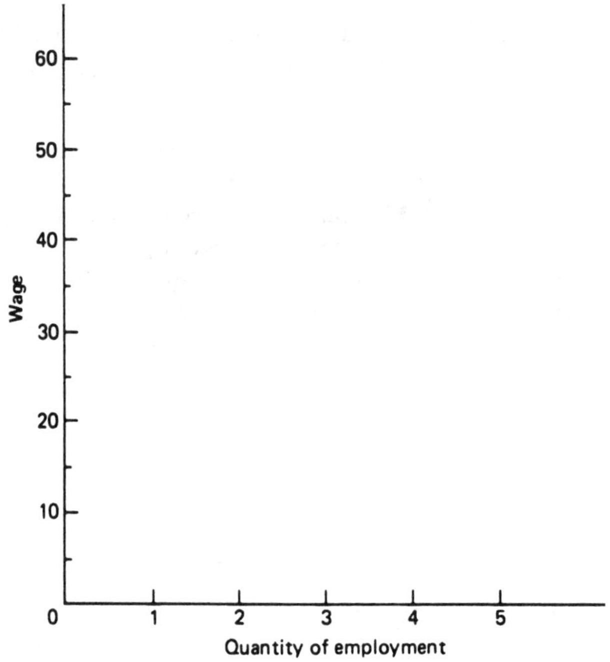

Figure 15.1

3. Figure 15.2 depicts a perfectly competitive labour market with no externalities. The equilibrium wage rate is _____ and the equilibrium quantity of employment is _____. Suppose a minimum wage of U is imposed. Then employment will be _____. Next, suppose the minimum wage is H. Then employment will be _____ and the difference between demand and supply will be _____. Fill in Table 15.3.

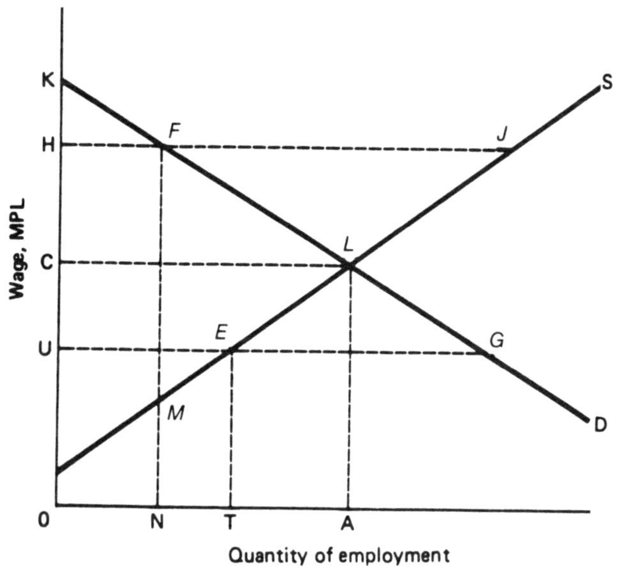

Figure 15.2

Table 15.3

	Efficiency loss is area:	Total labour income is area:	Income of other factors is area:
No minimum wage			
Minimum wage at U			
Minimum wage at H			

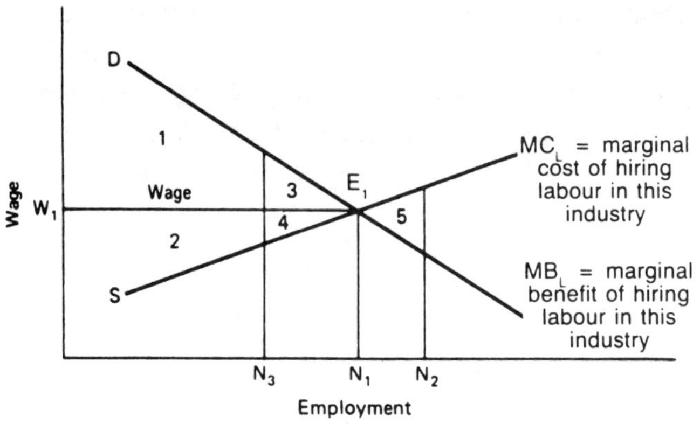

Figure 15.3

4a. (Note: This question requires study of the text, especially Figure 15-6.) The labour market in a perfectly competitive industry is shown in Figure 15.3. The marginal productivity of labour (VMP) in this industry is shown by the _____ curve, while the marginal productivity of labour elsewhere is shown by the _____ curve. The equilibrium is at _____, with wage _____ and employment of _____ workers. At this equilibrium, employers have (maximized, minimized) their profit by hiring labour up to the point where its marginal benefit – that is, the marginal productivity of labour in this industry as shown by the _____ curve – is equal to the marginal cost the employers face, as shown by _____. At the same time, employees have (minimized, maximized) their own net benefit by offering their labour up to the point where their marginal benefit – as shown by _____ – is equal to their marginal cost, shown by _____. This marginal cost to employees is called a (substitute, opportunity) cost, because it represents their potential earnings in their (least, most) attractive alternative job.

4b. If employment is at N_2, there is an efficiency (gain, loss) of area _____ because the (N_2 - N_1) extra workers employed would have (higher, lower) marginal productivity elsewhere – as shown by the _____ curve – than in this industry where their marginal productivity is shown by the _____ curve. On the other hand, if employment in this industry is at N_3, then there is an efficiency (gain, loss) because (N_1 - N_3) workers should be employed in this industry, but are not. These workers would have marginal productivity here shown by the _____ curve compared to their (lower, higher) marginal productivity elsewhere, as shown by the height of the _____ curve. Only at an employment level of _____ can one or the other of these types of efficiency losses be avoided.

ESSAY QUESTIONS

1. "The labour demand schedule slopes down for the same reason that the demand curve for a consumer good slopes down." Explain to what extent this is or is not true.

2. List and explain some influences that could shift the labour supply curve for an industry. In each case, indicate in which direction the shift would occur.

3. Over the past 50 years, the number of domestic servants in North America has fallen dramatically. Do you think this is because of the price and availability of labour-saving household appliances? Or is it due to rising wages in other occupations or generous social assistance programs? Or do both factors play a role? Explain how each affects the supply and demand for domestic help.

4. Discuss the influences that affect the elasticity of demand for labour, by first reviewing the influences affecting the elasticity of demand for a consumer good discussed in Chapter 6 in the text.

5. How would the supply of labour in a particular market be affected by a decrease in the cost of moving from one city to another?

6. Would you expect labour market discrimination to be more of a problem in a perfectly competitive industry or in a monopolistic industry?

ANSWERS

True-False: 1F, 2T, 3T, 4F, 5T, 6F, 7T, 8F, 9T, 10F, 11F

Multiple Choice: 1a, 2e, 3a, 4c, 5b, 6c, 7d, 8b, 9a, 10c, 11c, 12a, 13e, 14b, 15c, 16a, 17e, 18e, 19e, 20a, 21b

Exercises:

1a. Table 15.1 completed

W	O	MPP	MRP if P = \$10	MRP if P = \$15
0	0	—	—	—
1	12	12	120	180
2	19	7	70	105
3	24	5	50	75
4	28	4	40	60
5	30	2	20	30

2, 4

1b. Table 15.2 completed

Number of workers	Total physical output	MRP
0	0	—
1	10	\$50
2	19	45
3	27	40
4	34	35
5	40	30

3, \$135, \$120, \$15

2. Figure 15.1 completed

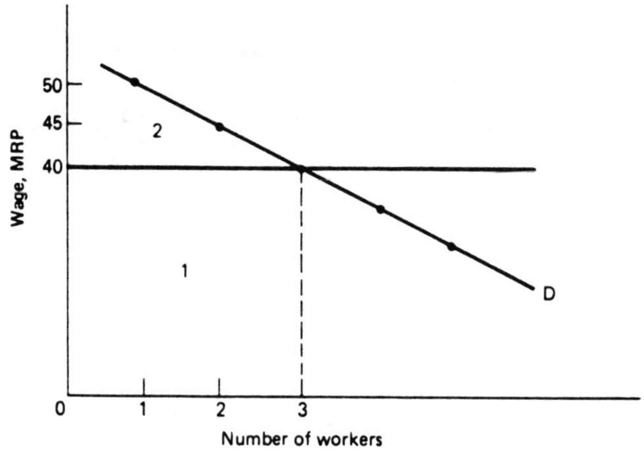

3. C, A, A, N, *FJ*

Table 15.3 completed

Zero	0CLA	KLC
Zero	0CLA	KLC
FLM	0HFN	KFH

4a. D, S, E_1, W_1, N_1, maximized, D, W_1E_1, maximized, W_1E_1, S, opportunity, most

4b. loss, 5, higher, S, D, loss, D, lower, S, N_1

ANSWERS TO PROBLEMS FROM THE TEXT

15-1. (a) Total revenue is $420 (21 units at $20). The total wage bill is $240 (4 workers at $60). The difference of $180 is the return to other factors of production.

(b) Total revenue is the total area of the first four bars in Figure 15-1; payments to labour is the area of these same bars below the horizontal line at $60, while the return to other factors is the area above that line.

15-2. If the product price falls to $10, the height of each bar in Figure 15-1 would be cut in half, as would the height of the firm's labour demand curve. At a wage of $60, the firm could hire 3 workers who would produce 18 units at $10, which would be just enough to pay the firm's wage bill.

15-3. **Table 15.1 (adjusted)**

Marginal Revenue Product vs. Value of Marginal Product

Workers	Output	MPP	Price	Total Revenue	MRP	VMP
0	0		—	0		
		5			$120	$120
1	5		$24	$120		
		7			$156	$161
2	12		$23	$276		
		6			$120	$132
3	18		$22	$396		
		3			$45	$63
4	21		$21	$411		
		2			$19	$40
5	23		$20	$460		

15-4. A minimum wage will be more likely to raise total income if labour demand elasticity is low. If elasticity is more than one, then a higher wage will lower labour income. And beware: Even if labour income is increased, it may be a questionable objective if it leaves many workers unemployed.

15-5. The tax shifts the supply curve up in Figure 15-3 (as in Figure 10-12). The gross of tax wage rate rises (the amount paid by employers) and the equilibrium quantity of labour hired falls. The wage paid to labour (the net of tax wage rate) falls. The excess burden of the tax is measured by the triangle formed by the area between the labour demand curve and the labour supply curve between the new and old equilibrium quantities of labour hired. The primary burden – the amount of tax paid – consists of a reduction in the surplus generated by the new equilibrium quantity of labour (payments to other factors plus profit) and in the total wages paid to labour at the new equilibrium quantity. An important implication of this diagram is that, although the tax is levied on employers, the burden is ultimately split between employers and labour – the (net) wage rate falls, although not by the full amount of the tax.

CHAPTER 16

Wages in Imperfectly Competitive Labour Markets

LEARNING OBJECTIVES

After you have studied this chapter in the textbook and the study guide, you should be able to

- Explain the purpose of unions and the role of collective bargaining
- Describe how union membership has changed in various periods of Canadian labour history
- Describe the changing relationship between Canadian and American union movements
- Explain the differences between Canadian and U.S. labour legislation in the question of compulsory union membership
- Show in a diagram the inefficiency that results when a union succeeds in raising wages (above the perfectly competitive wage) in an otherwise perfectly competitive labour market
- Outline the special ways that a union may improve efficiency
- Explain what is meant by monopsony
- Show in a diagram the inefficiency that results when a monopsonist succeeds in lowering wages (below the perfectly competitive wage) in an otherwise perfectly competitive labour market
- Show in a diagram how efficiency may be increased if a union is formed in a labour market that has previously been monopsonized
- Analyze bilateral monopoly, where market power is held by a union (a single seller of labour) on one side of the market and by a monopsony (a single buyer of labour) on the other

- Explain why a strike may occur even though there is a large collective loss from it

- Show why there may be large internal and external costs if labour negotiations break down and a strike occurs

- Identify three ways of trying to avert an imminent strike

- Explain the possible imbalance of bargaining power when a public service union negotiates with a government

- State four reasons workers get different wages

CHAPTER SUMMARY

The key objective in this chapter is to analyze what happens when labour markets are not perfectly competitive. Typically, the result is inefficiency, and this is compared with the efficient outcome when labour markets are perfectly competitive, as described in the previous chapter.

Elements of imperfect competition may appear on either side of the labour market. On the one side, workers may form a union which, as a monopoly (a single seller of labour services), is able to raise the wage rate. On the other side, there may be a **monopsony** firm (a single buyer of labour services) that is able to lower the wage rate. In either case, an inefficiently low amount of labour is hired. The interesting case of **bilateral monopoly** arises when there is a monopoly (a union) on the workers' side of the market, and a monopsony on the employer's side. Illustrations are provided to show how difficult and complicated wage bargaining can be in this case. In particular, special problems arise in any bargaining between a monopoly union of public service workers and their monopsony employer – the government.

History

There have been four distinct periods in the modern history of the Canadian labour movement.

1. During the 1920s and 1930s, union membership in Canada did not grow by very much. The most important labour organization, the Trades and Labour Congress of Canada (TLC), was essentially a federation of **craft unions** – like its U.S. counterpart, the American Federation of Labour (AFL). As a result, it did not appeal to unskilled workers in mass-production industries who did not belong to a

particular "craft." Furthermore, there was strong employer resistance to the growth of unions, and the labour legislation during that period made it hard for unions to overcome this resistance.

2. During the 1940s and early 1950s, union membership grew very rapidly in Canada. In part, the reason for this was the rapid rise in industrial unions, which brought the unskilled workers in mass-production industries into the union movement. Canada's **industrial unions** were organized in the Canadian Congress of Labour (CCL), the counterpart of the American Congress of Industrial Organizations (CIO). Furthermore, Canada's labour legislation changed during this period, with the right of workers to unionize becoming explicitly recognized; the 1945 Rand formula set a precedent by making it legal for a labour contract to compel all workers to contribute financially to the union.

3. In the decade between the early 1950s and early 1960s, union membership in Canada grew only slowly, in part reflecting the relatively slow growth of employment in industries in which unions have traditionally been important and in part reflecting continued strife between craft unions and industrial unions. However, this strife has gradually diminished, and most unions of either type are now affiliated with the Canadian Labour Congress (CLC), which was created in 1956 through a merger of the TLC and CCL. (In the United States, a similar merger created the AFL-CIO.)

4. Since the early 1960s, union membership has remained relatively stable in the aggregate, but its composition has been changing. Union membership in the private sector and in the traditional international unions has continued to grow slowly. Most of the growth in union membership in the 1960s and 1970s has occurred instead in national unions which are not affiliated with U.S. labour organizations. In particular, there has been rapid growth in union membership in the public service and, of course, public sector unions are national unions.

(In the United States, union membership as a proportion of the labour force has declined during the last few decades. Part of the reason for this has been public hostility to unions in the United States, as well as the passage of legislation such as the Taft-Hartly Act, which outlaws compulsory checkoff of union dues and gives the individual states the right to pass laws prohibiting **union shops** or **closed shops**. Closed shops and union shops are legal in Canada.)

Effects of Unions

A union gives workers a voice in presenting grievances to their employer. It also negotiates with management to establish **seniority rules** and improve working conditions. These benefit not only the workers but also the employer who is able to offer more attractive jobs and therefore reduce quit rates.

But the main objectives of a union are to protect the jobs and raise the wages of its members. According to recent estimates, unionized workers get anywhere from

10% to 30% higher wages than comparable non-unionized workers. If a union is established that raises the wage in a previously competitive labour market, there are three main effects: (a) there is a reduction in employment and, therefore, a loss of income for those workers who lose their jobs; (b) there is an increase in the wage rate and, therefore an increase in income for those workers who still have jobs; and (c) there is a loss in economic efficiency. Figure 16-2 in the textbook shows the effect of unionization in an industry, including both the **transfer effect** – labour gains at the expense of other factors of production – and the **efficiency effect** – employment is reduced below the competitive level.

The analysis in Figure 16-2 of the efficiency loss that results from a union is overly harsh because, in some ways not shown in this diagram, unions may improve economic efficiency. First, by giving workers a voice, unions provide them with an alternative to quitting or being fired when a problem arises. Thus, they save unnecessary costs of labour turnover. Second, by improving working conditions they can reduce the tension between workers and employers, and thus create a more productive atmosphere. Third, a union's bargaining power may simply offset the bargaining power of monopsonist employers; in this case, a union may increase efficiency. (Remember that our earlier discussion of the efficiency losses from a union applies only if the labour market is perfectly competitive otherwise.)

Monopsony

As a single employer of labour, a monopsony tries to exploit its market power by reducing wages. If it succeeds – in an otherwise perfectly competitive labour market – the three main effects will be to (a) transfer income from labour to other factors of production; (b) reduce employment; and (c) create an efficiency loss. Figure 16-3 in the textbook illustrates the economic effects of monopsony in an otherwise perfectly competitive labour market. There, it is shown that the monopsonist will pay a wage that is less than labour's marginal revenue product, resulting in a transfer from labour to other factors of production (e.g., capital). Also, it is shown that employment is reduced below the competitive level, resulting in a loss in economic efficiency.

Bilateral Monopoly

In this case of "two-sided" monopoly, market power is held both by a union on the one side, and by a monopsonistic employer on the other. This case is the most difficult to analyse.

To illustrate, suppose a union is formed in a labour market where a monopsonist employer has been keeping the wage rate below the perfectly competitive level. In this case, the formation of the union may raise the wage back toward the perfectly competitive level. If this is the outcome, the union will be simply undoing some of the effects of the monopsony. Specifically, the union will (a) transfer income back from other factors of production to labour, (b) increase employment, and (c) reduce the efficiency loss from monopsony.

However, it is not that simple to predict the outcome in this situation. For example, there is no guarantee that a newly formed union will only raise wages toward the perfectly competitive level; it may raise wages beyond this. If this happens we can no longer be sure that the union will increase efficiency. This is the basic problem in analyzing bilateral monopoly: We don't know where the wage will be set. All we know for sure is that the wage will be somewhere between the high wage the union seeks, and the lower wage the monopsonistic employer seeks. At what point the wage will be determined within this range depends on the bargaining power of each side. This, in turn, depends partly on the ability of each to outlast the other in the event of a **strike**. Thus, the bargaining power of the union depends upon the size of the union's strike fund. The bargaining power of the employer depends upon the size of its inventories of finished goods that it can continue to sell during a strike.

Strikes

In a sense, everyone is damaged by a strike. The employer loses profits and the labour force loses wages. Nevertheless, strikes do occur, because (a) each side may see a strike as a way of getting a more favourable wage rate than the other side's final offer on the eve of the strike; (b) each side may want to increase its future credibility and bargaining power by clearly demonstrating that it is prepared to allow a strike to take place; or (c) either side may make a bargaining mistake that prevents an agreement from being reached before a strike deadline. In comparison to other countries, Canada has a record of relatively frequent and long-lasting strikes. Nevertheless, in an average year the typical Canadian worker spends less than one day on strike.

One reason strikes pose an important issue for public policy is spillovers – that is, costs of strikes to people not involved in the bargaining. For example, a transit strike prevents people from getting to their jobs.

There are several possible ways of averting a strike when the two sides are unable to reach agreement on their own. (a) The government (federal or provincial, depending on who has the jurisdiction over labour relations in the industry involved) may appoint an outsider to act as a mediator or conciliate between the parties. (b) Both sides may agree to voluntary arbitration, in which a third party decides upon a settlement that both sides agree in advance to accept. (c) If they don't agree to voluntary arbitration, the government may force them to accept compulsory arbitration.

Unions of Public Service Employees

Unions in the public sector raise problems because they have such a strong bargaining position, for the following reasons.

1. There are large spillover costs to the voting public when public servants such as transit workers or the police go on strike. Thus, voters may exert great pressure on the government to settle the dispute.

2. Public servants know that, in the last analysis, it is typically easier for a government than for a private company to raise the funds necessary to pay a higher wage. The government can tax or borrow in a way that is not available to private employers.

3. A union has much greater bargaining power over a financially weak government than it would have over a financially weak private employer. The reason is that a strike won't force a government out of business, but it might drive a private employer bankrupt, in which case there are no jobs to negotiate about.

4. Because public service employees now constitute a large bloc of voters, politicians are reluctant to fight hard against their wage demands.

Because public servants have such a strong bargaining position, it is often suggested that they should not be allowed to strike, or even form a union. But this would raise a problem. If these workers cannot form a union, how can they defend themselves against a monopsonistic employer (the government)? If not with a union, what else?

Wage Differences

Wage differences can exist for at least five different reasons: First, there may be dynamic **wage differentials**. When new job opportunities open up in an industry, wages must rise temporarily to attract workers from other industries. Eventually, the influx of new workers will bring the wages back down. Second, compensating wage differentials give workers more pay for especially hazardous or unpleasant jobs. Third, monopoly or monopsony power may be greater in some labour markets than in others. Fourth, barriers to entry can keep wages artificially high in some jobs. Fifth, those with special talents and skills earn a higher wage because they are more productive, as we shall see in the next chapter.

IMPORTANT TERMS

1. Collective bargaining
2. Seniority rules
3. Craft union
4. Industrial union
5. Closed/union shop
6. Efficiency loss from unionization
7. Monopsony
8. Efficiency loss from monopsonization
9. Transfer effect from unionization/monopsonization
10. Bilateral monopoly
11. Strike
12. Wage differential

TRUE-FALSE

T F 1. Bilateral monopoly in the labour market means that employers are exercising monopsony power and labour is exercising monopoly power.

T F 2. An industrial union draws its members from any industry, provided they have a common skill (such as plumbing).

T F 3. The Canadian Auto Workers (CAW) is a craft union.

T F 4. Like Samuel Gompers' American Federation of Labour, the Trades and Labour Congress of Canada was an attempt to organize labour for a political class struggle, rather than for the pursuit of improved wages and working conditions.

T F 5. If wages are reduced below what they would be in perfect competition, there will be a loss in efficiency.

T F 6. A union will seek to raise wages, while a monopsonist will seek to lower them.

T F 7. Other things equal, a company producing perishable goods is more vulnerable to strike threats than one producing durable goods.

T F 8. The spillover cost of a strike must be less than the internal cost to the industry in which the strike occurs.

T F 9. Public service unions have recently been growing less rapidly than other unions.

T F 10. Compensating wage differentials would not exist if workers viewed all jobs as equally attractive.

T F 11. Unions necessarily contribute to inefficiency in the economy.

MULTIPLE CHOICE

1. When a union negotiates seniority rules, workers with seniority are typically:
   a. the first to be laid off and the first to be rehired
   b. the first to be laid off and the last to be rehired
   c. the last to be laid off and the last to be rehired
   d. the last to be laid off and the first to be rehired
   e. left unaffected in terms of being laid off or rehired

2. Craft unions draw their membership from:
   a. workers in companies that build pleasure boats
   b. workers in companies that build any boats
   c. all workers in a specific industry regardless of their skills
   d. all workers in a specific industry provided they have the same skill
   e. all workers from any industry provided they have the same skill

3. Unions, in Canada and elsewhere:
   a. negotiate higher wages
   b. negotiate improved working conditions
   c. have occasionally been getting voting seats on boards of directors
   d. act as a social forum for their members
   e. all of the above

4. According to labour market studies, unionized workers in Canada are estimated to earn wages that are higher than comparable non-unionized workers by:
   a. 6 to 12%
   b. 10 to 30%
   c. 35 to 40%
   d. 55 to 73%
   e. less than 4%

5. The Rand formula:
   a. specifies that all workers must contribute to the union, whether or not they are union members
   b. specifies that a strike cannot be held unless there has been a vote by all employees
   c. specifies that illegal strikes during the time the agreement is in force will be penalized
   d. was originally contained in a 1945 court decision
   e. all of the above

6. Labour contracts in Canada specifying a closed shop:
   a. were prohibited by a federal law passed in 1967
   b. are illegal for workers belonging to industrial unions
   c. are generally legal in Canada
   d. are the only kinds of labour contracts that are legal in Canada
   e. are required under the Rand formula

7. Which of the following provides the greatest barrier to entry into a work force?
   a. an open shop
   b. a closed shop
   c. a union shop
   d. the Rand formula
   e. right-to-work legislation

8. In a union shop, a firm:
   a. can hire only workers who are already union members
   b. can hire only workers who have already worked in a union shop
   c. can hire only workers who have already worked in an open shop
   d. can hire non-union workers provided they join the union within a brief specified period
   e. can hire any workers, who then have the option of joining or not joining the union

9. Which of the following is the clearest example of featherbedding?
   a. seniority rules
   b. sexual harassment on the job
   c. firefighters employed on diesel trains
   d. shorter work weeks
   e. the firing of technologically displaced workers

10. As a fraction of the non-agricultural labour force, union membership in the second half of the 1980s was about:
    a. 1/3 in Canada and 1/5 in the United States
    b. 1/4 in both Canada and the United States
    c. 1/3 in Canada and less than 1/10 in the United States
    d. 1/2 in Canada and just over 1/3 in the United States
    e. about 40% in Canada and about 25% in the United States

11. If a union formed in a perfectly competitive labour market successfully raises wages, then:
    a. income is transferred from other factors of production to all workers
    b. income is transferred from other factors of production to workers who still have a job in this industry
    c. there is an efficiency gain from increased employment
    d. there is an efficiency loss from increased employment
    e. there is an efficiency gain from reduced employment

12. Unions improve efficiency by:
    a. raising wages above what they would be under perfect competition
    b. reducing labour turnover by giving workers the chance to present their grievances rather than quit or be fired
    c. increasing labour turnover by negotiating higher wages
    d. increasing employment above its perfectly competitive level
    e. b. and d.

13. If a firm can hire only workers who are already union members, it is described as a:
    a. constrained shop
    b. closed shop
    c. union shop
    d. open shop
    e. restricted shop

14. Which of the following is most likely to occur if a union is introduced into a previously competitive labour market with no externalities?
    a. Total income to labour will decrease
    b. The income of some individual workers will increase
    c. Employment in that market will increase
    d. Incomes of non-labour factors of production will increase
    e. An efficiency gain will result

15. The introduction of labour-saving machinery:
    a. may create temporary unemployment, and result in worse jobs for labour in the long run
    b. may create temporary unemployment, but results in higher wages for labour in the long run
    c. may temporarily raise employment, but results in worse jobs for labour in the long run
    d. may create temporary unemployment, and results in lower wages in the long run
    e. has no effect on employment in either the short or the long run

16. Unions may have beneficial effects on efficiency:
    a. by removing labour's collective voice and thus reducing distractions in the workplace
    b. by reducing communication between labour and management, and thus reducing distractions facing managers
    c. by increasing quit-rates
    d. by reducing quit-rates
    e. by increasing management's market power to raise wages

17. Employment will be increased in an otherwise perfectly competitive labour market by:
    a. the introduction of a union whose main effect is to raise wages
    b. collusion by employers to act together like a monopsonist
    c. an increase in the minimum wage
    d. the introduction of a closed shop
    e. none of the above

18. A union's negotiating power will be increased most by:
    a. a large union strike fund
    b. a small union strike fund
    c. a right-to-work law
    d. large inventory holdings by the employer
    e. reduced tariff protection on the employer's output

19. In a labour market with a strong union, the creation of a monopsony bargaining association by employers tends to:
    a. raise wages even further
    b. lower wages
    c. transfer income from other factors of production to labour
    d. a. and c.
    e. none of the above

20. Baseball salaries before and after the players' escape from the reserve clause illustrate:
   a. how much unions can raise salaries
   b. how much unions can lower salaries
   c. how much monopsonists can raise salaries
   d. how much monopsonists can lower salaries
   e. the countervailing power of a union

EXERCISES

1a. In Figure 16.1, MC_L is supply and MB_L is demand in a perfectly competitive labour market with no externalities. The equilibrium wage is _____ and the equilibrium quantity of employment is _____. In perfect competition the income of labour is area _____ and the income of other factors is area _____.

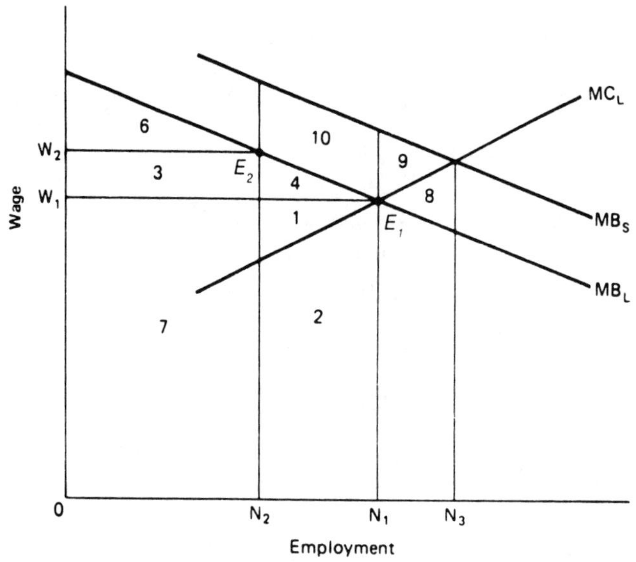

Figure 16.1

1b. Suppose now that a union is formed, which increases the wage to W_2. Then the quantity of employment will be _____, the income going to labour still employed in this industry will be _____, the income going to other factors will be _____, and the efficiency (gain, loss) will be _____.

1c. Now suppose that there is an external benefit from hiring labour in this activity. Specifically, suppose the workers being hired are musicians – they provide not only a direct benefit to their employer (the symphony orchestra) whenever they play in a concert, but also an external benefit because of their other contributions to the cultural life of the community. Because of this external benefit, the marginal social benefit of labour is MB_S rather than just the employers' benefit MB_L. Then the efficient quantity of employment will be _____. In perfect competition the wage will be _____, the quantity of employment will be _____, and the efficiency (gain, loss) will be _____.

1d. With this externality, if a union is formed to raise wages to W_2, then the quantity of employment will equal _____ and the efficiency (gain, loss) will equal _____.

2. In Figure 16.2, D represents the demand for labour while area 1 represents the external cost of a strike.

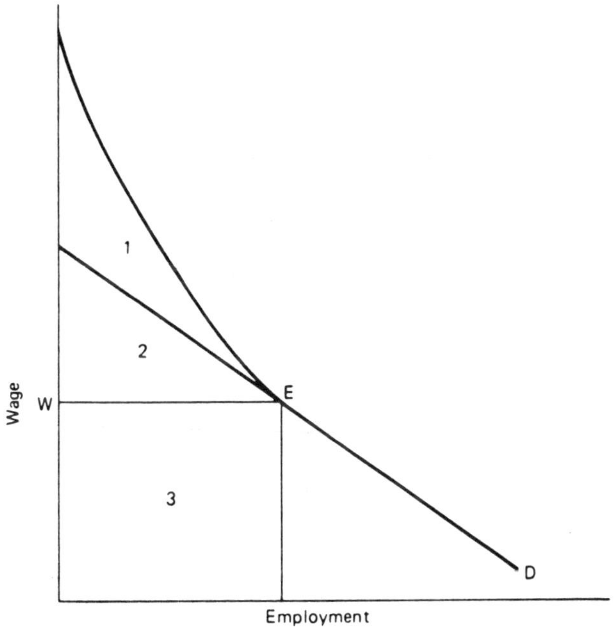

Figure 16.2

If a strike occurs, the cost to labour – in terms of lost wages – is area _____, while the loss of income by other factors in this industry is area _____. This means that the total internal cost to all factors in this industry is _____. In addition, there is an (external, internal) cost of area _____. Therefore, the total cost to society of a strike in this industry is _____. The problem with a strike is that the labour and management participants in the negotiation take into account only (external/internal) costs. No account may be taken of the additional cost to other groups shown as ____.

ESSAY QUESTIONS

1. Do you think that unions help or hinder the attempt to achieve (a) stable prices and (b) an equitable distribution of income?

2. If there is no union on one side of the market to raise wages, and no collusion or association by employers on the other side of the market to lower wages, compare the bargaining position of the individual worker and the individual employer.

3. Describe the conditions under which an increase in the minimum wage may increase the amount of employment.

4. Describe the spillovers if each of the following went on strike:
   a. Municipal garbage workers
   b. Air traffic controllers
   c. City police
   d. Steel workers

ANSWERS

True-False: **1**T, **2**F, **3**F, **4**F, **5**T, **6**T, **7**T, **8**F, **9**F, **10**T, **11**F

Multiple Choice: **1**d, **2**e, **3**e, **4**b, **5**e, **6**c, **7**b. **8**d, **9**c, **10**a, **11**b, **12**b, **13**b, **14**b, **15**b, **16**d, **17**e, **18**a, **19**b, **20**d

Exercises: **1a**. W_1, N_1, 7 + 1 + 2, 6 + 3 + 4
1b. N_2, 3 + 7, 6, loss, 1 + 4
1c. N_3, W_1, N_1, loss, 9
1d. N_2, loss, 1 + 4 + 9 + 10
2. 3, 2, 2 + 3, external, 1, 1 + 2 + 3, internal, 1

ANSWERS TO PROBLEMS FROM THE TEXT

16-1. This is entirely possible since both result in employment levels below what would prevail under perfect competition in the labour market. The transfer effect, however, is different. Under unionization, it favours labour; under monopsonization, it favours non-labour factors of production (e.g., capital).

16-2. If the association negotiates wages down to W_2, equilibrium is at E_2 and some employment is restored. Therefore, efficiency is improved. If, however, the association negotiates wages down to W_1, there is no change in employment, simply a reversal of the transfer effect. Therefore, the same level of inefficiency obtains.

16-3. If the minimum wage is set at the competitive level (i.e., W in Figure 16-4), then efficiency is clearly improved. If, however, the minimum wage is set above the competitive level, efficiency (and employment) may be reduced.

16-4. (a) It may be a way of helping an unprofitable firm avoid bankruptcy (which would lead to a loss of jobs for all workers).

(b) Efficiency improves: With the marginal worker being paid the competitive wage, the firm will expand its hiring to the competitive, efficient level. (The return to other factors of production will be lower than in the competitive equilibrium, because of the higher wages paid to some workers.)

(c) In one way, it may improve job security: It may help the firm stay in business. In another way, however, job security may be reduced: It is now in the firm's interest to put pressure on the more highly paid workers to leave, since they can be replaced by new workers who are paid a lower wage.

16-5. Recall that the theory of the second best states that efficiency may be improved by introducing offsetting distortions in the face of pre-existing distortions. Monopsony distorts the allocation of labour precisely because the monopsonist is able to exercise market power. Unionization confers market power on workers, thereby creating a potential offset to the distorting effects of monopsonization.

16-6. Answering this question will require some class discussion. First, begin to develop a table such as that shown below. From the demand curve, MB_L is read as the wage associated with each quantity demanded. From the supply curve, MC_L is read as the wage associated with each quantity supplied. Plot these curves, as in Figure 16-2 in the textbook. The competitive equilibrium is where $MB_L = MC_L$. At this point, W = 2,000 and L = 6,000

Quantity of Labour	Marginal Product in this Industry – MB_L	Marginal Cost of Labour to Society – MC_L	(a) Monopoly Union – Marginal Benefit to Unionized Labour	(b) Monopsony Firm – Marginal Cost of Labour to the Firm
1,000	4,500.00	333.33	4,000.00	666.67
2,000	4,000.00	666.67	3,000.00	1,333.33
3,000	3,500.00	1,000.00	2,000.00	2,000.00
4,000	3,000.00	1,333.33	1,000.00	2,666.67
5,000	2,500.00	1,666.67	0.00	3,333.33
6,000	2,000.00	2,000.00	-1,000.00	4,000.00

(a) The problem faced by the union is that, in order to have an additional unit of labour hired, the wage rate must fall. This lower wage applies to all units of labour – in other words, the "marginal benefit to unionized labour" is less than the wage rate, since incomes of existing workers will fall (this is rather like the MR curve for the monopolist, discussed in Chapter 12). Plot the "marginal benefit to unionized labour" curve on your diagram. The union will seek to place workers up to the point where the marginal benefit to unionized labour is just equal to the opportunity cost of the last unit employed – that is, where the marginal benefit to unionized labour curve cuts the MC_L curve. This occurs where L = 3,750. For this quantity of labour, the firm is willing to pay W = 3,125 (which is above the competitive wage rate of W = 2,000).

(b) The problem faced by the monopsonist is that, in order to hire an additional unit of labour, the wage rate must rise. This higher wage applies to all units of labour – in other words the marginal cost of labour to the firm exceeds the wage rate (as in Figure 16-3 in the textbook), since the wage paid to all workers must rise. Plot the "marginal cost of labour to the firm" curve on your diagram. The firm will hire workers up to the point where the marginal benefit is just equal to the marginal cost – that is where MB_L cuts the marginal cost of labour to the firm curve (as in Figure 16-3 in the textbook). This occurs where L = 4,286. In order to hire this much labour, the firm must pay a wage W = 1,428.66 (which is below the competitive wage).

(c) The union position results in the lowest level of employment, hence the greatest welfare (efficiency) loss. (See Figures 16-2 and 16-3 in the textbook.)

CHAPTER 17

Other Incomes

LEARNING OBJECTIVES

After you have studied this chapter in the textbook and the study guide, you should be able to

- Explain how the public receives an interest income for providing business with debt capital, and how the public receives a profit income for providing business with equity capital

- Explain how the demand for loanable funds is related to the marginal efficiency of investment schedule

- Explain the trade-off between pre- and post-retirement consumption, and the relationship between this and the interest rate

- Explain how the supply curve for savings results from consumers' choices between pre- and post-retirement consumption

- Show in a diagram how an interest rate ceiling imposed on a perfectly competitive market for loanable funds will affect efficiency and redistribute income

- Explain why it is a fallacy to suppose that interest rate ceilings necessarily help poor people

- Explain how relative factor prices influence decisions by individual firms

- Compare an investment in human capital and an investment in physical capital

- Describe the conditions under which investment in human capital could be less than the efficient amount, and the conditions under which it could be more than the efficient amount

- Explain why it is difficult to measure the rate of return on human capital

- Define the economist's notion of "rent" and explain why it can be earned not only by land, but by any factor of production

- Give three examples of rent, in addition to rent on land

- Describe how rent is capitalized in the value of land

CHAPTER SUMMARY

In the previous two chapters, we analyzed labour income. The objective of this chapter is to analyze other forms of income – specifically, interest, profits, and rent. About one-quarter of domestic factor income in Canada goes to factors of production other than labour. This chapter is about the income earned by other factors, that is, the income earned by capital and the income earned by land.

The Rate of Interest and Normal Profit

First, in discussing interest rates, we see how they are determined by supply and demand in the market for loanable funds. The demand for loanable funds – the marginal efficiency of investment curve (MEI) – reflects the potential investment projects that can be undertaken in descending order of profitability. Investment will occur up to the point where the rate of return on investment is just equal to the interest rate on the funds used to finance investment – the firm's cost of capital. As the interest rate falls, investment will rise – the demand curve for loanable funds therefore slopes downwards. The supply of loanable funds – the supply curve for savings – reflects individuals' choices between present and future consumption. As interest rates rise, future consumption becomes relatively cheap – a given amount of savings buys a larger amount of future consumption. Equivalently, as the interest rate rises, the opportunity cost of present consumption rises also. The supply curve for loanable funds therefore slopes upwards. The equilibrium rate of interest is found where demand and supply intersect. (In the textbook, this simple analysis is extended to show the efficiency and equity effects when the government intervenes to impose a ceiling on interest rates.)

Now, consider the income earned by physical capital such as plant and machinery. This income goes as:

a. interest to those who have made loans to business to buy plant and equipment – that is, to those who have provided **debt capital** to business;

b. profit to those who have provided funds to business to buy plant and equipment by buying shares (stock) in that business – that is, to those who have provided **equity capital** to business.

In practice, there is not one rate of interest, but many, because of differences in risk. The greater the risk that a borrower will be unable to repay a loan, the higher the rate of interest that this particular borrower will have to pay. Interest rates are also influenced by a number of other factors, such as the expectation of inflation and the length of term of the loan. In addition, the expectation of a change in future interest rates will affect today's interest rates.

An important policy question studied in this section is: What happens if the government imposes an interest-rate ceiling? If the market for loanable funds is perfectly competitive, there are likely to be four main effects of such a policy: (1) The public saves less because the interest reward for savings has been reduced. Consequently, fewer loans are made and there is less investment. (2) Because investment is reduced, there is an efficiency loss, shown by the familiar triangle in Figure 17-6. (3) There is likely to be an additional efficiency loss, because investment funds must be rationed, and the borrowers who do succeed in acquiring the limited funds may not be those with the most profitable investment projects. (4) Income is transferred from lenders to those borrowers who are still able to acquire loans. (They now pay a lower interest rate.)

However, it is a fallacy to suppose that interest-rate ceilings necessarily help the poor. The people who benefit are the borrowers who get the limited funds at a bargain price. But these borrowers may be quite rich, while those who don't get funds may be poor.

Normal profits are earned by owners of equity capital. Normal profit is defined as the return that could be earned in an alternative investment – in this case, the interest the owner could have earned lending these funds out instead.

Factor Prices and the Allocation of Scarce Resources

In a free market, the wage rate screens labour into its most productive use. (Employers with less productive jobs don't hire labour because they can't afford to pay the market wage.) Similarly, a free market screens investment funds provided by savers into the most productive investments, i.e., those with the highest MEI. (Businesses that want to invest in less productive projects can't do so, because they can't afford to pay the market interest rate.) In either case, the market price is a rationing device which ensures that the most productive activities will be undertaken.

Human Capital

Capital income is earned not only from investment in physical capital, but also from investment in **human capital** in the form of education and training. One form of human capital is a university or college education; another is apprenticeship, or on-the-job training. In this regard, an important issue is the divergence between the private and social returns to education.

There are two reasons investment in human capital may be less than the efficient amount:

1. Employers are sometimes reluctant to provide on-the-job training because trainees may quit and take their skills elsewhere.

2. There are often external benefits from education. For example, when a highly educated scientist discovers a cure for a disease, it benefits the entire population. Because such external benefits are not taken into account by those making the decision to invest in education, investment in human capital may fall short of the efficient level. This underinvestment in human capital provides a justification for government subsidies to education.

In practice, estimating the returns to a university education is very difficult for a number of reasons. For example, people with high incomes tend to have a lot of both education and talent. It's hard to sort out how much of their higher income is due to each.

Further complications arise if we wish to calculate the social return to education. For example, it is difficult to measure the external benefits of education. (How do you measure the benefits to society when a highly educated scientist discovers a new strain of wheat?)

Rent

Finally, this chapter analyses the concept of (economic) rent – the return to a factor of production above its opportunity cost (that is, above the income it could earn in an alternative activity). Rent is earned not only by land, but also by any other highly productive factor. Examples include the rent earned by highly skilled baseball players or business executives. The textbook gives five examples of economic rent:

a. The return to agricultural land because of differences in quality.
b. The return to urban land because of differences in location.
c. The return to mineral deposits because of differences in quality.
d. Above-normal profits earned in an industry with barriers to entry.
e. The income (above opportunity cost) of an individual with a valuable talent or skill. (See Figure 17-9 and Box 17-2.)

It is important to understand how rents are capitalized in the value of land. Suppose you own two plots of farm land, and one (A) earns more income – and therefore more rent – than the other (B). A will clearly be worth more; you can sell it for a higher price. But how high will its price go? The answer: it will rise until the rent it earns is about the same percentage return that you can earn elsewhere. For example, if you can rent it out for $200 a hectare and the interest rate you can earn by lending out your money instead is 10%, then you will be willing to sell it (and someone else will be willing to buy it) if its price rises to $2,000. Thus, rents on land (or on other things such as the right to produce agricultural commodities whose prices are regulated by marketing boards) determine the values of land, production quotas, and so on.

IMPORTANT TERMS

1. Debt capital.
2. Equity capital
3. Physical capital
4. Human capital
5. Marginal efficiency of investment
6. Opportunity cost of present consumption
7. Supply curve for savings
11. Economic rent
12. Capitalization

TRUE-FALSE

T F 1. Interest income is earned by those who provide equity capital.

T F 2. The marginal efficiency of investment curve measures the nation's stock of physical capital.

T F 3. An interest-rate ceiling benefits all those who wish to borrow.

T F 4. A substantial increase in the price of a factor of production will typically induce a firm to change the combination of factors it is using.

T F 5. If a ceiling is imposed on the price of any good or service, then any necessary rationing of this good or service is likely to lead to an efficiency loss.

T F 6. Factor prices act as a screening device to help allocate factors of production.

T F 7. Human capital is like physical capital in so far as it represents an expenditure today that is expected to pay off in the future.

T F 8. The costs of a university education include more than living, tuition, and book costs.

T F 9. The private rate of return to a university education is not necessarily the same as the social rate of return.

T F 10. Very little of the income of hockey star Mario Lemieux is rent.

MULTIPLE CHOICE

1. What is the annual rate of return on a machine that costs $10,000 and generates enough sales over its 1-year lifetime to cover labour, materials, and other costs, plus $12,000?
   a. 120%
   b. 20%
   c. 12%
   d. 10%
   e. 2%

2. The demand curve for loans reflects
   a. the marginal revenue product of labour
   b. the marginal efficiency of investment
   c. either a. or b. depending on whether the good being produced is labour or capital intensive
   d. the time preference of savers
   e. none of the above

3. Savers in our society receive an interest return because of their decision to
   a. buy domestic rather than imported goods
   b. speed up import purchases
   c. delay consumption
   d. speed up consumption
   e. deposit money in a bank savings account rather than to buy government bonds

4. An interest-rate ceiling helps all
   a. the rich who want to lend
   b. the poor who want to lend
   c. the poor who want to borrow
   d. borrowers
   e. those borrowers who can still obtain funds

5. Which of the following is the most likely result of an interest-rate ceiling in a perfectly competitive market for loanable funds?
   a. a transfer of income from poor borrowers to some lenders
   b. a transfer of income from all borrowers to some lenders
   c. a transfer of income from rich to poor
   d. a transfer of income from lenders to some borrowers
   e. a reduction in the amount of credit rationing

6. An interest-rate ceiling
   a. redistributes income, but has no effect on efficiency
   b. leads to an efficiency gain that is likely to be underestimated by the usual triangular measurement
   c. leads to an efficiency gain that is likely to be overestimated by the usual triangular measurement
   d. leads to an efficiency loss that is likely to be overestimated by the usual triangular measurement
   e. leads to an efficiency loss that is likely to be underestimated by the usual triangular measurement

7. A company in a shaky financial position pays
   a. a higher interest rate on its borrowing than it would if it were financially sound
   b. a lower interest rate on its borrowing than it would if it were financially sound
   c. the same interest rate on its borrowing as it would if it were financially sound
   d. a higher or lower rate, depending upon the rate of inflation
   e. a lower rate because of the expectation of inflation

8. Since the interest rate is greater than zero, we know that
   a. present goods are worth more than future goods. The reason is that a given amount of present goods can be transformed into more future goods.
   b. present goods are worth less than future goods. The reason is that a given amount of present goods can be transformed into more future goods.
   c. present goods and future goods have an equal value if interest rates are rising
   d. present goods and future goods always have an equal value
   e. nothing can be said about the relative value of present and future goods

9. A rightward shift in the marginal efficiency of investment is likely to
   a. decrease the rate of interest and decrease the amount of funds loaned
   b. decrease the rate of interest and increase the amount of funds loaned
   c. increase the rate of interest and increase the amount of funds loaned
   d. increase the rate of interest and decrease the amount of funds loaned
   e. increase the rate of interest and leave unchanged the amount of funds loaned

10. An increase by the public in its valuation of current (compared to future) consumption will
    a. decrease the rate of interest and decrease the amount of funds loaned
    b. decrease the rate of interest and increase the amount of funds loaned
    c. increase the rate of interest and increase the amount of funds loaned
    d. increase the rate of interest and decrease the amount of funds loaned
    e. increase the rate of interest and leave unchanged the amount of funds loaned

11. An increase in wages will induce a firm to
    a. hire more labour
    b. lower its prices
    c. use more labour-saving techniques
    d. use fewer labour-saving techniques
    e. produce more output

12. Minimum wage laws
    a. discourage on-the-job training of apprentices
    b. encourage on-the-job training of apprentices
    c. increase allocative efficiency
    d. transfer income from workers who still have jobs to other factors of production
    e. transfer income from workers who lose their jobs to other factors of production

13. An upward-sloping supply curve for loanable funds reflects
    a. the choice by individuals to reduce present consumption when the interest rate rises
    b. the choice by individuals to increase present consumption when the interest rate rises
    c. the choice by individuals to increase future consumption when the interest rate falls
    d. the choice by individuals to reduce future consumption when the interest rate rises
    e. none of the above

14. In unrestricted, perfectly competitive capital markets, the interest rate is a price that allocates funds
    a. to rich capitalists, at the expense of labour
    b. to the most productive set of investment projects
    c. to the set of investment projects which bankers decide are the least risky
    d. to the rich at the expense of the poor
    e. none of the above

15. A high-school education can be viewed as
    a. a bad investment, because it yields a lower return than a university education
    b. a bad investment, even though it yields a higher return than a university education
    c. a bad investment, because it yields a lower return than physical capital
    d. a good investment, even though it yields the same return as a university education
    e. a good investment, because it yields a higher return than physical capital

16. To estimate the social return to investment in higher education, the private rate of return should be
    a. adjusted downward to take account of government subsidies to higher education
    b. adjusted upward to take account of government subsidies to higher education
    c. adjusted downward to take account of the external benefits of education
    d. a. and c.
    e. left unadjusted in any of these ways

17. In explaining why the private and social returns to a post-secondary education differ, we must take into account
    a. the external benefits of a post-secondary education, but not its subsidization by the government
    b. its subsidization, but not its external benefits
    c. both its subsidization and its external benefits
    d. both, but only if they are roughly equal
    e. neither

18. Land may earn rent because it is
    a. productive in growing crops
    b. attractively located for business development
    c. the site of mineral resources
    d. the site of oil deposits
    e. any of the above

19. If the quantity of wheat that can be produced on a hectare of land doubles, while the quantity and cost of inputs remain constant, then the rent per hectare
    a. increases by 50%
    b. almost doubles
    c. doubles
    d. more than doubles
    e. none of the above

20. The income of the typical physician includes
    a. rent on innate talents
    b. a return to human capital accumulated in medical school
    c. a return to human capital accumulated as an intern
    d. none of the above
    e. all of the above, except d.

EXERCISES

1a. Figure 17.1 shows a perfectly competitive market for loanable funds. The equilibrium rate of interest in this market is _____ and the equilibrium quantity of loans is _____. In a competitive equilibrium the interest income received by lenders would equal _____.

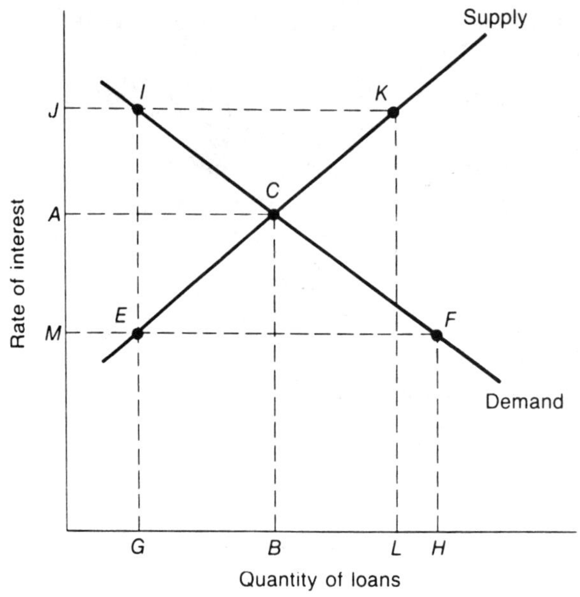

Figure 17.1

1b. If the government imposes an interest-rate ceiling at M, then the quantity of loans will be _____, the MEI will be _____, the excess demand for loans will be _____, the interest income received by lenders will be _____, and the size of the efficiency loss will probably be (more, less) than the area _____.

1c. If the interest ceiling is set at *J*, then the size of the efficiency loss will be _____.

2a. Figure 17.2 shows a perfectly competitive market for a factor of production, where D is the demand curve and S_1 is the supply curve. In a competitive equilibrium, the factor price would be _____ and the quantity of employment of the factor would be _____. The income received by the owners of this factor would equal _____ and the income received by the owners of all other factors would equal _____.

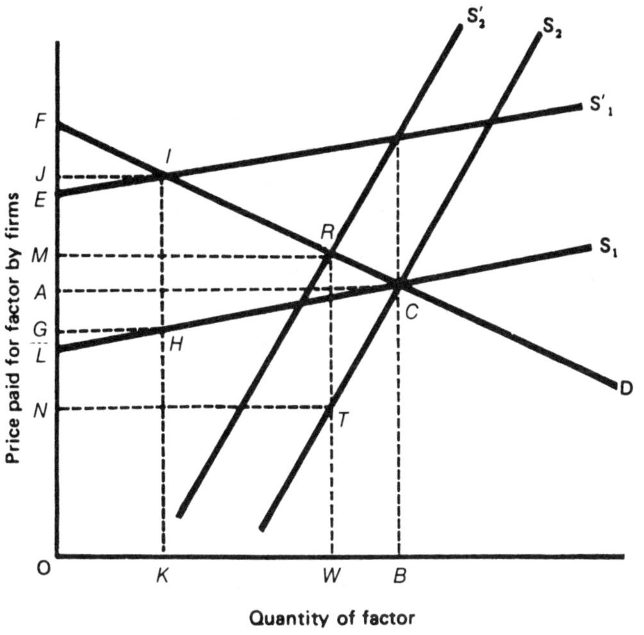

Figure 17.2

2b. Now suppose that a tax is imposed on the owners of this factor, equal in amount to *LE* per unit of the factor that they are supplying. This would shift the supply curve up vertically by the amount *LE*, so that the after-tax supply curve is the one labelled S_1. With the tax, the after-tax equilibrium price paid by firms for the factor will equal _____, the equilibrium price received by the owners of the factor will equal _____, the after-tax income accruing to owners of the factor will be _____, the amount of the tax collected will be _____, the income received by other factors will be _____, and the size of the efficiency loss will be _____.

2c. Now suppose that there is no tax; instead, suppose that supply shifts from S_1 to S_2. S_2 is (more, less) elastic than S_1. With supply curve S_2 the equilibrium factor price will be (no different, more, less) than with S_1, and the equilibrium quantity of employment of the factor will be (no different, more, less) than with S_1.

2d. With S_2 the same tax *LE* will shift the supply curve up to S_2'. With the tax, the equilibrium price paid by the firms for the factor will be _____, the after-tax equilibrium price received by owners of the factor will equal _____, the quantity of employment of the factor will equal _____, the after-tax income accruing to owners of the factor will equal _____, the amount of the tax collected will equal

_____, the income received by other factors will equal _____, and the size of the efficiency loss will equal _____.

2e. To sum up: If we consider the effects of a tax in the face of these two pre-tax supply curves S_1 and S_2, the one generating the greater tax revenue is (S_1, S_2); the one that produces the smaller efficiency loss from the tax is (S_1, S_2); the one generating the smaller reduction in employment is (S_1, S_2); the one generating the least reduction in the factor's after-tax income is (S_1, S_2), and the one reducing other incomes the least is (S_1, S_2).

ESSAY QUESTIONS

1. The discoverers of insulin, Banting and Best, did not become millionaires as a result of their discovery, despite the fact that it has probably saved millions of human lives. Explain what this means if we wish to compare the private and social rates of return to human capital.

2. Name several influences that affect the position of the MEI schedule, explaining in each case how the schedule is affected, and in what direction, by an increase in that influence.

3. Show how the income of a surgeon can be viewed as partly a wage, partly a return to human capital, and partly a rent. Which of these components would be increased by the surgeon's success in developing a more advanced surgical technique? By the surgeon's special recognition by the Royal College of Surgeons? How would the rent component be affected if licensing requirements were relaxed to permit more people to practise surgery? Explain.

4. As the interest rate rises, the price of bonds falls. Bearing this in mind, show how an increase in the rate of interest affects potential lenders differently from those who have already lent money by purchasing bonds. Show also how it affects potential borrowers differently from those who have already borrowed money by selling bonds.

5. Suppose that a factor had a totally inelastic supply. What would its opportunity cost be to society? Would it be accurate to classify all its income as rent?

6. Why is it difficult to measure the social rate of return on investment in human capital?

7. Decompose the effects on present and future consumption of an increase in the interest rate into an income effect and a substitution effect. Is it possible that the supply curve for loanable funds may be other than upward sloping?

ANSWERS

True-False: **1**F, **2**F, **3**F, **4**T, **5**T, **6**T, **7**T, **8**T, **9**T, **10**F

Multiple Choice: **1**b, **2**b, **3**c, **4**e, **5**d, **6**e, **7**a, **8**a, **9**c, **10**d, **11**c, **12**a, **13**a, **14**b, **15**e, **16**a, **17**c, **18**e, **19**d, **20**e

Exercises: **1a**. *A*, *B*, 0*ACB*

1b. *G*, *J* (or *GI*), *EF* (or *GH*), 0*MEG*, more, *ICE*

1c. zero because the ceiling is ineffective

2a. *A*, *B*, 0*ACB*, *AFC*

2b. *J*, *G*, 0*GHK*, *JIHG*, *FIJ*, *ICH*

2c. less, no different, no different

2d. *M*, *N*, *W*, 0*NTW*, *NMRT*, *MFR*, *RCT*

2e. S_2, S_2, S_2, S_2, S_2

ANSWERS TO PROBLEMS FROM THE TEXT

17-1. (a) An increase (decrease) in the interest rate will result in the rate of return on some investment projects falling below (rising above) the opportunity cost of the funds used to finance them. Accordingly, fewer (more) investment projects will be undertaken.

(b) The interest-rate ceiling has the effect of reducing the quantity supplied of loanable funds and increasing quantity demanded relative to the equilibrium – that is, there is an excess demand for loanable funds at i_2. At i_2, investors will seek to undertake projects such as *h* which would otherwise not have shown a potential profit. It's then a question of which projects are able to secure funding, and these may as easily be projects such as *h* assuming that banks do not discriminate among borrowers on the basis of the potential profitability of a project (i.e., they simply care that the borrowed funds are secure). The additional efficiency loss is, therefore, the forgone net return from potentially more profitable projects such as *j*.

(c) Similarly, rent controls result in an efficiency loss because MB > MC at the controlled price. With rationing error, this "loss" is increased since rental accommodation will not be allocated in accordance with willingness to pay; those who fail to get accommodation may, in fact, have a higher willingness to pay than those who do. The point is that, in order to maximize net benefits, supply should be allocated to those with the greatest willingness to pay – interference with the market mechanism, such as price controls, prevents the price system from ensuring this outcome.

17-2. Define the productivity of land as the value of the corn it can produce, minus the cost of shipping it to market. Then, the ring of farms surrounding Toronto has higher productivity (just like the higher productivity of land A in Figure 17-12 in the textbook). The ring of farms beyond the innermost ring has lower productivity, because of the greater transport cost involved in shipping corn to market. And so on.

17-3. A firm may pay high salaries to such individuals in order to acquire their human capital (experience in marketing, management, design, etc.). It may also wish to acquire their knowledge of the products and processes the competing firm is now using and developing, and of what that firm plans for the future.

17-4. Suppose interest rates are expected to fall next year because of a decrease in the demand for loans (a leftward shift in the MEI curve in Figure 17-5 in the textbook). In this case, lenders will increase their purchases of long-term bonds , to lock in the interest rate before it falls. Thus, the price of long-term bonds rises – that is, the interest rate today on long-term bonds falls.

17-5. This question relates to the divergence between private and social returns to education/training contained in Box 17-2. Generally, it is assumed that this divergence will result in an underinvestment in on-the-job-training. However, minimum wage laws may be changed to reflect the low productivity associated with on-the-job-training. Similarly, provincial governments may underprovide job training services because of interprovincial spillovers. This suggests a possible role for subsidies through the federal government.

17-6. To an economist, rent is the return of a factor of production in excess of its opportunity cost. In ordinary language, rent is periodic payments for the temporary use of various assets (such as apartments, rental cars, or farmland) owned by someone other than the user.

To an economist, the earnings of individuals such as professional athletes or movie and TV actors have a large rent component, but the public does not generally consider those earnings as rent. Payment for the use of an apartment is considered by the public as being rent, though to an economist it mostly reflects the opportunity cost of the capital invested in apartment buildings. Payment for the use of farmland would be considered rent by both economists and the general public.

17-7. Licensing in the medical profession is a barrier to entry; as such, this confers monopoly power on medical associations in setting fees, etc. Monopoly rents therefore accrue to the members of the association – the doctors. The objective of licensing is, of course, to ensure control of standards in the profession.

17-8. Correct, except for the last sentence. An increase in the price of oil does increase rent on existing oil fields.

17-9. A restricted set of cab operators would, in effect, act as a quota system; those who hold the quota rights receive the rents.

CHAPTER 18

Income Inequality

LEARNING OBJECTIVES

After you have studied this chapter in the textbook and the study guide, you should be able to

- Explain the reasons some people have more income than others
- Explain how the Lorenz curve is constructed and why it provides a good picture of the nation's income distribution
- Explain why the Lorenz curve may exaggerate the degree of inequality
- Identify the government policies that have been designed, at least in part, to make incomes more equal, and specify which of these has been most successful in achieving this objective
- Explain why the direct effects of policies designed to increase equality are at least partially offset by their negative indirect effects on incentives
- Demonstrate why it cannot be claimed that a free market leads to a fair distribution of income
- Demonstrate why complete equality of income is not necessarily fair; that is, show why equality is not the same as equity (fairness)
- Explain why it is reasonable to aim for some compromise between the extremes of a free market and complete equality
- Show why a conflict often exists between equity and efficiency
- Specify at least one policy where these two are not in conflict

CHAPTER SUMMARY

In the three preceding chapters, we have described how incomes are determined in our society. For example, some people have a higher income because of some innate talent or a large investment in human capital. Others may earn rent from land they own. Our first objective in this chapter is to summarize these economic reasons for differences in incomes, and complete that list with the additional reasons – such as just plain luck – that have not been dealt with in earlier chapters because they don't yield to economic analysis.

Our second objective is to examine the Canadian income distribution that results from all these influences. How much income inequality is there? This question is answered with a Lorenz curve which gives an immediate picture of how much of the nation's income is earned by low-income Canadians, and how much by high-income Canadians. The conclusion is that a great deal of inequality exists.

The third broad question we then address is: How effective are the government's programs of taxation and expenditure that have been designed, at least in part, to reduce inequality? The answer is that government expenditures, especially transfer payments, have had considerable effect, but taxes have had surprisingly little effect in equalizing incomes.

This then provides the background for tackling one of the most difficult issues in economics – the normative question: "How unequal should incomes be?" While economists cannot answer that question in a definitive way, they can throw a great deal of light on this issue. Specifically, we show that it is difficult to argue that either (a) income equality or (b) the free-market distribution of income is fair.

Why Is There Inequality?

There are at least eight reasons as to why some people may have more income than others: (1) their greater investment in human capital, (2) some innate ability on which they earn rent, (3) greater financial wealth, either because they have inherited it or saved it, (4) greater market power due to membership in a union or possession of some other form of monopoly power, (5) a willingness to work harder or longer hours, (6) discrimination in their favour in the labour market, (7) good connections and other benefits of family background, and (8) just plain luck – being at the right place at the right time. To illustrate how costly it can be if you are in the right place at the wrong time, consider the classic complaint of the failing stock-market speculator: "I got all the decisions exactly right; it was just the timing I got wrong."

While we don't have enough information to state precisely how much income inequality is due to each of these factors, there is some evidence that human capital may be the most important: In an early U.S. study it was found that as much as 60% of income differences were due to differences in human capital.

How Much Inequality Is There in Canada?

This question is answered by the **Lorenz curve** shown in Figure 18-1 of the text. This curve shows the percentage of the nation's income received by the poorest 20% of the population; by the poorest 40%; and so on. If everyone had exactly the same income each year, then the Lorenz curve would be the 45° "**complete equality**" line shown in that diagram. In this case, the poorest 20% would get 20% of the nation's income; the poorest 40% would get 40% of the nation's income; and so on. This is not true for the Canadian Lorenz curve shown in this diagram. Its large bow indicates a substantial degree of inequality.

Actually, this overstates the case. Even if there were perfect equality, with all families receiving exactly the same lifetime pattern of income, there would still be some bow in the Lorenz curve, since it measures income in a single year. The reason is that some families would be at the height of their earning power. They would be observed with far more income in that year than younger families who would be just beginning their careers at a low income.

How Much Do Government Expenditures and Taxes Reduce Inequality?

The Lorenz curve in Figure 18-2 in the text shows that government taxes and transfers reduce inequality by some 20 to 25%. That is, the area between the complete equality line and the Lorenz curve is reduced by between one-fifth and one-quarter. This reduction has been accomplished by three broad government programs:

1. Taxation. Taxes generally reduce inequality, because most taxes fall more heavily on the rich than on the poor.

2. **Cash transfer** programs, which include not only programs such as social assistance to needy families, but also Unemployment Insurance, Old Age Security, and family allowances.

3. **Transfers** in kind, such as education, housing, and health care services that are provided by the government.

Taken together, government transfers in cash and in kind are considerably more important than taxation in reducing inequality.

While these programs have the direct effect of reducing inequality, they also have an offsetting indirect effect. They increase inequality because they reduce the incentive for the poor to find and hold jobs. Furthermore, they reduce the incentive for families at all income levels to stay married. (When a family breaks up, its income is split between two smaller families, lowering the income per family. In particular, a break-up is very likely to create a single-parent family – usually headed by a woman – with low income. Government support to one-parent families obviously helps them – but it also reduces the financial incentive to stay together.)

What is a "Fair" or "Equitable" Distribution of Income?

This question cannot be answered with complete certainty, because it is a normative question of "what ought to be," rather than a positive question of "what is." Nevertheless, most people would agree on two points:

1. The outcome of the free market has no special claim to being fair. One reason is that there is no way of justifying huge profits to those who can exercise market power and raise price because they operate in markets that are not perfectly competitive. But there are problems that go deeper than this. Even if markets were perfectly competitive, it would be difficult to argue that their outcome would necessarily be fair. The example in the text is of the individual who makes no effort or contribution to the nation's output, yet who receives a very high income because he owns inherited agricultural land. The only claim for perfect competition – and it's an important one – is that, in the absence of externalities, it provides an outcome that is efficient. But no claim can be made that this outcome is necessarily fair.

2. At the other extreme, complete equality of income would not be fair either, because some people work harder and longer than others, and some people have more dangerous jobs than others. Most would agree that it is fair for such people to have a higher income. After reading this section, it is essential that you be able to explain why equality and equity are not the same. Equality means "being equal" while equity means "being fair."

With these two extremes – the free market's distribution of income and a completely equal distribution of income – being judged unacceptable, what is a reasonable compromise? Here are two of the guidelines suggested in the text:

1. Set **equality of opportunity** as our objective rather than equality of reward. View life as a race that should be fair, with all participants starting out together although, of course, not finishing that way. No cheating should be allowed: High incomes acquired by dishonest means should not be tolerated. There should be no handicaps; for example, no one should be denied the opportunity of an education because of discrimination. But this doesn't mean that everyone should be awarded a university degree – that should depend on what people are willing and able to do with their equal opportunity.

2. We should modify the rewards of the race. Some must finish last, but they should not be left in an impoverished state.

The Conflict Between Equity and Efficiency

Perhaps the most important concept in this chapter is this: In striving for equity, it must never be forgotten that there is typically (though not always) a conflict between equity and efficiency. To take the extreme case: If everyone were guaranteed an equal income, who would want to fight fires or work the long hours of the computer engineer? Equalizing the nation's income pie would reduce the size of that pie.

The Rawlsian Solution

The ideas of Professor John Rawls discussed in Box 18-1 of the text are of considerable interest because for some time many people thought he had the solution to the problem of what the nation's income distribution should be. Rawls suggests that we imagine everyone to be in an "original position," in which no one knows what his or her particular income will be. Then ask what kind of income distribution reasonable people would choose from behind this "veil of ignorance." They would be choosing a distribution of income – that is, an "income ladder" – without knowing on which of the rungs they themselves would be located.

Rawls argues that in these circumstances, everyone would agree to his "difference principle": There should be complete equality in the distribution of income, unless there is an unequal distribution that leaves everyone better off. But he arrives at this conclusion by supposing that all the people who make this decision would figure that with their luck, no matter what "income ladder" they may choose, they would end up on the lowest rung; so, they would choose an income distribution in which the lowest rung is as high as possible. In other words, they would chose the income distribution with the largest minimum income. This is the **maximin criterion.**

In this box, we give examples to show that Rawls' theory only applies to people who won't take a risk under any circumstances. Therefore, it just doesn't apply to average Canadians – let alone those who visit Las Vegas in search of risk. Thus, Rawls did not answer the question of what our income distribution should be. To this question, there may never be a clear answer.

IMPORTANT TERMS

1. Lorenz curve
2. Complete equality line
3. Transfers in kind
4. Maximin criterion
5. Cash transfers
6. Equity
7. Equality of opportunity

TRUE-FALSE

T F 1. Transfers-in-kind are those transfers that do not affect the distribution of real income.

T F 2. Government expenditures are more effective than taxes in reducing inequality.

T F 3. If government tax and transfer programs were to redistribute a large amount of a nation's income, part of a country's Lorenz curve might end up above the 45° line.

T F 4. Between 1951 and 1981, the income after taxes and transfers of the poorest 20% of Canada's population grew at least as fast as that of the rest of the population.

T F 5. If income is defined broadly to include both money and leisure, then fairness requires that those who take a lot of their income in one form (leisure) should get less in the other form (money).

T F 6. The only reason that complete equality is rejected as a target is that this division of the nation's income pie would shrink its overall size.

T F 7. Equity is a normative, rather than a positive issue.

T F 8. Scientific evidence indicates that complete equality is the only fair way of distributing the nation's income.

T F 9. The provable virtues of a free, perfectly competitive market have to do with its equity – not its efficiency.

T F 10. Equity requires that everyone be paid the same income.

T F 11. It is possible to have an absolutely fair competition, but a bad system of rewards.

MULTIPLE CHOICE

1. In about 1984, what proportion of the nation's net wealth (that is, taking into account a family's debts as well as its assets) was held by the least wealthy 25% of the population?
   a. 15%
   b. 12%
   c. 5%
   d. 3%
   e. essentially none at all; their average net wealth was about zero

2. In about 1984 how much of the nation's wealth was held by the richest 5% of the population?
   a. 8%
   b. 18%
   c. 28%
   d. 38%
   e. 58%

3. Early research on inequality in the United States tended to indicate that, in determining differences in income
   a. the least important influence is wealth
   b. the least important influence is family background
   c. the most important influence is human capital
   d. the least important influence is luck
   e. the least important influence is human capital

4. The Lorenz curve measures how close the nation's actual income distribution is to
   a. a fair distribution
   b. an equal distribution
   c. the distribution in the previous year
   d. the distribution that would exist if all markets were perfectly competitive
   e. the distribution that would exist if no markets were perfectly competitive

5. The greater the degree of income inequality
   a. the smaller the bow in the Lorenz curve (i.e., the closer the Lorenz curve is to the 45° line)
   b. the larger the bow in the Lorenz curve
   c. the steeper the initial slope of the Lorenz curve
   d. the higher the point the Lorenz curve eventually reaches
   e. none of the above

6. In 1990, what percentage of the total Canadian income (before taxes and transfers) was earned by the lowest-income 40% of Canadian families?
   a. less than 2%
   b. about 4%
   c. about 8%
   d. about 14%
   e. about 31%

7. Because all government taxes taken together are
   a. highly progressive, they are more effective than government expenditures in making incomes more equal
   b. highly progressive, they are less effective than government expenditures in making incomes more equal
   c. not highly progressive, they are less effective than government expenditures in making incomes more equal
   d. not highly progressive, they are more effective than government expenditures in making incomes more equal
   e. regressive, they are more effective than government expenditures in making incomes more equal

8. Putting an end to racial discrimination is likely to
   a. increase the bow in the Lorenz curve
   b. decrease the bow in the Lorenz curve
   c. change the Lorenz curve so that its bow is above rather than below the 45° line
   d. make the Lorenz curve start from a different initial point
   e. make the Lorenz curve end at a different point

9. If some individuals acquire more and more human capital, while others do not, then this is likely to
   a. increase the bow in the Lorenz curve
   b. decrease the bow in the Lorenz curve
   c. change the Lorenz curve so that its bow is above, rather than below, the 45° line
   d. make the Lorenz curve start from a different initial point
   e. make the Lorenz curve end at a different point

10. If we were to pursue only the goal of equity, we would find that our policies would
    a. always reduce efficiency
    b. often reduce efficiency
    c. always increase efficiency
    d. expand the size of the total income pie
    e. leave the size of the total income pie unchanged

11. It is difficult to argue that the free market would do a completely equitable job of distributing income because
    a. the free market is often not perfectly competitive; some people raise their income through the exercise of market power
    b. even if the free market were perfectly competitive, it would still often provide luxuries for the wealthy, without providing adequate necessities for the poor
    c. the free market is efficient
    d. a. and b.
    e. none of the above

12. The most difficult concept for economists to pin down is
    a. efficiency gain
    b. efficiency loss
    c. equity
    d. equality
    e. inequality

13. A policy of trying to equalize incomes completely has been criticized because it would
    a. be inefficient
    b. be unfair, because it would give people who work hard the same reward as those who do not
    c. require a change in our present system of inheritance
    d. shrink the total income pie
    e. all of the above

14. The major virtue of a perfectly competitive free market is its
    a. efficiency when there are no externalities
    b. efficiency when externalities do exist
    c. equity
    d. tendency to ensure equality of income
    e. tendency to ensure equality of wealth

15. A criticism of Rawls' theory is that it:
    a. is based on an unrealistic assumption about how people view risk
    b. concentrates only on the individual (or group) that is lowest on the income scale
    c. doesn't take into account those who are near to, but are not at, the bottom of the income scale
    d. is based on the maximin principle
    e. all of the above

16. John Rawls argues that income should be divided equally
    a. in all circumstances
    b. in no circumstances
    c. unless an unequal distribution benefits the majority
    d. unless an unequal distribution benefits at least a large minority
    e. unless an unequal distribution benefits everyone

17. According to Rawls' maximin criterion, which of the following income distributions is best?
    a. everyone gets $3,000 per year
    b. everyone gets $5,000 per year except for one person who gets $3,100
    c. half the people get $10,000 per year and the other half get $1,000
    d. everyone gets $20,000 per year except for one person who gets $2,900
    e. everyone gets $40,000 per year except for one person who gets $3,000

18. Which of the following is not an example of a transfer in kind?
    a. subsidized housing
    b. provincial health insurance
    c. government job-training programs
    d. Old Age Security
    e. free primary education

19. In the mid-1980s, taxes and transfer payments eliminated approximately what percentage of income inequality?
    a. 20 to 25%
    b. 30 to 35%
    c. 40 to 45%
    d. about half
    e. about 75%

20. The share of total income, before taxes and transfers, going to the richest 20% of Canadian families in 1990 was
    a. 20 to 25%
    b. 30 to 35%
    c. 40 to 45%
    d. about half
    e. about 75%

21. According to 1990 data, the share of total income (before taxes and transfers) going to the richest 20% of Canadian families was about how many times larger than the share going to the poorest 20% of families (that is, average family income among the richest 20% was about how many times larger than the average income among the poorest 20%)?
    a. about 3 times
    b. about 5 times
    c. about 8 times
    d. a little less than 10 times
    e. about 15 times

EXERCISES

1. Table 18.1 below gives the income distribution of a hypothetical economy, as in panel (a) of Table 18-1 in the textbook. In Table 18.2 below, fill in the cumulative income distribution in the last row.

Table 18.1

	Lowest 20%	Second 20%	Third 20%	Fourth 20%	Highest 20%
Percent of income	4	6	10	20	60

Table 18.2

	Lowest 20%	Lowest 40%	Lowest 60%	Lowest 80%	Total
Percent of income					

Plot this as a Lorenz curve in Figure 18.1 below, and label it L_1.

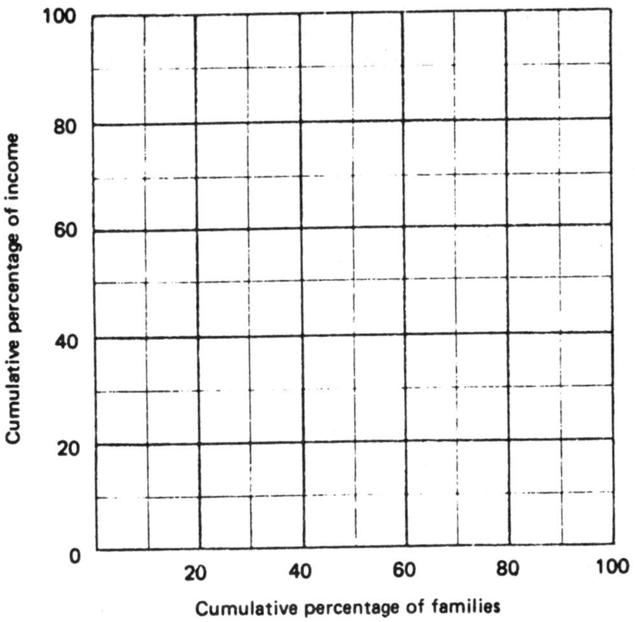

Figure 18.1

Suppose that the government then taxes away half the income of every family in the top 20% of the income distribution and gives it in equal amounts to every family in the lowest 60% of the distribution. Fill in the resulting income distribution in Table 18.3 and the resulting cumulative income distribution in Table 18.4.

Table 18.3

	Lowest 20%	Second 20%	Third 20%	Fourth 20%	Highest 20%
Percent of income					

Table 18.4

	Lowest 20%	Lowest 40%	Lowest 60%	Lowest 80%	Total
Percent of income					

Plot the Lorenz curve for income after taxes and transfers in Figure 18.1 and label it L_2. Note how important taxes and expenditures can be in reducing inequality, at least in theory.

2. Consider the five following ways of distributing income among five families in an economy:

   a. Four families receive $1,000 per year each, and the fifth family receives $600 per year.
   b. Four families receive $501 per year each, and the fifth receives $3,000 per year.
   c. Each family receives $500 per year.
   d. Four families receive $1,100 per year each, and the fifth family receives $5,600.
   e. Four families receive $5,000 per year each, and the fifth receives nothing.

   Fill in Table 18.5, giving the total national income according to each distribution.

Table 18.5

Distribution	Total national income
A	
B	
C	
D	
E	

Fill in Table 18.6 for each of the distributions, showing the cumulative percentages.

Table 18.6 (percent of income)

Distribution	Lowest 20%	Lowest 40%	Lowest 60%	Lowest 80%	Total
A					
B					
C					
D					
E					

Draw and label the Lorenz curve for each of these distributions in Figure 18.2.

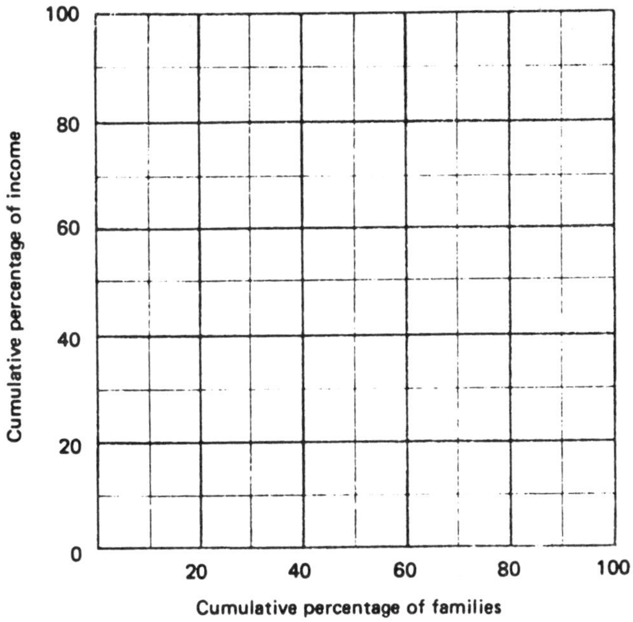

Figure 18.2

Indicate in Table 18.7 below the way that these distributions would be ranked according to Rawls' maximin criterion.

Table 18.7

Rank	Distribution
Best	
Second best	
Third best	
Fourth best	
Fifth best	

According to Rawls' ranking, does the best distribution have the largest total income? Does it have the least inequality as measured by the Lorenz curve?

The reason that egalitarians – that is, those who believe in equal incomes – were disillusioned by Rawls is illustrated in Figure 18.2, where we see that Rawls (does, does not) recommend the "complete-equality" distribution _____. Instead, he recommends distribution _____, which is one of the (most, least) equal of the distributions.

ESSAY QUESTIONS

1. "With a problem as perplexing as determining the best income distribution for the nation, the best approach is a simple one that strikes right to the heart of the matter: Make all incomes equal. This is philosophically and morally the fair and just solution." Do you agree? Explain your position.

2. In your view, is it possible for an unequal income distribution to be equitable? Use examples to support your position.

3. Is it fair for Steffi Graf to earn such a high income from doing something – playing tennis – that many others in the world enjoy?

4. In what way do you think the shape of the Lorenz curve would be affected by:
   (a) an end to racial discrimination
   (b) some individuals acquiring more and more human capital, while others do not
   (c) unemployment insurance
   (d) a highly progressive tax
   (e) a special new tax on wage income
   (f) a special new tax on incomes over $100,000

5. Marxists believe in the principle, "to each according to his needs, from each according to his abilities." Do you agree or disagree? Why or why not? Do you think that this principle would lead to a straight-line Lorenz curve? Why or why not? Do you think that a government that tried to put this principle into effect would run into problems?

ANSWERS

True-False: **1**F, **2**T, **3**F, **4**T, **5**T, **6**F, **7**T, **8**F, **9**F, **10**F, **11**T

Multiple Choice: **1**e, **2**d, **3**c, **4**b, **5**b, **6**d, **7**c, **8**b, **9**a, **10**b, **11**d, **12**c, **13**e, **14**a, **15**e, **16**e, **17**b, **18**d, **19**a, **20**c, **21**e

Exercises: **1**. Table 18.2: 4, 10, 20, 40, 100

Figure 18.1 completed

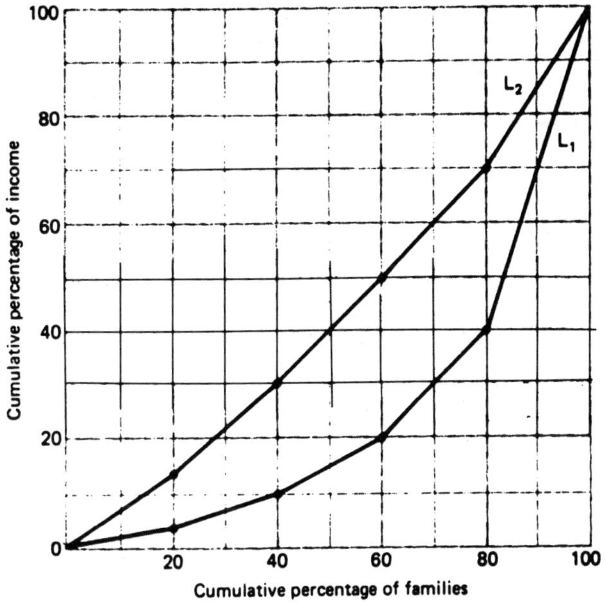

Table 18.3: 14, 16, 20, 20, 30
Table 18.4: 14, 30, 50, 70, 100

2. **Table 18.5 completed**

Distribution	Total national income
A	$ 4,600
B	$ 5,004
C	$ 2,500
D	$ 10,000
E	$ 20,000

Table 18.6 completed

Distribution	Lowest 20%	Lowest 40%	Lowest 60%	Lowest 80%	Total
A	13	35	57	78	100
B	10	20	30	40	100
C	20	40	60	80	100
D	11	22	33	44	100
E	0	25	50	75	100

Figure 18.2 completed

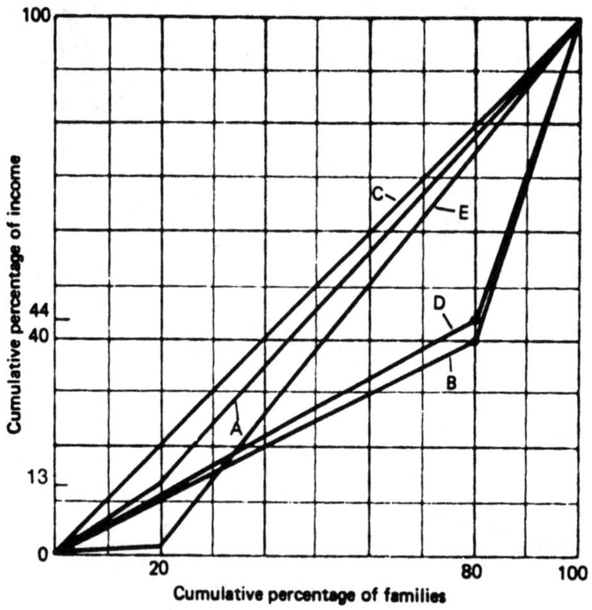

Table 18.7 completed

Rank	Distribution
Best	D
Second best	A
Third best	B
Fourth best	C
Fifth best	E

No, no, does not, C., D., least

ANSWERS TO PROBLEMS FROM THE TEXT

18-1. The one thing that is financially more rewarding than being the world's best is to have people think you are the world's best. Then they will pay a very large rent for your services (or for that matter, for your appearance at some function or on some board).

18-2. If there were no externalities, and if markets were perfectly competitive (two major assumptions), then free market prices of factors would help to maximize the total national income pie. However, while this would be efficient, there is no reason to believe that the distribution will be equitable.

18-3. This statement is basically true, and represents another view of the difficulties in Rawl's approach.

18-4. This is an excellent question for class discussion. Check with your government documents librarian to get data on provincial per capita incomes. Are different regions equally endowed with non-labour factors? Are regions comparable in terms of labour endowments? (Also, consider the implications of problem 18-5.) Discuss both regional development policies and the fiscal equalization program? Do these have different purposes?

18-5. Recall that a monopsonist will pay a wage below the competitive wage. Thus, if the labour market becomes perfectly competitive (a) the wage rate rises and (b) returns to non-labour factors of production will fall (i.e., the transfer effect).

PART FIVE

MICROECONOMIC ISSUES OF OUR TIME

CHAPTER 19

What Are the Gains from International Trade?

LEARNING OBJECTIVES

After you have studied this chapter in the textbook and the study guide, you should be able to

- Identify the three major sources of gains from international trade
- Explain why trade increases competition in the domestic Canadian market and reduces the market power of Canadian producers, thus generating an efficiency gain
- Explain why trade makes possible cost reductions because it provides opportunities to exploit economies of scale. Thus, income is increased and a wider variety of new products is available.
- Explain the difference between absolute advantage and comparative advantage
- Explain why countries export those commodities in which they have a comparative advantage, and how comparative advantage is determined by opportunity costs
- Explain the two respects in which international trade and technological change are similar, and the respects in which they are different
- Show the gains from trade in a supply/demand diagram by comparing the effect of trade on consumers with its effect on producers
- Identify the winners and losers from international trade
- Distinguish between trade in goods and trade in services
- Explain the efficiency gain from foreign investment in Canada

CHAPTER SUMMARY

Canadians in British Columbia gain from domestic trade with other Canadians in Alberta and Quebec. Similarly, Canadians gain from international trade with the Japanese and the Americans. The reasons are the same in either case. Our purpose in this chapter is to examine three broad sources of the gains from trade: (1) increased competition; (2) economies of scale; and (3) comparative advantage. This chapter also identifies the winners and losers from trade. While winners outnumber losers, and the nation as a whole benefits from trade, some Canadians are hurt. Their ability to organize themselves and apply political pressure is one of the main reasons that countries maintain restrictions on trade – restrictions that will be examined in the next chapter. Finally, this chapter introduces a particular form of trade in services (as opposed to goods), namely foreign investment in Canada.

The Sources of Gain

1. **Increased competition**. There are two important changes that face domestic producers when trade is opened up. First, they face a much larger market; they can now sell to people anywhere in the world. Second, they now face many more competitors. Canadian General Electric (CGE) no longer competes just against Electrohome and other Canadian producers; instead, it now competes with an additional group of producers from Japan, the United States, and elsewhere. Because of increased competition, oligopolists such as CGE and Electrohome lose much of their market power – their ability to influence price. Thus, they move closer to perfect competition, with the increase in efficiency that this implies. Similarly, a Canadian monopolist may, as a result of trade, find itself an oligopolist, with several foreign competitors; this industry also moves closer to perfect competition.

2. **Economies of scale**. Without international trade, each country must be self-sufficient; it must therefore produce a wide variety of products in the small quantity necessary just to satisfy its own needs. First, with trade, increased market size may make goods available that would otherwise not exist – that is, product variety may be increased. Boeing might not have been able to develop the jumbo jet if it had been able to sell it only in the U.S. market, rather than in the entire world. Second, with international trade, each country can specialize, producing only a few items in large volume and trading to get the rest. Large volume often means reduced cost; that is, there are economies of scale. And reduced cost means that we can produce and therefore consume more. In other words, our real income rises. It also rises because other countries are specializing and reducing their costs. Thus, the products we trade for, as well as the goods we produce ourselves, fall in cost.

3. **Comparative advantage**. To understand comparative advantage, you must first understand **absolute advantage**. Table 19-3 in the textbook can be used to clarify the

difference between the two. In the right-hand column of this table, we see that Canada has an absolute advantage in food because a Canadian worker can produce 3 units of food, whereas a worker in Britain can produce only 1. In other words, it only takes a third as many workers to produce food in Canada as in Britain. The input requirement – that is, the labour requirement – to produce food in Canada is lower than in Britain. (This is the definition of absolute advantage: a country has an absolute advantage in a good if the input requirement in that country is lower than that in other countries.)

Canada also has an absolute advantage in clothing. (A Canadian worker outproduces a British worker in clothing by 6 to 4, as shown in the first column of Table 19-3.) Because Canada has an absolute advantage in producing both goods, absolute advantage cannot be the key to explaining which country will produce what. If it were the key, then Canada would produce both goods, and Britain neither – and that is inconsistent with the two-way trade we observe.

What, then, does determine the pattern of production and trade? The answer is: comparative advantage. But in which product does Canada have a comparative advantage? The answer is: food, because this is where Canada's absolute advantage is greater; a worker in Canada can outproduce a worker in Britain by 3 to 1 in food, but by only 6 to 4 – that is, 3 to 2 – in clothing. Because Canada has a comparative advantage in food, Britain has a comparative advantage in clothing; that's where Britain's absolute disadvantage is least.

Using a more formal definition, we say that Canada has a comparative advantage in food if it has a lower opportunity cost of producing food than does Britain. This is, indeed, the case. In the second row of Table 19-3, we see the high opportunity cost of food in Britain. Since a worker who is now producing 1 unit of food could instead be producing 4 units of clothing, the **opportunity cost** (the alternative forgone) of producing that 1 unit of food is 4 units of clothing. Compare this to the lower opportunity cost of food in Canada, derived from the top row in this table: Since a Canadian worker who is now producing 3 units of food could instead be producing 6 units of clothing, the opportunity cost in Canada of each unit of food is 6/3 = 2 units of clothing. Because Canada has a lower opportunity cost of food than does Britain, Canada has a comparative advantage in food, and will specialize in this. Similar calculations for clothing will show that Britain has a comparative advantage here. With specialization in its products of comparative advantage, both Canada and Britain benefit, as is demonstrated in the calculations at the bottom of this table.

To sum up: Both absolute and comparative advantage refer to the cost of production. The difference is in how this cost is measured. For absolute advantage, cost is measured in terms of inputs required. For comparative advantage, cost is measured in terms of outputs forgone, that is, opportunity cost.

Here's an intuitive approach that may help you to understand better the gains from trade. Trade is the way a country can inexpensively acquire the goods in which it does not have a comparative advantage. Why produce these goods at home – where their opportunity cost is high – when they can be purchased from another country where their opportunity cost is low?

This gain from trade is further illustrated using the production possibilities curve shown in Figure 19-4 of the textbook. The gain comes when a country uses trade to move from point *B* to *D*. But you should be able to break down this move into its two components: (1) the move from *B* to *C*, as the country specializes in food, and (2) the move from *C* to *D*, as the country then trades food for clothing.

This production possibilities curve is also useful, as shown in Figure 19-5 in the textbook, when it is used to compare international trade and technological change. Both allow a country to consume a combination of goods lying beyond its current production possibilities curve. (Both may also be the source of unemployment that may have to be endured in the short run in order to realize income gains in the long run.)

The textbook also illustrates the gains from trade using familiar supply and demand diagrams. You should understand clearly why the nation gains from unrestricted exports, as shown in Figure 19-6, and unrestricted imports, as shown in Figure 19-7. We gain on the export side because we sell goods abroad for more than it costs us to produce them (or more than we lose when we switch these goods away from domestic consumption). At the same time, we gain on the import side because we can buy imports for less than it would cost us to produce them inefficiently at home; and imports also allow us to increase our consumption of bargain-priced goods from abroad. For both exports and imports there is a triangular efficiency gain shown in Figures 19-6 and 19-7. You should be able to confirm these gains in a diagram like Figure 19-8 that shows how trade affects consumers and producers. This technique then allows you to fill in the details on the second key question in this chapter.

Who Are the Winners and Losers?

Since opening our borders to an import lowers the domestic price of this good, consumers win and domestic producers lose. On the export side, there is also a conflict between these two groups – although the roles are reversed. Because opening foreign markets raises the price we can charge for our exports, producers win and consumers lose. Whenever trade policy is changed for a specific industry, a conflict between consumers and producers arises. This must be understood before turning to the contentious issues of trade policy discussed in the next chapter.

Trade in Services: Foreign Investment

A large amount of the capital being used in Canada has been provided by foreign savers (today mostly from the United States, but earlier from the United Kingdom).

The main reason Canada relies on a large amount of foreign saving is not that Canadians are less willing to save than people in other countries; instead, it is because Canada has a very large number of profitable investment opportunities in resource-based industries (like the mining industry) and elsewhere. Foreign capital in Canada includes both equity capital (mostly as a result of foreign direct investment) and debt capital (resulting from portfolio investment).

The presence of foreign capital in Canada has led to a much lower return on capital than would prevail if there were no foreign capital here. As a result, Canadian savers earn a lower rate of return on their capital than they otherwise would (and supply less saving than they otherwise would). However, the additional capital provided by foreign savers raises the value of Canadian output and leads to higher incomes to other Canadian factors of production (primarily labour). As Figure 19-11 in the textbook shows, the gain to these other factors of production (area 1) is larger than the loss to Canadian savers; hence, there is an efficiency gain (shown by areas 2 + 3 in the figure) from allowing foreign capital to come into Canada.

The efficiency gain shown in Figure 19-11 is computed on the assumption that the total return to foreign-owned capital (area 4 + 5 in the figure) is paid to the foreigners. In reality, however, part of the return represents a benefit to Canadians: that part which is paid to the government as taxes. (Foreign-owned firms pay corporate income tax at the same rate as Canadian-owned firms, and interest and dividends paid to foreigners are subject to Canadian "withholding tax.") Thus, the efficiency gain shown in Figure 19-11 may be an underestimate.

The possibility of efficiency gains provides an argument for letting foreign capital in with no restrictions. However, there are several arguments that can be used to justify some restrictions on the inflow of foreign capital. One argument noted in the text is that by limiting the amount of capital that we allow to come in, we may be able to attract it into Canada at a lower cost. (Other arguments against allowing unrestricted foreign investment in Canada – such as the possible erosion of Canada's political sovereignty or cultural identity if we get too much of it – are discussed in the appendix to Chapter 19.)

IMPORTANT TERMS

1. Economies of scale
2. Comparative advantage
3. Opportunity cost
4. Absolute advantage
5. International specialization
6. Terms of trade
7. Production gain on an export

8. Consumption gain on an import
9. Foreign direct investment
10. Cost of foreign capital

TRUE-FALSE

T F 1. Comparative advantage ensures that Canadian exports of any good will equal Canadian imports of that same good.

T F 2. International trade tends to transform a natural oligopoly into a natural monopoly.

T F 3. Although each member country in the European Community imposes tariffs in its trade with other member countries, it may trade freely with the rest of the world.

Table 19.1 Output per Worker

	Clothing	Food
in Canada	10	8
in Europe	2	4

T F 4. In Table 19.1, Europe has a comparative advantage in food.

T F 5. In Table 19.1, Europe has an absolute advantage in both goods.

T F 6. If Canada has an absolute advantage in a good, then Canada will necessarily specialize in that good.

T F 7. If Canada has a lower opportunity cost of producing good X than any other country, then Canada has a comparative advantage in X.

T F 8. While improved technology allows a country to consume more by moving to a higher production possibility curve, international trade allows a country to consume more without moving its production off its existing production possibilities curve.

T F 9. Large North American exports of grains following droughts overseas in the early 1970s benefitted North American farmers, hurt North American consumers, and resulted in an overall efficiency loss.

T F 10. If a country imports oranges, then producers of oranges in that country probably gain from international trade in oranges.

T F 11. An inflow of foreign capital into Canada is likely to harm both Canadian labour and Canadian capital owners.

MULTIPLE CHOICE

1. Manufactured goods are
   a. imported, but not exported by Canada
   b. exported, but not imported by Canada
   c. exported by Canada to Europe only
   d. imported and exported by Canada
   e. neither imported nor exported by Canada

2. Specialization and trade provide gains in
   a. domestic trade only
   b. foreign trade only
   c. domestic and foreign trade
   d. neither domestic nor foreign trade
   e. foreign trade, as long as countries do not have an absolute advantage

3. Which of the following is a possible result of international trade?
   a. a natural monopoly in the domestic market may be transformed into a natural oligopoly in the world market
   b. a perfectly competitive industry may be turned into a natural oligopoly
   c. a natural oligopoly may be turned into a natural monopoly
   d. a perfectly competitive industry may be turned into a natural monopoly
   e. large firms are able to exercise more market power because the size of the market is increased

4. International trade makes domestic firms more competitive in terms of
   a. price
   b. quality
   c. design
   d. the introduction of new products
   e. all of the above

5. International trade will lead a firm to introduce a new product if
   a. trade shifts demand to the right enough so that for the first time demand for the product overlaps its average costs
   b. trade shifts demand to the left enough so that for the first time demand for the product overlaps its average costs
   c. trade shifts demand to the left enough so that for the first time marginal cost of the product intersects its average cost
   d. trade shifts demand to the right enough so that for the first time marginal cost of the product intersects its average cost
   e. trade shifts demand to the right enough so that for the first time marginal cost of the product intersects its average variable cost

6. Under international trade we export those goods for which we have a relatively low
   a. materials cost
   b. wage cost
   c. accounting cost
   d. opportunity cost
   e. overhead cost

7. The idea of comparative advantage was developed by
   a. Adam Smith
   b. Karl Marx
   c. David Ricardo
   d. Alfred Marshall
   e. John Maynard Keynes

8. If Canada has an absolute advantage in a good, then Canada
   a. may or may not export that good
   b. will necessarily export that good
   c. will necessarily avoid exporting that good
   d. will necessarily import that good
   e. will necessarily avoid importing that good

Table 19.2 Output per Worker

	Clothing	Food
in Canada	6	3
in Europe	4	1

9. In Table 19.2, international trade would induce Canada to import
   a. food
   b. clothing
   c. both
   d. neither
   e. one or the other; we can't say which

10. In Table 19.2, Canada has an absolute advantage in
   a. both goods, and a comparative advantage in food
   b. both goods, and a comparative advantage in clothing
   c. both goods, and a comparative advantage in neither
   d. neither good, but a comparative advantage in food
   e. neither good, but a comparative advantage in clothing

11. In Table 19.2, Europe has an absolute advantage in
   a. both goods, and a comparative advantage in food
   b. both goods, and a comparative advantage in clothing
   c. both goods, and a comparative advantage in neither
   d. neither good, but a comparative advantage in food
   e. neither good, but a comparative advantage in clothing

12. In Table 19.2, Europe's opportunity cost of producing food is
   a. 3 units of clothing
   b. 6/3 = 2 units of clothing
   c. 6/4 = 3/2 units of clothing
   d. 4 units of clothing
   e. 3 units of food

13. If the lower right-hand number in Table 19.2 is changed from 1 to 2, then Canada has an absolute advantage in
   a. both goods, and a comparative advantage in food
   b. both goods, and a comparative advantage in clothing
   c. both goods, and a comparative advantage in neither
   d. neither good, but a comparative advantage in food
   e. neither good, and a comparative advantage in neither

14. A nation's real income can be increased by
    a. international trade, but not by improved technology
    b. improved technology, but not by international trade
    c. neither technology nor international trade
    d. both technology and international trade
    e. international trade, provided there is protection for competing domestic industries

15. International trade allows a nation to increase its income by
    a. reaching a point beyond its production possibilities curve (PPC)
    b. reaching a point inside its PPC
    c. reaching along its PPC to a point to the northwest and staying there
    d. reaching along its PPC to a point to the southeast and staying there
    e. staying at the same point on its PPC

16. When Canada imports a good
    a. every Canadian citizen gains
    b. Canadian producers and Canadian consumers of that good benefit
    c. Canadian producers and Canadian consumers of that good lose
    d. Canadian consumers lose, but Canadian producers gain
    e. there is an efficiency gain

17. The efficiency gain from the export of a good reflects a gain to
    a. consumers, plus a gain to producers
    b. consumers, minus a loss to producers
    c. producers, minus a loss to consumers
    d. consumers only
    e. neither

18. A sudden move to free international trade is most likely to cause short-term unemployment in which of the following industries?
    a. industries that don't export now, but could in the future
    b. industries that export only
    c. industries that export and sell domestically
    d. import-competing industries
    e. industries in which there are neither exports nor imports

19. Without trade in a world with two countries and two goods, real income will be
    a. higher in the country that has an absolute advantage in both goods
    b. lower in the country that has an absolute advantage in both goods
    c. higher in the country that has an absolute advantage in neither good
    d. higher in the country that has a comparative advantage in neither good
    e. higher in the country that has a comparative advantage in both goods

20. In a world with two countries and two goods, opening trade will
    a. benefit neither country
    b. benefit only the country with an absolute advantage in both goods
    c. benefit only the country with a comparative advantage in both goods
    d. be a way for each country to benefit
    e. benefit only the country with a comparative advantage in neither good

21. If during the last 50 years the Canadian government had been following a policy of not allowing any foreign capital into Canada, then
    a. Canadian wage rates would most likely have been higher than they currently are
    b. Canadian GDP would most likely be higher than it currently is
    c. the rate of return to capital in Canada would most likely have been higher than it currently is
    d. the amount of Canadian-owned capital used in Canada would most likely have been lower than it currently is
    e. none of the above

22. The amount of net direct foreign investment (that is, direct foreign investment in Canada less direct Canadian investment in foreign countries)
    a. was lower (as a proportion of GDP) in 1950 than during subsequent decades
    b. was negative during much of the 1970s and 1980s
    c. increases when a foreigner purchases bonds issued by Quebec Hydro
    d. has been larger than foreign portfolio investment since 1970
    e. increases whenever a foreigner buys shares in any Canadian corporation

EXERCISES

1a. Suppose that Figures 19.1 and 19.2 represent the markets for shoes in England and Spain.

Without international trade, the price in England would be _____ and the quantity produced in England would be _____. The price in Spain would be _____ and the quantity produced in Spain would be _____. With trade, price will (rise, fall) in England and (rise, fall) in Spain.

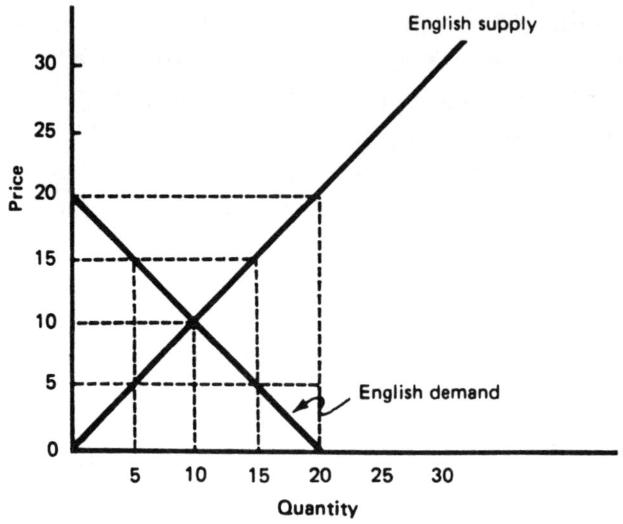

Figure 19.1

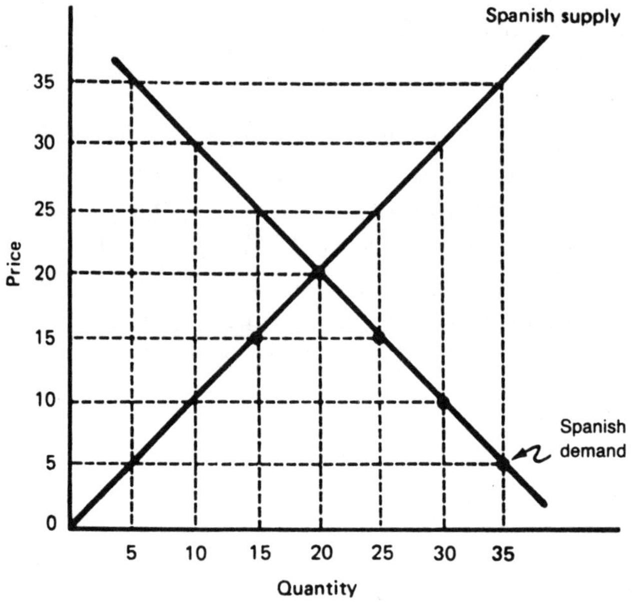

Figure 19.2

1b. With international trade the single price at which the total demand – that is, the English demand plus Spanish demand – equals the total supply is _____. At that price English demand is _____ and English supply is _____; Spanish demand is _____ and Spanish supply is _____. In this situation, (Spain, England) will export _____ units of shoes. England has a comparative (advantage, disadvantage) in shoes, as reflected by the (lower, higher) price and cost of shoes in England before trade.

2a. This exercise is designed to help you understand comparative advantage. In Table 19.3, suppose that for country A, each acre of land will produce 100 bushels of wheat or 30 bushels of corn, whereas for country B, each acre of land will produce 40 bushels of wheat or 20 bushels of corn. Suppose that each country has 4000 acres. Fill in Table 19.3, giving the production possibilities for A and B.

Table 19.3

A's Production Possibilities		B's Production Possibilities	
Thousands of bushels of wheat	Thousands of bushels of corn	Thousands of bushels of wheat	Thousands of bushels of corn
0	_______	0	_______
100	_______	40	_______
200	_______	80	_______
300	_______	120	_______
400	_______	160	_______

2b. Plot the PPCs for the two countries in Figure 19.3.

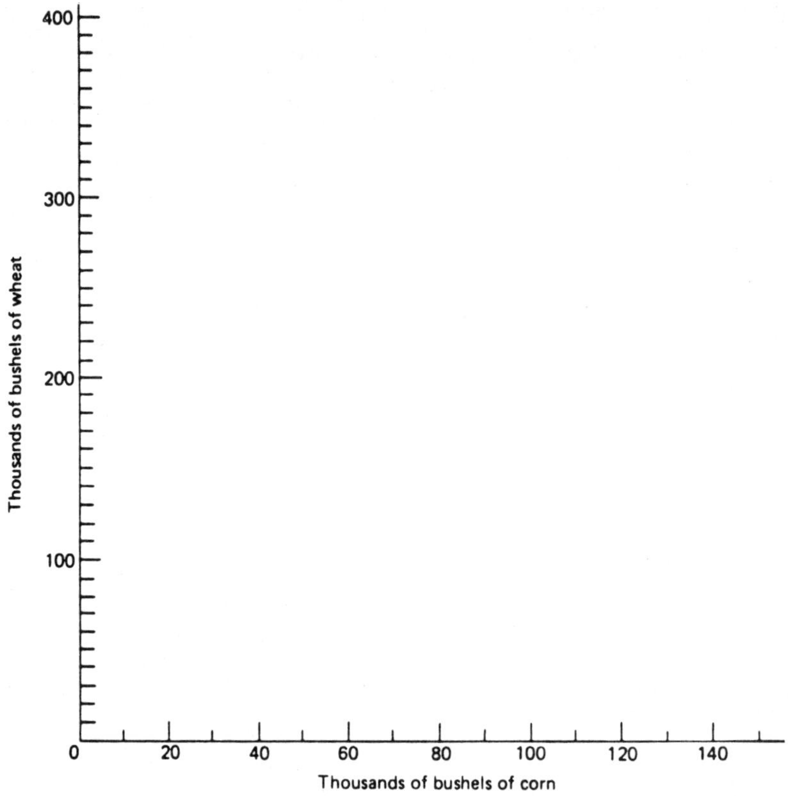

Figure 19.3

2c. Country _____ has an absolute advantage in producing corn; country _____ has an absolute advantage in producing wheat. Country _____ has a comparative advantage in producing corn; and country _____ has a comparative advantage in producing wheat. Suppose that, before trade, each country devotes half its land to each product. Then country B will produce and consume _____ thousand bushels of wheat and _____ thousand bushels of corn. Mark this on Figure 19.3. Also mark the production and consumption point for country A.

2d. Suppose that A and B were then to trade with each other at the price of 10 bushels of wheat for every 4 bushels of corn. (Note that this ratio of 10:4 is between A's pre-trade domestic exchange ratio of 100:30 = 10:3 cited at the beginning of this question, and B's ratio of 40:20 = 10:5. Therefore, it is a rate of exchange that will make trade beneficial for both countries.) Let's now see precisely why it is in B's interest to specialize in corn and purchase its wheat from A. If it does so, and devotes all its 4000 acres to corn, B will produce _____ thousand bushels of corn and _____ thousand bushels of wheat. B then keeps the original 40 thousand bushels of corn for its own consumption, and takes the additional 40 thousand it has produced and sells this for _____ thousand bushels of wheat. It is now able to consume the same 40 thousand bushels of corn as before, and 20 thousand (more, less) bushels of wheat. This 20 thousand bushels of wheat represents its (gain, loss) from specialization and trade. Graph B's specialization and trade with arrows in Figure 19.3, clearly indicating B's gains from trade.

Now plot similar arrows for A in Figure 19.3 to show how this exchange also benefits A. (Hint: A moves to the northwest along its PPC in order to produce the 100 thousand more bushels of wheat it needs to exchange with B. When it gives up this wheat to B, it acquires 40 thousand bushels of corn for it; this trade moves it back to the southeast. The question is: Does A go back to its original point or to a point superior to it and thus also acquire a gain from trade?)

Note how the trade arrows for the two countries have the same length and slope. They must; each trade arrow describes the exchange of 100 thousand bushels of wheat for 40 thousand bushels of corn. The only difference in the two arrows is the direction in which they are pointing. (They must point in opposite directions, because an export for one country is an import for the other.) Note also that gains from trade arise because the two PPCs have different slopes; therefore, it's possible to have a mutually beneficial trade arrow with a slope in between. If the two PPCs had the same slope, then opportunity costs would be the same in both countries. Consequently, neither country would have a _____ advantage, and mutually beneficial trade would (be possible, not be possible). We emphasize that we're concentrating here just on comparative advantage. Economies of scale also provide opportunities for mutually beneficial trade – but that's another story.

3a. In Figure 19.4, D is the Canadian domestic demand curve and MC is the Canadian marginal cost curve for a perfectly competitive good.

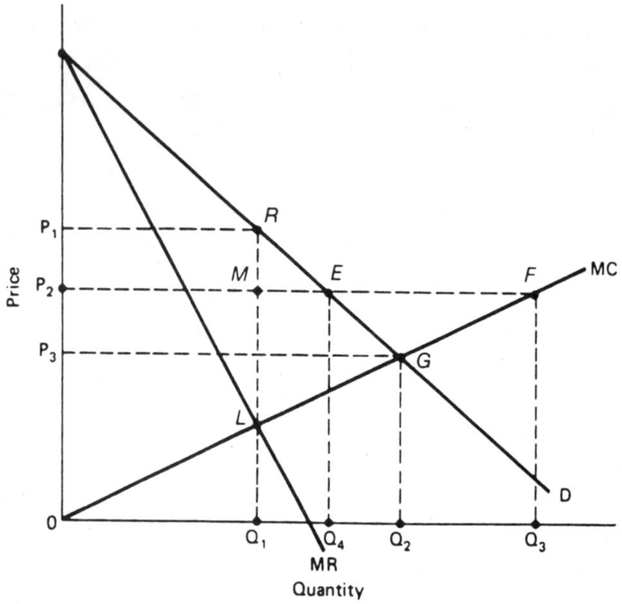

Figure 19.4

Suppose initially that there is no international trade. Then the amount _____ will be produced and the market price will be _____. Suppose now that international trade is introduced, and that it results in a price equal to P_2. Then consumption of the good in Canada will be _____, production of the good in Canada will be _____, and the difference between these amounts will be _____, which will be the amount of the good that Canada (exports, imports).

3b. As a result of allowing international trade in this good, producer gain (surplus) in Canada has gone (up, down) by the amount _____ and consumer surplus in Canada has gone (up, down) by the amount _____. Therefore, the net efficiency (gain, loss) to Canada is _____.

3c. Suppose next that there is no international trade in the good and that the market in Canada is an unregulated monopoly. Its marginal revenue will be the line _____. The monopolist will produce the amount _____ and will charge price _____. The efficiency (gain, loss) from monopoly will be _____.

Suppose now that international trade is introduced and that as a result the firm that used to have a monopoly in Canada is forced to behave as a perfect competitor, taking price as given.

Suppose as before that with international trade the market price is P_2. Then consumption of the good in Canada will equal _____, production of the good in Canada will equal _____, and the difference between these two amounts equals _____, which will be the amount of the good that Canada (exports, imports).

3d. As a result of allowing international trade in this good, the total revenue received by the producer in Canada has gone from _____ to _____, so the net gain in total revenue equals the rectangle _____, minus the rectangle _____.

3e. But the producer's cost has increased by the four-sided figure _____; thus the net gain to the producer equals the triangle _____, minus the rectangle _____. At the same time, consumer surplus (rises, falls) by _____; thus the net gain to the country (that is, the net gain to consumers plus the net gain to the producer) equals area _____. Shade in this area.

3f. In this case trade brings two efficiency gains: the standard gain from trade that results even in a world of perfect competition, shown by area _____, plus a gain because trade also ends monopoly inefficiency, as shown by area _____. Both gains make up the area _____, thus confirming our conclusion in part **e**.

3g. Does this illustrate a special case in which it is possible for international trade in a specific commodity to benefit both the consumers and the producers of that commodity?

4a. In Figure 19.5, the curve D = MEI represents the demand for capital funds in Canada, S_{Can} is the supply of funds from Canadian savers, and S_t is the total supply curve of funds, including foreign funds. The curve S_{tt} is the total supply curve of funds if a tax, given by the vertical distance T = (*CG*) = (*AF*) is imposed on the earnings of foreign capital.

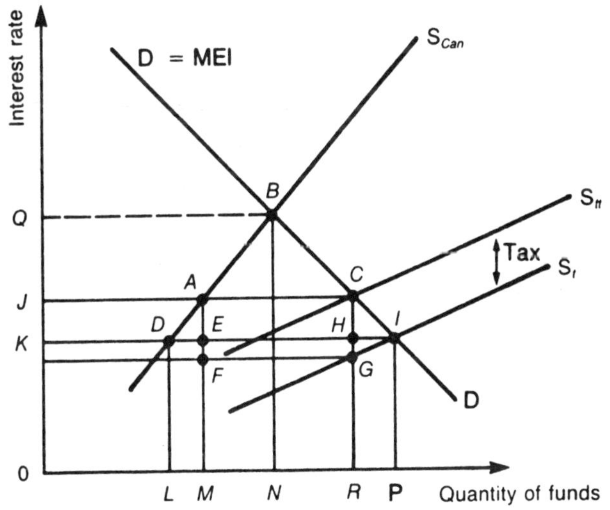

Figure 19.5

If no foreign capital is allowed into Canada, the amount of funds used in the economy will be _____ and the return to capital will be _____.

4b. If foreign capital is allowed to come in and there is no tax, the total amount of funds used in the Canadian economy will be _____, of which _____ will be supplied by foreign savers. The total return on the foreign capital will be equal to the rectangle _____, and the efficiency gain will be the triangle _____.

4c. If a tax T is imposed on the earnings of foreign capital, the total supply curve shifts up to S_{tt}. The amount of foreign capital used in Canada will shrink to _____. The total return going to foreign capital owners (after payment of the tax) will be the rectangle _____. Canadian taxpayers will benefit by the tax paid by the foreign capital owners; the revenue from this tax is the rectangle _____. This tax revenue, plus the triangle *ABC*, is now the total net benefit to Canadians of having this amount of foreign capital invested in Canada.

(The imposition of the tax will increase the gain to Canada from having foreign capital here if the tax paid by the foreigners is greater than the reduction in the net gain to Canadian factors of production as the tax is imposed; that is, if the tax revenue rectangle is greater than the area *DICA*.)

ESSAY QUESTIONS

1. Who gains and who loses from a tariff that prohibits the import of a certain good? Do the gains outweigh the losses, or vice versa? Explain.

2. Looking ahead to the next chapter, can you think of any goods that we would not want to export, no matter how great the net economic benefits might be? Hint: Americans now trade military aircraft and equipment with Canada, and this trade provides economic benefits to both countries. Would you recommend that the Americans do the same with the Soviet Union?

3. "One of the gains from international trade is that it induces firms to reduce or eliminate technical inefficiency." Is this true? Why? Did we miss this point, or was it covered under one of our four broad sources of gains from trade?

4. Why do you think the leaders of the Canadian Auto Workers argue that the government should take steps to limit the number of Japanese autos imported into Canada? If you were one of these leaders, what would be your attitude towards a similar restriction on Canadian imports of steel? Why?

5. Why might trade between Ontario and Quebec benefit both provinces? In your answer, you may want to define the concept of an "export to another province" and an "import from another province."

6. A recent slogan has been "Trade, not aid. If we reduce Canadian restrictions on imports from the less developed countries, they will benefit, and so will we." Do you agree or disagree? Explain why.

7. Can you name any activities in your province that have developed as a result of inter-provincial specialization – that is, specialization between provinces? Any activities that have developed as a result of international specialization?

8. If the United States and Canada have an approximate balance in their trade, which country is more dependent on that trade? Why?

9. "There is no trade in cement between Australia and Germany. The reason is that transport costs on so bulky and heavy an item more than cancel out the gains from trade." Explain this statement. Do you agree with it? Does this mean that transport costs influence trade patterns? Explain how high transport costs in a good may explain "cross-hauling" – for example, the export of potatoes from Prince Edward Island to New York at the same time as potatoes are being imported into western Canada from the United States.

10. Suppose Canada imposes a high tariff on the imports of a good such as washing machines. Thus, whenever a washing machine is imported, Canadian taxpayers benefit from the tariff collected by the government.

    Suppose now that a foreign firm comes into Canada and establishes facilities to produce a large number of washing machines in Canada; as a result, there is a sharp reduction in the number of washing machines imported into Canada, and the government loses the tariff revenue that would have been collected on the imported machines.

    If we want to measure the net benefit to Canada of this foreign investment, how should we treat the loss of tariff revenue? Is it generally in Canada's interest to have foreign firms invest in production facilities in Canadian industries that are protected by tariffs? Is the possibility of foreign investment relevant when we try to measure the efficiency loss from imposing a tariff?

ANSWERS

True-False: **1F, 2F, 3F, 4T, 5F, 6F, 7T, 8T, 9F, 10F, 11F**

Multiple Choice: **1d, 2c, 3a, 4e, 5a, 6d, 7c, 8a, 9b, 10a, 11e, 12d, 13c, 14d, 15a, 16e, 17c, 18d, 19a, 20d, 21c, 22b**

Exercises: **1a.** $10, 10, $20, 20, rise, fall

1b. $15, 5, 15, 25, 15, England, 10, advantage, lower

2a. and **2b. Table 19.3 completed**

A		B	
Wheat	Corn	Wheat	Corn
0	120	0	80
100	90	40	60
200	60	80	40
300	30	120	20
400	0	160	0

2c. *A, A, B, A,* 80, 40

2d. 80, zero, 100, more, gain, comparative, not be possible

3a. Q_2, P_3, Q_4, Q_3, Q_4Q_3, exports

3b. up, P_2FGP_3, down, P_2EGP_3, gain, *EGF*

3c. MR, Q_1, P_1, loss, *RGL*, Q_4, Q_3, Q_4Q_3, exports

3d. P_1RQ_10, P_2FQ_30, MFQ_3Q_1, P_1RMP_2

3e. LQ_1Q_3F, *MLF*, P_1RMP_2, rises, P_1REP_2, *RLFE*

3f. *EGF, RLG, RLFE*

3g. yes

4a. 0*N*, 0*Q*

4b. 0P, *LP*, *LDIP*, *DBI*

4c. *MR, MFGR, FACG*

ANSWERS TO PROBLEMS FROM THE TEXT

19-1. Yes, both may benefit – even in the special case where cost curves in both countries are exactly the same. Economies of scale mean that the AC curve for each product is falling. As Britain specializes in good *X*, the average cost of producing it is reduced. As Canada specializes in good *Y*, the average cost of producing it also falls. With specialization and the reduced cost of producing each good, resources are released that can be used in other productive ways. Therefore, each country may benefit – even though neither may have a comparative advantage. (In other words, both countries may benefit, even though there is no difference in their cost curves. Of course, if cost conditions do differ – if comparative advantage does exist – then this is a further source of benefit.)

19-2. This can be shown using a PPC as in Figure 19-5(*a*); or using supply and demand curves as in Figure 19-7. Note in any of these cases that trade is being reduced, rather than increased, so the analyses are reversed.

19-3. (a) Now Britain does not have an absolute advantage in the production of either good; it does, however, have a comparative advantage in clothing production. The opportunity cost of clothing production in Britain is now 1/4 unit of food, whereas the opportunity cost of clothing production in Canada is 2/5 units of food.

(b) In this case, the opportunity cost of clothing production is the same in both countries (1/4 unit of clothing) – hence, neither country has a comparative advantage. Therefore, there is no potential gain from trade.

19-4. At point *K*, consumption of both clothing and food has increased relative to point *B*. The gains from trade may be measured by passing a line through point *B*, parallel to line *CD*. The vertical distance between these two lines measures, in units of clothing, the gains from trade. (Equivalently, the horizontal distance between the two lines measures, in units of food, the gains from trade.)

19-5. This is precisely the situation modelled in Figure 19-7 in the textbook. The efficiency gain associated with free trade in oil will be areas 1 + 2. If, however, we now price oil below the world price, there will be both a production loss – domestic production falls below the efficient level – and a consumption loss – domestic consumption rises above the efficient level. The transfer effect in this case consists of a loss to producers (price has fallen) and to taxpayers (who foot the bill for the subsidy on imported oil) in favour of consumers (who pay the subsidized price). Figure 21-7 in the textbook illustrates the resulting efficiency loss.

19-6. The argument here essentially parallels that on p. 403 of the textbook, except that here the sequence is reversed – starting from a situation of free international capital movement, suppose that international capital flows are now prohibited.

19-7. (a) First, construct the corresponding demand and supply schedules (like Tables 4-1 and 4-2) and plot the supply and demand curves. The equilibrium price (in the absence of trade) is $P = 6$. The corresponding equilibrium quantity is $Q = 500$.

(b) At a world price of $P = 9$, Canada would export this good. At this higher price, producers gain, consumers lose. The (welfare) gain to producers is an area similar to $PCAP_A$ in Figure 19-6.

(c) The loss in consumers' surplus is an area similar to $PBAP_A$. (Note: Since the producers' gain exceeds the loss in consumers' surplus, there is an overall efficiency gain, similar to areas 3 + 4 in Figure 19-6.)

(d) At $P = 9$, $Q_s = 800$, $Q_d = 200$. Six hundred units will therefore be exported.

(e) The value of this export is 9 x 600 = 5,400.

19-8. (a) (This question is similar to 19-7 and refers back to Figure 19-7 in the textbook.) In the absence of trade, the equilibrium price is $P = 70$, and the corresponding quantity is $Q = 13{,}000$.

(b), (c), (d), (e) Since price falls with free trade, consumers gain and producers lose. Canada will import 9,000 units. The value of this import is 40 x 9,000 = 360,000.

CHAPTER 20

International Trade: Policy Debates

LEARNING OBJECTIVES

After you have studied this chapter in the textbook and the study guide, you should be able to

- Explain the various non-economic reasons why trade barriers still exist
- State three fallacious economic arguments for protection, explaining why they are fallacious
- State eleven economic arguments for protection that contain some element of truth, and the difficulties with each of these arguments
- Describe the historical development of international trade policy in Canada and elsewhere in the world, including the multilateral efforts at trade liberalization over the last 50 years, with special reference to the creation of the GATT and the Kennedy, Tokyo, and Uruguay Rounds
- Evaluate the European Community (EC) with special reference to the problems it raises for North American exporters
- Outline the terms of the Canada/U.S. Free Trade Agreement (FTA) and the North American Free Trade Agreement (NAFTA)
- Assess the benefits and/or costs of free trade for Canada
- Give several examples of non-tariff barriers, explaining why each distorts trade
- Explain the concept of tariff escalation and its significance to Canada
- Explain the effects of tariffs or quotas that reduce exports

CHAPTER SUMMARY

Even though the gains from trade have been evident since the days of Adam Smith, and even though **tariffs** have been on a downward trend over the last 50 years, many **trade barriers** still remain. We are still a long way from free trade. The primary objective of this chapter is to answer the question "How is it possible that these barriers still exist? Can they, or can they not, be justified?" We will also address a number of other important and closely related questions: What are the historical developments that have moved Canada and other nations toward freer trade? As we have been moving two steps forward, what are the new barriers to trade that have been moving us one step back? Another issue of particular significance to Canada is, of course, the 1989 **free trade agreement** with the United States **(FTA)** as well as the 1994 **North American Free Trade Agreement (NAFTA)**. What are the likely advantages and disadvantages to Canada as the provisions of NAFTA are implemented?

The trade barriers that remain throughout the world – and new ones that have been introduced – have been defended by their supporters as "in the national interest." Do the arguments they use make sense?

Arguments for Protection

Several of the arguments for protection have little to do with economics. The main non-economic reason for protection is political. The loss that results from allowing a good to be freely imported is felt very heavily by the few people who specialize in producing that good domestically; in many cases, their jobs are threatened by the competition of imports. These people will often vote for a politician who promises to work for restrictions on such imports. In the debate over the FTA during the 1988 election, the fear that the agreement would lead to major job losses was a major theme in the Liberal and NDP campaigns opposing it. As we saw in the last chapter, the damage to those who become losers under free trade is likely to be more than offset by the benefits to the winners – all the people who are able to enjoy a wider variety of less expensive goods, or who get jobs in the expanding export industries. But these expected gains by the winners are either hypothetical, or widely dispersed over the public as a whole, with the benefit received by each individual being relatively small. Thus, winners usually vote for other issues on which they feel more deeply, and the politician who promises to work for restrictions on imports is often elected. Thus, trade restrictions that make no economic sense may still be introduced for political reasons.

In some countries, especially the United States, tariffs and other trade restrictions have also been justified by considerations of national security. The argument here is that some industries produce goods that are vitally important to a country's national defence. If there were no trade restrictions protecting domestic producers from import competition, some of these industries might not survive. But this would leave the country in a vulnerable position in times of war. However, in small countries that belong to military alliances (such as NATO), this national security argument loses much of its validity if the country's military needs can be supplied from other countries within the alliance.

A third non-economic argument for protection is especially relevant to a small country like Canada which is geographically close to, and has extensive economic relations with, a large neighbour: that restrictions on trade may be needed in order to protect and foster the small country's unique cultural identity. Because of scale economies in such industries as book and magazine publishing, TV programming, or filmmaking, it is difficult for domestic producers to compete with American publishers, filmmakers, and so on. But if Canadians read primarily foreign books and magazines and watch foreign-made movies and TV programs, will it be possible to preserve our separate and distinct identity?

Because many Canadians feared that the answer was no, they pushed hard for special provisions in the FTA to protect our cultural industries and, in the end, the Americans agreed to put in a number of safeguards for cultural industries.

Now let's turn to the economic arguments that have been used to try to justify protection. Many have resurfaced of late in the debate over NAFTA. Some are fallacious, but some contain an element of truth.

1. "Buy Canadian because it keeps our money at home. When we buy goods from Italy we lose our money to the Italians." This argument is fallacious. When we buy Italian goods, our money eventually comes back when the Italians buy our goods. The Italians want our goods, not our money.

2. "We can't compete with cheap foreign labour." This argument is also fallacious. Labour in many foreign countries is less expensive because it is less productive. Our higher productivity means that, on average, we can compete with cheap foreign labour. We do particularly well in goods in which we have a comparative advantage (where our productivity advantage more than offsets our higher wage rate). We can't compete where we don't have a comparative advantage (where our productivity advantage does not offset our higher wage rate). In the recent NAFTA debate, many opponents focused on the relatively low Mexican wage rate, but failed to take into account the low productivity of Mexican labour.

3. "Tariffs should be tailored to equalize costs at home and abroad." This, too, is a fallacious argument. According to the theory of comparative advantage, we gain from international trade because there are differences in costs between countries. Tailoring tariffs to eliminate these differences would eliminate trade, and all the gains it provides.

4. “If we buy steel from Hamilton rather than Japan, employment will rise in Hamilton rather than Japan.” There is a grain of truth in this argument. Restricting imports of steel from Japan may stimulate employment in Hamilton at least in the short run. However, there are two problems. First, Japan may retaliate with her own restrictions against our exports, and this will reduce employment in Canada. Thus, we don’t get employment gains after all. In short, we are following a “beggar-my-neighbour” policy that doesn’t provide employment benefits, but results in shrinking trade and a loss of the gains from trade. Second, blocking out Japanese competition makes it more difficult to control costs and prices in Canadian industries. If Canadian workers don’t feel that they have to compete with the Japanese, they will be less restrained in their wage demands. We saw in Chapter 20 that one of the gains from trade is that it makes our economy more competitive. We lose this gain whenever we protect our industries.

5. “Restricting trade will diversify a nation’s economy.” This may be true for some countries. Trade may lead a country to specialize in producing just a few goods. If world prices drop for these few goods, the country will suffer from having “put all its eggs in one basket.” But even though Canada does have very large exports of a few primary products such as wheat, timber, and natural gas, it also exports a whole range of other primary and manufactured products as well. Thus, a lack of diversification in international trade is not a serious enough problem in Canada to justify increased tariff protection. Moreover, heavy specialization may sometimes put a country in a particularly favourable position if the world price of its main export good rises; a prime example is the group of OPEC countries which produces almost nothing but oil.

6. “We need to protect our infant industries.” This argument is sometimes valid. Without the protection of trade restrictions, some industries may never reach the size where they can realize the economies of scale necessary to compete in world markets. However, there are three difficulties with this argument. (a) **Infant industries** never seem to grow up. They typically continue to demand protection, and no government wants to lose votes by cutting the apron strings. (b) Even if an industry were to “grow up,” it still might not be able to compete effectively. (c) If the infant industry really does have a promising future, then why aren’t private lenders willing to lend it enough money to survive until maturity?

7. “Restricting imports may reduce the price we have to pay for them.” This may make sense if Canada buys so much of a good that a cutback in this demand (as a result of a Canadian import restriction) would reduce the world price. However, the Canadian demand for most goods represents only a very small

fraction of the world demand for those goods. Hence, Canada's ability to influence the world prices for the goods it imports is very limited.

8. "Restricting imports may reduce our vulnerability to a cutoff in foreign supplies." Cutbacks in oil supplies from OPEC countries in the 1970s made clear the force of this argument. But oil is special; for most other commodities, the risk of having our supply cut off is minimal. If one country stops selling to us, we can turn to other sources of supply.

9. "Use protection to engineer (that is, create) a comparative advantage." Just as past accumulation of capital by some nations has given them a comparative advantage in products that require a lot of capital, the accumulation of human capital in protected high-tech industries today could give us a comparative advantage in those industries in the future. There is some truth in this, but:
   a. It is similar to the infant industry argument, and subject to the same criticisms.
   b. Like other arguments it assumes that our trading partners won't retaliate.
   c. Protecting one high-tech industry like computer chips increases the cost of other high-tech industries that use chips.

10. "Protect industries with positive externalities." High-tech industries are again a good example. (There were huge external benefits to the general public when AT&T developed the transistor.) It's true that positive externalities justify a subsidy, but protection may be the worst kind – again, since it invites retaliation.

    There are only a few strong arguments for free trade. However, the many arguments against it are often seriously flawed and universally assume partners won't retaliate if we protect. So, don't just count the number of arguments. The case for free trade is still a strong one.

Non-tariff Barriers

There are several kinds of **non-tariff barriers to trade**:

1. **Quotas** are quantitative limits on imports. These include the **voluntary export restraints (VERs)** that Canada and the United States pressured the Japanese into imposing on their exports to North America. The United States subsequently removed this pressure and the Japanese were free to drop the VERs on shipments to the United States. However, they did not. Why should they? The United States and Canada had shown them how to profitably cartelize their export sales to North America. Because of this, the Japanese auto companies were making more profit in North America than in Japan.

An alternative form of quota is a limit that a country imposes on its own total imports of a particular good.

2. Health or quality standards. An example is the European ban on hormone-fed beef from North America. How much is this a policy to protect health and how much is it a policy to block out import competition? It is hard to say.

3. Bureaucratic red tape can be used to discourage imports. An example was the French requirement that all imported VCRs be cleared through the tiny, inland customs house at Poitiers – the same town that Frederic Bastiat used to satirize protection 150 years ago. (See Box 20-1.)

History of Canadian Trade Policy

Perhaps the most important period in Canadian trade policy was the 1880s, when the Conservative government under Sir John A. Macdonald introduced very high tariffs as part of its National Policy – aimed at stimulating Canada's manufacturing industry and promoting interprovincial trade. Since that time, Canada's tariffs have generally been falling (except during the early 1930s when Canada and many other countries raised tariffs as a way of stimulating domestic aggregate demand and reducing unemployment). Since the Second World War, the trend toward lower Canadian tariffs can be partly explained by Canada's participation in the programs of multilateral tariff reductions negotiated by most of the world's industrialized countries under the **General Agreement on Tariffs and Trade (GATT)**. Especially important international tariff reductions came as a result of the "Kennedy Round" of tariff negotiations in the late 1970s. The "Tokyo Round" of negotiations dealt not only with tariffs, but also with "non-tariff" barriers (NTBs), such as import quotas, special customs procedures which make import trade more costly, and the discrimination in government purchasing against imported goods. A new round of multilateral negotiations – the Uruguay Round – began in 1986.

From the viewpoint of Canada and the United States, the process of multilateral tariff reductions has been especially important since the formation of the European Economic Community (EEC) in the late 1950s. Since the countries that are members of the EEC have abolished tariffs on trade with each other, Canadian and U.S. exporters (who still face a tariff on their sales to an EEC importer) are at a disadvantage relative to suppliers in any EEC country. (For Canada, this problem became especially important in 1973 when the United Kingdom, one of Canada's important trading partners, joined the EEC.) However, this disadvantage has become less severe since the EEC has participated in all multilateral agreements to reduce tariffs on all imports.

The 1988 Canada/United States Free Trade Agreement (FTA)

Proponents of free trade have long argued that it is in Canada's interest to ultimately abolish all tariffs and other restrictions on Canada-U.S. trade. Advocates of such an agreement have argued that the resulting gains from industrial specialization and from an increased ability for Canadian firms to exploit economies of scale could lead to a large increase in Canada's GDP. Some studies conducted in the mid-1980s suggested that this increase would be as much as 8 to 9% of GDP. (However, other analysts predicted gains as small as 1 to 2%.) Furthermore, free trade advocates argued that an important objective of a free trade arrangement would be to protect Canada against the effects of future protectionist moves by the United States, in the form of increased tariffs or NTBs.

Following the recommendations of the MacDonald Commission in 1985, Canada formally requested that the United States enter into negotiations about an agreement. The United States accepted, and during 1986-88, a draft agreement was negotiated. Following an election completely dominated by this issue, the victorious Progressive Conservatives brought in legislation ratifying the agreement, which came into effect on January 1, 1989.

The main provisions of the agreement stipulated that all tariffs and many other obstacles to Canada-United States trade were to be eliminated over a ten-year period ending in 1998. In addition, there was provision for joint Canada-United States scrutiny of application of existing trade laws by either country to restrict imports from the other, and for continued negotiations over the issue when either country will be allowed to impose such restrictions.

Because the agreement is so recent, it is still too early to assess what its main effects will be. Critics argue that an elimination of our tariffs on imports from the United States will make it impossible for most of our manufacturing firms to stand up against the increased competition from U.S. firms. Hence, Canada's manufacturing sector will shrink substantially, with considerable job losses, and we will be pushed further in the direction of producing mostly primary products (being "hewers of wood and drawers of water"). Further, free trade will greatly increase our political dependence on the United States, in the critic's view. However, other observers are more optimistic and suggest that even though some manufacturing industries will contract as a result of increased international competition, others will remain competitive by specializing in the production of a narrower range of products for both the U.S. and Canadian markets; still others will expand as they increase their export sales when U.S. tariffs are eliminated. Moreover, while increased trade with the United States in one sense makes us more vulnerable to political pressure from that country (since Canadian producers become more dependent on the U.S. market), in another sense the agreement may reduce our vulnerability: Under the FTA the United States has agreed to refrain from imposing certain types of restrictions on imports from Canada.

The 1994 North American Free Trade Agreement (NAFTA)

NAFTA is the result of trilateral negotiations involving Canada, the U.S., and Mexico. NAFTA will have three principal impacts:

1. It will provide Canadian exporters with improved duty-free access to the Mexican market with its high growth potential;

2. It will provide Canadian consumers with the benefits of duty-free imports from Mexico;

3. It will provide Canadian industry with the low-cost Mexican inputs necessary to keep it competitive.

In effect, NAFTA creates a North American trading bloc – fortress North America. Because it has made rules of origin more demanding – rules that ensure a certain amount of North American content in goods shipped across internal borders – NAFTA provides a degree of protection to North American manufacturing interests. For many items, however, participants move to the same common external tariff – zero – obviating the need for rules of origin. Finally, NAFTA involves parallel accords in which each country agrees to allow its two partners to impose penalties on it if it fails to enforce its own labour laws or environmental laws. NAFTA came into effect on January 1, 1994. As with the FTA, it will be some time before we can quantify its economic (and other) effects.

The Uruguay Round

A problem that continues to be important for Canadian international trade is the problem of tariff escalation. Because importing countries often have higher tariffs on processed goods than on raw materials, there is a tendency for the processing of many Canadian raw materials to be done in the importing country rather than in Canada. In order to promote more processing in Canada, Canadian trade negotiators have been trying to get our trading partners to reduce the escalation in their tariff schedules.

The ongoing GATT (General Agreement on Tariffs and Trade) negotiations are multilateral negotiations involving most of the industrial nations of the world. The 1993 completion of the Uruguay round has resulted in further trade liberalization in both goods and services. Of particular importance is the agreement to reduce subsidies on agricultural exports and the replacement of quotas with explicit tariffs, to be gradually eliminated over the next decade.

Appendix 20-A

The appendix to chapter 20 illustrates the economic effects of tariffs and quotas. Both tariffs and quotas will result in a distinct output effect and a consumption effect. Price rises – given completely elastic world supply at a given "world price," the domestic price will rise by the full amount of the tariff. There will be increased domestic output, replacing imports. Domestic consumption falls. Associated with these, there will be resulting efficiency losses (see Figure 20-3 in the textbook).

An important difference between a tariff and a quota is that the former generates revenues for government, whereas the latter creates rents for those who hold the quota rights. Moreover, if the quota rights are held by foreigners, then these rents flow out of the country, compounding the losses resulting from inefficient production and consumption levels. In such a case, a quota becomes a much more costly protectionist device than is a tariff. One example of such a case is that of voluntary export restraints (VERs).

IMPORTANT TERMS

1. Trade barrier
2. Tariff
3. Quota
4. Non-tariff barrier to trade (NTB)
5. Infant industry
6. The General Agreement on Tariffs and Trade (GATT)
7. FTA
8. NAFTA
9. Rules of origin
10. Voluntary export restraint (VER)

TRUE-FALSE

T F 1. Tariffs are often imposed because producers have more political influence than consumers.

T F 2. When international trade is opened up in a good, Canada as a whole gains only if we end up exporting that good.

T F 3. Diversifying an economy may reduce the gains from trade.

T F 4. If Canada were to increase restrictions on imported steel, this would tend to increase employment in Hamilton in the short run.

T F 5. After an infant industry has been supported by the government for a year or two, political pressure to remove the protection becomes almost irresistible.

T F 6. Canadian processing of raw materials before they are exported to foreign countries is discouraged because many of the countries with which we trade have lower tariffs on unprocessed raw materials than on processed goods.

T F 7. Because wages in Canada are higher than in Mexico, it follows that costs of production are also higher – and this justifies protecting our goods from cheap Mexican products.

T F 8. One of the strongest arguments for trade restrictions is that they keep us from losing our dollars to foreigners.

T F 9. If the government were to do nothing about our unemployment problems, this would constitute a "beggar-my-neighbour" policy.

T F 10. By restricting its imports, a large country may be able to improve its terms of trade, but for a small country such a strategy is unlikely to work.

MULTIPLE CHOICE

1. The national security argument for protecting essential defence industries:
   a. has been opposed by economists since the days of Adam Smith
   b. is not heard as often in Canada as it is in the United States
   c. is justified as a method of creating employment, but can't be justified in any other way
   d. all of the above
   e. none of the above

2. If we take into account the interests of both producers and consumers, then restrictions on the imports of Japanese cars into Canada are:
   a. in the interest of the nation as a whole, and in the interest of the province of Ontario
   b. in the interest of the nation as a whole, but not in the interest of the province of Ontario
   c. not in the interest of the nation as a whole, nor in the interest of the province of Ontario
   d. not in the interest of the nation as a whole, but it may well be in the interest of the province of Ontario
   e. not in the interest of Ontario, and has little or no effect on the nation as a whole

3. The strongest political pressure for a change in trade policy usually comes from:
   a. producers lobbying for import restrictions
   b. producers lobbying for export restrictions
   c. consumers lobbying for import restrictions
   d. consumers lobbying for export restrictions
   e. consumers lobbying for a reduction in trade restrictions

4. In dealing with a serious problem of unemployment, a country that trades heavily should normally look first to:
   a. increasing tariffs
   b. increasing quotas
   c. increasing other non-tariff barriers
   d. restricting its exports
   e. domestic monetary and fiscal policy

5. Which of the following arguments for protection makes economic sense?
   a. we should tailor tariffs so as to equalize costs at home and abroad
   b. when we import, the country loses money that wouldn't be lost if we produced domestically instead
   c. we can't compete with cheap foreign labour
   d. for a large country such as the United States, restricting oil imports may significantly reduce the world price of oil
   e. all of the above

6. Problems that arise when a country protects an infant industry include:
   a. the industry's cost may never fall below those in foreign countries, because foreigners may enjoy some natural advantage
   b. it may be very difficult to know when infant protection has become an old age pension
   c. the new industry may hire a large number of employees whose voting power may make it difficult to remove protection later – even when it is no longer justified
   d. all of the above
   e. none of the above

7. A beggar-my-neighbour policy involves:
   a. encouraging the purchase of essential materials from abroad
   b. export controls to prevent the sale of our natural resources to foreign countries
   c. import restrictions designed to capture employment from foreign countries
   d. subsidies to encourage imports of foreign natural resources
   e. subsidies to encourage imports of foreign luxury goods

8. The infant industry argument for protection makes sense if the infant is:
   a. able to compete against foreign firms now, but not in the future
   b. not able to compete against foreign firms now, but will be able to in the future
   c. won't be able to compete now or in the future
   d. will be able to compete now and in the future
   e. won't be able to compete now; the future is irrelevant

9. "If I buy a radio from India, I get the radio and India gets the dollars. But if I buy a Canadian-built radio, I get the radio and the dollars stay here." This argument is:
   a. misleading because the Indians seldom keep the dollars they earn from us in trade; they eventually spend them on our goods
   b. misleading because the dollars I spend buying a Canadian-built radio also leave this country
   c. correct; this is why we should stop trading
   d. correct; we should trade only for political reasons
   e. true for radios, but not for most goods we import

10. The argument that an industry with positive externalities should be protected is most similar to the argument that:
    a. a polluting industry should be taxed
    b. a polluting industry should be subsidized
    c. a polluting industry should be left alone
    d. vaccinations should be subsidized
    e. vaccinations should be taxed

11. If an industry has large positive externalities:
    a. it must be protected
    b. it should be protected
    c. it should be subsidized, with protection being the best method
    d. it should be subsidized, but not by protection because this invites retaliation
    e. it should be subsidized, but not by protection because this guarantees against retaliation

12. Non-tariff barriers are:
    a. designed solely to restrict trade
    b. designed solely to improve health standards
    c. designed solely for other non-trade reasons
    d. sometimes designed to restrict trade, and sometimes designed to improve health standards; but in either case, they restrict trade
    e. justified so long as they provide a benefit, regardless of their cost

13. The National Policy introduced by Sir John A. Macdonald:
    a. was a policy intended to nationalize the Canadian oil and gas industry
    b. proposed the establishment of a free trade arrangement with the United States as a means of raising Canada's national income
    c. was an early version of the CBC program "The National"
    d. introduced high tariffs on imported goods as a means of promoting trade between Canada's provinces
    e. provided a large subsidy for VIA Rail passenger service

14. Canadian tariffs today are:
    a. higher than in the 1930s
    b. slightly lower
    c. much lower
    d. about the same
    e. higher in most goods, but lower in some

15. Under the Canada/United States free trade agreement:
    a. all tariffs and non-tariff barriers will be eliminated by 1992
    b. all tariffs will be eliminated by 1998
    c. all tariffs will be eliminated by 1995, but existing non-tariff barriers will remain
    d. Canada is obliged to eliminate several of its existing social programs
    e. none of the above

16. With free trade between Canada and the United States, it is likely that Canada will:
    a. give up the production of industrial goods in order to concentrate on agricultural goods
    b. give up the production of agricultural goods in order to concentrate on industrial goods
    c. give up one industry (say, electrical machinery) in order to specialize in another (say, chemicals)
    d. give up the production of some items of electrical machinery in order to specialize in other items of electrical machinery; and do the same in chemicals
    e. in both electrical equipment and chemicals, produce an even wider range of items than at present

17. According to estimates by Harris and Cox, a Canada/United States free trade agreement will lead to an increase in Canadian GDP of:
    a. 0.5 to 1%
    b. 4 to 5%
    c. 8 to 9%
    d. 14 to 15%
    e. a small decrease in Canadian GDP

18. The concept of "tariff escalation" refers to:
    a. the policy of charging higher tariffs on more expensive goods
    b. the tendency for countries to raise their tariffs in order to reduce unemployment during the Great Depression
    c. the policy of countries importing raw materials to charge higher tariffs on raw materials in order to drive down the price of such imports
    d. the policy of some countries to charge lower tariffs on imports of unprocessed raw materials than on imports of other goods
    e. the policy of charging higher tariffs on goods imported from low-wage countries

19. The formation of the European Economic Community:
   a. was one of the reasons for the severe scarcity of agricultural goods in the early 1980s
   b. has made it easier for Canadian firms to compete against the French in the German market
   c. has made it more difficult for Canadian firms to compete against the French in the German market
   d. has made it more difficult for Canadian firms to compete against the Japanese in the German market
   e. has had no effect on Canadian firms competing in the German market

20. In the Kennedy Round, participating countries cut their tariffs by about a third. In the Tokyo Round that followed:
   a. almost no further progress was made
   b. no further progress was made
   c. participating countries cut their remaining tariffs by about 10%
   d. participating countries cut their remaining tariffs by roughly another one-third
   e. participating countries cut their remaining tariffs by roughly 90%

21. The Tokyo Round resulted in an average tariff reduction of about:
   a. 5%
   b. 15%
   c. 25%
   d. 35%
   e. 45%

22. The Uruguay Round resulted in
   a. further tariff reductions
   b. the substitution of tariffs for quotas on certain agricultural products
   c. provided for enforcement of environmental laws
   d. all of the above
   e. just a. and b.

23. NAFTA provided for
   a. free trade in goods and services
   b. enforcement of labour and environmental laws
   c. a strengthening of rules of origin
   d. all of the above
   e. none of the above

24. Tariffs result in
   a. a loss in consumers' surplus
   b. a transfer from consumers to producers and to the treasury
   c. efficiency losses
   d. all of the above
   e. just a. and c.

EXERCISES

This exercise covers the same ground as the appendix to the chapter. You will probably be able to do the exercise and find it helpful, even if you are not being asked to study the appendix. However, if you get stuck, you can refer to the appendix for help. In any case, first try to do the exercise on your own.

1a. Figure 20.1 shows the domestic Canadian supply and demand for a good that is traded internationally. Without international trade the price would be _____ and the quantity produced would be _____. If this good is available on the world market at a price P_2, then the price in Canada, under free trade, will be _____. Domestic production will be _____, domestic consumption will be _____, and the country will (import, export) the amount _____. As a result of this international trade, the (gain, loss) to consumers is area _____, while producers are (better, worse) off by area _____. If we consider both producers and consumers, the effect of international trade on the nation, on balance, is an efficiency (gain, loss) of area _____.

1b. Suppose that the government imposes a tariff on this good, shown by arrow t. Suppose that this has no effect on the world price of the good. Because of the tariff, the domestic price will (rise, fall) to _____. (Importers who are willing to bring this good in for a price P_2 will need this higher price to compensate them for the tariff t that they now have to pay the government.) The quantity of imports will be _____. As a result of the tariff, consumers (gain, lose) area _____, while producers are (better, worse) off by area _____. Moreover, the government is now collecting a tariff t on imports of _____, for a total revenue of area _____. Therefore, there is a net (gain, loss) to the nation from this tariff of areas _____.

1c. Now suppose that, instead of this tariff t, the government imposes an import quota that restricts imports to the quantity *FG*. With imports of *FG*, P_2 (is, is not) an equilibrium price, because the demand for this good at price P_2 is (more than, less than) the domestic plus imported supply. Thus, price will be (above, below) P_2. P_3 (is, is not) an equilibrium price because, with imports *FG*, the demand for this good at P_3 is (more than, less than, equal to) the domestic plus imported supply. Thus, this quota of *FG* is the quota equivalent of tariff _____, because both raise the domestic Canadian price by _____, and reduce imports to _____.

1d. Because of the quota, the price in the domestic market will rise to _____, consumers will (gain, lose) area _____, and producers will (gain, lose) area _____. Suppose that the quota rights are held by foreigners exporting to Canada. They can then make a profit by acquiring this good outside Canada for _____ per unit and selling it in Canada for _____. The revenue the government gets from the imposition of this quota is _____. Therefore, the net effect on the nation of this quota is its effect on producers and consumers, which is a (gain, loss) of area _____.

1e. When the Canadian government imposes an import quota, and gives away these quota rights to foreigners, then a quota will result in a (larger, smaller) amount of (gain, loss) to the nation than will an equivalent tariff. The additional (gain, loss) from the quota occurs because duty revenue is collected by the Canadian government if there is a (tariff, quota), but is not collected if there is this type of (tariff, quota). Instead, this revenue goes as profit to (Canadian producers, foreign holders of quota rights).

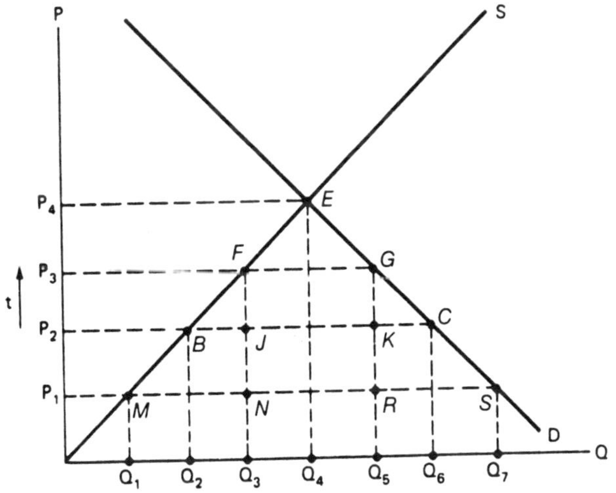

Figure 20.1

ESSAY QUESTIONS

1. When a country is in a severe recession, the political pressure to reduce imports becomes stronger. Why? Critically evaluate such a proposal.

2. It is sometimes argued that trade restrictions protect our high standard of living from being eroded by competition from low-income countries. Evaluate this. Do trade restrictions erode our standard of living or increase it for the nation as a whole? For the industry that's being protected? What, then, of NAFTA?

3. Even though the complete elimination of tariffs in all countries would be likely to promote economic efficiency both in Canada and throughout the world, Canadian policy makers of course have no control over tariffs in foreign countries, and we cannot expect to be able to persuade all other countries to remove their tariffs on imports from Canada. On the other hand, it would be possible for Canada to eliminate unilaterally all tariffs on imports into Canada even if other countries do not reduce their tariffs on imports from us. Discuss arguments for and against such a unilateral tariff elimination.

4. Explain carefully how a tariff tends to reduce the benefits of international specialization.

5. Consider a tariff high enough, not just to reduce, but to completely prevent imports (a "prohibitive" tariff). How would it affect consumers? producers? the nation as a whole? Would the government collect any duty revenue from such a tariff? From a tariff that only reduces imports?

6. The text argued that a country may improve its terms of trade by restricting imports. In 1973 the oil-producing countries of OPEC managed to improve their terms of trade by restricting their exports. Explain carefully what are the similarities and differences between the "terms of trade" argument for restricting imports and the "terms of trade" argument for restricting exports.

ANSWERS

True-False: 1T, 2F, 3T, 4T, 5F, 6T, 7F, 8F, 9F, 10T

Multiple Choice: 1b, 2d, 3a, 4e, 5d, 6d, 7c, 8b, 9a, 10d, 11d, 12d, 13d, 14c, 15b, 16d, 17c, 18d, 19c, 20d, 21d, 22e, 23d, 24d

Exercises: **1a.** P_4, Q_4, P_2, Q_2, Q_6, import, *BC*, gain, P_4ECP_2, worse, P_4EBP_2, gain, *EBC*
1b. rise, P_3, *FG*, lose, P_3GCP_2, better, P_3FBP_2, *FG*, *FGKJ*, loss, *FJB* and *GKC*
1c. is not, more than, above, is, equal to, t, t, *FG*
1d. P_3, lose, P_3GCP_2, gain, P_3FBP_2, P_2, P_3, zero, loss, *FGCB*
1e. larger, loss, loss, tariff, quota, foreign holders of quota rights

ANSWERS TO PROBLEMS FROM THE TEXT

20-1. This statement can't be true, since it is possible to raise a tariff so high that it eliminates all imports – and therefore any duty paid on them. Thus, as tariffs are increased from an initial zero level, duty revenue rises at first; but eventually it must fall.

20-2. (a) Since trade is now being cut off, rather than opened up, just reverse the analysis in Figure 19-8. Price rises rather than falls. (That is, all gains in Figure 19-8 become losses, and vice versa.)

(b) Eliminating exports has exactly the opposite effect as allowing exports in the first place.

(c) If exports are eliminated, it does not make any difference how this occurs. Export restrictions may be imposed for political reasons.

20-3. In one respect, tariff and transport costs are the same: They both deter trade. But, in another respect, they are different. If Canadian exporters were to incur higher costs because they went back to using clipper ships, this would be a waste – money down the drain. But if they incur a higher cost because they pay a foreign tariff, this is not all waste. Instead, some is a transfer from exporters to the foreign countries that are now collecting duty revenue.

20-4. Assume that there is a perfectly elastic world supply at price P_w – that is, Canada is a price taker on world markets. Draw a demand and supply diagram like Figure 20-3(*b*) in the textbook, but set P_w above the intersection between the demand and supply curves. The country would be an exporter of the good under free trade. An export tax *t* reduces the domestic price from P_w to P_t, by the amount of the tax. Producers lose as a result of the lower price. Part of this is reflected as a gain in consumers' surplus (a transfer from producers to consumers), part as an increase in government revenues (a transfer from producers to the treasury). The balance reflects efficiency losses resulting from an inefficiently high level of domestic consumption (the consumption loss) and from an inefficiently low level of production (the production loss). Nonetheless, a country might choose to levy an export tax if firms are foreign owned. In that case, the transfer from producers to domestic consumers and the treasury is an income transfer from foreigners – the country is better off, notwithstanding the induced consumption and production inefficiencies.

Equally well, if a trading partner threatens to introduce tariffs, an export tax will have the same effect on trade flows but will generate revenues for the domestic treasury rather than the foreign treasury.

20-5. A country may choose to voluntarily restrict its exports rather than have its partners introduce tariffs or other forms of protection such as import quotas. The issue comes down to the transfer effects associated with the various alternative methods of distorting free trade. For example, VERs will be equivalent in their economic effects to import quotas in the foreign country. VERs, however, provide a means of effectively appropriating quota rights, generating an income transfer from foreigners. Of course, a country's ability to do this sort of thing will depend on the degree of international competitiveness.

20-6. (a) First, you should plot the demand and supply curves on a sheet of graph paper. In the absence of trade, the equilibrium price would be well above the world price. Canada will, therefore, import snowmobiles. At P = \$6,000, domestic consumption (read from the demand curve) will be 25,000.

(b) At P = \$6,000, domestic production (read from the supply curve) will be 5,000.

(c) Imports of 20,000 snowmobiles, valued at \$6,000 each amount to \$120,000,000.

(d) The tariff would raise the domestic price by \$4,000 per unit to \$10,000. This would reduce domestic consumption to 17,000 snowmobiles of which 8,000 would be imported.

(e) At pre-tariff prices, the value of this import is \$48 million. At post-tariff prices, the value of this import is \$80 million. Since imports (foreign exports) have fallen by 12,000, there is a loss to foreign producers of \$72 million.

(f) Canadian consumers lose. The reduction in consumers' surplus is (see Figure 20-3(*b*) in the textbook) \$84 million.

(g) The gain to producers (area 3 in Figure 20-3) is \$28 million. The gain to the treasury (area 4 in Figure 20-3) is \$32 million.

(h) There is a net welfare loss to Canada of \$24 million (reflected in areas 1 + 2 in Figure 20-3).

CHAPTER 21

Natural Resources: Are We Using Them at the Right Rate?

LEARNING OBJECTIVES

After you have studied this chapter in the textbook and the study guide, you should be able to

- Distinguish between renewable and non-renewable resources
- Distinguish between common property and privately owned resources
- Describe the internal and external costs of extracting a common property resource, and explain why both of these are internal costs if the resource is privately owned
- Describe the maximum sustainable yield of a renewable resource and explain why harvests involve no future costs if the population of a species is greater than this; and why problems arise if the population is harvested down to a level below this
- Explain why simple projections of the use and availability of resources yield misleading predictions
- Explain why a perfectly competitive market in a natural resource may be efficient if the resource is privately owned, but not if it is common property
- Outline the principal measures which may be taken to induce appropriate conservation of a common-property resource
- Describe the efficient pricing pattern for a non-renewable resource and explain why conservation doesn't mean to simply stop using a non-renewable resource
- Describe how Canadian oil prices were controlled in the 1970s and early 1980s, and some of the practical problems that were encountered

- Explain the efficiency and transfer effects – domestic and international – of this policy, and how it affected the amounts of oil produced, consumed, and imported

- Present an argument for raising the domestic price of oil above the world price

CHAPTER SUMMARY

Since no one owns the fish in the sea, they are a **common-property resource**, and provide a good illustration of one of the central problems addressed in this chapter: Common-property resources are inadequately conserved in a free, perfectly competitive market. The reason is that fishing involves two costs – (1) the internal costs incurred by those who fish, such as the boats, nets, labour, and so on, and (2) the external cost that falls on future generations because there is less of this resource available to them. If the resource is common property, fishing firms don't pay any attention to this second cost. The fishing firm, for example, that ignores the external costs it is imposing on future generations will produce more than the efficient amount. (Its output decision is influenced by its internal costs, but not by the external costs it creates.)

Policies to Reduce Inefficiency in Resource Extraction

There are three possible ways to reduce inefficiency:

1. Set a physical limit on the catch. The problem with this approach is that it does not use the market mechanism. Instead, a government official restricts the catch (perhaps by putting a limit on the size of nets or size of boats). Too severe a physical restriction may be worse than no restriction at all.

   The two alternative ways to increase efficiency do use the market mechanism:

2. Impose a tax or fishing fee on fishermen according to the number of fish they catch – specifically, impose a tax on them equal to the external costs they generate.

3. Create **property rights**; let the fish be privately owned. While this is not possible in the oceans or Great Lakes, it might be in inland lakes or ponds. (And it certainly is feasible for many other resources – such as timber – that are already privately owned to a substantial extent.) Once the schools of fish are privately owned, the owners will take into account both the harvesting costs and the cost of having a reduced catch in the future. (It is their future catch that will be

reduced.) Thus, this future external cost is internalized once the resource is privately owned. Since the private owners will take all costs into account, the result is an efficient one. But it won't be equitable, unless the new owners are charged in some way for the asset (the fish) that they now own.

Special Problems of Non-renewable Resources

Since schools of fish can eventually reproduce themselves, they are a **renewable resource**. On the other hand, there are other resources, such as coal, oil, or base metals that are not renewable. The key questions with such resources are: Will we run out, and if so, when? What can we do to prevent this? Simple projections of present trends point to an eventual doomsday, when rising population overtakes our limited resources. But such projections are over-simplified, because they do not allow for the adjustments that will take place as resources become scarce.

One of the most important kinds of adjustment is this: As a resource becomes more scarce, it becomes more expensive. This, in turn, leads to: (1) a substitution in production for the scarce resource by other factors that are more plentiful; (2) a substitution in consumption by goods that require less of the scarce resource; (3) discovery and development of substitutes.

What Is the Efficient Pricing Pattern of a Non-renewable Resource?

The answer, illustrated in Figures 21-5 and 21-6 in the textbook, is that its price should keep rising as it becomes scarcer and scarcer; this will generate increasing pressure to conserve, for example, by using substitutes instead. It is important to understand why its price should not be the same in each year. This would be inefficient because $100 of a resource this year is worth more than $100 next year; used this year in investment it can grow to more than $100 next year. Therefore, it's efficient to use more this year and less next year – and a relatively low price this year and high price next year will generate that pattern.

It is also important to understand why, in a perfectly competitive market, the price of a resource will not (as well as should not) be the same in each year. If it were, the resource holders would sell it all off this year, and earn interest on the proceeds. (This is better than holding it until next year, selling it then for the same price, and earning no interest.) The price difference leaves them indifferent and therefore happy to sell it in either year.

Oil

Under the influence of OPEC – and, in particular, the Saudi Arabians – the world price of oil rose over ten times between 1973 and 1982. To provide some relief to oil users, the government instituted a policy of holding the domestic Canadian price down below the rapidly escalating world price. Full detail on the effects of this price ceiling – and the problems it raised – cannot be provided without a diagram, and you should be sure you have mastered Figure 21-7 in the text before proceeding. However, three of the broad effects of this price control policy can be sketched out.

1. There were winners and losers. The winners were oil users – from Sunday drivers to the giant power-generating companies and their customers – who benefited because the price of oil was kept down. However, this lower price hurt oil producers in Western Canada, as well as the governments in the producing provinces whose royalty revenues were reduced.

2. There were two efficiency losses, shown by the two shaded triangles in Figure 21-7. One arose because the low price encouraged inefficiently high levels of oil consumption, while the other arose because the low price discouraged domestic oil production (resulted in an inefficiently low level of production).

3. To reduce the negative effects on production, the government added a twist to this policy and thus created a "blended price system." Under this system, the price of "new" currently produced oil was not kept down. It was allowed to rise to the world price. Thus, domestic production of oil would not, it was hoped, be discouraged after all. On the other hand, the price of "old" oil (that was already being produced, and would continue to be produced almost regardless of price) was still kept low. Finally, the price that oil buyers paid was a "blended" average of these various prices (including, in addition, the high world price of imported oil). Because Canadian oil users were paying the average of what these various kinds of oil cost, it was not necessary for the government to provide any subsidy of the kind typically required by a price-control policy. Unfortunately, however, it was an imperfect solution. Because it did not allow the domestic price paid by oil users to rise to the world price, Canadian consumption and, hence, imports of oil continued at a relatively high level. Furthermore, the system with different producer prices for new and old oil was difficult to administer because new and old oil cannot be physically distinguished. In the mid-1980s, the control system was gradually dismantled and, following the decline in world oil prices in 1986, the gap between the world price and the domestic Canadian price essentially disappeared.

Even though the world price of oil in the late 1980s and early 1990s has fallen well below its previous peak, energy policy remained an important issue. For one thing, there was the question of what steps could be taken to prevent another crisis if OPEC were once again to restrict oil exports. Furthermore, we have become more aware of the potential damage that carbon dioxide emissions (to which oil is a major contributor) may be doing to the world's climate. This raises the question: To what degree will North American energy users turn to other forms of energy such as natural gas and – perhaps most important in the long run – how soon will nuclear fusion (as opposed to the fission technology in use today) be developed to the point where it can, to a substantial degree, replace oil as a source of energy? As the 1990s began, that date was still a long way off.

IMPORTANT TERMS

1. Renewable resource
2. Non-renewable resource
3. Common-property resource
4. External cost associated with resource harvesting/extraction
5. Maximum sustainable yield
6. Property rights
7. Reservation price
8. Dynamic efficiency
9. National Energy Program (NEP)

TRUE-FALSE

T F 1. Under perfect competition, the rate of extraction of a privately owned resource is generally greater than the efficient rate.

T F 2. Those harvesting a common-property resource take into account only the harvesting cost – not the cost to society of having less of this resource available in the future.

T F 3. For a common-property resource, supply is determined by the marginal extraction cost only.

T F 4. A competitive equilibrium in the market for a privately owned natural resource is generally inefficient.

T F 5. If it were possible to tax those who fish for each fish caught, then, in theory, it would be possible to eliminate the efficiency loss that results because the oceans are not privately owned.

T F 6. An open border to fishermen from foreign countries would make the harvesting of fish more efficient, just as a border open to imports of foreign goods makes production within a country more efficient.

T F 7. Conservation requires that non-renewable resources not be used at all.

T F 8. Allowing the domestic price of oil to rise to the world price makes us more dependent on foreign supplies.

T F 9. A policy of keeping the domestic price of a resource below the world price results in an inefficiently low level of domestic production.

T F 10. Raising the domestic price of oil above the world price will put upward pressure on the world price.

MULTIPLE CHOICE

1. In a perfectly competitive market, the last unit of a privately owned resource will be sold for:
   a. more than its reservation price
   b. less than its reservation price
   c. its reservation price
   d. more than its conservation price
   e. less than its conservation price

2. The height of the supply curve for a common property resource reflects:
   a. the extraction cost
   b. compensation for the reduced amount available in the future
   c. the extraction cost less compensation for the reduced amount available in the future
   d. the extraction cost plus compensation for the reduced amount available in the future
   e. the extraction cost or compensation for the reduced amount available in the future, whichever is larger

3. Which of the following is a common-property resource?
   a. fish
   b. timber on privately owned land
   c. an oil company's reserves
   d. coal
   e. copper

4. In analyzing resource use, economists use the term "reservation price" to mean:
   a. the lowest bid a seller will take in an auction
   b. the highest bid a buyer will pay in an auction
   c. the cost of harvesting or extracting a resource today
   d. the amount necessary to compensate for the reduced availability of the resource in the future
   e. c. and d.

5. The reservation price of a resource will decrease if:
   a. the expected future cost of extracting the resource rises
   b. the expected future price of the resource rises
   c. the expected future price of the resource remains constant
   d. auction prices have remained constant
   e. auction prices have been rising

6. The sustainable yield for fish (a renewable resource)
   a. is the amount that can be harvested while still leaving next season's population constant
   b. is independent of the fish population
   c. increases with the size of the fish population
   d. both a. and c.
   e. none of the above

7. A reasonable conservation objective for the fishery is to
   a. freeze the catch at market determined levels
   b. set quotas that are consistent with sustainable yields
   c. set quotas below the sustainable yield until the population has reached the level consistent with the maximum sustainable yield
   d. close down the fishery once and for all
   e. none of the above

8. Efficient pricing of a non-renewable resource requires that
   a. price rises at the rate of interest
   b. price is the same in every year
   c. quantity extracted is the same in every year (ceteris paribus)
   d. quantity extracted falls from year to year (ceteris paribus)
   e. both a. and d.

9. Between 1973 and 1982, the world price of oil (in U.S. dollars) rose from:
   a. less than $3 a barrel to $13 a barrel
   b. less than $3 to $23
   c. less than $3 to over $30
   d. $13 to $23
   e. $13 to over $30

10. The rapid increase in the price of oil in the 1970s:
    a. could be fully justified as a conservation measure
    b. could be partly justified as a conservation measure, but also reflected the exercise of monopoly power
    c. could not be justified, even in part, as a conservation measure
    d. represented a transfer from OPEC countries to oil-importing countries
    e. discouraged North American conservation efforts

11. Which of the following is a valid reason for raising the domestic Canadian price of oil above the world price?
    a. it would increase the revenues of oil exporters such as Venezuela and Mexico, with whom Canada has always had good diplomatic relations
    b. it would encourage consumers to substitute oil for natural gas
    c. it would, indirectly, make us less vulnerable to an interruption of international oil supplies
    d. b. and c.
    e. none of these reasons is valid

12. Keeping the domestic price of oil below the world price under the NEP:
    a. encouraged production and consumption
    b. discouraged production and consumption
    c. discouraged consumption and encouraged production
    d. encouraged consumption and discouraged production
    e. encouraged consumption, but had no effect on production

13. Under the "blended oil price" policy of the 1970s and early 1980s, which was highest?
    a. the price received by sellers of old oil
    b. the price received by sellers of new oil
    c. the price paid by buyers of new oil
    d. none of the above because these prices were all the same
    e. the policy was so confused that there was no way of telling

14. A substantial part of any increase in energy prices in Canada constitutes a transfer from
    a. Central Canadians to Western Canadians
    b. Canadians to foreign owners of the multinational oil companies that operate in Canada
    c. foreign owners of the multinational oil companies that operate in Canada to the federal treasury
    d. Central Canadians to the Alberta treasury
    e. mainly b. and d.

15. Putting a common-property resource under private ownership may raise which of the following problems?
    a. the resource will be harvested too rapidly
    b. if the new owners have monopoly power, they may use it to restrict the extraction of the resource more severely than conservation requires
    c. if the new owners have monopoly power, they may use it to increase the quantity extracted of the resource
    d. unless the new owners are charged adequately for this asset, it is unfair for society to provide them with such a windfall gain
    e. b. and d.

16. The creation of private property rights over what was previously a common property resource:
    a. is not legal for the government to do
    b. would raise problems of fairness if the government were to sell these rights to a private owner for a price below their market value
    c. would decrease the efficiency of the extraction of the resource
    d. would have no effect on the extraction of the resource
    e. would forever leave us with the same level of inefficiency in the extraction of the resource

17. An efficient pattern of resource use requires that:
    a. the resource be priced at the same level each year
    b. the price falls each year by the amount of the interest rate
    c. the price rises each year by the amount of the interest rate
    d. the cost of extracting the resource exceeds its price by the amount of the interest rate
    e. the cost of extracting the resource is less than its price by the amount of the interest rate

18. In a perfectly competitive framework, if a non-renewable resource is being extracted efficiently, and more is extracted next year than this year, then:
    a. the demand next year must have unit elasticity
    b. the demand this year must have unit elasticity
    c. the demand neither year must have unit elasticity
    d. the demand must be greater this year than next
    e. the demand must be greater next year than this

19. Conservation means:
    a. to stop using any of the resource at all
    b. to not use any of the resource until it is displaced by a substitute
    c. to use the resource in an efficient pattern over time, starting today
    d. to use the resource in an efficient pattern over time, starting as soon as its price starts to fall
    e. to use it in an efficient pattern over time, starting as soon as its price stabilizes

20. Which of the following policies is the least efficient way of responding to a higher world price of oil?
    a. limit the growth of GDP
    b. conserve more
    c. encourage more domestic production
    d. intensify the search for alternative sources of energy
    e. encourage energy-efficient technology

21. Allowing the domestic price of oil to increase to the world price results in:
    a. increased oil imports
    b. efficiency losses
    c. no change in efficiency
    d. increased domestic consumption of oil
    c. reduced domestic consumption of oil

EXERCISES

1a. Figure 21.1 depicts a perfectly competitive market for a natural resource. The demand curve is D, the marginal cost of extraction is the height of the curve labelled S, and the marginal external (future) cost is the difference between the height of S and S'. The efficient quantity (assuming no external benefits) is _____, and this quantity will be demanded if the price is _____. If the resource is privately owned, the price will be _____, the quantity extracted will be _____, and the size of the efficiency loss will be _____.

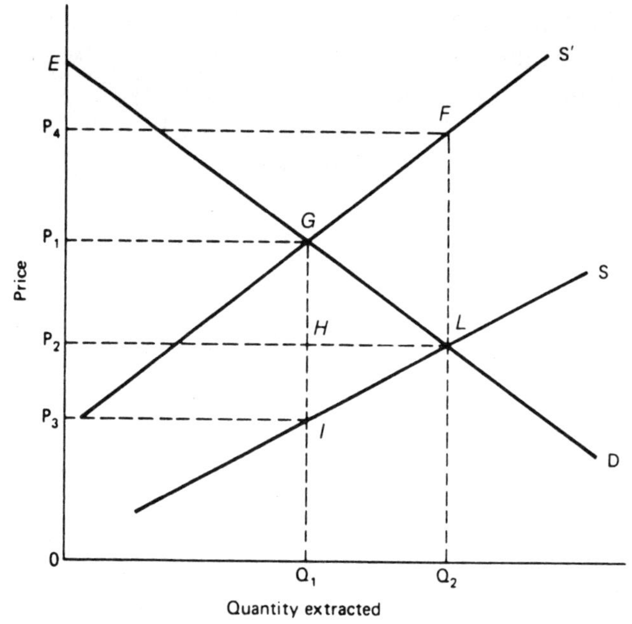

Figure 21.1

1b. If the resource is not privately owned, the price will be _____, the quantity extracted will be _____, and the size of the efficiency loss will be _____. The efficiency loss could be eliminated by a (tax, subsidy) on extraction equal to _____ per unit.

2a. In Figure 21.2, a price ceiling of P_1 is imposed on the domestic oil market. Domestic production is _____, consumption is _____, and (exports, imports) are _____. Because importers have to buy oil at the high world price P_2 and sell it domestically for only P_1, the government must compensate them by paying them a subsidy of _____ per barrel, times the _____ barrels they are importing, for a total government subsidy payment of area _____.

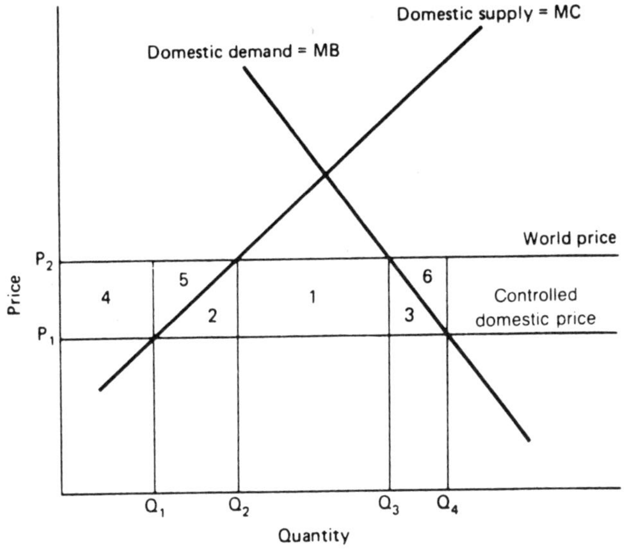

Figure 21.2

2b. When this price control is removed, price becomes _____, domestic production (increases, decreases) to _____, and domestic consumption (increases, decreases) to _____. (Imports, Exports) consequently (increase, decrease) to _____. Consumers (gain, lose) area _____ while producers (gain, lose) area _____ and the government (gains, loses) area _____ of (subsidy, tax) it no longer has to (pay, impose).

2c. When all these gains and losses are taken into account, the net (gain, loss) from decontrolling price is _____. This can be broken down into its two components: (1) The efficiency gain of area _____ because consumers are no longer buying oil they value at less than its true cost (the world price); and (2) the efficiency gain of area _____ because domestic firms are now producing oil for less than it previously cost to import. At the same time, there has been a transfer from consumers to _____ and _____.

ESSAY QUESTIONS

1. Explain how the problem of excessive use of a common property resource is similar to the problem of environmental pollution (discussed in the next chapter). To deal with each of these problems, the government sometimes considers

quantity restraints. Explain why you think these policies are effective or ineffective in dealing with each of these problems.

2. How does private ownership help to eliminate the inefficiency that exists when a resource is publicly owned (common property)? Would inefficiency be eliminated just as well if ownership were given to a single owner who then had a monopoly? What new problems might be created by allowing the resource to be monopolized?

3. "One of the shortcomings of the market mechanism is that private business interests are concerned, not with the future but, instead, with how much profit they can earn right now. We need the government to regulate the rate of extraction of natural resources to protect future generations from being deprived of their rightful share of resources." Do you agree or disagree? Why?

4. "If the population of a species is now greater than the point of maximum sustainable yield, and if firms are now harvesting at a rate just large enough to maintain a constant size of population, then by increasing the rate of extraction they can harvest more now and more in the future." Explain this statement, using a diagram similar to Figure 21.2. If the cost of extraction is zero, what is the opportunity cost of raising the rate of extraction in this situation? Is this a case of being able to get something for nothing?

5. The strict auto emission standard imposed by North American governments during the 1970s achieved its primary purpose of reducing pollution. But it had an unfavourable side effect because it increased our consumption of gasoline and thus damaged our attempts to conserve oil. Could the benefits of reduced pollution have been achieved without damaging the conservation effort if a policy of a higher oil price had been implemented instead? Explain.

6. Explain some of the external costs of producing and using oil. In your view, how do these costs compare with those arising from the production and use of natural gas? Coal? Nuclear fission?

ANSWERS

True-False: 1F, 2T, 3T, 4F, 5T, 6F, 7F, 8F, 9T, 10F

Multiple Choice: 1c, 2a, 3a, 4e, 5a, 6a, 7c, 8e, 9c, 10b, 11c, 12d, 13b, 14e, 15e, 16b, 17c, 18e, 19c, 20a, 21e

Exercises: **1a.** Q_1, P_1, P_1, Q_1, zero

1b. P_2, Q_2, *GLF*, tax, P_1P_3

2a. Q_1, Q_4, imports, Q_1Q_4, P_1P_2, Q_1Q_4, 5 + 2 + 1 + 3 + 6

2b. P_2, increases, Q_2, decreases, Q_3, imports, decrease, Q_2Q_3, lose, 4 + 5 + 2 + 1 + 3, gain, 4 + 5, gains, 5 + 2 + 1 + 3 + 6, subsidy, pay

2c. gain, 5 + 6, 6, 5, producers, the government

ANSWERS TO PROBLEMS FROM THE TEXT

21-1. Yes, it could be justified on conservation grounds (if, for example, such an agreement were to restrict the catch from, say, Q to Q^* in Figure 21.1). However, if the fish exist only in this area (so these owners monopolize its supply), there may be a natural temptation to restrict the catch even further as a means of exercising market power to raise price.

21-2. The unit you are thinking of not using this year has a value, when extracted today, of P_1. (The height of the demand curve – i.e., the marginal productivity of this resource – is P_1.) Moving along PP' to the right, we see that this unit extracted today and put to productive use would have an increase in value to P_5 by year 5. This is more than its value if it is "held in the ground" and not extracted until year 5.

The demand curve in year 5 – that is, the marginal productivity of the resource if extracted then – lies below P_5. Therefore, extract and use it now: Then its value will grow to P_5 in year 5. That's better than extracting it in year 5 when its value will be below P_5.

21-3. There is no further timber growth at point *C*. The proper timing of a timber harvest is every 30 years at point *B*. (This is where a straight line from the origin is tangent to the yield curve. This maximizes the slope of the line – that is, maximizes the average annual yield.)

21-4. (a) We might have been impressed by it. But if we had known as much as we know now about how economies adjust, we would have been sceptical.

(b) Similarly, we are sceptical of a "doomsday conclusion" on oil today.

21-5. (a) Holding the price down increased domestic consumption and decreased domestic production relative to what they would have been at the world price – imports were, therefore, greater than would otherwise have been the case. The international transfer was reduced. If all domestic oil production was foreign owned, the amount of transfer would have been reduced by the amount of producers' loss resulting from the lower price.

(b) You should disagree with this statement. If anything, the NEP pricing policy reduced the potential transfer from domestic users (Central Canadians) to foreign owners of multinational oil companies operating in Canada. The answer hinges on the degree of foreign ownership. (Of course, there was also a reduced potential transfer from domestic users to the Alberta treasury.)

CHAPTER 22

The Economics of Protecting the Environment

LEARNING OBJECTIVES

After you have studied this chapter in the textbook and the study guide, you should be able to

- Explain why pollution involves a form of externality (external cost)
- Explain why perfect competition does not lead to efficiency when there is pollution or any other kind of external cost
- Show the efficiency loss from pollution in a diagram similar to Figure 22-2 in the textbook
- Explain why we cannot and should not attempt to eliminate pollution completely. Rather, the question is: How far should pollution be cut back?
- Explain why pollution can be interpreted as a common-property problem
- Explain why proper assignment of property rights, regardless of to whom they are assigned, may correct for the pollution problem
- Explain the relevance of transactions costs
- Demonstrate why the policy of imposing a physical limit on pollution is a far less efficient way of reducing it than imposing a tax on emissions
- Show why imposing physical limits on pollution but allowing pollution rights to be bought and sold is at least as efficient as a tax would be
- Critically evaluate the policy of subsidizing pollution-control equipment
- Explain how the responsibility for protecting the environment is divided between the federal and provincial governments in Canada

- Describe some of the problems with the methods currently used by Canadian governments to control pollution
- Explain some of the problems that arise when pollution spills over provincial or international boundaries
- Explain how recycling reduces the pollution problem (and, as a favourable side effect, also reduces the problem of resource depletion studied in the previous chapter)
- Discuss the issues relating to energy and the environment and the potential role for a carbon tax

CHAPTER SUMMARY

Many people think that environmental pollution is simply a bad thing that should be prevented. They believe that it has nothing to do with economics and that economic considerations such as cost are irrelevant. Pollution, they contend, should be cleaned up, regardless of cost. The principal objective in this chapter is to show that pollution is, in fact, an economic problem – one that involves many of the principles that have already been developed in the textbook. Moreover, if economic considerations are ignored, pollution will be much more costly to control. Society will waste valuable resources in the clean-up effort. Or to put the same point another way: Our limited available funds for cleaning up will give us far less improvement in the environment if we ignore costs.

Pollution as an External Cost

Pollution is an **external cost**, because it is not borne by those responsible for it. For example, when smoke from a factory soils someone's clothes, the factory owner doesn't have to pay the cleaning bill.

Why Does a Perfectly Competitive Market Fail to Deal with the Pollution Problem?

When there is an externality like pollution, the "invisible hand" of a perfectly competitive free market does not provide an efficient outcome. The reason is that there is a violation of one of the conditions in Chapter 11 that allows perfect competition to deliver an economically efficient outcome. The condition that is violated is that the marginal cost to producers (MC) must be the same as the marginal cost to society (MC_S). This condition does not hold when there is an external cost such as pollution, because MC_S is more than MC. The difference between the two is the marginal external cost MC_E, as illustrated in Figure 22-1 in the textbook.

Efficiency requires that the marginal benefit to society (shown by the demand curve) be equal to the marginal cost to society MC_S. In Figure 22-2 of the textbook, we see that this efficient outcome is at E_2. However, this is not the equilibrium in a perfectly competitive free market. The reason is that, as always in such a market, supply reflects the cost facing producers. But this is only their private cost MC. The external cost of their actions is a cost they don't have to face. Because supply reflects private cost MC only, the perfectly competitive equality of demand and supply is at equilibrium E_1 rather than the efficient E_2. Thus, perfect competition is inefficient; too much output of this polluting good is produced (Q_1 rather than the efficient output Q_2). The efficiency loss is measured by the shaded triangle in this figure. Be sure you can explain this triangle: For each of the units of "excess" output between Q_2 and Q_1, **social cost** MC_S exceeds benefit D. There is, therefore, a net cost involved in producing each of these units – with the sum of all these costs being the triangle.

What Principles Should Guide our Antipollution Policy?

The above analysis suggests a simple way that the government can make a perfectly competitive market efficient. Impose a tax on polluting producers equal to the external cost they are creating; that is, impose tax r in Figure 22-2 of the text. This tax now becomes one of the costs producers have to face. In other words, the "external cost is now internalized," because it has now become a cost that producers have to face. Since producers will have to take this external cost – along with all their other costs – into account in making their supply decisions, the supply curve shifts up from S_1 to S_2. Supply now reflects both **internal** and external costs, and the perfectly competitive equilibrium of demand and supply is at the efficient point E_2. Thus, with this simple imposition of a tax, the perfectly competitive market does yield an efficient outcome after all. Adam Smith's invisible hand does work, because, with this tax, the government is applying the appropriate pressure on the market, and then letting the market work.

Figure 22-2 in the text illustrates another important principle: Polluting output can be cut back "too much." Limiting it to Q_3 is even worse than a "hands-off" policy that would allow output to continue unrestricted at Q_1. (At Q_3, the efficiency loss FE_2G would be even greater than the shaded efficiency loss triangle associated with Q_1.)

Finally, the conclusion from Figure 22-2 – that in an unregulated industry with polluting firms, competitive markets will not lead to the efficient amount of output (and pollution) – is similar to the conclusion from Figure 21-1 in the previous chapter – that overharvesting results in an efficiency loss when unregulated firms exploit a common-property resource. Pollution can also be interpreted as a common-property problem. So, for example, if those living downstream have the property right to clean water, they would then be able to sue or charge any polluting firm an amount that compensates them for any damage they incur. In Figure 22-2, this would be r per unit of pollution. The economic effects are identical to those of the tax solution. The difference is that with a tax there is a transfer from polluters to government; with **property rights** assigned to the downstream residents, there is a transfer from polluters to those who suffer directly from the pollution. Indeed, strictly from the point of view of economic efficiency, it does not matter to whom property rights are assigned. Even if those living upstream are assigned the property right to pollute, those living downstream would have an incentive to pay to have pollution reduced. The point is that, by creating property rights, you also create markets for the right to pollute. This makes it possible for the invisible hand to work properly and an efficient outcome will result from the market mechanism.

Antipollution Policies: The Canadian Experience

Canadian governments have not used the methods of taxing polluters as a way of controlling pollution; instead, they have favoured imposing limits on the allowable amounts of pollution that individual firms may emit. (The federal government has taken the lead in setting standards for the quality of air and water; however, the constitutional authority for setting and enforcing limits on allowable pollution rests with the provincial governments.) Another method has also been used: subsidizing the purchase of pollution-control equipment. On the whole, these programs have resulted in a substantial reduction in pollution, but most economists believe that they could have been designed to be more efficient. They make the following criticisms:

a. Because governments have not attempted to conduct systematic benefit-cost analyses of different types of pollution control, there has been little consistency in the limits set on allowable pollution: Some limits have probably been too restrictive, while others have not been restrictive enough.

b. Even if the total physical limit were to be set correctly (for example, at Q_3 in Figure 22-3 of the text) imposing restrictions on individual polluting firms is a much more costly way of reducing pollution (by, say, a half) than is the imposition of a pollution tax. Under a pollution tax of T, pollution would be cut back by those firms that have the lowest cost of pollution reduction – that is, firms to the right of Q_3 that can cut pollution at a cost shown, for example, by the short arrow. Thus, the total cost of reducing pollution would be minimized. On the other hand, when a physical limit on pollution is imposed on each firm, some of the reduction in pollution must be undertaken by firms to the left of Q_3 at the relatively high cost shown by, for example, the tall arrow. There is the same reduction in pollution, but it is achieved at an unnecessarily high cost.

In the United States, environmental agencies have recently begun to introduce a third method which, like a pollution tax, also lets the market work and therefore reduces pollution at minimum cost. This is a policy of imposing a physical limit on pollution but then allowing permits to pollute to be bought and sold at a market price. This "price of polluting" acts as a deterrent just like the tax T, ensuring that pollution will be cut back at minimum cost.

A fourth method that governments have used has been to subsidize pollution-control equipment. However, this has involved problems:

a. The government has often failed to ensure that the pollution-control equipment it has subsidized is used effectively.

b. Pollution-control equipment provides, at best, an "end-of-pipe" solution that is often more costly than other solutions such as using cleaner inputs. (For example, less polluting Western coal could be used in power plants.) Again, either a pollution tax or a system of tradeable permits would be a lower-cost policy because it would give firms not only the incentive to "cure" pollution, but also the incentive to find the least expensive cure.

Political Problems Plaguing Pollution Prevention

Even though Canadian and American governments have had remarkable success in slowing down and even reversing the deterioration of the environment, there are signs that further progress will be difficult. One reason for this is political. The lobbying efforts mounted by the firms opposing specific antipollution policies are likely to be more intensive than the lobbying by representatives for the beneficiaries. For a particular firm, preventing tighter antipollution rules may be a matter of life and death, while for those who benefit from anti-pollution policies, the effects of the rules applied to any single firm are of negligible importance. Furthermore, the pollution issue is sometimes complicated by the fact that pollution spills over boundaries. For example, some of the air pollution generated in Ontario spills over into Quebec; pollution of the Great Lakes by industrial firms on the American side of the lakes is of concern to Canadians as well as to American fishermen and swimmers; emissions of sulphur dioxide by U.S. power plants also affect Canadians. The problem here is this: How does one ensure that the government that has jurisdiction over the polluting firms takes into account the benefits accruing to residents in other jurisdictions when they decide how tightly to control their polluters?

Recycling

Recycling can play an important role in reducing the amount of pollution because it disposes of polluting wastes (such as empty beer cans). Such a policy would also mean that we will need to extract fewer natural resources from our environment. If we produce new beer cans out of old ones, we won't need to use as much bauxite.

Energy and the Environment

Alternative energy sources have (1) different implications for the costs of production and (2) different implications for the environment. In the 1990s, as concerns over the greenhouse effect have assumed centre stage, there has been increasing support for a simple but effective way of reducing those forms of pollution that contribute most significantly to global warming. In particular, there appears to be a strong case for a **carbon tax.** This would provide an incentive to cut back on the use of fossil fuels and to seek more energy efficient-low carbon technologies.

IMPORTANT TERMS

1. Internal cost
2. External cost
3. Social cost
4. Pollution and property rights
5. Effluent fees
6. Marginal cost of reducing pollution
7. Optimal amount of pollution
8. Transboundary pollution
9. International externality
10. Carbon tax

TRUE-FALSE

T F 1. Restricting industrial growth is one of the best measures for controlling pollution.

T F 2. Inefficiency occurs if producers do not take external pollution costs into account.

T F 3. Marginal external cost equals marginal social cost minus marginal private cost.

T F 4. The main effort of Environment Canada has been to collect the taxes that the government has imposed to discourage pollution.

T F 5. A pollution tax "internalizes an externality" because the producer is forced to face not only internal costs, but also the external costs imposed on society.

T F 6. Without government intervention, the marginal cost of having pollution would be zero.

T F 7. Setting an arbitrary physical limit on pollution will always be better than doing nothing at all.

T F 8. The problem with pollution is that, in the absence of government intervention, firms view it as an internal cost.

T F 9. A problem with the federal standards for maximum allowable rates of pollution emissions is that they are the same in provinces with relatively clean air as in provinces or cities where the air is already heavily polluted.

T F 10. Assigning environmental property rights to private industry will necessarily result in environmental disaster.

T F 11. If both the U.S. and Canadian governments agree to take into account the benefits to the citizens of the other country as well as to their own citizens when setting water quality standards for the Great Lakes, the lakes are likely to be cleaner than they would be if each country considers only the benefits of its own citizens.

MULTIPLE CHOICE

1. An example of an externality being internalized occurs if:
   a. an export firm is required to raise the price of a good it is also selling in the home market
   b. an export firm is required to export less and sell more goods on the home market instead
   c. a producer is forced to face the external cost its product imposes on society
   d. a producer is forced to face the internal cost its product imposes on society
   e. a tax is imposed on the producer equal to the marginal social cost of the good

2. In a perfectly competitive market, the marginal benefit of a polluting good will equal its marginal social cost if:
   a. a tax is imposed on the good equal to its marginal external cost
   b. a tax is imposed on the good equal to its marginal internal cost
   c. a subsidy is provided equal to the marginal internal cost
   d. a subsidy is provided equal to the marginal external cost
   e. the government does not intervene with either a tax or subsidy

3. In a perfectly competitive market for a polluting good where the government is following a "hands-off policy":
   a. less than the efficient amount will be produced
   b. more than the efficient amount will be produced
   c. the efficient amount will be produced
   d. price will be equal to the efficient level
   e. price will be higher than the efficient level

4. In the face of external costs, efficiency can be achieved in a perfectly competitive market by setting a tax equal to:
   a. the marginal social cost of producing the good
   b. the marginal internal cost of producing the good
   c. the marginal external cost of producing the good
   d. the total social cost of producing the good
   e. the total internal cost of producing the good

5. Airplanes flying low over houses near airports cause "noise pollution." The most efficient policy to deal with this would be to:
   a. rely on the "invisible hand" to take care of the problem
   b. provide a subsidy to each airline depending on the total amount of noise it creates in the affected neighbourhoods
   c. impose a tax on each airline depending on the total amount of noise it creates in the affected neighbourhoods
   d. impose limits on the number of flights of each airline
   e. subsidize airlines that install noise-abatement devices

6. The marginal external cost of a polluting good is equal to:
   a. its marginal social cost plus its marginal internal cost
   b. its marginal social cost less its marginal internal cost
   c. its marginal internal cost less its marginal social cost
   d. its marginal internal cost or its marginal social cost, whichever is greater
   e. its marginal internal cost or its marginal social cost, whichever is less

7. As time passes, pollution becomes a more difficult problem to deal with because the marginal cost of reducing pollution (MCR):
   a. shifts to the left, while the marginal cost of pollution (MCP) is rising
   b. shifts to the right while MCP is rising
   c. shifts to the right while MCP is falling
   d. shifts to the left while MCP is falling
   e. remains stable while MCP is rising

8. An effluent fee is:
   a. any tax imposed on the wealthy
   b. a special tax on the wealthy who pollute
   c. a tax on each unit of pollution
   d. a subsidy provided to polluters to encourage them to use cleaner fuels
   e. a subsidy provided to polluters who install pollution-abatement equipment

9. Which of the following is not a good example of an international externality?
   a. congestion of Canadian highways by American tourists
   b. leakage of chemicals from a plant on the Canadian side of the Niagara River
   c. smoke from a U.S. power plant that causes acid rain in Canada
   d. cutting down trees in Canada to produce newsprint for U.S. newspapers
   e. radioactive fallout in Sweden from a nuclear accident in the Ukraine

10. If a physical limit is set on the amount of pollutants each firm can emit:
   a. pollution will be cut back at minimum cost – that is, by the firms that can do so least expensively
   b. pollution will cut back at zero cost
   c. the result will surely be an improvement on leaving pollution uncontrolled
   d. the result will surely be inferior to leaving pollution uncontrolled
   e. it is not clear how the result will compare with leaving pollution uncontrolled

11. To determine the appropriate tax on pollution in a lake where there are many polluting industries, the government must have information on:
   a. the marginal cost of reducing pollution (MCR) and the marginal cost of having pollution (MCP)
   b. MCP but not MCR
   c. only the marginal benefit of reducing pollution (MBR)
   d. the marginal cost of pollution control equipment
   e. the marginal benefit of pollution control equipment

12. If one is to argue – along with Ronald Coase – that property rights should be created to deal with water pollution, then the question of who actually owns these rights:
    a. must be resolved by giving them to local governments
    b. must be resolved by giving them to polluting firms
    c. is more important from the point of view of equity, than of efficiency
    d. is more important from the point of view of efficiency, than of equity
    e. is important from neither an equity nor an efficiency point of view

13. If a physical limit is set on the amount of pollutants each firm can emit:
    a. pollution will be cut back, but at a higher cost than necessary
    b. pollution will be cut back, at the minimum possible cost
    c. there will be no change in the amount of pollution
    d. there will be an increase in the amount of pollution
    e. nothing can be said about the pollution that will result

14. The least-cost way of reducing pollution in a lake is to:
    a. encourage all firms to cut back their pollution by the same percentage
    b. force all firms to cut back their pollution by the same percentage
    c. let the firms with the highest profits cut back the most
    d. force the firms with the lowest profits to go out of business
    e. provide an incentive for firms with the lowest cost of reducing pollution to make relatively large cutbacks

15. If permits to pollute in a lake can be bought and sold, and sell for a price T, then pollution will be reduced:
    a. by those firms that can do so at a cost of less than T
    b. by those firms that can do so at a cost of more than T
    c. in equal proportion by all firms
    d. by firms that can externalize this internality
    e. by all firms that are physically able to do so, regardless of the cost

16. Consider the following three policies to reduce pollution:
    1. imposing physical limits on pollution
    2. imposing physical limits on pollution and allowing trade in pollution permits
    3. imposing a pollution tax

    The methods that use the market mechanism are:
    a. 1 and 2
    b. 1 and 3
    c. 2 and 3
    d. 1, 2, and 3
    e. 2 only

17. The government's policy of subsidizing the purchase of pollution control equipment can be criticized because it:
    a. places too great an emphasis on "end-of-pipe" treatment
    b. places too little emphasis on "end-of-pipe" treatment
    c. has led to an overemphasis by the government on how efficiently this machinery will subsequently be operated
    d. has been supported by inadequate short-term financing during its construction
    e. none of the above

18. The recycling of wastes:
    a. can reduce the rate of depletion of natural resources
    b. can increase the rate of depletion of natural resources
    c. is economically efficient, no matter how costly it may be
    d. causes pollution
    e. has no effect on pollution

19. The carbon tax proposal would
    a. tax different kinds of carbon-based fuels at the point of production and in proportion to the amount of carbon they contain
    b. tax different kinds of carbon-based fuels at a uniform level
    c. provide an incentive for adopting energy efficient technologies
    d. penalize coal
    e. all but b.

EXERCISES

1a. Figure 22.1 represents the market for a good that causes pollution.

If the market is perfectly competitive, output will be _____, market price will be _____, marginal social cost will be _____, and the marginal external cost will be _____.

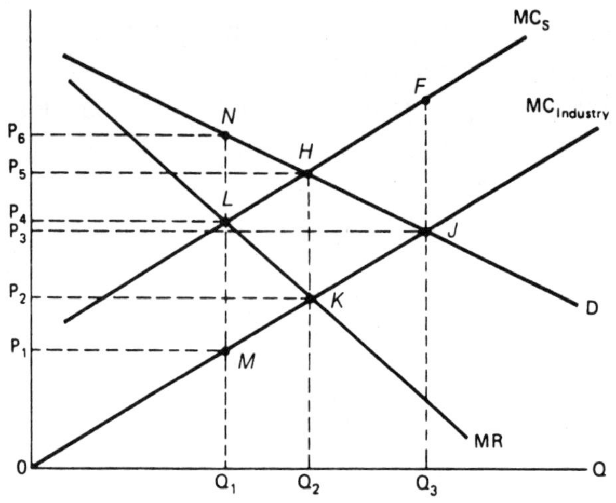

Figure 22.1

1b. If the commodity produces no external benefits, then the optimal output is _____. This output would be attained under perfect competition if the producers were faced with a tax of _____ per unit. This would result in a market price of _____. Without this tax, the efficiency loss will be area _____.

1c. Suppose that these firms were able to collude to form a monopoly. Then, the level of output (with no tax) would be _____, the market price would be _____, and the efficiency loss would be _____.

1d. Assume that the marginal external cost is constant – i.e., that the lines MC_S and $MC_{industry}$ are parallel, with $LM = HK = FJ$. Now suppose that the government imposes the same tax on the monopolist that it earlier charged to the perfect competitors. In this case, the monopolist will produce an output of _____, it will charge price _____, and the efficiency (gain, loss) will be area _____. Thus, a per unit tax on a polluting monopolist (will, will not) necessarily lead to greater efficiency.

2. If pollution is left uncontrolled in Figure 22.2, the amount of pollution will be _____. If the government imposes a tax T to reduce pollution, it will be cut back to _____. Those firms to the (right, left) of Q_1 will stop polluting while those firms to the (right, left) of Q_1 will continue to pollute.

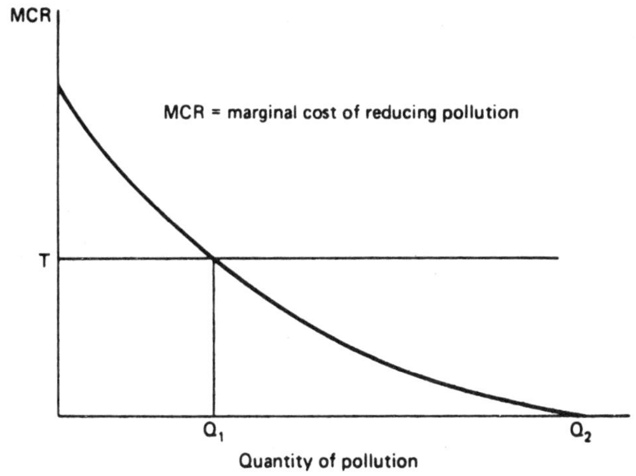

Figure 22.2

3a. If MCP_1 in Figure 22.3 is the marginal cost of having pollution and MCR is the marginal cost of reducing pollution, then, in the absence of any pollution tax, the quantity of pollution will be _____, MC*R* will be _____, and MC*P* will be _____. The economically efficient reduction in pollution is to quantity _____. This will result if firms are charged a tax of _____ per unit of pollution.

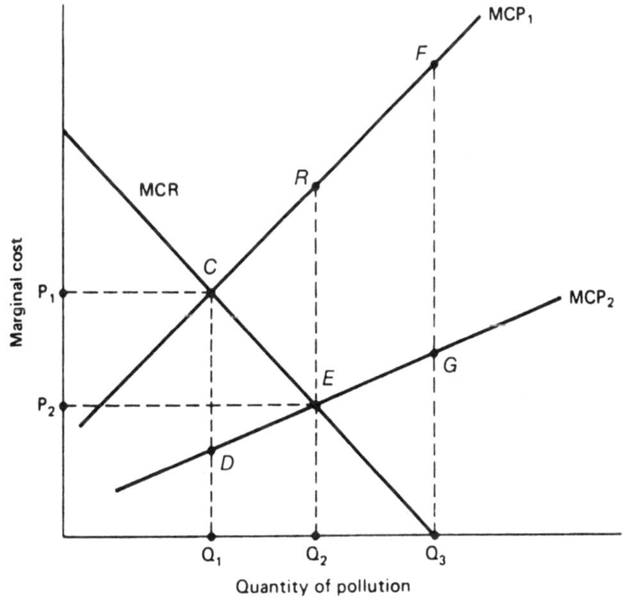

Figure 22.3

3b. Now suppose that the marginal cost of having pollution is MCP_2 instead of MCP_1. Then the economically efficient amount of pollution is _____. This will result if firms are charged a tax of _____ per unit of pollution. The efficient amount of pollution in this case is (more, less) because pollution is (more, less) damaging.

4. Now suppose that the marginal cost of having pollution is really MCP_1 but that the government makes a mistake and estimates it to be MCP_2. The government erroneously uses MCP_2 and sets the tax on pollution at _____. The resulting quantity of pollution is _____, which is (more, less) than the economically efficient amount. At this level of pollution, MCR is _____ and the true MCP is _____. There will be an efficiency (gain, loss) from the government's estimating error equal to area _____. Thus, we (may, may not) conclude that if the government underestimates the problem it will take inadequate action to counter it; that is, the government will set too low a pollution tax.

5a. The two lines in Figure 22.4 below show the marginal cost of reducing pollution MCR for two smoke-polluting firms (which are otherwise identical). Bars are added for detail. Reducing smoke pollution is less costly for firm (A, B). Suppose each firm is presently required by law to limit its output of smoke to 10 units, as shown by the dark vertical line. Both firms together generate 20 units of pollution. Now suppose that a government official decides, after reading this book, to impose a pollution tax instead of limiting each firm's smoke. If the official sets the tax at $650 for each unit of smoke emitted, then firm A will (cut back, expand) its emissions to _____ units of smoke, and B will (cut back, expand) its emissions to _____ units. Both firms together generate (more, less, the same) pollution as before. The firm with the higher MCR has (increased, decreased) its pollution and the one with the lower MCR has (increased, decreased) its pollution.

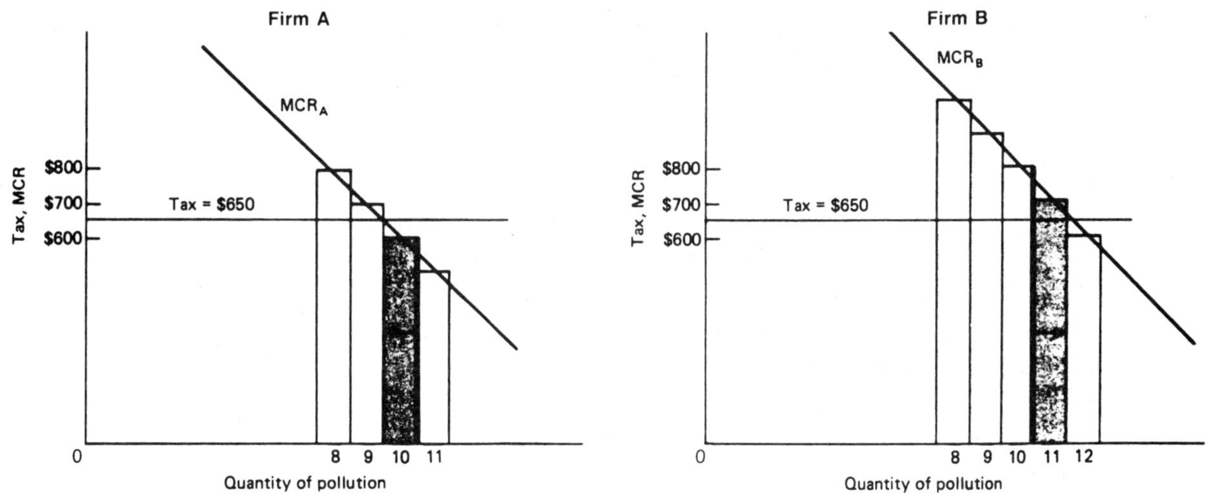

Figure 22.4

5b. Firm A's pollution-reduction costs have (increased, decreased) by _____, while firm B's pollution-reduction costs have (increased, decreased) by _____. Thus, the total pollution reduction cost of the two firms has (increased, decreased, stayed the same), while the total amount of pollution by the two firms has (increased, decreased, stayed the same). Therefore, the tax is (more, less) efficient in keeping down costs than the previous limits on pollution.

6a. Suppose that a company can produce a car that runs on gasoline, or one that runs on a newly invented fuel that sells for the same price, but that reduces the emission of pollutants by 50%. Unfortunately, the car using the new gasoline costs $200 more to construct. Suppose that, in all other respects, the two cars perform equally well, so that consumers do not care which fuel a car uses; if given the choice, they will buy the car with the lower purchase price. Therefore, with no regulations, the car producer will build the car using (gasoline, new fuel).

Suppose it is also possible to install an "end-of-pipe" pollution-control device on all its cars, which also reduces emissions by 50% but costs $500. Again, suppose that consumers do not care whether or not a car has this device. Then the auto producer will build the car using (gasoline, new fuel), and (with, without) the device. The cars (will, will not) pollute the atmosphere; but the car companies don't take this into account because this is an (external, internal) cost.

6b. Now suppose a government agency wants to cut back auto emissions by 50%. Therefore, it requires the company to install the pollution-control device. The company will now build cars using (gasoline, new fuel), and with the device. The cost to society of this end-of-pipe reduction in pollution is $_____ per car.

Now, suppose instead that the government merely requires the auto producer to cut back the emissions from its cars by 50%, leaving it up to the company to decide how to do this. Then, the cost to the company of complying with this requirement would be $_____ per car if it installed the device, or $_____ per car if it switched to the new fuel. Therefore, it would choose the (device, new fuel). In this case the cost to society of the reduction in pollution would be $_____ per car.

6c. In this example, the policy of telling the company how to reduce pollution is $_____ (more, less) costly per car than the policy of simply telling them to do it and leaving all the details to them. If, instead, the agency had told the company to do it by making cars that use the new fuel, the cost to society would have been (more than, less than, the same as) the cost of just telling them to do it. What general rule does this example suggest about the relative cost of telling companies to comply compared with telling them exactly how to comply?

ESSAY QUESTIONS

1. "One advantage of using taxes rather than physical limits to control pollution is that the former policy harnesses the forces of the marketplace to help find an efficient solution, whereas the latter policy does not." Do you agree or disagree? Explain your answer.

2. Explain why, in selecting the specific least-cost method of reducing pollution, private firms will do at least as good a job as government agencies, and often better.

3. In recent years, a large Canadian distillery has paid for the tickets to enable people to travel free on the Toronto subway system on New Year's Eve. Explain how this self-imposed tax has helped to promote economic efficiency by internalizing an external cost.

ANSWERS

True-False: **1F, 2T, 3T, 4F, 5T, 6F, 7F, 8F, 9T, 10F, 11T**

Multiple Choice: **1**c, **2**a, **3**b, **4**c, **5**c, **6**b, **7**b, **8**c, **9**d, **10**e, **11**a, **12**c, **13**a, **14**e, **15**a, **16**c, **17**a, **18**a, **19**e

Exercises: **1a**. Q_3, P_3, Q_3F, *JF*
1b. Q_2, *HK*, P_5, *HFJ*
1c. Q_2, P_5, zero
1d. Q_1, P_6, loss, *NLH*, will not
2. Q_2, Q_1, right, left
3a. Q_3, essentially zero, Q_3F, Q_1, P_1
3b. Q_2, P_2, more, less
4. P_2, Q_2, more, Q_2E, Q_2R, loss, *CRE*, may
5a. A, cut back, 9, expand, 11, the same, increased, decreased
5b. increased, \$600, decreased, \$700, decreased, stayed the same, more
6a. gasoline, gasoline, without, will, external
6b. gasoline, \$500, \$500, \$200, new fuel, \$200
6c. \$300, more, the same, telling them exactly how to comply will cost more unless the government happens to pick the least-cost method – in which case it doesn't matter

ANSWERS TO PROBLEMS FROM THE TEXT

22-1. If property rights are assigned to the polluter, there will be a transfer from the pollutee to the polluter – a payment to "buy" reduced pollution. If property rights are assigned to the pollutee, there will be a transfer from the polluter to the pollutee – compensation for damages done.

22-2. Using Figure 22-2 in the textbook, the total subsidy required will be area $Q_1E_1E_2Q_2$. Social costs, however, fall by the area under S_2 (the marginal social cost curve) between Q_1 and Q_2. The net benefit to society is, therefore, the difference between these two – the shaded triangle.

22-3. Clearly not – pollution is an inevitable by-product of industrialization. The issue is achieving the optimal level of pollution and this involves a comparison of the marginal benefits of further pollution reduction and associated marginal costs. Even in Figure 22-2, it is clear that reducing pollution to Q_3 involves a greater efficiency loss to society than does the status quo.

22-4. As is clear from Figure 22-3 in the textbook, closing down all firms is less efficient than doing so on the basis of their "willingness to pay" for the right to continue polluting.

22-5. If the economic break-even point were achieved – making nuclear fusion economically competitive with oil – there would be a substitution away from oil in order to eliminate the pollution damages associated with fission. Oil prices would tumble. If only the energy break-even point were achieved, since energy generation would remain extremely expensive relative to oil, the effects on oil prices would be less dramatic, but may fall in anticipation of the economic break-even point soon being achieved.

22-6. In one sense, the target rate of crime should obviously be zero. Through education and the solution of social abuses that lead to crime, we should be trying to eliminate the desire of people to engage in crime. However, this is utopian: In the last analysis, there will always be some people left who want to commit crime. In such circumstances, the target should be to eliminate most – but not all – of this crime. The more we reduce crime, the more difficult and costly further reductions become. Even if half the population were engaged in police work, it is doubtful that crime could be eliminated altogether.

Another way of reducing crime is to make it more likely that someone who is arrested will be convicted. We could do so by setting up laws that make it easier to convict a suspect. But this too involves a cost. To see why, first note an essential problem: We don't know which suspects are guilty and which are innocent. (If we knew that, we wouldn't need to have trials.) The easier we make it to convict a suspect, the more likely it becomes that the guilty will (correctly) be convicted; but it also becomes more likely that an innocent individual will erroneously be convicted. And every time we jail an innocent individual, this is a cost of our policy of reducing crime by making convictions easier.

CHAPTER 23

Public Goods and Public Choice

LEARNING OBJECTIVES

After you have studied this chapter in the textbook and the study guide, you should be able to

- Demonstrate why a free, perfectly competitive market provides less than the efficient amount of a good with external benefits

- Measure, in a diagram like Figure 23-1 in the textbook, the efficiency loss resulting from the private provision of a good with external benefits

- Show why efficiency requires a good to be subsidized by an amount equal to the marginal external benefit it provides (assuming that there are not high costs of administering the subsidy)

- Define and fully explain the concept of a public good

- Construct the marginal social benefit curve (a) for a public good, and (b) for a private good, making clear the difference between the two

- Explain why the "free-rider" problem makes it difficult for the government to estimate the benefits of a public good simply by asking people how highly they value it

- Show why it may be necessary to view as a public good any wildlife species that is becoming extinct

- Explain the concept of "option demand" and demonstrate its significance in dealing with such a wildlife species

- Explain why ensuring that products and jobs are safe requires dealing with a lack of information rather than an externality

- Demonstrate why information problems justify government intervention

- Show why information problems are more serious for health than for safety
- Demonstrate why benefit-cost analysis is important in designing government regulations
- Explain why benefit-cost analysis involves many problems; for example, this approach often requires us to attach a value to a human life
- Demonstrate why government policy becomes inconsistent, with too few lives saved, if no attempt is made to put a rough-and-ready value on a human life
- Give the reasons for believing that when the government provides a good or service – whether or not this is in response to a failure by the free market – major problems remain, such as internal problems in government decision making, problems in defining the public interest, and the problems of bureaucracy; that is, efficiency is still not guaranteed

CHAPTER SUMMARY

The last chapter dealt with external costs. In this chapter we use a parallel approach to analyze external benefits – that is, the benefits of a product that are enjoyed by others, above and beyond the internal benefits enjoyed by those who buy it. When **external benefits** exist, a free perfectly competitive market does not produce an efficient outcome. There is too little free-market production of such a good, just as there was too much production of a good with an external cost in the last chapter. The solution is to subsidize the good with the external benefits, just as the good with the external costs was taxed in the last chapter.

A further objective of this chapter is to extend this analysis of external benefits to describe the concept of a **public good**. A flood-control dam is an example of a public good, because no one can be excluded from enjoying its benefits, regardless of who pays for it. Typically, with such a broad distribution of benefits, no specific individuals play a significant enough role as purchasers to be prepared to buy the good. So, if it is to be provided at all, it must be the government that purchases it.

In addition, the chapter explores product safety and job safety as an economic problem. Here too, costs cannot be ignored.

Finally, this chapter describes the difficulties a government faces in trying to decide whether or not intervention is justified, and the more general problems that arise whenever the government provides the public with any good or services. Even when the private market fails, and a good must be provided by the government (if it is to be supplied at all) problems remain.

Why is there too little production of a good with an external benefit?

The Inefficiency of a Private Market When There are External Benefits

A free, perfectly competitive market delivers less than the efficient output of a product with an external benefit because the marginal cost of the product (supply) is equated to its marginal private benefit (demand), rather than to its marginal social benefit. The reason is that, in deciding on their demand for the product, buyers take account of only the private benefit it will provide them, and ignore the external benefit it will provide to others. With the demand curve therefore reflecting only private benefit and any external benefit being ignored, it is no surprise that too little is produced, as Figure 23.1 demonstrates. The appropriate government policy is to subsidize this product by the amount of the external benefit it provides (assuming there are not substantial costs in administering the subsidy). Such a subsidy will increase the demand for the product and thus increase its output to the efficient amount.

Public Goods

In the case of products with an external benefit that we have been describing so far – such as gardening – you will receive an external benefit if your neighbour pays $100 for gardening services. But, of course, you will get an even larger benefit if you pay the gardener the $100 yourself in order to have the gardening done on your own lawn rather than on your neighbour's. Thus, the benefits you get depend on who buys the service. A public good can be viewed as the extreme case of a good with an external benefit, where the amount of benefit that an individual gets is just as great if someone else buys as it is if he or she were to buy it. In other words, the individual cannot be excluded in any way from enjoying it. For example, you get the same benefit from cleaner air, whether or not you help to pay for antipollution measures. That is not true of a private good. You can't enjoy a movie or a restaurant meal unless you pay for it. This is the reason that the benefits of a private good are horizontally summed in Figure 23-2 of the textbook, while the benefits of a public good are vertically summed in Figure 23-3.

The Free-rider Problem

If you will get the same benefit whether or not you help pay for a good, why not be a "**free rider**" and not pay at all (or pay as small a share as you can get away with)? The incentive for people to ride free raises problems for an entrepreneur who believes (let's suppose, correctly) that the benefits people would get from a public good – such as a flood-control dam – exceed its costs and it, therefore, should be built. How can it be financed, when everyone the entrepreneur asks to contribute to it tries to minimize that contribution by understating the benefits the dam would provide? In short, each individual has an incentive to be a free rider, enjoying the benefits of the dam without contributing to it. Since all individuals have this incentive to understate the benefits of the dam, it appears not to be justified, and does not get built.

Suppose the government, rather than a private entrepreneur, tries to evaluate the dam by asking people how highly they would value it. If they think they will be taxed according to their answer, they will understate. On the other hand, if they think their taxes won't be affected by the project, they will tend to overstate their benefit – as a means of slightly increasing the chance that the project will be undertaken. In this case, they have nothing to lose, since the cost they incur is not affected by their overvaluation.

An Alternative Approach by the Government

In view of the difficulties in trying to get people to answer accurately, the authorities generally reject the approach of asking people for their evaluation of a project. Instead they often use a "benefit-cost" analysis based on a completely different kind of information. To use the example in the text, they may estimate the benefit of a dam by examining how frequently floods have occurred without it, and the average crop loss.

This approach may be superior, but it still involves major problems. For example, those who are running this analysis may have a vested interest in having the dam pass the benefit-cost test because they may hope to be employed in its construction. Or they may simply be trying to please their employer – a government that has promised this dam in the last election. They may therefore add benefits – perhaps at an inflated value – until these benefits exceed the costs, and the project is justified. Such an inflation of benefits may be easy, especially if one of the benefits of a flood-control project is to save lives. It is very difficult indeed to attach a dollar value to a human life.

The Environment as a Public Good

One solution to excessive environmental pollution is the use of effluent charges. However, when the environment is deteriorating of its own accord, its preservation may be viewed as a public goods problem. Government protection of the environment is justified if the costs of protection are less than the benefits which accrue to all members of society.

Government Intervention to Ensure Safe Jobs and Safe Products

1. How is government intervention to ensure safe jobs and safe products to be justified? If firms under pressure let products or workplaces become dangerous, the health and safety of the firm's customers or labour force may be compromised. This seems like an externality, but it isn't. The damage is not to an innocent bystander (like those living on a polluted river). Instead, it is to the firm's customers or labour force who are parties to the transactions, and who can consequently take some action to curb the damage the firm is doing to them. For example, airline passengers can avoid an unsafe airline and workers can insist on a premium wage for dangerous jobs – provided they know the risks involved. The evidence is that workers do insist on some premium in risky jobs, but not enough to compensate adequately.

   Thus, the major problem is the lack of information about exactly what risks to health and safety there really are. By the time the public finds out an airline is dangerous, lives have been lost. This justifies safety regulations by the Department of Transport. As another example, workers can't know the cancer risks from handling chemicals. This justifies government intervention to ensure that chemicals are labelled.

2. Risks to health are a greater problem than risks to safety. Workers can see risks to safety such as an unprotected buzzsaw, and can insist that it be safely installed. There is a much greater information problem with health. A cancer risk from chemicals that may kill people 20 years later cannot be "seen." Therefore, government intervention to provide information and to prevent risk is even more strongly justified where there is a health risk than where there is a safety risk; however, both are important.

3. The airlines provide two exceptions to these general principles:
   a. There is a huge information problem with safety in the air. Unlike the case of a buzzsaw, where information about risk becomes available when one person is injured, information about risk on an airline may become available only after hundreds are killed. Since the information cost the public faces in this case is so high, the government is justified in imposing safety standards.
   b. Government regulation of airline safety is further justified by externalities. A crash may not only kill the parties to the transaction (the passengers and crew), it may also kill innocent bystanders on the ground who are not parties to the transaction. (They have nothing to do with flying.)

Evaluating a Government Regulation with Benefit-Cost Analysis

A regulation cannot be justified just because it has a desirable objective such as improving health and safety. It must be effective in achieving that objective; that is, it must provide substantial benefits. And those benefits should exceed its costs. The purpose of benefit-cost analysis is to perform just such a test.

One might expect that whenever policy makers are considering a new regulation, they would perform such a benefit-cost analysis. Unfortunately, this is not always the case. In some recent legislation, it is expressly stated that regulations must be enforced regardless of their costs.

If we take a benefit-cost approach to analyze a proposed new regulation, it is first necessary to estimate costs, such as the operating costs of the agencies that administer the regulations, and the costs incurred by firms in complying with the regulations.

Even greater problems are encountered in estimating the benefits of a regulation. For example, one of the benefits may be the saving of lives – and no one wants to put a value on a human life. It is far easier to say that the value of a life is infinite, and leave it at that. But that's not how we value our lives. We all take some small risk with our lives whenever we take a trip in a plane – or, for that matter, an even bigger risk when we travel by car. We don't sit at home and avoid the risk, as we would if we truly believed that our lives had an infinite value. But while it's easy to argue that the value of a life is less than infinite, it's very difficult to be more specific.

Even if the complete information necessary for a full benefit-cost test is not available, it is still possible to make government policy more effective using fragmentary information. To use an example cited in the text, a regulation imposing an arsenic standard has been saving lives at an estimated cost of $70 million per life. Alternatively, lives could be saved at a cost of only about $100,000 each by building more railroad overpasses. Obviously, we should switch to this policy; if we did, we could save the same number of lives at much lower cost. Or, to put the same point more appropriately, we could use our limited funds to save far more lives.

Other Problems with Government Expenditure Decisions

More generally, when decision-making shifts from the private marketplace to the government – as indeed it must in the case of a public good which the private market fails to deliver – then a new set of special problems arises:

1. Typically, private firms stop producing goods if they are no longer profitable – or, if they fail outright from the start – because these firms would lose money otherwise. On the other hand, government projects that are no longer justified

are much more difficult to terminate for two reasons: (a) no politician wants to admit that a project may have been a mistake, for fear of losing the next election as a result; and (b) there is no natural check, like the bankruptcy of a private firm, to force termination of a government project.

2. Political votes are not as specific and frequent as the economic votes that people cast everyday when they are deciding what to buy with their money. Thus private auto companies get a clear message of the models the public wants and does not want. Not so with public goods. It may be two or four years before the next election when the public can vote on how it likes or dislikes the dam and the other goods and services the government is providing. And even if people do approve of what the government is doing – and vote for it in the next election – it's hard to know whether the election victory is due to the dam the government has built, or to its foreign policy, or to some other completely different issue. (Public opinion polls make this problem less severe, but don't remove it.)

3. Special interest groups can exert an inordinate influence on government decision making. Even if you have no particular interest in the government spending money on a proposed new road in northern Alberta, it probably doesn't pay you to invest a great deal of energy and resources in opposing it, since it may add only a trivial 10 cents to your tax bill. But those directly affected in the area have a strong incentive to support it and lobby for its construction. Thus, a few large benefits concentrated in one area may politically outweigh many small, widely dispersed costs, even if the sum of all these small costs exceeds the benefits economically.

4. Politicians are mainly interested in projects with benefits that are both obvious to the public and immediate. (If they don't have a payoff before the next election, it may be too late.) Thus, politicians often do not take a long-term point of view; there is a tendency for much government effort to be centred on short-term decision making.

5. The job of implementing – and sometimes initiating – government policies is performed by a bureaucracy. There is a constant tendency for bureaus and their budgets to expand, in part because of the incentives for bureau chiefs to expand their personnel. Accordingly, bureaus tend to grow beyond the efficient size. This tendency is not checked by the threat of economic loss or bankruptcy that faces a private firm that overexpands.

IMPORTANT TERMS

1. External (spillover) benefit
2. Internalizing an externality
3. Public good
4. Non-excludability
5. Non-rivalry
6. Free riders
7. Public choice
8. Public interest

TRUE-FALSE

T F 1. Internalizing externalities means that producers are forced to face any external costs of their actions; and buyers are allowed to enjoy any external benefits generated by their purchases.

T F 2. One benefit of having the government provide public goods such as flood control dams is that these decisions are easily reversible.

T F 3. The reason private firms can't be relied on to produce a public good is that they would externalize the internal benefits.

T F 4. The marginal social benefit curve of a public good can be constructed by vertically summing the individual demand curves.

T F 5. You cannot be excluded from enjoying the benefits of a public good even if someone else pays for it.

T F 6. Benefit-cost analysis is designed to ensure that the total benefits of a policy will equal its total costs.

T F 7. It is generally more difficult to cut out an expenditure program in the private sector than in the public sector.

T F 8. The public can be more specific in expressing its preferences for goods by voting in elections than by making purchases in the marketplace.

T F 9. It may make sense to vote for a party that has promised to make a certain government expenditure, even though you don't want this expenditure at all.

T F 10. Politicians prefer policies with costs and benefits that are obscure.

T F 11. Government policy should ensure that no damage whatsoever occurs to the environment.

MULTIPLE CHOICE

1. In producing two goods (one with an external benefit, the other with an external cost) a free, perfectly competitive market will generate:
   a. too much output of the good with the external benefit, and too little of the good with the external cost
   b. too little output of the good with the external benefit, and too much of the good with the external cost
   c. too little output of the good with the external benefit, and just the right amount of the good with the external cost
   d. too little of both
   e. too much of both

2. Which of the following comes closest to being a private good with no external benefits?
   a. national defence
   b. painting the outside of your house
   c. painting the inside of your house
   d. hiring a gardener
   e. the police force

3. If the government follows a "hands-off" policy, then the production of a perfectly competitive good with an external benefit will result in:
   a. marginal external benefit being greater than marginal social benefit
   b. marginal external benefit being equal to marginal social benefit
   c. marginal social cost being equal to marginal social benefit
   d. marginal social cost being greater than marginal social benefit
   e. marginal social cost being less than marginal social benefit

4. If a good has an external benefit, the government can ensure an efficient outcome by introducing a:
   a. tax equal to the external benefit
   b. tax greater than the external benefit
   c. subsidy less than the external benefit
   d. subsidy greater than the external benefit
   e. none of the above

5. If there are substantial administrative costs in subsidizing a good with an external benefit, the government should:
   a. tax it instead, to provide the same result
   b. subsidize the good regardless
   c. cancel the subsidy regardless
   d. cancel the subsidy if the efficiency gain it would produce is less than the administrative costs
   e. cancel the subsidy if the efficiency gain it would produce is greater than the administrative costs

6. The internal benefit of a good is the:
   a. benefit enjoyed by those who haven't purchased it
   b. benefit enjoyed by the individual who has purchased it
   c. benefit enjoyed by free riders
   d. benefit enjoyed by the government, even though the public has purchased it
   e. benefit enjoyed by the public, even though the government has purchased it

7. An example of internalizing an externality occurs when:
   a. a firm building a ski lift buys a restaurant at the bottom of the hill
   b. a firm buys from a domestic supplier a good that it used to buy from abroad
   c. a city government subsidizes exterior home improvements
   d. a. and c.
   e. b. and c.

8. In defining the marginal benefit to society of a public good:
   a. the demand curves by individuals are horizontally summed
   b. the demand curves by individuals are vertically summed
   c. the demand curves by individuals are horizontally summed and then vertically summed
   d. we use the same technique that was used to derive the market demand curve for a private good from the individual demand curves
   e. we take the demand curve of the individual who is most eager and able to buy the good

9. With a public good:
   a. anyone can participate in the benefits except the actual purchaser
   b. everyone can participate in the benefits including the actual purchaser
   c. no one can participate in the benefits except the purchaser
   d. only free riders participate in the benefits
   e. free riders are prevented from participating in the benefits

10. Estimates that the government collects from individuals on how highly they value public projects tend to be unreliable because:
    a. if people feel they will be taxed according to the value they state, they will tend to understate
    b. if people feel they will be taxed according to the value they state, they will tend to overstate
    c. if people feel they will not be taxed according to the value they state, they will tend to overstate
    d. if people feel they will not be taxed according to the value they state, they will tend to understate
    e. a. and c.

11. A free rider is someone:
    a. who cannot be excluded from enjoying the benefits of a project even though this individual has paid nothing to cover its costs
    b. who can be excluded from enjoying the benefits of a project
    c. who is trying to encourage the government to continue its transportation subsidies
    d. who has paid more than a fair share of the costs
    e. who has paid his or her fair share of the costs

12. A species of wildlife in the wilderness:
    a. cannot die out unless it is adversely affected by human action
    b. will die out if it is left unprotected
    c. may die out if it is left unprotected
    d. will be prevented from dying out by free market forces
    e. should not be protected by the government because of option demand

13. Almost all studies estimate the value of a human life in the broad range:
    a. $330,000 to $5 million
    b. $3 million to $6 million
    c. $4.5 million to $15 million
    d. $100 million to $200 million
    e. $1 billion to $3 billion

14. In controlling the release of new drugs:
    a. there is a cost of delay for further testing, but no benefit of delay
    b. there is a benefit from delay, but no cost
    c. there is neither a benefit nor a cost from delay, because health is a non-economic issue
    d. there is a cost and benefit of delay; the cost is that lives may be lost because a life-saving drug can't be used yet
    e. there is a cost and benefit of delay, but neither can be specified

15. In their daily decisions, most people implicitly value their own life as worth:
    a. an infinite amount
    b. zero
    c. about half their current year's income
    d. some value between a. and c.
    e. some value between b. and c.

16. Workers who take risky jobs:
    a. protect themselves fully by insisting on a higher wage that will completely compensate for the risk
    b. protect themselves partly by insisting on a higher wage that will partly compensate for the risk
    c. don't protect themselves at all
    d. settle for a lower wage
    e. settle for the same wage but lower fringe benefits

17. Benefit-cost analysis often involves the following problem:
    a. questionable projects that have been promised in an election campaign may be justified by exaggerating benefits
    b. questionable projects that have been promised in an election campaign may be justified by underestimating costs
    c. it is very difficult to place a value on a human life
    d. projects may be evaluated by those with a conflict of interest – for example, engineers who may eventually be employed in building the projects
    e. all of the above

18. Typically, a government bureau that is a monopoly will produce:
    a. too much output, while a private monopoly will produce too little
    b. too little output, just like a private monopoly
    c. too much output, just like a private monopoly
    d. the right amount of output, while a private monopoly will produce too little
    e. too little output, just like a private oligopoly

19. Suppose you voted for the NDP in 1988 because you were opposed to free trade with the United States, even though you thought that the economic policies of the Progressive Conservatives were superior. Then this illustrates the problem that:
    a. public expenditure decisions are hard to reverse
    b. special interest groups have an inordinate influence on public decisions
    c. bureaucrats are not subject to the normal check of bankruptcy
    d. political votes are difficult to interpret because they are not as specific as market place votes
    e. free riders are difficult to deal with

20. Many economists have argued that our farm subsidy programs are inefficient – that what farmers gain from higher food prices is less than what consumers lose. But these programs continue. According to the principles explained in this chapter, which seems the most likely explanation?
    a. food is a public good
    b. the farmers' special interest is politically stronger than the consumers' general interest
    c. the farmers' special interest is politically weaker than the consumers' general interest
    d. consumers do not adequately recognize the benefits of good food and must be forced to pay for them through taxes
    e. farmers have more votes than non-farmers

21. Reversing a decision is more difficult for a government than a private firm because:
    a. this admission of error may damage the government in the next election
    b. business executives generally prefer to admit mistakes than to continue to lose money
    c. politicians don't directly suffer out of pocket when they continue uneconomic expenditures
    d. all of the above
    e. b. and c.

22. Logrolling:
    a. never damages the public interest
    b. always damages the public interest
    c. always promotes the public interest
    d. sometimes damages the public interest, and sometimes promotes it
    e. has an effect which is impossible to assess, no matter how much information is available on individual preferences

23. If the government asks individuals their valuation of a public good, they will:
    a. overstate if the government will tax them according to their stated valuation
    b. understate if the government will tax them according to their stated valuation
    c. understate if the government will finance the project without taxing them
    d. neither understate nor overstate if the government will finance the project without taxing them
    e. neither overstate nor understate if the government will tax them according to their stated valuation

24. Option demand is the demand for:
    a. a good, not because you want to use it now, but because you may want to use it in the future
    b. a good, not because you want to use it now, but because you are certain to want it in the future
    c. any public good that provides benefits now and in the future
    d. any private good that provides benefits now and in the future
    e. a good which is a private good now, but may be a public good in the future

25. In the case of a natural oligopoly, the appropriate role for the government is likely to be to:
    a. enforce competition legislation
    b. regulate price
    c. provide the good itself
    d. leave the market alone
    e. encourage price discrimination

EXERCISES

1a. Figure 23.1 below shows the supply curve *S* and demand curve *D* for a perfectly competitive good that provides external benefits. Assume for now that there are no external costs of producing this good, and ignore MC_S.

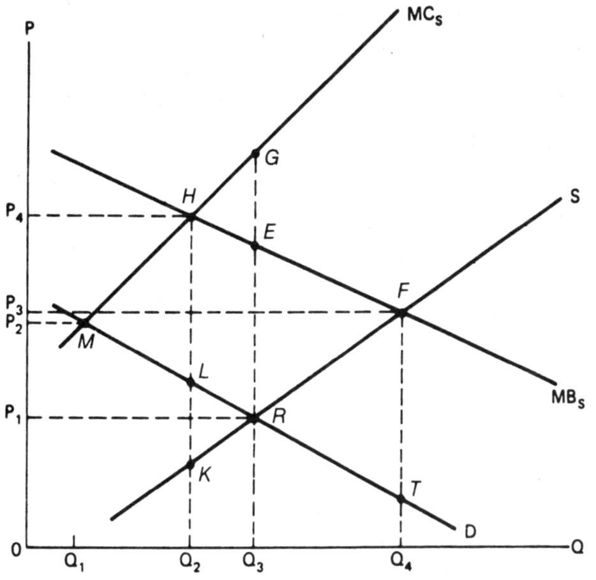

Figure 23.1

In an unregulated market, the quantity that is produced is _____ and the market price is _____. If the marginal social benefit curve is MB_S, then the economically efficient quantity is _____ and the marginal external benefit is _____.

1b. The efficiency loss from relying upon the private market for the provision of this good is _____. The government could eliminate this efficiency loss by offering a per unit (subsidy, tax) of _____ to the producers of this good.

1c. Now suppose that the good involves external costs as well as external benefits. (An example would be a dam that provides flood control to farmers downstream but that floods out farmers upstream.) Let the curve labelled MC_S represent the marginal social cost of producing the good. Then the efficient amount of production of the good is _____. At that level of production, the marginal external cost would be _____ and the marginal external benefit would be _____. With no tax or subsidy, the private market would produce (more, less) than the economically efficient amount and the efficiency loss would be _____. This efficiency loss could be eliminated if the government were to (tax, subsidize) the production of the good by _____ per unit.

2. Figure 23.2 shows the marginal private benefit MB_A and MB_B that individuals A and B receive from a public good (a waste-treatment plant). In Figure 23.2(*c*), show the marginal social benefit, assuming that A and B are the only members of society affected by the project.

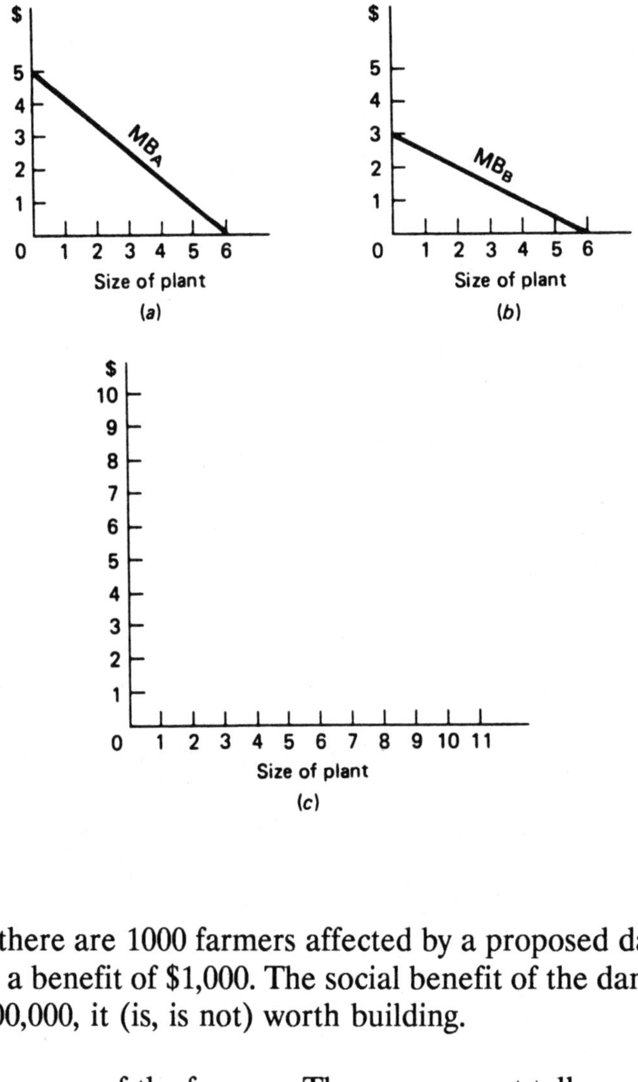

Figure 23.2

3a. Suppose that there are 1000 farmers affected by a proposed dam. Each of them would receive a benefit of $1,000. The social benefit of the dam is $_____. If the dam costs $500,000, it (is, is not) worth building.

3b. Suppose you are one of the farmers. The government tells you that it intends to tax farmers according to how much each says the dam will be worth to him or her. If you tell the truth, it will cost you $_____. If you say $2,000, it will cost you $_____. If you say no benefit, it will cost you $_____. You will have an incentive to (understate, overstate, reveal accurately) how much it is worth to you. Other farmers (will, will not) have the same incentive to provide this sort of answer, so the chances are that the dam (will, will not) be built – an (efficient, inefficient) outcome.

3c. As another example, suppose that the same 1000 farmers would get the same true benefits from the dam, but now suppose that the cost of building the dam is $1,500,000. In this case the dam (should, should not) be built. But suppose that now the government says that if it goes ahead with the dam it will tax the millions of taxpayers a few cents each to finance it. Your taxes will be scarcely affected. The only question the government has is: Should it go ahead or not? That depends on how highly farmers value it. If the government goes ahead, you will have a net gain (value to you of the dam minus your new taxes) of _____. You will maximize your chances of getting this gain if you (understate, overstate, reveal accurately) your benefit, and thus (increase, decrease) the chance that the dam will be built. Other farmers (will, will not) have the same incentive to give the same sort of answer, so the chances are that the dam (will, will not) be built – an (efficient, inefficient) outcome.

4. The Apex Company employs 2000 individuals working on high-steel construction. The firm has to pay its labour force a $1,000 per person wage premium each year in order to attract workers who are willing to risk their lives. The risks on this job raise the mortality rate by 2/1000; that is, the chance a worker will be killed during a year is 2/1000 higher than in other jobs. The question is: Should the government introduce a safety regulation that will reduce the risk by 1/1000, if this regulation costs $1.5 million (including both government administration costs and compliance costs by the firm)?

To answer this, we need to know the value of a human life. Because each worker is willing to take a 2/1000 chance of dying in return for an extra $1000 of pay, clearly, those workers value their lives at ($5 million, $500,000, $1,000, $500) which is the wage premium of $_____ divided by the _____ increase in risk.

Although this cannot be predicted precisely in advance, the expectation is that this regulation would save _____ lives, which is the _____ risk reduction from this regulation times the 2000 workers employed. Since each worker values his or her life at $_____, the benefit of this regulation is $_____. This is (greater than, less than, the same as) the $1.5 million cost of the regulation. Thus, this regulation (passes, fails) this benefit-cost test, and it would be (introduced, rejected).

ESSAY QUESTIONS

1. Explain carefully whether or not each of the following might be considered to be a good with an external benefit:
   a. the Canadian Olympic Team
   b. your telephone
   c. driver safety lessons
   d. television programs

2. If the government asks people to reveal how much they would benefit from a public good, will they tell the truth? If the government asks them to reveal how much they are being damaged by a good with an external cost, will they tell the truth? Why or why not? How will their answers be affected if the government tells them that it is thinking of providing them with protection from this external cost, with this protection to be financed out of the government's general tax revenues?

3. Many industries pay lobbyists to influence regulatory agencies, House of Commons or Senate committees, and other government agencies and officials in Ottawa. Sometimes these lobbyists spend a lot of time promoting the idea that their industry is a source of external benefits. Why would the firms in an industry pay lobbyists to do this?

4. Criticize the following statement: "The government should not be providing money for vaccination programs. If people are unwilling to pay the full cost of vaccinations without subsidy, then vaccinations fail the market test and should not be provided at all."

5. Show why the value of a human life may have to be taken into account in calculating both the benefits and costs of regulation of new drugs by the Department of Health and Welfare.

6. Explain why you agree or disagree with the following statement: "You can rely on the government to provide you with the goods you want at a reasonable price just as much as you can rely upon private business firms. The reason is that the party in power wants you to be pleased with what it provides so that you will vote for it in the next election, just as a private business firm wants you to be pleased with what it provides so that you will buy the product again."

7. It has been argued that when the government spends more money, it provides a great deal of benefits to a small number of people and a very small cost to a

large number of people (namely, taxpayers). Give an example. Why does a government judge that such a policy is in its interests? Will it necessarily be in the nation's economic interest?

ANSWERS

True-False: **1**T, **2**F, **3**F, **4**T, **5**T, **6**F, **7**F, **8**F, **9**T, **10**F, **11**F

Multiple Choice: **1**b, **2**c, **3**e, **4**e, **5**d, **6**b, **7**d, **8**b, **9**b, **10**e, **11**a, **12**c, **13**a, **14**d, **15**d, **16**b, **17**e, **18**a, **19**d, **20**b, **21**d, **22**d, **23**b, **24**a, **25**a

Exercises: **1a**. Q_3, P_1, Q_4, *ER* (or *FT*)

1b. *EFR*, subsidy, *TF*

1c. Q_2, *KH*, *LH*, more, *HGE*, tax, *LK*

2. Figure 23.2(c) completed

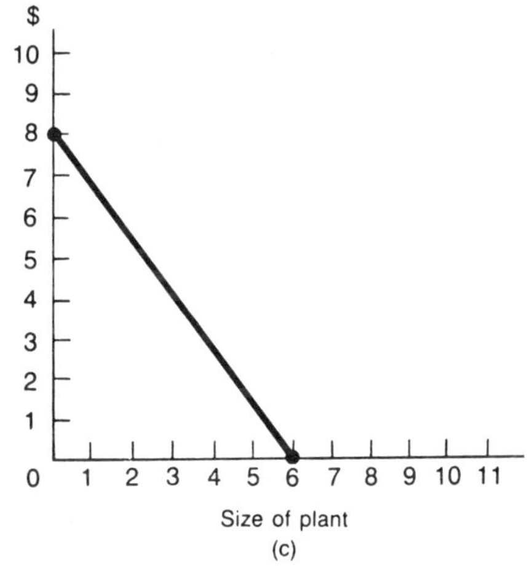

3a. $1 million, is

3b. $1,000, $2,000, 0, understate, will, will not, inefficient

3c. should not, almost $1,000, overstate, increase, will, will, inefficient

4. $500,000, $1,000, 2/1000, 2, 1/1000, $500,000, $1 million, less than, fails, rejected

ANSWERS TO PROBLEMS FROM THE TEXT

23-1. (a) Since marginal social benefit rises with the addition of individuals, supply should increase also, such that the marginal social benefit is again equated to marginal cost.

(b) Practising exclusion would make those individuals who are excluded worse off, while making remaining users no better off. As such, society is made worse off by practising exclusion – efficiency is not served (see Box 11-2 in the textbook).

23-2. Benefits include:

a. Reduced congestion on other arterial roads;
b. Time saved by those who must travel into the city (note that the purpose of the trip will be at issue here);
c. Reduced risk of accidents and loss of life

Costs include:

a. Construction costs;
b. Costs of acquiring the right of way (this will include direct costs of acquiring the land as well as indirect costs associated with, for example, breaking up existing neighbourhoods);
c. Costs associated with noise and inconvenience during construction;
d. Costs associated with increased roadway and parking congestion downtown.

23-3. The free-market equilibrium is at E_1 in Figure 23-1, where marginal cost S is equal to D_1, the marginal private benefit. A subsidy paid to the seller in an amount equal to the divergence between marginal social benefit and marginal private benefit at output Q_1 shifts the supply curve down by the amount of subsidy. Sliding down along D_1, the new equilibrium output is therefore at Q_2, the efficient level. The effects of such a subsidy are independent of the party to which the subsidy is paid.

23-4. It may not be clear that the crash was caused by inadequate safety precautions, rather than terrorism or bad luck. Yes, it does illustrate this difficulty. Even after two crashes, it still may not be clear (although, as crashes increase, the odds become stronger in favour of the "inadequate safety" explanation).

23-5. The line between these two cases may be drawn by an appeal to reason. It is unreasonable to expect an auto company to make cars that will stand up to a train. (This would bankrupt the auto companies.) At the same time, it is unreasonable for them to produce a car that explodes on contact.

It's hard to draw a line based on "reasonableness" since each person's view of what is reasonable differs. But, in practice, such a line must be drawn. This line is drawn in general by parliament, and, in particular, by the regulatory agencies (or, in case of appeals, by the courts).

CHAPTER 24

Government Policies to Reduce Inequality: Can We Solve the Poverty Problem?

LEARNING OBJECTIVES

After you have studied this chapter in the textbook and the study guide, you should be able to

- Describe how the poverty line is defined
- Explain why, over long periods of time, our definition of the poverty line tends to drift up to a higher level of real income
- State the factors that increase the likelihood of a family being poor
- Describe the government policies that attack the causes of poverty, and the policies that reduce its symptoms
- Distinguish between policies directed at reducing the causes of poverty and those directed at reducing the symptoms of poverty, and give examples of each
- Describe some problems that exist in our present welfare system
- Explain the concept of the implicit tax in a welfare program and why this is important in evaluating such programs
- Critically evaluate the guaranteed minimum income proposal
- Argue the case that income maintenance programs are the cure for poverty
- Argue the opposite case that such programs are the cause of poverty
- Describe how a negative income tax program would work
- Explain the theoretical advantages of a negative income tax program

- Explain why three objectives come into conflict when the government is trying to design a negative income tax: (1) to raise the minimum income to an acceptable level; (2) to increase the incentive to work, and (3) to keep the costs of the program from escalating

- Describe some results of experimental studies on the negative income tax

- Explain the pros and cons of a wage subsidy

HIGHLIGHTS OF THE CHAPTER

The objective of this chapter is to evaluate what we are now doing – and what we might possibly do in the future – to alleviate the grinding effects of poverty on the poorest individuals in our population. Specifically, we will address three sets of questions: (1) How is the **poverty line** defined, and who are the poor below it? (2) What policies do the federal and provincial governments now have in place to reduce poverty, and how successful have they been? (3) What income maintenance programs have been proposed to replace the present income support systems, and how likely is it that they would be successful?

The broad questions that are addressed in this chapter are:

How Is the Poverty Line Defined?

The most common definition of poverty is based on poverty lines (called "low-income cutoff" lines) estimated by Statistics Canada for different groups of families or individuals. It is defined by finding the income level at which the average family or individual would have to devote as much as 56.2% of income to the basic necessities of life – namely, food, clothing, and shelter. (Studies have shown that as family income increases, families spend a smaller and smaller proportion of income on these necessities.) Any family or individual below this low-income cutoff line is defined as being poor. The estimated poverty line is different for urban and rural families and for large and small families. In 1991, the poverty line for an urban family of four was $29,601 per year, while for the equivalent rural family it was $20,188. The poverty line is adjusted every year to take inflation into account. It also drifts higher in real terms over long periods of time because our idea of what is barely acceptable tends to increase.

Who Are the Poor?

Table 24-1 in the text shows that the incidence of poverty in 1990 was highest in

Quebec and the Prairies. The rate for Ontario was less than 10%, substantially below the national average. Table 24-2 shows how various characteristics of families and individuals affect the likelihood of poverty. Families (or individuals) are more likely to be poor if (1) the head of the household is female; (2) the head of the household has little education; (3) the family or individual has been unable to find full-time work; (4) the family has three or more children. You should be able to explain how each of these factors is related to poverty.

What Are the Government Policies that Reduce Poverty?

Several government programs attack the causes (as opposed to the symptoms) of poverty: (1) subsidizing investment in human capital, such as free primary and secondary schooling and subsidized job training under the National Training Act; (2) laws and programs that are intended to reduce the extent of poverty that arises from disability and illness, including laws regulating safety in the workplace and universal health insurance; (3) other policies, such as provision of subsidized day care, to make it easier for women in low-income families to earn an income outside of the home.

The programs that help alleviate the symptoms of poverty include several universal **social insurance programs** of government transfer payments in cash or in kind: **Old Age Security**, the **CPP/QPP**, **Unemployment Insurance**, provincial health insurance programs. These programs have become very expensive and are going to become even more costly as the proportion of old people (who receive a large proportion of these payments) in Canada's population increases during the next several decades.

Other government transfer programs are targeted; that is, they are designed to help poor people only. These include the federal **Guaranteed Income Supplement (GIS)**, which goes to poor people whose only source of income is Old Age Security, the federal **Integrated Child Tax Benefit**, and provincial **social assistance** (or "welfare") programs.

How Successful Have Government Anti-poverty Policies Been?

The incidence of poverty in Canada has declined rapidly during the twentieth century. As Figure 24-1 in the textbook illustrates, since 1961, the estimated proportion of families living in poverty has declined from about 4 in every 10 to about 1 in every 8. Some people argue that most of the credit for this is due to our welfare programs. They also argue that these programs have given us the additional, "non-economic" benefit of knowing that we live in a decent society that provides for the poor.

However, critics point to a number of problems with our current welfare programs. One problem arises because the system imposes an "**implicit tax**" on any income the poor may earn. When a poor family earns another $1,000 of income, it may consequently have to give up, say, $800 of welfare benefits it receives from the government. (Sometimes it's more than this, sometimes less.) This $800 is called an 80% "implicit tax" because, from the point of view of the poor, it's as though they had $800 of their additional $1,000 of income "taxed away." If they only get $200 net benefit when they go out and earn $1,000, why bother? It is critical that you understand this concept of an implicit tax, and why a high rate of this tax weakens the incentive of the poor to work. For some families in our present welfare system, this implicit tax has been very high indeed – in some instances approaching, or even exceeding, 100%. In such cases, the poor who earn another $1,000 will lose $1,000 of welfare payments from the government. Their income doesn't increase at all; they have no monetary incentive to get a job.

What Are the Proposals to Replace the Present Welfare System?

1. **A guaranteed minimum income (GMI)**. Under this program, shown in Figure 24-3 of the textbook, the government would guarantee a family a minimum income of, say, $10,000. Any shortfall in the family's earnings would be covered by a payment from the government. The problem with this policy is that it has a built-in 100% implicit tax that leaves no incentive for the poor to go to work. If they do, and earn another $1,000, their welfare payments from the government are reduced by this same amount. It doesn't matter whether they earn $5,000 or $6,000. Their income is fixed by the government at a $10,000 level. So they don't benefit at all when they earn that $1,000 more. Ensure that you fully understand this scheme before you proceed.

2. A **negative income tax (NIT)**. This proposal also provides the poor with a guaranteed minimum income; but, in addition, it provides them with an incentive to go out and earn income on their own. This program is illustrated in Figure 24-5 in the textbook. The implicit tax in this program can be set at, say, 50% (rather than the 100% implicit tax in the GMI proposal above). Thus, a family that earns another $1,000 of income has its payments from the government reduced by only $500. It therefore gets a net benefit of $500, which provides it with an incentive to work. Note that the "income-after-subsidy" line *CA* that was completely flat in the *GMI* proposal in Figure 24-3 – and, therefore, provided no incentive to work – has now been replaced by the upward-sloping line *CQ* in Figure 24-5. Since some of the benefit from increased income can now be kept – it is no longer all lost – there is an incentive to go to work.

If, as its proponents recommend, the negative income tax were to replace the entire inconsistent set of present welfare policies, it would provide another benefit. It would be more equitable because all the poor would be treated alike; all would face the same minimum income, and the same implicit tax. However, this policy would not be problem-free. Like any other anti-poverty program it could not simultaneously achieve the three desirable but conflicting goals of (1) providing an acceptable minimum income for everyone, (2) preserving the incentive for people to work, and (3) keeping costs down. As an example of how these goals may conflict, suppose the government decides to achieve the first goal by raising the minimum income level from $10,000 to $12,000. This will shift the "income after" line CQH in Figure 24-5 up by $2,000 throughout its whole length, thus increasing the grey "subsidy gap" that the government must fill. Thus, this measure may conflict with objective (3) of keeping costs down.

Unfortunately, results of NIT experiments in the United States suggest that, in practice, the negative income tax doesn't work as well as many economists had hoped. In fact, compared with even the existing welfare system, it had disappointing results because it was not successful in inducing people to work more.

A Wage Subsidy

Disappointment in the NIT experimental results has led some to suggest this alternative: a **wage subsidy** that would provide financial assistance to the poor by increasing their wages. Because it would increase the reward for work (the wage rate) it is hoped that this scheme might provide a stronger work incentive. Its main drawback is that it would remove any guaranteed minimum income, and thus would provide no assistance to those individuals who, because of age or disability, cannot work to support themselves. Accordingly, some method would have to be devised to "tag" such people, so that they could qualify for special government support. While such a system would be necessary, it would be far from foolproof. One problem is that some of the able-bodied who do not want to work may try to have themselves fraudulently tagged as disabled.

Concluding Remarks

In the analysis of the GMI and NIT proposals, the focus has been on the cost of a welfare system, in terms of the reduced incentive to work by the recipients of welfare. But there is another cost as well – the cost of raising the taxes from the general public to finance the welfare expenditure. There is evidence that there is about a 25-35% loss when taxes are raised, because those who are taxed are left with less incentive to work. Make sure – in Figure 24-4 of the text – that you can clearly distinguish between these two costs – that is, the disincentive to work imposed on the public that has to pay for welfare payments, and the disincentive to work of the poor who receive the welfare payments.

IMPORTANT TERMS

1. Poverty line
2. Social insurance programs
3. Old Age Security (OAS)
4. Canada Pension Plan (CPP) and Quebec Pension Plan (QPP)
5. Unemployment Insurance (UI)
6. Health Insurance
7. Benefit clawback
8. Targeted transfer programs
9. Guaranteed Income Supplement (GIS)
10. Integrated Child Tax Benefit
11. Social Assistance ("welfare")
12. Implicit tax
13. Guaranteed Minimum Income (GMI)
14. Negative Income Tax (NIT)
15. Wage subsidy

TRUE-FALSE

T F 1. By 1991, only one Canadian family in 20 was below the poverty line.

T F 2. Average real family income in the 1920s was well below the poverty-line income in 1991.

T F 3. The poor are located in the lower left-hand corner of the Lorenz curve.

T F 4. The poverty-line income estimated by Statistics Canada is lower for a family in an urban area than for a comparable family in a rural area.

T F 5. The poverty line is not adjusted over time to take account of inflation, because inflation is not the problem.

T F 6. Unemployment insurance benefits are an example of an in-kind transfer.

T F 7. Families in which the head of the household is a woman are more likely to be poor than are other families.

T F 8. Transfer programs such as social assistance relieve the symptoms of poverty rather than attacking its causes.

T F 9. Under a guaranteed minimum income, all Canadians would receive the same income after taxes and subsidies.

T F 10. The implicit tax in a welfare system is the sum of the benefits lost divided by the additional earned income.

T F 11. All Canadian provinces have about the same proportion of families living in poverty.

MULTIPLE CHOICE

1. In 1991, Statistics Canada estimated that the poverty-line income for a rural family of four was:
   a. more than $17,000 per year
   b. higher than the poverty line for an urban family of four
   c. the same as the poverty line estimated for 1982
   d. about the same as for a single individual in a city
   e. less than $12,000

2. By recent standards, the proportion of the population living in poverty in the early 1960s was about:
   a. 1 in 10
   b. 1 in 5
   c. 1 in 3
   d. 50%
   e. 2 out of 3

3. It becomes impossible to lift all Canadians out of poverty, if we define poverty as:
   a. the bottom half of the income distribution
   b. any income less than $10,000
   c. the bottom tenth of the income distribution
   d. a. or c.
   e. b. or c.

4. Select the correct word to put in the blank spot: It is _____ better to attack the causes of poverty than its symptoms.
   a. always
   b. usually
   c. seldom
   d. almost never
   e. never

5. In the 1920s, a family with a real income close to today's poverty line would have been considered well off. This reflects the fact that:
   a. productivity has decreased
   b. our standards of what constitutes a poverty line income have risen
   c. government welfare programs have been reduced
   d. population has expanded
   e. food was cheaper in 1920 than it is today

6. The percentage of all families with annual incomes below Statistics Canada's low-income cutoff:
   a. was estimated to be about 1/3 of all families in the early 1960s
   b. decreased more during the period 1960-80 than during 1980-86
   c. was estimated to be less than 15% in 1990
   d. was higher in Quebec than in the rest of Canada in 1990
   e. all of the above

7. Which of the following government transfer programs is not specifically targeted at people with low incomes?
   a. Unemployment Insurance
   b. social assistance programs
   c. child tax benefit
   d. Guaranteed Income Supplement
   e. low-income housing

8. Which of the following kinds of government programs relieve only the symptoms of poverty?
   a. those that subsidize investment in human capital
   b. social assistance payments under the cash deficit method
   c. universal health insurance
   d. policies to reduce unemployment and disability
   e. subsidized day care

9. Which of the following government programs does not create an implicit tax on the recipients?
   a. social assistance payments
   b. child tax benefit
   c. Guaranteed Income Supplement
   d. subsidized housing
   e. Old Age Security payments

10. Which of the following combinations accounted for the largest share of total federal and provincial government expenditures in 1991?
    a. hospital and medical insurance, Unemployment Insurance, and Old Age Security
    b. social welfare assistance, Unemployment Insurance, and Old Age Security
    c. hospital and medical insurance, family allowances, and the child tax credit
    d. Old Age Security, social welfare assistance, and family allowances
    e. Unemployment Insurance, Guaranteed Income Supplement, and Workers' Compensation

11. A guaranteed minimum income:
    a. would increase efficiency by increasing the incentive to work
    b. would be very costly, especially because it would reduce the incentive to work
    c. would cost less than we would expect, because it would increase the incentive to work
    d. would have no effect on the incentive to work
    e. would have no effect on efficiency

12. A guaranteed minimum income has an implicit tax on very low income families of:
    a. 0%
    b. 25%
    c. 50%
    d. 75%
    e. 100%

13. The income-maintenance program that would provide the poor with the largest incentive to work is one in which the "income-after-subsidy" line:
    a. has zero slope
    b. has a slope close to zero
    c. has a slope of 30°
    d. has a slope of almost 45°
    e. has a negative slope

14. The estimated "leak in the welfare" bucket in which income is transferred to the poor has been estimated at about:
   a. zero when taxes are collected, and 50% when the welfare expenditures are made
   b. 30% when taxes are collected, and 60% when the welfare expenditures are made
   c. 30% when taxes are collected, and 20 to 25% when the welfare expenditures are made
   d. 50% when taxes are collected, and 20 to 25% when the welfare expenditures are made
   e. 50% when taxes are collected, and zero when the welfare expenditures are made

15. The maximum implicit tax on any family facing the present set of federal and provincial welfare policies may be:
   a. about 50%
   b. about 80%
   c. just under 100%
   d. 100%
   e. more than 100%

16. A family will have the strongest financial incentive to stop working if the implicit tax it faces is:
   a. zero
   b. so close to zero that the difference is not significant
   c. 50%
   d. almost 100%
   e. more than 100%

17. If a family living in government-subsidized housing is required to pay 25% of its income in rent, then for this reason alone it is facing an implicit tax of:
   a. zero
   b. 25%
   c. 75%
   d. 100%
   e. 125%

18. A welfare program that pays you $5,000 if you earn nothing, and $4,500 if you earn $2,000, has an implicit tax of:
    a. zero
    b. 25%
    c. 40%
    d. 50%
    e. 105%

19. Which of the following should offer the greatest work incentive to the very poor?
    a. no taxes or subsidies
    b. the present welfare system
    c. a wage subsidy
    d. a guaranteed minimum income
    e. a. and d. equally

20. With a negative income tax, an increase in the implicit tax rate will:
    a. increase the slope of the "income-after-tax" line
    b. decrease the slope of that line
    c. leave the slope of that line unchanged
    d. raise the point where the income-after-tax line intersects the vertical axis
    e. lower that point

21. Suppose a negative income tax is set up with the minimum income set at $8,000, and the implicit tax rate set at 50%. In this case, a subsidy would be paid by the government:
    a. to no one
    b. only to those earning less than $4,000
    c. only to those earning less than $8,000
    d. only to those earning less than $12,000
    e. only to those earning less than $16,000

EXERCISE

Consider the following four tax-subsidy programs:

A. Every family earning less than $5,000 receives enough subsidy to give it an income of $5,000 after taxes and subsidies. On every dollar earned over $5,000, a family must pay a 20% tax.

B. Every family receives a subsidy of $5,000, but then pays a 50% tax on every dollar earned.

C. Every family receives a subsidy of $3,000, but then pays a tax of 30% on every dollar earned.

D. Every family receives a subsidy of $3,000 but then pays a tax of 50% on every dollar earned.

In Figure 24.1, plot the line for each program showing how a family's income after taxes and subsidies is related to its income before taxes and subsidies. For each program, indicate in Table 24.1 the marginal tax rates on income earned above $5,000.

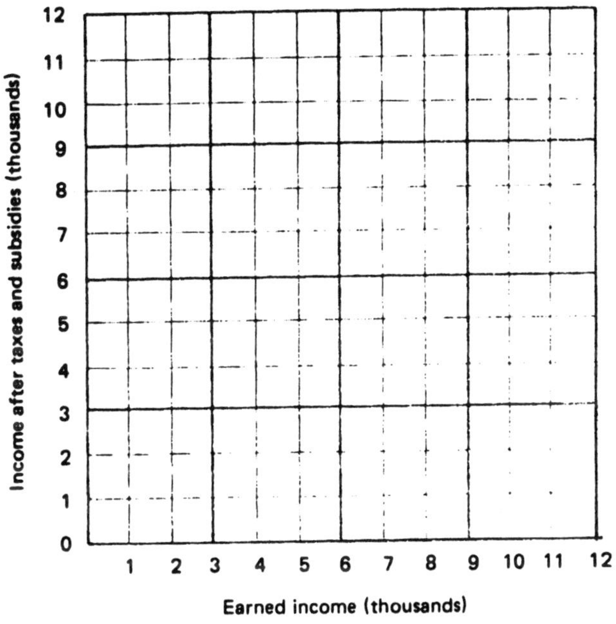

Figure 24.1

Table 24.1

Program	Marginal tax rate on income earned above $5,000
A	
B	
C	
D	

Suppose that the distribution of earned incomes (before taxes and subsidies) in the economy is given by Table 24.2.

Table 24.2

Annual income before taxes and transfers (thousands of dollars)	0	3	5	6	10	15	20	50
Number of families earning this income	1	2	4	4	3	2	1	1

In Table 24.3 fill in the net tax (i.e., tax minus subsidy) paid to each family under each of the programs.

Table 24.3

Income (in thousands)		**0**	**3**	**5**	**6**	**10**	**15**	**20**	**50**
Net tax of each family under program:	A								
	B								
	C								
	D								

In Table 24.4 show the total net taxes collected – that is, total taxes collected minus total subsidy paid. Assume that, regardless of the tax-subsidy program that is imposed, there is no change in the amount of work and, therefore, no change in the earned income of each family. In other words, the income distribution in Table 24.2 doesn't change, regardless of the tax-subsidy program.

Table 24.4

Program	Total net taxes
A	
B	
C	
D	

ESSAY QUESTIONS

1. "Universal social insurance and welfare programs may be desirable, but they are totally unproductive. They don't add anything to the nation's capacity to produce." Do you agree with this statement, or not? Explain your answer. (Use provincial medicare as one of your examples.)

2. If you observe that the children of the poor are poor, and that the children of the rich are rich, does this prove the ability of the rich to secure a high income for their children (by providing them, for example, with special educational opportunities)? Or does it reflect different genetic capabilities? Or both? Discuss.

3. If the main ill effect of social assistance programs is to encourage fathers to leave home so their families can qualify for welfare, what do you think of maintaining the program but disqualifying any family whose father has abandoned them?

4. If the government gave equivalent cash transfers instead of subsidized housing, education, or other types of assistance in kind, would the recipients be better off? Why? Would their children be better off? Why does the government provide assistance in kind?

ANSWERS

True-False: 1F, 2T, 3T, 4F, 5F, 6F, 7T, 8T, 9F, 10T, 11F

Multiple Choice: 1a, 2c, 3d, 4b, 5b, 6e, 7a, 8b, 9e, 10a, 11b, 12e, 13d, 14c, 15e, 16e, 17b, 18b, 19c, 20b, 21e

Exercise:

Figure 24.1 completed

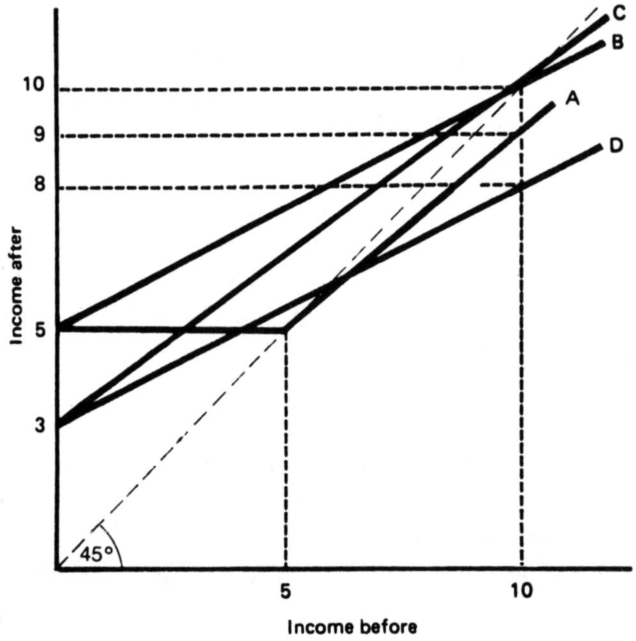

Table 24.1 completed

A	20%
B	50%
C	30%
D	50%

Table 24.3 completed

-5,000	-2,000	0	200	1,000	2,000	3,000	9,000
-5,000	-3,500	-2,500	-2,000	0	2,500	5,000	20,000
-3,000	-2,100	-1,500	-1,200	0	1,500	3,000	12,000
-3,000	-1,500	-500	0	2,000	4,500	7,000	22,000

Table 24.4 completed

A	10,800
B	0
C	0
D	36,000

ANSWERS TO PROBLEMS FROM THE TEXT

24-1. A family facing an implicit tax of 90% (or 105%) will lose 90 cents (or $1.05) in benefits from the government for every additional $1 of income it earns. If it faces an implicit tax of 90%, it will have very little incentive to work, since it will only be able to keep 10 cents on the dollar. If its implicit tax is 105%, this family would be better off not earning additional income; it can have a higher income by working less.

24-2. Leaks in the transfer bucket are illustrated in Figure 24-4 in the textbook. The "cost" to Canadian society of income transfers to the poor will include the excess burden associated with collecting the taxes required to pay for the transfers as well as the excess burden associated with transfer programs themselves. Administrative costs are only a small component of the leak.

24-3. (a) The new figure will be similar to Figure 24-5, but the line *CH* will be flatter, intersecting the 45° line at about $14,300 (rather than at $20,000).

(b) The incentive to work has been reduced: a family now gets to keep only $300 out of each $1,000 it earns (rather than $500 per $1,000 in Figure 24-5).

(c) The implicit tax has risen. It is now 70%, rather than 50% in Figure 24-5.

(d) Yes, they are: the higher the implicit tax, the lower the incentive to work.

(e) If each family continues to work the same amount as before, the total government subsidy is less than before, since each family's subsidy has been reduced.

However, because the incentive to work has been decreased, some families are now likely to work less, and thus move to the left in the diagram. Such a move increases the subsidy they will receive. On balance, therefore, it is not clear whether the total subsidy the government pays out will increase or decrease.

(f) Because some families are now likely to reduce the work they do (that is, move to the left in the diagram), the transfer bucket has become leakier.

(g) In this case, the line *CH* shifts down by $2,000, in a parallel fashion, starting at $8,000 on the vertical axis and intersecting the 45° line at an income of about $16,000. In comparison with Figure 24-5, the incentive to work may not be affected much, because the implicit tax remains the same (at 50%). However, a family that does not work at all will now have an income of only $8,000, not $10,000. This may induce some families to work more, simply to eke out a bare living.

The total amount of subsidy the government pays is likely to be reduced in this case. This is both because each family is subsidized up to a lower level, and because some families that previously contributed nothing or very little to their own support are now likely to feel that they have to work more, given the reduced support level.

24-4. The answers here are highly subjective. This is an excellent question for class discussion. Suggest it to your instructor.

cut here

STUDENT REPLY CARD

In order to improve future editions, we are seeking your comments on

Study Guide to accompany Microeconomics, Fourth Edition, by Blomqvist, Wonnacott, Wonnacott, and Hobson

Please answer the following questions and return this form via Business Reply Mail. Your opinions matter. Thank you in advance for sharing them with us!

Name of your college or university: ____________________

Major program of study: ____________________

Course title: ____________________

Were you required to buy this book? ________ yes ________ no

Did you buy this book new or used? ________ new ________ used ($________)

Do you plan to keep or sell this book? ________ keep ________ sell

Is the order of topic coverage consistent with what was taught in your course?

cut here

fold here

Are there chapters or sections of this text that were not assigned for your course? Please specify:

Were there topics covered in your course that are not included in the text? Please specify:

What did you like most about this text?

What did you like least?

If you would like to say more, we would appreciate hearing from you. Please write to us at the address shown on the reverse of this page.

cut here

fold here

cut here

Postage will be paid by

MAIL POSTE

Canada Post Corporation / Société canadienne des postes

Postage paid
if mailed in Canada

Port payé
si posté au Canada

Business Reply

Réponse d'affaires

0183560299 01

0183560299-L1N9B6-BR01

Attn.: Sponsoring Editor
College Division

MCGRAW-HILL RYERSON LIMITED
300 WATER ST
WHITBY ON L1N 9Z9

tape shut